I0036841

America's
Protectionist
Takeoff
1815-1914

The Neglected American School of Political Economy

MICHAEL HUDSON

Enlarged, revised and updated version of *Economics and Technology in 19th-Century American Thought – The Neglected American Economists.*
First published 1975 by Garland Publishing, Inc., New York & London

© 2010 Michael Hudson / ISLET-Verlag
Set in Baskerville
Typesetting & Layout by Cornelia Wunsch
All rights reserved

www.michael-hudson.com
www.islet-verlag.de

Hudson, Michael, 1939-
America's Protectionist Takeoff 1815–1914:
The Neglected American School of Political Economy
Michael Hudson.

ISBN 13: 978-3-9808466-8-4

DEDICATION

I dedicate this book to the memory of Gus Kelley and Sam Ambaras,
antiquarian economics booksellers in New York City,
who provided me with the raw materials
for this volume a half-century ago.

CONTENTS

IV. FROM BORDER-STATE PROTECTIONISM TO THE EMERGING NEW YORK MAINSTREAM

V. HENRY CAREY'S GENERATION AFTER THE CIVIL WAR

VI. SOME OPPONENTS OF THE PROTECTIONISTS

VII. THE GENERALISTS

VIII. THE AMERICAN SCHOOL'S TECHNOLOGICAL OPTIMISM VERUS THE PESSIMISM OF EMPIRE

IX. POLITICAL ORIGINS OF THE U.S. DEPARTMENT OF AGRICULTURE: SOIL CHEMISTRY AND INTERNATIONAL TRADE THEORY 1840–62

X. OBSOLETE FACTORS IN THE INTERNATIONAL ECONOMY

PREFACE

When I began my economic studies in 1961, my mentor Terence McCarthy advised me to focus on the flowering of classical theory in the 19th century. For starters he suggested that I read every book cited in the bibliography of Marx's *Theories of Surplus Value*, which he had just translated—its first publication in English. Because many of these books were too rare to be available in the library at New York University where I was enrolled, I haunted the New York bookstores. Despite their rarity, most 19th-century economics texts could still be picked up for only a few dollars, as there was little demand for books deemed intellectually obsolete. I soon became friends with New York City's three dealers in rare economics books: Augustus Kelley, Samuel Ambaras and Sidney Millman. Kelley hired me to review and recommend books for his burgeoning reprint company, paying me in kind for many years out of his enormous inventory.

Being a contrarian by nature, I selected titles I had never heard of, by authors who did not appear in the literature. Among the most neglected writers were the 19th-century American protectionists. Not even ostensibly encyclopedic studies of American economic thought paid much attention to them, treating them patronizingly as anomalies rather than the men who designed the nation's rise to industrial supremacy. Political histories of the United States tended to focus on the Democratic Party, as if the Republicans (and the Whigs before them) had no distinct economic program, much less a body of theory more realistic and empirically relevant than those of Malthus and Ricardo to which the Democratic Party subscribed.

The protectionist doctrine that shaped America's industry and agriculture is out of fashion in today's free-trade world. Academically, it went beyond the narrow boundaries of today's economics discipline by deeming public policy and technology central to economic theorizing, not "exogenous." Analyzing what was needed to increase productivity, the American School emphasized that wages and prices had to be high enough to sustain rising living and educational standards for labor, and investment in rising energy mobilization by capital. To me, this broad scope is what made these writers so interesting. I felt as if I were discovering a lost civilization—that which the United States sought to become along much different economic lines, socially and intellectually more secular than was the case in Europe, and free of its class antagonisms thanks to its "Economy of High Wages" doctrine.

While I was searching for a dissertation topic along these lines in 1964, the wage and price guidelines that President John F. Kennedy had proposed for the steel industry were still in the news. These guidelines called for wages to be increased in keeping with productivity. This seemed to explain productivity simply by employees working harder, without reference to capital investment or technology resulting from research and development. I was surprised that employers did not respond by arguing that capital and development costs should be factored into productivity calculations. If they increased wages in proportion to the rise in output per man-hour, would this deter them from investing in labor-displacing plant and equipment and increasing energy use per production worker?

The NYU professor teaching growth and productivity models was Solomon Fabricant, moonlighting from his day job as research director at the National Bureau of Economic Research. When I suggested reviewing the history of concepts of productivity and explanation of its growth over time as my dissertation topic, he urged me to find something else to write about, because the National Bureau had defined productivity simply as output per manhour, that is, output divided by labor time. But when I asked about capital productivity, Prof. Fabricant pointed out that Edward Denison and Robert Solow had correlated the quantity of labor and the dollar value of capital investment with output. The statistical residual unexplained by this simple correlation was deemed to be technology. Without further explanation it seemed to be produced freely by the momentum of scientific progress. No attempt was made to go below the surface and analyze why productivity occurred when and where it did (or did not), or who received its benefits—labor via wages, or industrial capital via profits, or finance via interest or the government via taxes and user fees?

It has become fashionable among economists to take a given variable, plug it into a historical ratio with some other statistical series, and seek a correlation. Any time series can be correlated with any other. What is not correlated can be defined narrowly or broadly, simplistically or in a more complex way. It can be called "technology," "public policy," divine intervention or whatever one wants. Denison called the unexplained variable left over from statistics on labor and capital investment "technology." The implication was that like capital formation, it occurred independently from public policy. This afforded an excuse to avoid examining the role played by tariff and tax policy, public infrastructure investment in education and living standards. It assumed that technology was simply "there," supplied by scientific advance throughout the world on terms equally available to all—with no environmental constraints. 19th-century writers never would have formulated so simplistic and policy-free an approach.

When I said that I wanted to review the ideas of earlier economists regarding productivity, Prof. Fabricant reminded me that he had shown his displeasure at my term paper critiquing the Harrod-Domar formulae for economic growth based crudely on labor/capital proportions. I had suggested that capital could be labor-displacing rather than calling forth an increase in employment proportional to the historical correlation between capital investment and employment. He explained was that the history of thought was a waste of time. "If ideas no longer are held, it is because they have been found wanting as economic theory has moved toward today's state of perfection." All my proposal could do was distract attention from the perfection of modern-day orthodoxy.

It was clear that I had to find another dissertation topic. Over one of my frequent lunches with my friend and professor Gerhardt Bry (who also worked at the National Bureau) I mentioned the ideas of one of the American economists whose book I had just found: E. Peshine Smith, a major influence on Henry Carey and author of an energy theory of capital and economic growth. Prof. Bry suggested that this topic might seem suitably antiquarian not to antagonize NYU's Economics Department.

If it seemed non-controversial, this was simply because economic historians have ignored Peshine Smith as if the American School never existed. The modern abhorrence of protectionism expunged from history the logic that guided U.S. industrialization under Republican leadership from 1860 through 1912. The American School's trenchant critique of free trade and the theorizing of Ricardo, Malthus and other British writers caused a cognitive dissonance in the minds of professors eager to promote a view of American history driven by an inexorable drive for free trade and westward expansion as Manifest Destiny.

Actually, westward expansion was a Democratic Party policy to extend slavery and plantation agriculture. In an epoch when protective tariffs were the principal source of revenue for the federal government (that is, until the 16th Amendment created the federal income tax in 1913) the South based its cotton and tobacco production on foreign markets, seeking to feed its slaves with low-priced grain from the West. The Whig and Republican industrial program called for concentrating industry in the Eastern urban centers, whose population would be fed by farms that would find their major market at home, not abroad. But industrialization threatened to bid up food prices, eroding the competitiveness of plantation agriculture. This prompted the Democratic Party to urge free trade, small government and credit aimed mainly at export financing, not industry. The slave states in particular decried industrialization and urbanization as culturally decadent rather than the key to economic progress. At issue was the kind of cultural, social and political structure America would develop and national trade policy would act to bring about.

By the late 20th century few Republicans were interested in their party's original protectionist plank. "Open trade is not just an economic opportunity, it is a moral imperative," President George W. Bush declared in a May 7, 2001 speech. "Trade creates jobs for the unemployed. When we negotiate for open markets, we're providing new hope for the world's poor. And when we promote open trade, we are promoting political freedom." But for 19th-century Republicans, free trade led to international dependency and industrial unemployment, blocking economic progress. America's position as an industrial latecomer called for active government subsidy of industry, protective tariffs, public spending on infrastructure and freedom from British financial power.

During the course of my research I ordered microfilms of Smith's correspondence with Henry Carey and others from the University of Pennsylvania's archives, and tracked down related protectionist literature by following the trail from the bibliography mentioned in each book I discovered, largely with the help of my book-dealer friends who told me that I was their only buyer for such material. The dissertation was approved in 1968.[1]

When I taught the graduate courses in trade theory at the New School during 1969–72, some of my students suspected that I had made up "Peshine Smith" as a fictitious alter ego. And indeed, I was inspired to write a history of theories of trade and development largely as a result of the ideas I learned while studying the American critique of Ricardian logic. In today's jargon, free trade theorizing was agenda-oriented, adopting a series of unrealistic axioms and assumptions to create a logic that would lead along a narrow path to an anti- protectionist conclusion.[2]

In my lectures I emphasized that a logical corollary of the theory of economic growth was the theory of obsolescence. The faster capital and labor productivity rises in leading nations, the further these economies leave low-productivity industry and agriculture behind. This perception had struck economists even before Adam Smith. I was invited to give a paper on this topic for the Catholic Economic Association, which had just changed its name to the Association for Social Economics. At its 1971 meeting I read a paper on "Obsolescent Factors in the International Economy," published in the March 1972 *Review of Social Economics* and included in this volume (chapter X).

---

[1] Michael Huckleberry Hudson, *E. Peshine Smith: A Study in Protectionist Growth Theory and American Sectionalism*, Ph.D. Dissertation, New York University, 1969.

[2] I have published these lectures as *Trade, Development and Foreign Debt: Theories of Polarization and Convergence in the International Economy* (Pluto Press 1992, now in press in a second, expanded edition).

Ever since the Department of Agriculture published its centenary 1963 annual report *A Century of Service* describing its origins as responding to the needs of agriculture, I had sought to write a corrective to show the lead taken by industrial protectionists warning against the free-trade idea that America's economic advantage lay in exporting slave-based plantation products in exchange for English manufactures. This met with the usual cognitive dissonance as unearthing the political dynamics leading to the Department of Agriculture was not the orthodox position, so the paper went unpublished. I include it in this volume (as Chapter IX).

In 1975 a reprint company, Garland Press, asked me to select books from my library to reprint and write introductions for them. I used the opportunity to dismantle my dissertation and write new biographies of the major American protectionists. It was published under the title *Economics and Technology in 19ᵗʰ-Century American Thought. The Neglected American Economists*. As a collection of introductions to these reprints, my summaries attracted no attention at all. Only about a hundred copies of the book were printed, as the publisher set a price so far above printing costs that sales broke even at only fifteen or twenty copies.

Shortly after its publication I surveyed the idea of America as a new civilization for the National Endowment for the Humanities through a contract with the Hudson Institute, where I was Chief Economist. My aim was to describe how the idea of high-wage labor becoming more productive — and consolidating its position by raising educational and cultural levels to best apply industrial and agricultural technology — led naturally to an analysis of how a high-consumption society would differ from that of Europe. Class conflict was played down in favor of the "harmony of interest" doctrines promoted by Henry Carey's school, which tended to theorize along "cooperative" materialistic lines in which economic development was driven simply by man's increasing efficiency at exploiting nature rather than his fellow man.

The American School thus replaced the classical economic idea of class conflict with that of international conflict, not only among economies ultimately but among different social organizations. And that, of course, became America's unwillingness to join any international organization that would have power to dictate its own policy, and indeed for not viewing itself as a member of the European parties to the Great War that broke out in 1914. It led to America's demand that its Inter-Ally arms debts be repaid after the war, to its insistence on veto power in the United Nations after World War II, and to its historical "go-it-alone" stance in global diplomacy. I have been told that all copies of my report except for my own copy have been lost or destroyed, so I include it in the present volume.

It took a few decades for interest in Peshine Smith and the American School to arise, mainly in foreign countries. In Japan, where Smith had served as advisor to the Mikado more than a century earlier, Bill Totten asked me in 1993 to summarize Smith's relevance for an on-line publication he edited, Our World. In Norway, Erik Reinert organized a "reality economics" group. Its members included Arno Daastøl who pursued research relating to Friedrich List's strategies for industrialization, in particular its immaterial aspects, and Ha-Joon Chang, who wrote "Kicking Away the Ladder" in 2002. I provided a summary of my chapter on Smith from the present volume in the book that Prof. Reinert edited.[3] More recently, I juxtaposed the American School's technological optimism to the logic for expansionist empire-building in a paper delivered in Wuhan, China, on Nov. 8, 2009 for the Chiniese translation of the present book (chapter VIII).

The most natural market for such ideas would seem to be today's "late-comer" nations. They find themselves today in a position analogous to that of the United States at the outset of the 19th century when it required tariff protection, industrial and agricultural subsidies to avoid becoming merely a "hewer of wood and drawer of water." The economic logic behind America's rise to industrial and agricultural domination deserves to be understood, and also its subsequent emulation of trade strategy, repeating that of Britain, seeking to bury the knowledge of its catch-up path. Once in a dominant position, lead nations find their interest to lie in preaching the gospel of free trade rather than protectionism, and ignoring the degree to which technology and productivity growth are a product of active government subsidy.

* * *

The 1975 version of this book consisted of biographical summaries of the major advocates (and some opponents) of the American School of political economy. My hope in republishing their writings was to provide raw material for a re-examination of how America sponsored industrialization and agricultural modernization. In view of the fact that almost nothing has been done to elaborate this history in the 33 years since this book was published, it may be appropriate here to provide a broad perspective on why these writers were so important.

At its most idealistic, American economic thought aimed at creating a society free of the class antagonisms that were impoverishing labor in Europe and its colonies. The doctrines of Malthus and Ricardo made this conflict

---

[3] "Technical Progress and Obsolescence of Capital and Skills: Theoretical foundations of 19th-century U.S. industrial and trade policy," in Erik S. Reinert, ed., *Globalization, Economic Development and Inequality: An Alternative Perspective* (Cheltenham: Edward Elgar, 2004).

seem natural and inevitable. Rejecting these ideas, the American School sought to create a new civilization socially and intellectually as well as economically. It was a civilization more innovative than passively traditional, more pragmatic than ideological, more secular and hence less subject to authority. (That is why I include John W. Draper in this volume.) The basic logic was that if low-wage nations with relatively low-productivity labor were to catch up, governments needed to shape prices and incomes to subsidize capital investment and provide basic infrastructure to minimize the cost of living and doing business over time. Without such "catch-up" protectionism the international economy would polarize more and more as leading nations consolidated their income and productivity advantages in agriculture as well as industry, capped by a rising creditor advantage as well.

Eight major themes are paramount in the development of this doctrine:
(1) a labor productivity explanation of wages, including what today is called human capital to explain why employers of high-wage labor could undersell low-wage producers;
(2) an energy measure of capital productivity;
(3) a concept of soil fertility and agricultural productivity as the product of capital investment rather than stemming from Ricardian "original and indestructible powers";
(4) a doctrine of urban-rural balance and the virtues of population density as a political antithesis to Manifest Destiny;
(5) public infrastructure investment as a distinct factor of production, whose role is to lower the cost of doing business;
(6) regulation of banking and finance as a leading public utility;
(7) a broad historical and sociological view of economic analysis; and
(8) a materialistic and secular but non-Marxian technological view of economic evolution

These eight elements created a uniquely American alternative to the free-trade ideas that followed from Ricardian value theory, the population ideas of Malthus, and Europe's liberal opposition to government power in an epoch where parliaments were dominated by post-feudal landholding aristocracies and monopolies carved out of the public domain. The United States owed no land rent to a hereditary aristocracy. It did endow the railroad barons with vast land grants, but subsequently passed legislation to regulate passenger fares and freight rates. The idea was to break up industrial trusts and regulate natural monopolies as public utilities, including power companies and, in time, phone companies and broadcasters.

xiii

THE THREE MAJOR ECONOMIC PHILOSOPHIES DEVELOPED DURING 1815 TO 1914

RICARDIAN POPULATION THEORY	MARXISM	THE AMERICAN SCHOOL
Population and Wage Theory		
Assumes all labor to be of equal productive powers. Hence, densely populated countries have the lowest wage levels.	A supply-and-demand theory of wages determined by the "reserve army of the unemployed." The state will employ surplus labor under socialism. (Implicit agreement with the Ricardians.)	The Economy of High Wages doctrine: Productivity gains tend to exceed wage gains, enabling high-wage labor to undersell "pauper labor." Hence, profits and wages may rise together. Higher income slows the growth of population, pushing up wages all the more. Also, higher wages spur capital substitution, increasing labor productivity. Finally, higher population density increases productivity, and therefore increases wage levels.
Agricultural productivity and land rent		
Diminishing returns. Soil has "original and indestructible powers." Capital application will not affect relative soil fertility.	Ditto	Soil fertility is a product of agricultural chemistry and the application of capital. Agribusiness enjoys increasing returns as population increases and a circular flow develops between city and countryside. Land rent becomes increasingly a form of profit.
Concept of capital		
Capital is viewed mainly as a cost, ultimately in the form of embodied labor. The growth in society's economic surplus appears only as an incidental "externality." Ignores the non-cost aspects of capital, including "social capital" and public investment.	Also laissez faire, despite Marx's recognition that foreign trade exploits less developed regions. Foreign trade is exploitative—but by developing industrial capitalism, it brings the day of socialism nearer.	Capital's net productive powers exceed its (labor-) cost to an increasing degree. This increases society's economic surplus, transforming the character of labor and society.
Theory of Foreign Trade		
Foreign trade is necessary to stave off higher food prices in the highly populated industrial nations. Otherwise, food prices and land rents rise, eating into profits. The gains from trade are shared equitably among developed and less developed countries.	Land rent stems from private property relationships. Socialism will dissolve the institutions of private property, equalizing the return to labor.	Foreign trade exploits the raw-materials exporters. Protective tariffs are needed to promote industrial capital and high wages. Free trade leads to soil-depleting modes of cultivation. High-wage labor exploits low-wage labor. Hence, younger countries are more amenable to industrialization, with their educated labor, than pauper-labor countries. Industry is needed to develop modern agriculture; just the reverse of the Smith-List theory of development stages.
Scope of Political Economy		
Wealth, capital and economic rent increasingly ignored in favor of utility theory concentrating on personal psychological welfare. Less and less political and social theory.	Increasingly a theory of how to transform society's political institutions (its "political integument") that block progress.	Pro-statist in tariff policy and internal improvements, but not domestically. Capital theory evolved into a materialist view of history shaping consumption and production.

(1) *A labor productivity explanation of wages*

A central concern was to explain how a high-wage economy such as the United States could hope to undersell manufactures produced by "pauper labor" in Europe and its former colonies. The explanation was that productivity growth tended to exceed wage gains. The American system of political economy, wrote Peshine Smith in 1852, "rests upon the belief, that in order to make labor cheap, the laborer must be well-fed, well-clothed, well-lodged, well-instructed, not only in the details of his handicraft, but in all general knowledge that can in any way be made subsidiary to it. All these cost money to the employer and repay it with interest."[4] Along similar lines Jacob Schoenhof wrote in 1884: "It is not by reducing wages that America is making her conquests, but by her superior organization, greater efficiency of labor consequent upon the higher standard of living ruling in the country. High-priced labor means better food and better living, and these supply the American workman with the energy and nerve-power for which he is so justly celebrated. High-priced labor countries are everywhere beating 'pauper-labor' countries."[5] It cost money to eat well, keep in good health and grow strong, and above all to pursue higher education and training as industry became more skill-intensive.

Republicans argued that protective tariffs were needed to promote the capital investment that would make American labor more productive, and that employers would find their interest to lie in paying workers more. Whereas Ricardian theory depicted a wage/profit tradeoff in which wage gains were paid at the industrial capitalist's expense, the Economy of High Wages doctrine showed that highly paid labor was sufficiently more productive to make it attractive to employers.[6] This explained why a high-wage economy would be able to undersell and out-produce low-wage economies, establishing a harmony of interests between labor and capital (an interest not reflected in the strike-breaking activities and opposition to labor unions so often experienced in practice).

---

[4] See below, pp. 181f.

[5] *Wages and Trade in Manufacturing Industries in America and Europe* (New York: 1884), p. 19. See below, pp. 227–37.

[6] Some British writers did note the wage-productivity feedback, but they are dismissed (in footnotes if they are mentioned at all) as being merely "mercantilist," much as the American School writes were dismissed as "protectionists" as if this meant that they were economically illiterate. The idea that higher wages might be a precondition for rising productivity was never incorporated into mainstream economic doctrine. But I describe the long pedigree for views opposing today's "race to the bottom" ideology in *Trade, Development and Foreign Debt* (London: 1992), pp. 72f. and 225f. regarding Josiah Tucker, and 180f. regarding Adam Smith.

The productivity explanation of wage levels provided an argument for why protective tariffs would promote higher living standards than could be achieved by exporting cotton, grain and other raw materials to England. In contrast to the Democrats' advocacy of westward expansion, workers in industrial pursuits were paid out of what they produced, not by the "backwoods" principle of what they could eke out on the land. Industrialists would not pay workers more just because these men could do better by becoming homesteaders out west. Shifting emphasis to the industrial demand for labor, protectionists argued that what enabled employers to pay high wages were the sales proceeds and profits they earned.

(2) *An energy measure of capital productivity*

Classical British political economy distinguished cost-value, reducible ultimately to the cost of labor, from prices that included rents and other property or financial claims that had no counterpart in inherent cost of production. Isolating economic rent as a cost-free and hence socially unnecessary "free lunch" was part of Europe's fight to free itself from the vestiges of feudalism's military conquest of the land. The American School was more concerned with how industrial technology lowered costs (and increased output) by productivity gains, above all by capital productivity in terms of energy use per man-hour. Peshine Smith in particular viewed capital supplying raw energy as replacing manual labor in the "lower" tasks of production. Even in agriculture, land was like a machine, using energy and becoming industrialized into what would be called agribusiness.

Capital technology in all sectors required rising educational levels, leading Smith and his contemporaries to develop the concept of "human capital," breathlessly rediscovered by neoclassical economists in the 1950s. The political corollary was that labor and capital productivity was largely a function of government tariff and subsidy policy. Protective tariffs were needed to enable industrial investment to cover its expensive start-up costs, thereby saving America from becoming a raw-materials exporter with low-productivity labor.

(3) *A view of soil fertility and agricultural productivity as the product of capital investment*

Ricardian rent and trade theory assumed soil fertility to be intrinsic, neither enhanced by the application of capital nor depleted by farming methods. By contrast, the research of Justus Liebig and other soil chemists showed that fertility needed to be maintained by crop rotation or by the application of fertilizer to convert the soil's chemical composition into crops. What Ricardo imagined to be economic rent as a gift of nature thus was better viewed as profit on capital invested in the land and in harvesting its crops.

This perception as to the variable productivity of land led the American School to apply the cost of environmental protection to trade theory by pointing out that in contrast to rising industrial productivity, plantation agriculture—headed by Southern slave production of cotton and tobacco—exhausted the soil. The cost of replenishing its fertility as a byproduct of exporting plantation crops and minerals did not appear on the "market" balance sheet of gains or losses from trade, but it nonetheless existed as what today would be called an "externality," a cost not reflected in market pricing. The Whigs sought to document this environmental soil-renewal cost in the Patent Office's 1849 report, the second volume of which was written by Daniel Lee.[7]

The result was that contrary to what orthodox history might expect, it was not the farming regions that supported creation of a Department of Agriculture. Rather, it was industrial protectionists who argued that the dominant form of market crop production being pursued in the United States—plantation export agriculture—was economically destructive. I therefore survey the prehistory of this government agency as a new essay in this volume.

(4) *A doctrine of urban-rural balance*

Inasmuch as soil depletion was a major dynamic behind westward expansion as Southern slave owners pressed for Manifest Destiny, the economic ideas developed in the tariff debate led to the question of what kind of society the United States would become: a self-sufficient urban industrial economy enjoying rising productivity and wage levels, or a slave-based rural raw-materials export economy increasingly dependent on Britain for its manufactures and high-technology products. Peshine Smith and Henry Carey advocated to "putting the consumer by the side of the producer" by returning urban nightsoil (human feces) as fertilizer to the countryside to increase soil fertility. Their alternative to Manifest Destiny was to promote a flowering of industry alongside farming areas so as to free the nation from dependency on any foreign source of supply, if not indeed to achieve outright autarchy.

(5) *Public infrastructure as a fourth factor of production*

Protectionists viewed infrastructure investment as a vehicle on which to spend tariff revenue. Simon Patten described public investment as a "fourth" factor of production alongside labor, land and capital. Rather than being an economic burden as occurred when taxes were levied to pay for war, "in an industrial society the object of taxation is to increase industrial prosperity" by lowering costs. Taxes spent on internal improvements would be "burdenless"

---

[7] See below, pp. 297–313.

if invested in projects such as transport infrastructure in the form of canals and railroads to lower distribution costs, and a postal service and public education to increase productivity. The classic example was the Erie Canal, which lowered farm rents in upstate New York by making cheaper Western grain available. The return to public investment in the form of transportation and other infrastructure was measured not by the earnings it generated, but by its ability to lower the economy's overall cost structure. "Parks, sewers and schools improve the health and intelligence of all classes of producers," elaborated Patten, "and thus enable them to produce more cheaply, and to compete more successfully in other markets."[8]

(6) *Banking and finance as public utilities*

The legacy of British banking in the United States was a system based mainly on trade financing and speculation, prompting Democrats such as Thomas Jefferson and Andrew Jackson to fight against a central bank and branch banking so as to prevent bankers from becoming powerful enough to siphon off the economic surplus. It was in France and Germany that banking developed more along industrial lines, coordinated with government planning and a heavily military element in the case of Germany. But the continental European industrial model never gained a foothold in America. What was unique was the government acting as the main credit creator during the Civil War by issuing greenbacks. The subsequent Greenback and Populist Parties (not dealt with in this volume) urged the Treasury to provide bank credit and earn interest on behalf of the public domain, but little attempt was made to establish government banking as a serious alternative to New York, Philadelphia, Boston and Chicago. The main concern was to counter the deflationary price pressures resulting from the government's attempt to roll gold prices back to their pre-Civil War levels. This raised the debt burden on agriculture in particular, imposing financial austerity on the national economy and spurring a pamphlet literature on monetary reform and predatory interest extraction.

---

[8] "The Theory of Dynamic Economics," in *Essays in Economic Theory* ed. Rexford Guy Tugwell (New York: 1924, Knopf), p. 96, originally in *The Publications of the University of Pennsylvania, Political Economy and Public Law Series* 3:2 (whole No. 11), 1892. "If a state is military in character and passive in its [economic development] policy," Patten explained, "it is a consumer of wealth and not a producer. Its expenses must then be met by taxation based upon moral or political ideals." Europe's aristocratic governments, prone as they were to military adventurism, developed their tax policy "at a time when the state was a mere military organization for the defense of society from foreign foes, or to gratify national feelings by aggressive wars." In view of the fact that Patten was the first economics professor at the nation's dominant business school of the day, the Wharton School at the University of Pennsylvania, the neglect of American School economics is all the more remarkable.

(7) *A broad historical and sociological view of economic analysis*

In creating an alternative to the free-trade emphasis on current market prices, incomes and productivity, the American School extended the scope of economic logic to focus on long-term development not reflected in market prices. Taking into account soil and resource depletion, capital productivity and technology, education and infrastructure investment led American economic analysis to develop on lines that came to be called institutionalist. This focus developed alongside socialist and Progressive Era critiques of market forces in their political context. Both schools advocated a greater government role in shaping market forces, in contrast to the individualistic lines endorsed by Democratic political leaders and the free-trade curriculum maintained at the oldest and most prestigious Anglophile colleges.

(8) *A materialistic and secular but non-Marxian technological view of economic evolution*

American materialism rejected socialist doctrines of class conflict and pessimistic warnings of impoverishment based on diminishing returns and population growth on the one hand, and also Europe's sanctimonious and authoritarian religion bolstering the authority of that continent's hereditary aristocracies and vested financial interests. Instead of focusing on class conflict and viewing capital as income exploited from wage-labor, the American School viewed capital accumulation as the technological ability to exploit nature—not land and natural resources as in Ricardian economics, but natural energy, mainly a function of the progress of science and technology. American economists thus were materialist in a non-Marxist way, advocates for industrial capital rather than criticizing it. Whereas the focus of classical European political economy was how to purify industrial capitalism from the rentier legacy from feudal conquest of the land and the imposition of groundrent, American writers were technological optimists postulating a harmony of interests between capital and labor—and agriculture too, which they analyzed as an application of capital to the land or what in time would be called "agribusiness." This approach led to the analysis of land as capital, and even its conflation at the hands of John Bates Clark in the 1890s.

Yet most historians have focused on the Democratic Party's political and economic policies. The topics of Manifest Destiny, slavery and abolitionism, land speculation and the creation of wealth American families from insider land and financial dealings have crowded out discussion of the debate over government economic policy to promote industry and technology. Partly this neglect of Whig and Republican political economy reflects the fact that the first major American academic alternative to British free-trade economics did not emerge until the 1880s and 1890s. Trained in German universities, the new generation of economists brought back to the United States a social-democratic ideology of public regulation of markets. This itself stemmed in no small part from Friedrich List, whose ideas were formed largely in the United States in the 1820s and 1830s in association with Mathew Carey's Philadelphia circle.

In Simon Patten the American School found a synthesis with the German political economy in which most late 19th-century U.S. economists were trained. Along with other German-trained economists, he formed the American Economic Association to serve as the equivalent of Germany's Verein für Sozialpolitik. As usual, free traders opposed the new organization. J. Laurence Laughlin at the University of Chicago, along with Frank Taussig at Harvard, Arthur T. Hadley at Yale and the social Darwinist William Graham Sumner refused to join. The free-trade strongholds at Columbia University, Harvard and Yale promoted the pragmatic "value-free" approach of John Bates Clark, along with English individualism.

One byproduct was a secularist critique of religious dogma at the nation's land grant colleges and newer academic centers such as Cornell, as well as business schools such as the Wharton School at the University of Pennsylvania. Leading American historians found in the Arab Renaissance a vehicle to contrast to the Inquisition's Catholic Church's stifling of intellectual freedom. Washington Irving wrote on the Alhambra, William Hickling Prescott on the conquest of Peru and Mexico, and Henry Carey Lea on the Spanish Inquisition, a theme picked up John Draper, Simon Newcomb and Simon Patten. The common denominator with the American School's economic views was the emphasis on empirical analysis as a check on the tendency of deductive reasoning to deteriorate into a dogmatic and distorted world-view.

After World War I the German-trained economists were isolated as "institutionalists," a group that included Thorstein Veblen and most academics who analyzed land and monopoly rent as an overhead to be minimized by being regulated or taxed away. Even in the business schools, which had been founded to counter free-market logic, the theorizing of Clark and British marginalists replaced the American School of technologically oriented economics. Having little use for this broader protectionist body of theory, the victorious free-trade ideology proclaimed itself to be the new perfection of method and content. The economic doctrine that shaped early American public policy was forgotten, a condition in which it remains today. America's leaders no longer found it in the national interest to broadcast a global understanding of the logic and that of British imperial strategists as to how free trade served to crush foreign industry in its cradle, explanations gleefully quoted by American protectionists.

Today, foreign countries might equally well cite the early U.S. analysis of the dynamic at work—from the victim's vantage point. The logic guiding American economic policy during the Republican half-century from 1860 to 1912 aimed at countering the "lock-in" effect of existing productivity disparities under free trade.

In appropriating the lead-nation status hitherto occupied by Britain, the United States has adopted a status quo thinking that causes cognitive dissonance in acknowledging the policies developed by the American School of political economy. Having replaced Britain as the world's major industrial and creditor power after World War I, the United States adopted free trade and open financial markets on precisely the grounds that its early protectionists criticized Britain for doing. American economic strategists had learned the lesson that free trade benefits the strong at the expense of the weak. Instead of examining the path by which the United States built up its economic strength, foreign countries have adopted today's free-market Washington Consensus "Do as we say, not as we have done" as a timeless policy guide. This approach misses the strategy by which the United States rose to industrial supremacy after the Civil War. Loss of the American School's critique of free-trade logic has left the road open for an acceptance of neoliberal ideology that is blocking countries from upgrading their labor, industry and agriculture, locking countries that fail to protect their home markets into a syndrome of economic obsolescence.

INTRODUCTION

Among the many American economists of the two generations spanning the Treaty of Ghent in 1814 and outbreak of civil war in 1861, only Friedrich List and Henry Carey have gained recognition. Daniel Raymond has received some attention as a precursor of List, Mathew Carey as a leading journalist and publisher, and the Canadian-American economist John Rae as an anticipator of various theories of productivity and interest. There have been some excellent studies of post-Civil War theorists of technology and society, as John W. Draper, Simon Newcomb, Simon Patten, and Thorstein Veblen. But no serious scholarship has been published on Alexander Everett, Calvin Colton, E. Peshine Smith, Stephen Colwell, Francis Bowen, Van Buren Denslow and lesser lights. No attempt has been made to relate their economic theories to their regional context and self-interest, or to the evolution of American materialism, social Darwinism, and ultimately the attempt to create in America a new civilization differing fundamentally from that of the Old World.

Even in the decades following the Civil War when protectionism was firmly establishing itself as national policy, American academicians ignored the substantial contribution to economic theory made by the American School of economists. The reason is that this school was uniformly protectionist, whereas academic orthodoxy continued to be dominated by laissez-faire ideology. We are thus faced with the anomaly that while increasingly protectionist policies were being enacted by Congress, their academic defense was muted. Matters hardly were helped by the fact that by the 1870s the protectionists clustered around Henry Carey had become somewhat of a sect, cut off not only from the mainstream of laissez-faire academic economics but even from the third generation of protectionists returning from Germany with a greater social idealism.

Representative of this period's academic attitude was C. F. Dunbar's summary comment in 1876 that American writers had contributed "nothing towards developing the theory of political economy..."[9] European economists

---

[9] Charles F. Dunbar, "Economic Science in America, 1776–1876," *North American Review* 121 (1876), reprinted in his *Economic Essays* (ed. Sprague; New York, 1904). This deprecation was endorsed by Dunbar's fellow American, Henry W. Farnam in his "Deutsch-amerikanische Beziehungen in der Volkswirtschaftslehre," in *Die Entwicklung der deutschen Volkswirtschaftslehre im neunzehnten Jahrhundert* (Schmoller Festschrift), Vol. I (Leipzig, 1908).

paid more serious attention to the theoretical contribution made by American protectionists. The German historical school and its admirers in France produced studies of List and his indebtedness to American protectionist thought. Dühring in Germany, Ferrara in Italy, and followers of Bastiat in France elaborated Carey's "optimistic" theory of economic growth. Works of Carey and Peshine Smith were translated into French, Italian and German during the 1850s to 1870s. The Irish historical economist Cliffe Leslie wrote a number of articles on the American School. An Italian, Ugo Rabbeno, published one of the earliest studies of American protectionism. To be sure, he observed, "in the crowd of American protectionist writers and their contradictors … rarely indeed is originality to be met with, and mere commonplace abounds; and in the advocates of protection, many are the errors which do not even need refutation, whilst their adversaries repeat ad nauseam the old theoretical arguments dogmatised by liberalism: and in general, both sides are so engrossed with the attack and defence of their respective positions and the interests depending on them, that it is vain to expect any impartial scientific conclusions from their labours." Nonetheless, he stressed, "whilst the aspect of American liberalism … is marked by an almost complete want of originality, and forms no particular code of doctrines, originality is, on the other hand, to be found in some of the more eminent advocates of protection, and they have inspired, to a greater or less extent, all of their contemporaries."[10]

Some interest in the early protectionists developed in reference to their rent theories. Frank Fetter was especially struck by their general identification of rent with interest (and implicitly of land with capital). Fetter in fact believed that a major factor in the neglect of these early writers was precisely "the dominance of the Ricardian economics in America, especially after J. S. Mill's work gave it a new vogue among American readers." Finding the anti-Ricardians "strangely neglected by later generations of American students,"[11] he urged his student John R. Turner to write his dissertation on rent theory among the antebellum American economists.

One cannot but agree with Turner that "students of the history of economic thought have inexcusably neglected the early American economists."[12] Nonetheless, his book failed to ignite any great interest in these writers. A decade later, in 1932, M. R. Eiselen wrote a dissertation on *The Rise of Pennsylvania Protectionism*, although this was mainly a study in local political history rather

---

[10] Ugo Rabbeno, *The American Commercial Policy: Three Historical Essays* (London, 1895), p. 288.
[11] Introduction to John R. Turner, *The Ricardian Rent Theory in Early American Economics* (New York, 1921), pp. vii, viii.
[12] *Ibid.*, p. xv.

than economic theory. Ernest Teilhac's *Pioneers of American Economic Thought in the Nineteenth Century* (1935) concentrated only on Daniel Raymond, Henry Carey and Henry George. Carl William Kaiser's dissertation on the *History of the American Protectionist – Free Trade Controversy* (Philadelphia, 1939) provided a catalog of arguments relating directly to the tariff debate, but did not investigate any of the theories developed by protectionists beyond the confines of their most immediate application to the tariff controversy. Michael J. L. O'Connor's *Origins of Academic Economics in the United States*, published in 1944, contains much valuable thinking on the ante bellum protectionists, as well as an exhaustive bibliography. Indeed, O'Connor shows the neglect of the early protectionists to be all the more strange in view of their association with a number of the nation's colleges — especially the University of Pennsylvania following the Civil War — and the adoption of books by Colton, Peshine Smith and Bowen as texts, as well as Henry Carey's *Principles of Social Science* (particularly in Kate McLean's one-volume summary) and, after the Civil War, books by Carey's followers Robert Ellis Thompson at the University of Pennsylvania and William E. Wilson at Cornell University.

Nonetheless, Joseph Dorfman's six-volume review of American economic thought glossed over the protectionists, omitting altogether such men as Mathew Carey, George Tibbits and Erastus Bigelow, devoting but four pages to Alexander Everett, half a page each to Calvin Colton and Van Buren Denslow, three confused pages to E. Peshine Smith, and eight pages to Simon Patten. Dorfman devoted scarcely a word to Henry Clay, Andrew Stewart or other politicians whose speeches expounded the protectionist doctrines of the American School. Horace Greeley is described simply as a utopian socialist, and the largest space — ten pages — is devoted to Francis Bowen, certainly the least original of the self-proclaimed American School.

Largely responsible for Dorfman's cursory treatment was his view that "there were too many conflicting interests involved in the protectionist cause to make it anything more than a jumble of opportunistic motives."[13] This is a curious reason indeed, for free trade was just as sectionally opportunistic and diverse in its motives as it came to be expounded in the Northeast, the slave South and the rural West. In fact, it is precisely the sectional divisions and loyalties dividing the Northern protectionists that make their position interesting as an indicator of the evolution of American political-economic development as a differentiated whole.

---

[13] Joseph Dorfman, *The Economic Mind of American Civilization*, Vol. 11 (New York, 1946), p. 596.

The major reason for Dorfman's dismissal of the American protectionists seems to be his dislike for non-laissez-faire policy and doctrine. In this respect his work is unfortunately prejudiced, *for the nineteenth century American economic mind, to the extent that it was original, was highly protectionist.* Dorfman has prejudiced himself (and thus a generation of potentially interested scholars) from investigating the concepts and theories developed by the American School regarding wages, profits, rent, business cycles, population, productivity and economic growth—precisely those theories that were most original and characteristically American in the period covered by his work.

Nor was interest in the ante-bellum economic writers stimulated by Schumpeter's judgment that Dunbar's flippant dismissal of them in 1876 "has not been invalidated by the information made available by more recent research. It is indeed not true if we take account of problems raised, suggestions made, and factual work done, but it is true if we emphasize the word theory."[14] Among the protectionists, however, were some who developed theories which, though novel in their time, are today taken for granted, such as the (marginal) productivity theories of wages and interest, and the theory of non-competing groups. Others developed concepts now exciting economists as modern innovations, such as the treatment of educational skills as a representative form of capital, the theory of technological obsolescence, capital as a form of energy-conversion vehicle, a concept of soil fertility much more dynamic than that found in orthodox Ricardian economics of the day, an analysis of the nature of international dependency and terms-of-trade exploitation, and an elaboration of the changing nature of labor and land as economic inputs during the course of technological evolution.

Members of the American School sought to ground their economic thought in the natural sciences and comparative history rather than in the deductive trains of moral philosophy and teleology that characterized British political economy. They developed an economy-of-high-wages doctrine and elaborated it as a form of Social Darwinism. They argued against the bland Ricardian assumption of the neutrality of money in international trade. They sought to extend abstract economic categories into their sociological and historical-institutional setting, and to trace the relationship between economic and technological evolution and the transformation of social forms, including what today is being revived as the debate over "postindustrial" economic society.

That these innovations were made specifically by protectionists is not surprising in light of the fact that the fundamental question underlying the U.S. tariff debate was the nature and consequences of industrial growth.

---

[14] Joseph Schumpeter, *History of Economic Analysis* (New York, 1954), p. 514.

International trade was viewed as only one element of a much broader system of economic considerations. In fact, it is only because protective tariffs were the common policy conclusion of these economists that they have come to be grouped together as "protectionists," and the term is somewhat unfortunate. They referred to themselves as members of the American School, and their investigations far surpassed the confines of trade theory as such. The term American System was popularized by Henry Clay during the 1820s as a slogan for his program of protective tariffs, internal improvements and a national bank.

This program was defended by protectionists of varying sectional loyalties, whose common ground was an attempt to controvert the doctrines of Ricardo and Malthus that had come to be used as doctrinal support for the Democratic Party's program of free trade and limited federal activity. The most original minds among the protectionist writers were those seeking to supplant the Ricardo-Malthus long-term model of economic growth (emphasizing distribution within a relatively stagnant economy characterized by diminishing returns) with one more optimistic as to the evolution of industrial civilization's rapidly expanding productive powers and rising wage levels.

There can be no doubt that protectionist growth theory was often permeated with bias and designed to serve specific sectional interests. It was the product of partisan and politically active men, often journalists and pamphleteers who had close contact with Whig and (after 1854) Republican leaders. Alexander Everett during the 1820s to 1840s, and Francis Bowen in the 1850s, provided an economic theory supporting the policies of the Webster Whigs from their native Massachusetts. Calvin Colton was the official biographer of Henry Clay and edited his works, enunciating a protectionist doctrine particularly attractive to the northern border states and their allied non-abolitionist classes further north. Henry Carey's economic thought reflected the protectionist needs of his native Pennsylvania.

The writings of these economists reflect the sectional antagonisms developing within the Whig Party during the 1840s between the Northeast Seaboard, inland industry, and the border states. Peshine Smith, by contrast — in many respects the most original of the American School — was a protege of William Henry Seward, the ideological leader of the Republican Party during the 1850s. He was representative of the upstate New York protectionists that dominated U.S. foreign policy following the Civil War. The two Sewards (elder and son), along with Hamilton Fish and Peshine Smith, all from upstate New York, were the four highest-ranking State Department officers during the 1860s, and felt their regional background quite strongly.

The sectional aspect of the leading controversies in American economic thought becomes all the more apparent when it is borne in mind that protectionist doctrine was closely interwoven with the theory of population and agricultural productivity. Indeed, what has become known under the portmanteau term "tariff debate" was more accurately a debate as to the dynamics of economic growth itself. *Its major issue was whether the nation should remain primarily agricultural or industrialize*, whether the South should become the focal point of a westwards-expanding slave system, or the Northeastern and Middle Atlantic states become the focal point of an increasingly industrial national economy.

Southerners and Northern free traders adopted the doctrines of Malthus and Ricardo to argue that industrialization, immigration and concentration of America's population in an urban East would soon bring about diminishing returns in agriculture, eroding living standards and ultimately the very institutions of democratic society. It was a Democrat who coined the phrase *Manifest Destiny*, and Malthusian doctrine which depicted America's vast land area as its great economic advantage over more "mature" nations.

The protectionist Whigs, by contrast, pointed to the economic burden sustained by America as a result of its great land expanse relative to the sparseness of its population. An expensive transport overhead was needed to distribute the country's output, while the large distances separating urban consumers from Western farmlands rendered uneconomic the return to the soil of urban wastes, and thereby contributed to soil depletion. A compact urban-rural balance was necessary to achieve optimum farming practices, and an increasing population density to achieve optimum economies of scale, rising wage levels and higher living standards. Westward expansion would thus forestall the benefits of industrialization.

Among the proponents of industrialization, representatives of each geographic region claimed to enunciate the truly "American" school of political economy. The major sectional division occurred over the role to be played by foreign commerce after industrialization had occurred and all available lands filled up. The Boston protectionists Everett and Bowen reflected their region's commercial shipping interests in asserting that although increasing population density enabled increasing returns to occur in manufacturing, it resulted in diminishing returns in agriculture once "optimum" density was reached. In this respect they endorsed the Ricardo-Malthus doctrine: Because of diminishing returns, they argued, once America's soil came to be fully cultivated, the nation would have to emulate Britain's example and export its manufactures in exchange for foreign raw materials. They believed that this could occur on favorable terms of trade, and thus would not impair incomes and living standards.

By contrast, Henry Carey and his followers, and later Simon Patten and what became known as the "Chinese Wall" school, argued for America to aim at total self-sufficiency and virtual economic isolation from foreign countries, at least from those more industrially advanced such as England. They claimed that increasing population density normally was accompanied by increasing returns in agriculture as well as in industry, and concluded that population growth could occur indefinitely without requiring the United States to become a net importer of food and raw materials.

Gradually an anti-Ricardian and anti-Malthusian doctrine was built up that made a lasting contribution to economic thought and policy. Among its formulators were some excellent minds which, although not unaffected by special interest considerations, pierced the fog of polemical discussion to develop important truths. Nonetheless, the contribution made by the American School remains neglected. The idea persists that these writers possessed, in Schumpeter's words, "hardly more than traces of an impulse to develop analytic tools," and that they were little more than a group of "would-be theorists who disdained to learn the art of theorizing."[15]

Studies paving the way for a new integration of the varied strands of American political-economic ideology have concentrated mainly on its post-Civil War flowering into full-blown systems. Among the most valuable of these studies are Richard Hofstadter's *Social Darwinism in American Thought* (1944), Donald Fleming's *John William Draper and the Religion of Science* (1950), and Daniel Fox's *The Discovery of Abundance: Simon N. Patten and the Transformation of Social Theory* (1957). The present study concentrates on the pre-Civil War roots of this ideology. It portrays the evolution of American economic idealism in geographic motion, shifting its political base on numerous occasions as dictated by regional self-interest but always remaining economic at base. It is in this economic respect that American social and national idealism stood apart from British political philosophy as a system. The latter remained essentially a teleological moral philosophy which concentrated on ideal ends, not the analysis of processes and their superstructures such as is found in the United States.

American economic idealism was as much a materialist protest against orthodox moral philosophy as was European Marxism. Like Marxism, it increasingly widened its scope beyond the confines of marketplace economics to comprehend social and historical analysis in its broadest sense. Unlike Marxism, it was characterized not by a doctrine of class conflict but of man's struggle to master the forces of nature for the benefit of labor and capital together. Hence its ability to comprehend not only protectionism but populism,

---

[15] Joseph Schumpeter, *History of Economic Analysis* (New York, 1954), pp. 514, 676.

and to include in its ranks such seeming anomalies as Horace Greeley and Henry George. Hence, too, the ever-present tension between Henry Carey's followers—the second generation of American protectionists, which pretty much ignored the fact that their doctrine was being used to support increasingly powerful industrial trusts—and the American national economists who returned from Germany with a greater degree of sympathy for domestic social reforms, men such as Simon Patten and his colleagues who took the lead in forming the American Economic Association in 1886.

The American School and its successors inspired Brooks and Henry Adams to trace the social consequences of man's growing command over nature's energy resources. Most important from the standpoint of today's simplistic textbook view of American history, it argued against tendencies that are now viewed as monotonic in American history: westward expansionism and Manifest Destiny, the rise of America as an export power, its growing military role played in foreign continents, and the about-face made by American economic orthodoxy following World War I when the United States, having supplanted Britain as the world's economic lead-nation, adopted in its turn the doctrines of laissez-faire against which it had struggled for the first hundred and fifty years of its existence. Present-day American economics students are taught modernized versions of the doctrines of Ricardo and Malthus which were controverted more than a century ago by the American School. Today's view of the evolution of American economic and political thought thus diverges from the historical setting of this evolution, and is more a product of contemporary orthodoxy than that of the original contributors to and formulators of this broad-ranging ideology.

I. Review of the Literature

THE REACTIONARY ROLE PLAYED BY THE COLLEGES IN FORMING DISTINCTLY AMERICAN IDEALS

The economic doctrines unique to America in the nineteenth century developed almost entirely outside of the nation's academic centers—mainly by journalists and reverends in the retinues of the leading Whig and (after 1854) Republican politicians, and by a few businessmen. This non-academic nexus has led modern observers to dismiss the American School's protectionist theories of trade and development as little more than a special-interest lobbying effort. But when we look at the substance of this theorizing we find a principled and well-informed alternative to the free-trade theory taught in most colleges. With few exceptions the academic presentation of economics in the clerical schools of the Northeast and the major Southern colleges followed the free-trade policy conclusions of British moral philosophy. Critics rejected this not because they were anti-intellectual but because they found the doctrines of David Ricardo and Thomas Malthus unduly pessimistic in rationalizing the status quo as natural and inevitable—including U.S. dependence on England in exchanging its rural agricultural products (headed by slave plantation crops) for urban manufactures.

Rejecting free trade as a timeless and universal policy, protectionists held that no *a priori* rule was appropriate to guide nations at all stages of their development. Arguing that institutions and historical circumstances differed among nations, they accused British liberalism of claiming an unwarranted universality of scope and using circular reasoning to rationalize the status quo and its trade patterns as being natural and inevitable. Much as today's Third World and Asian countries criticize the free market orthodoxy of mainstream economics, so the 19th-century American School pointed out that free trade doctrine reflected Britain's own self-interest in seeking to consolidate its status as workshop of the world. It also served the commercial interest of Southern agricultural exporters and their allies among New England shipping interests and the New York and Philadelphia banking houses in opposing a national industrial tariff policy.

Policy makers who reject the free market doctrines underlying today's global diplomacy thus could find no better backing than the trade and development theory that enabled the United States to end up outstripping Britain as the

11

workshop (and creditor) of the world. After the Civil War the nation rejected free trade, seeking to transform the existing status quo by shaping markets to improve productivity, profits and wage levels in tandem.

Early economic teaching as moral philosophy

Political economy was not originally a separate subject, but was taught as a branch of moral philosophy, typically by men trained in theology or law. It usually covered one of the three terms in the senior year, after the moral philosophy course. A favorite early textbook was the Cambridge Rev. William Paley's Principles of Moral and Political Philosophy (1785), followed by texts by Rev. John McVicker (1825), Rev. Samuel P. Newman (1835), Rev. Francis Wayland (1837), Rev. Aaron L. Chapin (1878), and Rev. Arthur Perry (1866). Their books described how economic growth should occur under a "natural" free-trade order leading to the existing status quo, and how income was distributed under current production conditions. Rather than seeking to develop a manufacturing base, academicians in the Southern and Northeastern states found America's economic strength as well as democratic political foundation to lie in its agrarian base. They feared that once the Western lands were fully occupied and the country was forced to begin industrializing, wages would fall, profits would follow suit and the country's political institutions would crumble.

In this respect their theories transplanted the doctrines of Malthus and Ricardo. As Wesley Mitchell has noted, "the attitude of early American economists is reminiscent of the American poets who wrote many a verse to the skylark without observing that the skylark is not an American species. It is a sort of literary tradition carried on by men whose minds are not primarily concerned with economics and people who are not thinking hard about problems other than the formal ones which they found in older books and which they reproduced and solved with their own panegyrics upon the harmony of economic organization."[16]

This degree of abstraction was not disinterested. Academic economics in the United States was as partisan as it was in other countries. Texts departed from the exposition of general principles to pamphleteer, and professorial chairs served as pulpits from which were attacked protective tariffs, communism, and slavery or abolition, depending on the location of the college.

"The earliest northern colleges," wrote Michael O'Connor in his comprehensive *Origins of Academic Economics in the United States*, "were Harvard (1636) and Yale (1701), seminaries for training Congregational ministers. Since the Church was the state Church, these colleges were essentially state institutions...

---

[16] Wesley C. Mitchell, *Types of Economic Theory, From Mercantilism to Institutionalism* (New York: 1969), Vol. II, p. 224.

The Presbyterians created Princeton (1746). In 1751 Franklin's forerunner of the University of Pennsylvania came into existence, and a Church-of-England head was appointed in 1754. Columbia, predominantly Anglican, was founded (1754) in New York. The Baptists set up Brown (1764) in Rhode Island; and the Dutch Reformed, Rutgers (1770) in New Jersey."[17] Dartmouth (1769) began as a Congregationalist missionary college for the Native Americans ("Indians") on the frontier.

Richard Hofstadter has warned against the notion "that Harvard and the other colonial colleges were at their inception no more than theological seminaries … In fact … the founding fathers of colonial education saw no difference between the basic education appropriate for a cleric and that appropriate for any other liberally educated man. The idea of a distinctly theological seminary is a product of modern specialism, sectarian competition, and of a reaction to the threat of secularism in the colleges. Such an idea was outside their ken. … in Harvard's first two generations, only half the graduates became ministers and the remainder went into secular occupations."[18] However, these secular graduates were brought up with a religious ideology centered on the moral philosophy course, and colonial college presidents were clergymen.

Benjamin Franklin tried to establish a more secular trend by appointing laymen as the first trustees of his Pennsylvania Academy in 1751. His *Proposals for a Complete Education of Youth* (1749) suggested "a course of instruction which, although dealing primarily with history," presented it in a predominantly secular economic setting. "He proposed that information be given in the curriculum on the history of commerce, on the invention of the arts, on the rise of manufactures, on the progress of trade, and the change of its seats together with the reasons and causes therefore."[19] However, O'Connor notes, "the Church of England soon increased its control over the college in Philadelphia," moving it away from the aims of its original trustees.

Columbia College likewise initiated a few independent courses in commerce and government, but "gradually became an Anglican appendage. … In 1775 Columbia's president was chased back to England, and in 1784 the Regents appointed by the state legislature formally took over the school." Similarly Brown University, which under Baptist control had acted as a force for tolerance and whose trustees "gave representation to four sects, and … rejected religious discrimination," gave way as "Brown came under the educational influence of Princeton and tended to follow the standard northern ideas on

---

[17] Michael J. L. O'Connor, *Origins of Academic Economics in the United States* (New York: 1944), pp. 64f.

[18] Richard Hofstadter, *Anti-Intellectualism in American Life* (New York: 1963), p. 60.

[19] O'Connor, *Origins*, p. 66.

curriculum."[20] As Cliffe Leslie observed in 1880, a distinguishing feature of American political economy "is the conspicuousness of a theological element." However, this element was highly elastic as to its implications for public policy. "Assumptions respecting the Divine will and designs are employed by both protectionists and free-traders in support of their theories. The Malthusian theory is controverted as atheistic in tendency, and contrary to the commandment to replenish the earth. ... Down to recent time, also, the lecturers on political economy in American Colleges were for the most part, as many of them still are, ministers of religion. This circumstance is itself connected with a more general cause; for political philosophy has been left to a theological class, who have worked their professional ideas into it, because the laity were engaged in more lucrative pursuits."[21]

It was this worldliness that led commercial interests to supplant the early theocracy after the American Revolution. A kind of clerical-aristocratic philosophy emerged as a counterpoise to democracy. As O'Connor describes, "the Clerical School of political economy was a social instrument," developed when the elite of the Northeast "consisted of merchants, bankers, and their professional associates. On the whole, the teachings of the clerical school developed in harmony with the needs and interests of this elite." The result was not a high level of intellectual scholarship. "In 1826 Wadsworth made the complaint that our colleges initiate nothing and 'have to be dragged along by public sentiment.'" Harriet Martineau, writing in 1837, "was especially critical of Boston gentlemen and New England merchants because they were so conspicuous in the proslavery mobs. She said the merchants 'have kept the clergy dumb ... overawed the colleges, [and] given their cue to the newspapers,' on the slavery issue." The college president was a "gentleman" who easily dominated the school, his main task being to raise funds from leading merchants ("the giving men") and teaching the moral philosophy course, usually including political economy as its final semester. "In the clerical political economy the mercantile Northeast found elements which proved valuable in counteracting the claims of democrats and protectionists."

From the vantage point of most college administrations the function of higher education was conservative and quiescent, aimed at instilling moral and political views consonant with the existing division of property and social power. O'Connor cites Jane Marcet's claim that "youth and innocence may be molded into any form you choose to give them," and Rev. Chalmers' bold statement that

[20] O'Connor, *Origins*, pp. 66ff.
[21] Thomas E. Cliffe Leslie, "Political Economy in the United States" [1880], in *Essays in Political Economy*, 2nd ed. (London, 1888), pp. 137–39.

We affirm that reason will make anything palatable to the lower orders; and, if only permitted to lift her voice in some cool place, as in the class-room of a school of arts, she will attain as firm authority over the popular mind, as she wields now within the walls of parliament. And political economy, the introduction of which into our popular courses has been so much deprecated, will be found to have pre-eminence over the other sciences, in acting as a sedative, and not as a stimulant to all sorts of turbulence and disorder. It will afford another example of the affinity which exists between the cause of popular education, and that of public tranquillity. Of all the branches of that education, there is none which will contribute more to the quiescence of the multitude, than the one for whose admittance into our mechanic schools we are now pleading.[22]

The resulting economic doctrine opposed the nationalism threatening to alter New England's established trading patterns by insulating the American economy from that of England. The Clerical School was cohesive largely because it found a ready-made whole in British thought. It was mindful of its regional economic loyalties, trying "to repel the Jacksonian challenge to vested banking interests" as well as the religious skepticism characteristic of the labor movement by 1830. Clerical textbooks "usually ignored the slavery issue. Since the cotton planter had largely abandoned Jeffersonianism, it was possible for the Northeastern clerics to regard him as an ally against the Western democracy, as well as against protectionism."[23]

Moral philosophy served as the "matrix of the social sciences" especially in colleges in the Northeast, literally "seminaries of learning" that remained under sectarian domination longer than in other regions of the country.[24] Only outside of academia at the hands of the American School did this matrix take on a natural science base, evolving into what Auguste Comte called Sociology or Social Physics, a secularization of economic thought akin to the spirit of early Jeffersonianism.

Religious protestations might in principle have been used to justify protectionist policies, as evidenced by the ministers to be found among the protectionists (Colton, Colwell and William Ellis Thompson), much as Bishop Berkeley, Josiah Tucker and others are to be found among the British "mercantilists." So it was by no means religious leanings alone that led to the particular views of economic writers citing theological justification. Once having formulated their views, they rationalized how these might be fitted into the divine natural order of society so as to give minimum offense to their Christian audience. It is difficult to gauge the extent to which religious sentiment was inserted for rhetorical

---

[22] O'Connor, *Origins* p. 92, citing Jane Marcet, *Conversations on Political Economy* (London, 1816), pp. 119f. and Thomas Chalmers, *The Christian and Civic Economy of Large Towns* (Glasgow, 1821–26), Vol. III.

[23] O'Connor, *Origins*, pp. 276, 70, 75, 97, 278.

[24] *Ibid.*, pp. 1f.

purposes, but at least it is clear that the religious sentiments often voiced by the American School of economists did not interfere with their materialistic technological foundation of economic theory.

The Southern context

The Jeffersonian initiative in building a popular educational system and introducing political economy into the college curriculum reflected "the agrarian republicanism of the Virginia dynasty dominating the National Government in the early decades of the century." He wished to construct "a model, nonclerical, state university as 'the future bulwark of the human mind in this hemisphere,'"[25] an institution that would "give to every citizen the information he needs for the transaction of his daily business ... and, in general, to observe with intelligence and faithfulness all the social relations under which he shall be placed." This dream was fulfilled in 1819 when the University of Virginia was established at Charlottesville, less than four miles from Monticello.

Jefferson "considered intercourse with England 'contaminating' and condemned its cultural influence." In 1817 he had translated Destutt de Tracy's *Treatise on Political Economy* for use as the prospective university's major economics textbook. De Tracy opposed payment of interest by banks, and condemned paper money as a combination of robbery and monopoly. He also identified the interests of the poor with those of society generally. But use of his book never really spread, and O'Connor points out that a Jeffersonian economics as such never developed. "After Jefferson died, reaction in Southern political economy became plainly evident. The politics of the Cooper school was broadly in favor of slavery and against the new democracy."

Thomas Cooper started out as an English radical and abolitionist, served time as a Pennsylvania protectionist, moved South in 1819 to become a protégé of Jefferson, and ended up an increasingly reactionary president of the University of South Carolina during 1820-1834. O'Connor describes the emerging Southern School as "primarily concerned with defending the Southern planter from the protectionist onslaught of Carey's Pennsylvanians. Cooper's group found that the handiest weapon in this struggle was an adaptation of Ricardian political economy. ...Jeffersonianism, allied as it was with the early progressive spirit of Pennsylvania and the West, expressed a philosophy of leadership advocating change. The Cooper school, on the other hand, was actuated by the need to conserve and defend. ...There was a Southern tendency to be critical of banks, or at least neutral on the issue. Southerners often claimed that the economic position of Northern laborers was not at all unlike that of slaves. ...

---

[25] *Ibid.*, pp. 19, 23f. See also p. 68.

[But t]hey never so much as endorsed the cause of the Northern worker."[26] Mitchell describes Cooper "as singularly unobservant" of the economic differences between the United States and England: "He wrote his treatise on British models and had nothing to say in a systematic way about the extraordinary difference between the economic organization of the community where he was writing and that of England. One would have thought that a person concerned with economic problems in South Carolina at the time would have felt it incumbent to show in his treatise what modifications in British views were necessary to take into account the great institution of slavery. But the alterations are not found in Cooper's treatise."[27]

In sum, the Jeffersonians never developed their political idealism into any systematic economic doctrine partly because of the South's anti-industrialism and its growing espousal of slavery. A slave system hardly could be expected to develop an Economy of High Wages doctrine. Nor were Northeastern writers interested in idealizing a self-sufficient, American economy isolated from the growth of international commerce.

Sectional interests and the content of economic theorizing

To understand economic theorizing in pre-Civil War America, we must recognize four regional schools of economic thought: the Northeastern clerical school, tied closely to British laissez faire orthodoxy; the Southern school, inspired initially by Jefferson and then degenerating into the Cooper school; the Middle Atlantic protectionist school led by Carey *père et fils*; and the Boston School of protectionism as a kind of hybrid of the latter two schools. These schools diverged broadly in their methodology, content, and degree of optimism or pessimism about the prospects of economic evolution.

Originally federalist, the Bostonian and kindred Northeast increasingly opposed strong government intervention in economic life. It felt its economic interest to lie more with England and the South than with the Middle Atlantic industrial states. Southern plantation interests likewise led the region to espouse laissez faire doctrine. Both these regions thus found their commercial interest to lie in popularizing British economic orthodoxy averse to industrial protectionism.

Economists in each region usually started with a given policy conclusion — especially on the tariff — which bore special relevance to their local interests, and then tried to rationalize the policy they intuitively felt appropriate for their

---

[26] *Ibid.*, pp. 61f. See also pp. 48ff. Cooper's *Lectures on the Elements of Political Economy* was published at Columbia, South Carolina, in 1826. He was succeeded as president of this university by the equally reactionary Francis Lieber.

[27] Mitchell, *Types of Economic Theory*, p. 223.

time and circumstances into a full-blown logical system. I do not mean to say that this policy inspiration of their doctrines means that their objectivity was willfully twisted to serve political and economic self-interest, but simply that most economic theories are time- and space-bound. This explains why each region's leading economists tended to ally themselves with one another, as no "American" environment yet existed as such.

For instance, the theories enunciated by the Boston protectionists Alexander Everett, Willard Phillips and Francis Bowen — all Philips, Exeter and Harvard graduates, and all active in New England publishing and political life — stand in sharp contrast to the theories of economists from other regions. Although they "tended to censure the clerical colleges, they were closer to the elite than were the earlier nationalists. The Bostonian group gave little outspoken approval to their mid-Atlantic predecessors," notes O'Connor, and "were very much more conservative towards institutions such as banks."[28] According to John Rae, Alexander Everett was "scared" of Mathew Carey's work. Everett and his fellow Bostonian Caleb Cushing supported industrial tariffs, but endorsed the Malthusian and Ricardian doctrines of economic and social stagnation that the Democratic Party held could be staved off only by westward expansion.

Neither New England nor Southern economists acknowledged the discoveries by Liebig and others in agricultural chemistry that controverted the Ricardian concept of soil on which this expansionist doctrine rested. Everett was more Malthusian than George Tucker of Virginia in his debate with the latter, and Bowen's attempt at anti-Malthusianism was no more successful. This helps explain Peshine Smith's disdain for Bowen and Cushing, typical of the attitude of Middle Atlantic protectionists. It was left to Carey's school to achieve a solid anti-Ricardian complement to anti-Malthusianism. Their protectionism was rejected by the commercial and shipping interests of New England and by the cotton interests of the South. Both these regions accepted America's trade dependency as a raw-materials exporter to England as rationalized by the Ricardian doctrine of comparative advantage. The implication was that the nation must become increasingly trade-oriented, and ultimately imperialistic, reasoning backwards in a static and increasingly abstract circle to defend this worldview.

By contrast, the American School became increasingly isolationist, looking to the internal market rather than abroad, optimistic in seeking to develop America as nothing less than a new civilization rather than being pessimistic as to the prospects for labor and its living standards.

---

[28] O'Connor, *Origins*, pp. 45, 60.

Mid-Atlantic leadership in creating an American School of political economy

The most uniquely American economic philosophy was developed by protectionists in the Middle Atlantic states, especially Pennsylvania, upstate New York and Maryland. But their views found little reception in universities. (The University of Pennsylvania did not introduce a course explicitly on political economy until 1855, taught by the free trader Henry Vethake.) The leading American protectionists centered first around Mathew Carey in Philadelphia and included Hezekiah Niles, Daniel Raymond and Friedrich List, and later around Mathew's son Henry. This latter group represented the culmination of the self-entitled American School of political economy. E. Peshine Smith, Stephen Colwell, Horace Greeley, William Elder and Robert Ellis Thompson, as well as Van Buren Denslow and Simon Patten of Illinois shared a common denominator that coincided with the policies advocated by their region's leading congressional representatives such as Andrew Stewart and later William "Pig-Iron" Kelley of Pennsylvania, and William Henry Seward and Hamilton Fish of upstate New York in the State Department after the Civil War.

These Middle Atlantic states represented the nascent industrial center of America. But prior to the Civil War, industrialization required protective tariffs in the face of British industrial supremacy. The divergence between the American School and that of orthodox British free trade doctrine reflected the nation's diverging self-interest from that of England. The aim of making America economically and also culturally independent of England is especially marked in the treatises of Mathew Carey, William Jarvis, Daniel Raymond and William Jennison. These protectionists were self-made men, publicists and entrepreneurs rather than academic types.

The Congressional speeches and official reports of Alexander Hamilton, Alexander Dallas, Henry Clay, Andrew Stewart and other politicians are of major theoretical value, and it was natural for major protectionists to attach themselves to political leaders. Mathew Carey influenced Stewart, as the Boston protectionists Alexander Everett and Caleb Cushing (although Democrats) seem to have influenced Daniel Webster. Everett was a personal and legal aide to John Quincy Adams in his early career. Calvin Colton became the biographer and economic theoretician for Clay. Peshine Smith was legal counsel and advisor to Seward throughout the latter's career as governor of New York, senator and Secretary of State. Philadelphia's protectionists were tied closely to Pennsylvania politics, coordinated by Henry Carey after the Civil War.

Expressing the self-interest of the Middle Atlantic states, the American School found itself increasingly at odds with Southern and Northeastern self-interest, as well as with the class and political prejudices of these two regions:

19

their anti-labor attitude, their deflationary hard-money sympathies and opposition to a national bank, their opposition to as active a program of federal internal improvements, their support for westward expansion, and their belief that national and world economic development would mean a growing role played by foreign trade, in contrast to the more autarchic economic doctrines of Henry Carey's school. The latter combined optimism as to America's long-term potential with a demonstration that rising income levels for all classes — including labor — could be realized without reordering the political structure of capitalism. This optimism denied the need for westward expansion (not to speak of imperialism) to sustain the nation's rising income levels. Let America develop its home market and it need not depend upon England, or later on foreign conquests in the Far East.

The American School thus sought to dispel the doctrine of implicit class antagonism implied by Malthus, Ricardo and other British writers anticipating an increasing polarization of society that would impoverish most citizens. Rather than viewing workers and capitalists as competing for shares of a declining per capita income, it foresaw labor earning a growing share of an expanding per capita national income, while profits on invested capital likewise would rise. Workers would accumulate their own capital in the form of educational and working skills, enabling craftsmen to become entrepreneurs and property owners in their own right. And whereas academic theory held (at least initially) that low-wage countries would conquer high-wage nations in industrial competition, the American School anticipated that the nation's high income and educational levels would give it a growing industrial superiority.

Members of this school sought to develop a broad theory of productive powers and social evolution. At its highest level it grounded its reasoning in the natural sciences, stressing the relation between technology, social transformation and national development. This school included political figures (Henry Clay, Andrew Stewart, William Henry Seward, William Kelley etc.), journalists (Mathew and Henry Carey, Hezekiah Niles, Friedrich List and Horace Greeley), ministers (Calvin Colton, Stephen Colwell and Robert Ellis Thompson), lawyers (Daniel Raymond, Peshine Smith) and, in the final stage of the tariff controversy, industrialists such as Erastus Bigelow, Joseph Wharton, John Welsh, John Roach and assorted lesser lights.

The academic mainstream continued to promulgate the Ricardian concept of soil as possessing an inherent and permanent level of fertility, and of labor as possessing a similar intrinsic rate of productivity. The protectionists, especially the second (post-1848) generation, drew upon the new discoveries in agricultural chemistry and physiology to demonstrate man's ability to improve or exhaust the soil's productive powers, and to enunciate the Economy of High

Wages doctrine describing how the superior efficiency of highly-paid labor was in the capitalist's interest. These theories controverted the Ricardian theory that an increasing share of wealth would be reaped by owners of raw-materials resources (*e. g.*, by farmers and mine owners) as diminishing returns spread throughout the world, and the Iron Law of Wages (which stated that wage rates tended to settle at subsistence levels). Economies would become rich, the American School claimed, not by exporting raw materials and living off natural resource rent, but by industrializing to earn high income by a positive wage-productivity feedback.

The pragmatic foundation of American "anti-intellectualism"

Hofstadter finds a generally anti-academic attitude throughout the 19th century. "As popular democracy gained strength and confidence, it reinforced the wide-spread belief in the superiority of inborn, intuitive, folkish wisdom over the cultivated, over-sophisticated, and self-interested knowledge of the literati and the well-to-do. Just as the evangelicals repudiated a learned religion and a formally constituted clergy in favor of the wisdom of the heart and direct access to God, so did advocates of egalitarian politics propose to dispense with trained leadership in favor of the native practical sense of the ordinary man with its direct access to truth. This preference for the wisdom of the common man flowered, in the most extreme statements of the democratic creed, into a kind of militant popular anti-intellectualism."[29] It would be more apt to call it contra-rianism, for it arose out of a conscious, often highly intellectual repudiation of the doctrines broadcast by the colleges.

As Leslie observed, "in England it was not philosophers and professors, but manufacturers and politicians, who carried free trade: in America the manu-facturers and most energetic politicians are against it, and can point to a so-called national system of political economy on their side, while the opposite system labours under the suspicions attaching to a foreign origin."[30] It thus was not academic theory that was responsible for foreign policy in America, any more than in England.

To be sure, much of the anti-academic attitude of the early protectionists stemmed from their frustration at being unable to develop a systematic defense of industrial tariffs beyond a mere "doctrine of exceptions" to the rules and precepts of British political economy, developed largely on an *ad hoc* political basis. It is no coincidence that the term "self-made man," which Hofstadter takes as the epitome of anti-intellectualism, was coined by Henry Clay in a

[29] Hofstadter, *Anti-Intellectualism*, pp. 154f.
[30] Leslie, *Political Economy*, p. 142.

speech delivered in the Senate in 1832. "Denying that the tariff would give rise to a hereditary aristocracy, he maintained, to the contrary, that nothing could be more democratic; it would give further opportunities for men to rise from obscurity to affluence. 'In Kentucky, almost every manufactory known to me is in the hands of enterprising and self-made men, who have acquired whatever wealth they possess by patient and diligent labor.'"[31]

Hofstadter finds such businessmen to be anti-intellectual Babbitts. Many undoubtedly were, just as many pious fools taught in the universities. But the textile and carpet manufacturer Erastus Bigelow wrote a sizeable treatise arguing against British political economy. The iron manufacturer Stephen Colwell wrote valuable economic studies, as did Friedrich List and Andrew Stewart (railroad and canal promoters), and "self-made" publishers such as Mathew Carey, Hezekiah Niles and Horace Greeley. The fact that many of the most creative proponents of industrialization were not businessmen, should prevent their economic philosophy from being dismissed as a narrow "businessman's culture." But this is part of the modern era's prejudice against recognizing that non-academic protectionist theorizing was refined into a broad economic doctrine capable of holding its own with the British theories taught in most universities.

Hofstadter thus is partial in representing the founding of American business schools as being "at times anti-intellectual centers dedicated to a rigidly conservative set of ideas." They described themselves as supporting inductive principles and historical study rather than the deductive philosophy taught by mainstream American colleges. It was not on anti-intellectual grounds that Henry Carey Baird, founder of the first publishing firm in America to specialize in technical industrial books, called in 1885 for technical schools to supplant the classical grammar schools that produce "too many 'gentlemen' and 'ladies,' so called."[32] It was an attempt to make the educational system more responsive to the industrial ideology being formulated outside the universities.

Hofstadter is not incorrect when he states: "This view of human affairs lent itself too readily to the proposition that the sum and substance of life lies in the business of practical improvement; it encouraged the complacent notion that there is only one defensible way of life, the American way, and that this way had been willfully spurned or abandoned by peoples elsewhere. Many Americans found the true secret of civilization in the Patent Office."[33] But it was the Patent Office's report of 1848 that described how the phenomenon of "mining the soil" by plantation crop production undermined the Ricardian theory of

---

[31] Hofstadter, *Anti-Intellectualism*, p. 255, quoting Daniel Mallory, ed., *The Life and Speeches of the Hon. Henry Clay* (New York: 1844), vol. II, p. 31.

[32] *Ibid.*, pp. 262f., 258.   [33] *Ibid.*, p. 239.

soil fertility as having "original and indestructible powers," on which he based his theory of comparative advantage. And it was patents that provided the foundation for rising productivity, and hence the replacement of labor by capital.

The view of class harmonies was elaborated into a distinctly American form of idealism based not on the exploitation of labor but the exploitation of nature by energy-driven technology. The American materialist economists, sociologists and historians went far beyond what began merely as a "doctrine of exceptions" in formulating an optimistic materialism in place of the pessimistic British doctrines of Malthus and Ricardo. By the mid-19th century, supporters of industrialism were able to construct broad and comprehensive analytic systems to explain why protective tariffs were in America's national interest rather than being an inefficient diversion of resources as depicted in Ricardian doctrine. Hofstadter emphasizes the tendency of businessmen and their supporters to voice anti-intellectual sentiments without stressing that it was a particular form of anti-academicism being voiced—opposition to the British moral philosophy and free trade political economy. Industrialization was defended above all on grounds of technological potential and the relationship between technology and society—an approach that found little room to fit into the academic curriculum.

Few American colleges of the day were willing to admit protectionists. The University of Maryland turned down Mathew Carey's offer to donate $500 per year to endow a chair of political economy for Daniel Raymond. Carey and his friends met with a similar lack of success when they tried to obtain a teaching position for Friedrich List. And few businessmen for their part were interested in financing a protectionist textbook, partly because manufacturers of the day were little more than workmen or master craftsmen with scant funds available for such projects.[34] Industrial tariff protection was supported more as an economic and political ideal than as a lobbying effort by businessmen.

At least the post-1848 second generation of protectionists found more academic success in the United States than abroad. In Britain, Leslie observed, Isaac Butt taught at the University of Dublin, and Gustav Schmoller popularized the school of historical economics in Germany, "but no regular text-book of the principles of political economy, advocating protection ... has been published in any country in Europe. In the United States, on the other hand, protection is set forth in formal economic text-books—for example, the

---

[34] See for instance Charles Patrick Neill, *Daniel Raymond: An Early Chapter in the History of Economic Theory in the United States*, Johns Hopkins University Studies in Historical and Political Science, Fifteenth Series, No. 6 (June 1897), pp. 18–21, and O'Connor, *Origins*, p. 35.

treatises of Carey, Thompson, Peshine Smith, Bowen and Wilson taught by the professors of several colleges."[35] However, protectionists were appointed to university positions only on an isolated basis. Their early appointments can be counted on the fingers of one hand. In 1852, Rev. Calvin Colton was appointed to a newly created chair of "public economy" at the Episcopalian Trinity College in Hartford, Connecticut, which he filled until his death in 1857. Bowen was appointed to Harvard in 1853, teaching his kind of protectionism for two decades and writing a textbook on *Principles of Political Economy* in 1856 that ran through five editions and was used at the University of Pennsylvania after 1859, at Trinity College after Colton's death, and at a few other colleges. It ran through six more editions after being revised in 1870 as *American Political Economy*.

Peshine Smith sought help from Henry Carey and Thurlow Weed to obtain a teaching position, and did indeed teach mathematics for two years at the University of Rochester, but was unable to obtain a post teaching political economy. However, his *Manual of Political Economy* (1853) went through nine printings by 1897, and was used at Princeton during 1858-61, at Geneva (Hobart) College, and at Cornell University during 1871-74 by William E. Wilson, who wrote his own protectionist textbook on *First Principles of Political Economy* in 1875 (which went through four subsequent editions through 1891). Also in 1875, Rev. Robert Ellis Thompson, who had been teaching the protectionist economics course at the University of Pennsylvania since 1869 — the first of Carey's followers to obtain such a position — published his textbook on *Social Science and National Economy*, republished in 1882 and thereafter as *Elements of Political Economy, with Special Reference to the Industrial History of Nations.*

Creating new types of colleges to teach a new approach and content

In reforming an educational curriculum (or for that matter a government agency) it often is easier to start afresh by creating a new institution to replace the old. Perceiving that a new start can avoid the inertia involved in retaining an existing and administration, the Republicans established state land-grant colleges after the Civil War. Only then did the materialist strain within American thought achieve serious academic representation — not only by the American School of economists but also by historians such as John W. Draper at New York University and Andrew Dickson White at Cornell. And starting with the Wharton School of Finance and Economics at the University of Pennsylvania in 1881,

[35] Leslie, *Political Economy*, pp. 140f.

the business community endowed business schools to provide an alternative to the free-trade ideology taught in the most prestigious colleges of the Northeast and the South. These new institutions were the path of least resistance to create what today is recognized to be the distinctly American approach to economic thought and national industrial policy.

But for the more theocratic institutions, the tendencies described by O'Connor remained dominant. The first separate professorship of political economy (as distinct from moral philosophy) was established in 1871 by Harvard for Charles F. Dunbar, largely to shift the economics course away from Bowen, whose mildly expansionary monetary views offended the college administration. Yale appointed Francis Amasa Walker professor of political economy in 1874, and Johns Hopkins adopted the new chair in 1876. "When 'economics' succeeded 'political economy,' a scientific symbolism largely replaced religious references in the textbooks," concludes O'Connor. "But despite the altered diction and type of conception, the texts in general continued to express rather similar basic attitudes."[36]

The most important development in the academic fortunes of protectionist doctrine was the Wharton School — the first business school, soon emulated by the Universities of California, Chicago and Wisconsin. The Philadelphia iron magnate Joseph Wharton specified that the institution should teach "how a great nation should be, as far as possible, self-sufficient, maintaining a proper balance between agriculture, mining, and manufactures, and supplying its own wants ... how by suitable tariff legislation a nation may keep its productive industry active, cheapen the cost of commodities, and oblige foreigners to sell to it at low prices, while contributing largely toward defraying the expenses of its government; and lastly, the necessity for each nation to care for its own, and to maintain by all suitable means its industrial and financial independence, the right and duty of national self-protection must be firmly asserted and demonstrated."[37] Rev. Thompson became the school's dean and first economics professor, succeeded by Edmund James in 1883 and joined by Simon Patten in 1886.

Patten, James and Richard Ely took the lead in founding the American Economic Association in 1885, largely to promote the historical and institutionalist principles they had learned in Germany. Indeed, one can trace a line

---

[36] O'Connor, *Origins*, p. 288.

[37] Joseph Wharton, *Is a College Education advantageous to a Business Man?* (Philadelphia: 1890), pp. 32–34, quoted in Ugo Rabbeno, *The American Commercial Policy: Three Historical Essays*, 2nd ed. (London, 1895), p. 385. Wharton gave an initial $100,000 donation towards founding this school, with an additional $25,000 for a library, and by the time of his death in 1902 had increased his endowment to a total $500,000. The University of Pennsylvania's political economy library was in large part donated by the protectionist bibliophile Stephen Colwell.

from Friedrich List and the first generation of protectionists who protested against British economic doctrine on historical grounds, through Schmoller and other members of the German historical school back to America via the students studying in Germany from about 1880 onward. However, proponents of laissez faire captured the association fairly quickly. Envisioning only a narrow scope for political economy as that discipline narrowed into "economics" at the turn of the 20th century, it came to eschew the sociological and historical dimensions that occupied the attention of most American economists who had been trained in Germany. The economic writers best remembered today are Henry George and Thorstein Veblen, whose disdain for mainstream economists was reciprocated by the latter. History, social science and sociology departments became the path of least academic resistance to protectionist theories, as tariffs and institutional development could be studied there as historical phenomena arising under particular historical circumstances. Establishment economists came to view the subject as merely of antiquarian interest.

Technological optimism as the basis for the harmony of interests—and indeed, a new civilization

In Europe the major materialist movement was that of Marxism, inexorably linked with the doctrine of class conflict. But in America the materialism of Carey's school was associated with an optimistic doctrine of class harmonies, elevating materialism to a form of idealism. Carey helped broaden political economy into sociology, a branch of knowledge conceived in the Comtian sense of integrating all other disciplines. It did so in a way that described how man's conquest of nature was raising the status of most labor from merely manual to more skilled and intellectual tasks, improving productivity, output and living conditions accordingly. This doctrine rejected British orthodoxy on the ground that it largely ignored how the physical sciences were transforming knowledge and technology. The American School chose to examine the causes leading to society's enrichment, not the class conflicts leading to immiseration. What Simon Patten called the Economy of Abundance was enabling acquired characteristics to shape a new social psychology, in contrast to Europe with its class conflicts and vicious political system.

The economic advisors who shaped America's protectionist industrial strategy looked to active state intervention to shape society into a superior form than that of Europe. They advocated universal manhood suffrage, high educational standards, better labor conditions—especially state support to improve women's and children's working conditions—public charity, and infrastructure spending. And they were active abroad as well as at home. In 1872, Peshine Smith went to Japan to serve as legal advisor to the Mikado, the first of many Republican economists, agronomists and other aides who formed a "brains trust" to help shape Japanese development after the Meiji Restoration. But their ideas got little hearing within the narrow confines of U.S. college curricula until the 1880s as new types of public universities were formed. In fact, there was little opportunity to fit these ideas into the academic curriculum for most of the 20th century. The nation as a whole, particularly its industrialists, found their self-interest to lie in promoting free trade throughout the world, for much the same reason as England had found a century earlier: American industry and farming had come to lead the world in productivity and comparative costs. The nation's policy makers accordingly accepted academic laissez faire orthodoxy as government policy as it became a creditor power as well as the world's supreme industrial and agricultural competitor.

This policy shift occurred not because of what the universities taught, but because America's evolving role in world affairs called for freer trade. Harvard and other prestige universities espoused the factor-price equalization theorem, dropping the Economy of High Wages doctrine that even free traders such as Taussig had come to accept by World War I. As the United States appropriated Britain's position of world leadership, its politicians and diplomats appropriated its former mother country's economic doctrines, above all its free market rationalization of the status quo. There was little reason to adhere any longer to the idealism that had marked the break from England's laissez faire doctrine. What had emerged as a uniquely American formulation of economics and sociology became a thing of the past.

DISTINGUISHING CHARACTERISTICS OF THE AMERICAN SCHOOL

C. P. Neill's monograph on Daniel Raymond: *An Early Chapter in the History of Economic Theory in the United States* (1897) and G. B. Mangold's review of *The Labor Argument in the American Protective Tariff Discussion* (1908) are the first two serious American studies of the history of protectionist economic theory in the United States. Neill demonstrates the basically different points of reference of early American protectionism from that of British orthodoxy: the concern with the growth of national wealth and output rather than with the distribution of money incomes; the concept of capital, labor, and land in terms of their productive powers, not simply their earnings relative to their costs of production; and the related areas in which "American writers have exerted an influence upon the development of [economic] science to an extent that has not heretofore been conceded." Mangold's study demonstrates the extent to which these theories were developed in reference to the tariff debate, with the scope and focal point of each party's doctrine relating to its tariff position.

In no area of nineteenth-century American thought is the link between economic theory and political self-interest clearer than in the realm of wage theory in its application to international trade (and to a lesser extent westward expansion). As the country's economic and political conditions evolved, protectionists and free traders shifted positions on the correlation between population density and wage levels, and between wage levels and foreign trade patterns.

Early advocates that America remain an agrarian and raw-materials exporting country argued that its relatively high wage levels pre-empted it from early industrialization. As long as workers could support themselves on sparsely populated Western lands, raising foodstuffs and exchanging them for European manufactures at favorable prices, there was little to be gained from industrializing. Protectionists from Alexander Hamilton through Mathew Carey found themselves obliged to argue that American wage rates were not all that much higher than those of England, and that even if they were, the United States enjoyed lower industrial costs in areas such as raw materials and water power: "the disparity in this respect between some of the most manufacturing parts of Europe and a large proportion of the United States is not nearly so great as is commonly imagined," asserted Hamilton in his *Report on Manufactures*. "It is also much less in regard to artificers and manufacturers than in regard to country laborers ... and the disparity which does truly exist is diminished in proportion to the use which can be made of machinery." Foreign manufacturers faced higher costs for raw materials, land rent, taxes and transport charges, whose combined weight "cannot be estimated at less than fifteen to thirty percent ... [and] are more than a counterpoise for the real difference in the price of labor."[38]

In 1824, Henry Clay was still playing down the implication that high wage rates left America unsuited for industrial self-sufficiency: "the argument assumes that natural labor is the principal element in the business of manufacture. That was the ancient theory. But the valuable inventions and vast improvements in machinery, which have been made within a few past years, have produced a new era in the arts ... we must no longer limit our views to the state of ... population and the price of wages ... Capital, ingenuity in the construction and adroitness in the use of machinery, and the possession of raw materials, are those which deserve the greatest consideration ... The state of our population is peculiarly favorable to the most extensive introduction of machinery. We have no prejudices to combat, no persons to drive out of employment."[39]

American protectionists thus emphasized not only that production costs of varying types differed among nations, but that production functions themselves differed. International trade not only threw industrial labor in one country into competition with that in foreign countries, it threw the capital of one nation into competition with the labor of others. *Nations that fostered the most rapid accumulation of capital would emerge industrially supreme.*

These arguments initally were put forth at a time when protectionists were not looking to the votes of labor for support. Most industrialists hoped to keep American wage levels as low as possible, and many campaigned to block laborers from acquiring Western lands except through land speculators. In fact, only in the first decade following the Revolution could laborers migrate freely to Western lands. Under Hamilton's tenure as first Secretary of the Treasury, public lands were sold mainly to speculators, with credit being granted

---

[38] Alexander Hamilton, *Report on the Subject of Manufactures* (1791), in Frank Taussig, ed., *State Papers and Speeches on the Tariff* (Cambridge, 1893), pp. 34–37. Mangold gives a somewhat garbled account of this statement in "The Labor Argument in the American Protective Tariff Discussion," *Bulletin of the University of Wisconsin*, #240 (August, 1908), p. 16. In fact, Mangold's seeming quotations are usually paraphrases which must in all cases be checked carefully against the originals for authentication.

[39] Henry Clay, Speech in the House of Representatives, March 30 and 31, 1824, in Taussig, ed., *op. cit.*, p. 291. See also pp. 269f.

exclusively on purchases of ten or more square miles (nine square miles after 1796). Not until 1830 did substantial reform begin to be effected (made permanent in 1842), permitting colonists who squatted on and cultivated the waste lands to secure tracts not exceeding 160 acres. The Homestead Law was passed in 1862.

Pointing to the depression experience of 1819–20, protectionists argued that industrialization would employ women, children and seasonal farm labor that would remain idle in agriculture. Tariff protection would provide a more stable internal market without the depressions and unemployment that occurred under America's existing trade pattern. It also would attract immigrants, especially skilled laborers, while the spread of mechanized production would mitigate the influence of America's relatively high wage rates. The choice was not really between whether American labor should produce agricultural or industrial commodities, it was whether much of this labor would be employed in manufactures or not at all. Growth in the country's urban industrial population would sustain a thriving home market for farm and plantation products. It followed that industrial tariffs would render the United States economically independent of England, by protecting industries that had been brought into being by America's commercial isolation during the Napoleonic Wars. Nearly all these arguments had been made in Hamilton's *Report on Manufactures*, with the exception of references made to the new industries that had been fostered during the War.

The institution of universal male suffrage in the 1820s obliged protectionists to formulate their arguments with an eye towards demonstrating labor's self-interest in high tariffs. In the past it had been argued that the accumulation of American machinery would, if anything, lower wages by supplanting labor. This argument was dropped in favor of the pauper-labor doctrine, which stressed that tariffs protected labor and its wage rates rather than simply capital and its profit rates. Free traders argued all along that it was not desirable for Americans to undersell foreign manufacturers, or to be brought into direct market competition with them, because they must equal or surpass them not only in skill and machinery, but also in human degradation: "We must drive our laborers from the fields to those dismal and demoralizing abodes where they sink into hopeless stupidity and penury; where health and morals frequently become victims to hard labor and to the laws of poverty and hunger," stated one opponent of industrialization in 1821.[40]

---

[40] Quoted in Mangold, *op. cit.*, pp. 47f.

The protectionists appropriated this thesis, pointing out that the equalization of poverty need not occur if America protected its labor and capital by high tariffs. This could enable sufficiently high wages and profits to be paid to sustain high domestic living standards *and* new investment. As Stanwood describes this turnabout, each side in the tariff controversy took over "the position of the other, and [found] in the situation ground for supporting its own cause. The protectionists aver that wages are higher in this country than elsewhere, and they put that fact forward as a reason for a high tariff, to protect high wages ... The free traders deny that wages are really higher here than abroad, taking into account their purchasing power ..." *e.g.*, that free trade would lower the expenses of manufactures bought by laborers, thereby increasing the real value of their money wages.[41]

In 1827 the Harrisburg Convention asserted that "a nation whose labor was dear could not without ruin carry on commerce with one whose labor was cheap,"[42] at least not without seeing its own wage rates depressed to that of its trading partners. Protectionists also continued to exploit the unemployment argument for high industrial tariffs, pointing out that many laborers did not care to abandon their profession and become farmers, but would be forced to do so in the absence of protective tariffs. This pauper-labor argument became especially pronounced after 1828, and remained a mainstay in the protectionist arsenal until it was dropped for a while during 1848–60, only to reappear stronger than ever for more than half a century following the Civil War.

The early protectionists—and later, those of Carey's school—denied the factor proportions theory of industrial advantage commonly held in the early nineteenth century. According to this theory, high population density connoted world industrial advantage because of the low wages industrial workingmen were obliged to receive in densely populated, highly-competitive urbanized nations such as England. Free-traders emphasized that American wage levels were high and would remain so as long as the nation possessed abundant Western lands. This was the so-called "backwoods theory" of high wage levels: open migration to Western lands (at that time, lands west of the Alleghenies) reduced the supply of available urban labor, resulting in high wages simply on supply-and-demand grounds. Protectionists replied that relative supply factors alone were not sufficient to explain America's high industrial wage levels. There also must be a real product high enough to sustain these levels. This developed into the marginal-productivity explanation of wage rates. It was not

---

[41] Edward Stanwood, *American Tariff Controversies in the Nineteenth Century* (Boston, 1903), Vol. I, p. 225. On this point see also Mangold, *op. cit.*, pp. 98f.
[42] See Mangold, *ibid.*, pp. 68, 84ff.

the superabundance of land but of capital, the protectionists argued, that enabled high industrial wages to be paid — and not a superabundance of labor but of capital that provided nations with world advantage under conditions of mechanized production. The factor endowment theory maintaining that densely populated nations enjoyed industrial advantages might have held true before the industrial revolution, but it no longer was valid. Capital was displacing labor with increasing cheapness.

Free-traders argued that America would all too soon become a manufacturing power. As its Western lands began to fill up, the backwoods safety valve would close and population growth henceforth would be confined largely to the cities. The increasing supply of urban labor would press down wage rates, enabling America to compete with England only as its working class became more miserable. This was a uniquely American interpretation of Ricardian doctrine. Ricardo had argued that the onset of diminishing returns in agriculture increased wage costs to the capitalist, by forcing up the price of food (while channeling a rising proportion of income into the hands of landowners). According to orthodox Ricardianism, the filling up of American lands would work to raise American money wages, not lower them — although real wages would be eroded.

On a more long-term interpretation of Ricardianism, land-rich countries like America ultimately would gain the world's industrial advantage. As lands filled up in England and the more densely populated nations, money wages would rise (along with land rents), increasing industrial costs. The centers of industry would shift away from the high food-cost (and thus high-wage) countries to the low food-cost (hence low-wage) countries, with the result that America might in time become the seat of world industry. This logical culmination of the Ricardian system seems to have occurred to no one in the nineteenth century, if only because it was too far in the future for economists who were not accustomed to think in terms of long-term limits of growth.

The debate over wage levels and industrial advantage prior to the Civil War was linked directly with the parallel debate over the effect on wage levels of westward expansion. Free traders found their political base largely in the South, which wanted to bring more land under the slave (plantation) system of cultivation in order to maintain their world monopoly in cotton. This required a parallel expansion into non-slave territories so as to feed the growing slave labor force with low-priced foodstuffs. The protectionists wished to hold labor in the East, where increasing population density would lead to greater efficiency of production, hence a greater real product out of which to pay industrial wages.

Free traders continued to depict industrialization in terms of aggravated conflict "between man and money—between capital and labor." Only the free availability of Western lands could support labor's wage rates, the expansionists and free traders argued: Only maintenance of the United States as a primarily agricultural, raw-materials exporting country could sustain democracy in working order. "Whilst the tariff does not enhance the wages of labor," the famous Walker Report argued in 1846, "the sales of the public lands at low prices, and in limited quantities, to settlers and cultivators, would accomplish this object … the power of the manufacturing capitalist in reducing the wages of labor would be greatly diminished."[43]

Mangold's book breaks off in 1847, just at the point where the wage/tariff controversy was about to undergo another turn at the hands of Henry Carey and E. Peshine Smith. Although the pauper-labor argument had become a staple of protectionist logic at the hands of Colton and other first-generation protectionists, Carey and his followers saw that it assumed an implicit antagonism between labor and capital. *Enlightened capitalists would find their self-interest and competitive power with foreign nations not in paying low wages but in paying high wages, because highly-paid labor was much more efficient than pauper labor.* Protectionism was needed to maintain employment—by increasing capital to employ labor, along with what British economists called the wages fund—and to provide federal revenues to extend educational facilities and related internal improvements.

Increased association and division of labor in the Eastern states, argued Carey in his *Past, Present and Future* (1848), would increase America's productive powers sufficiently to sustain rising wage rates out of an expanding product. But Western migration would retard the rise of labor productivity in the East, holding down the nation's output and wage levels. Shortly thereafter Carey's associate, Peshine Smith, drew upon Liebig's investigations in physiology to demonstrate that although well-fed and well-clothed labor might cost more to its employer on a *per diem* basis, it more than made up for this in the form of increased work capacity. High *per diem* wage rates connoted low unit-labor costs. *The exploited factor in production was nature, not labor.* Industrialization favored increasingly skilled labor, leaving manual tasks to be performed by machines rather than by men, who were freed to steadily elevate their status in economic society. Hence the evolution of protectionism, indeed isolationism, into an economic and social ideal.

---

[43] Quoted in Mangold, *ibid.*, pp. 101f. The full passage may be found in Taussig, ed., *State Papers and Speeches*, p. 242.

This idealism paled after the Civil War, especially with the growth of trusts. Protectionists found the more sophisticated arguments of Peshine Smith and Carey to be too tenuous, and reverted to the old pauper-labor argument for protective tariffs. True, this argument presumed identical production functions among nations and overlooked the correlation between high wages and high productivity. It also overlooked the tendency for developing economies to substitute machinery for manual labor. But the pauper-labor argument was easy to grasp, and was thus more workable from a political point of view.

Furthermore, now that the slave system was broken, protectionists dropped their opposition to westward expansionism. The economy-of-high-wages doctrine was thus left to free traders to exploit, and passed into the hands of men like Francis Amasa Walker, Jacob Schoenhof, and Frank Taussig. If high *per diem* wage rates connoted low unit labor costs, they argued, then America did not really need tariff protection.

Common to all parties in the debate was the rise of the economy-of-high-wages doctrine, which viewed the production process in terms of technological factors rather than simply money factors. English thought of the period followed the wages-fund doctrine in asserting that an increase of capital tended to raise wage rates (and lower profit rates), because the wages fund was a financial pool of money to be divided among the labor force on a supply-and-demand basis. The American economists emphasized that an increase of capital would increase productive powers by much more than its cumulative cost in terms of labor. Capital was to be thought of not simply as embodied labor (although this tended to determine its financial return, to be sure) but in terms of the hundreds of manpower-equivalents of work effort for which it substituted. *The increase in industry's physical stream of output far surpassed the growth in industrial revenues, thanks to the growing powers of nature tapped by mechanized industry.*

This view of capital in terms of the doctrine of productive powers rather than in simple financial terms is stressed in Neill's study of Daniel Raymond, who helped focus American protectionist doctrine on what Lauderdale had called public wealth as distinct from private riches. Raymond viewed capital as a productive factor in its own right, capable of performing tasks which human labor simply could not do, such as introducing absolute uniformity of production (hence the mass production of interchangeable parts). To the English, the concept of technology referred to the "mix" of capital, labor and land viewed as distinct factors of production. To the American School it meant a broader social system of organization, with capital substituting for both labor and land under conditions of increasing returns and increased real earnings of all classes.

THE TARIFF CONTROVERSY IN ITS SECTIONAL ASPECTS: 1776–1860

At its birth the United States was formed as a compound of two competing economic systems: a nascent Northern industry (still largely in its household phase) associated with an essentially family-farm agriculture, and the slave South with its plantation system. In this dual economy the North sought to promote an urban-rural balance between domestic agriculture and industry, each sector growing as it consumed the products of the other. The South, by contrast, looked increasingly to foreign markets for its cotton, tobacco and other plantation products.

This economic division was reinforced by a similar national division along political lines. The Northern Federalists supported a strong national government, the Southern Jeffersonians favored a decentralized system safeguarding states' rights. Until the 1820s this political division was muted by the somewhat countervailing political attitudes of North and South towards England. The South showed itself willing to promote domestic industry as the price necessary to achieve economic and hence political and military independence from England. The North, especially those seaboard states whose politics were strongly influenced by international shipping interests, felt that it had much more to gain by protecting its commerce with England than in promoting its modest industry.

The War of 1812 interrupted this commerce, and channeled Northern capital away from shipping into producing manufactures previously obtained from England. By the end of the war a fairly sizable industry had developed. But its prosperity was thwarted by restoration of normal trade with England. Northern federalism became protectionist—while the South moved economically closer to England, abandoning its early ideals of American economic independence from its former mother country. The interests of these two regions, whose divisions apparently had been reconciled during the four decades spanning the Declaration of Independence in 1776 to the Treaty of Ghent, now diverged over an expanding range of issues: America's economic relationship with England in the 1810s, the tariff in the 1820s, states' rights and the money and banking system in the 1830s, westward expansion in the 1840s, and the extension of slavery into new territories in the 1850s.

All these controversies were incidents in the basic conflict between the plantation system and urban industry, each with its own requirements as to the country's domestic and foreign policy. The seeds of the political tensions that finally erupted in Civil War lay in the uneven rates of economic and political absorption of the West. At stake was whether the United States should remain basically agricultural or should deliberately foster its industrialization.

As early as 1776 the British economist Josiah Tucker anticipated the tensions that the tariff debate would create within the United States: "the Southern independent Republics will never consent to prohibit the Introduction of the Manufactures of Old England merely for the Sake of encouraging (to their own Loss) the Manufactures of New England (a People whom they both hate, and despise) nor will the New Englanders give a Monopoly to the Southern Provinces against themselves. Therefore as both will act separately, according to their respective local Interests; the English Manufactures will find an easy Admission with very little, or no Obstruction."[44] Implicitly, Tucker concluded, America would remain an economic satellite of England because of its political divisions. But not until after 1816 did these sectionalist tensions rise to dominate the consciousness of most Americans. It was towards England that they felt their greatest hostility, a feeling held most of all by the southern Jeffersonians.

The major sectional antagonism perceived was between East and West. As Rufus King of New York put matters in 1786, "every Citizen of the Atlantic States, who emigrates to the westward of the Alleghany is a total loss to our confederacy ... Nature has severed the two countries by a vast and extensive chain of mountains, interest and convenience will keep them separate, and the feeble policy of our disjointed Government will not be able to unite them. For these reasons I have ever been opposed to encouragements of western emigrants. The States situated on the Atlantic are not sufficiently populous, and losing our men is losing our greatest source of wealth."[45] Still, the West became mainly as the decisive swing-region in the implicit long-term economic and political struggle between North and South. At the Virginia ratification convention of 1787, William Grayson prophesied that the "contest of the Mississippi involves the great national contest; that is whether one part of this continent shall govern the other. The Northern States have the majority and

---

[44] Josiah Tucker, *A Series of Answers to Certain Popular Objections against Separating From the Rebellious Colonies, and Discarding them Entirely: Being the Concluding Tract of the Dean of Gloucester on the Subject of American Affairs* (Gloucester, 1776), pp. 44f.

[45] Quoted in Frederick J. Turner, *The Significance of Sections in American History* (New York, 1932), p. 28.

will endeavor to retain it."[46] And it was indeed the North that was destined to increase its economic and political weight in the union, by virtue of its more rapid population growth, magnetism for immigration, and industrialization.

North-South antagonisms nonetheless remained muted during the interruption of trade with England during the War of 1812. To be sure, Alexander Hamilton's *Report on Manufactures* (1791) alluded to the fact that: "It is not uncommon to meet with an opinion, that though the promoting of manufactures may be the interest of a part of the Union, it is contrary to that of another part. The Northern and Southern regions are sometimes represented as having adverse interests in this respect. Those are called manufacturing; these, agricultural States; and a species of opposition is imagined to subsist between the manufacturing and agricultural interests."[47] But he anticipated that experience would gradually dissipate this view: "the aggregate prosperity of manufactures, and the aggregate prosperity of agriculture, are intimately connected" by the growth of home-market reciprocity of demand between the two sectors. The South would find its interest to lie in endorsing industrial protection and creating a thriving Northern market, just as would the agricultural West.

This view glossed over a fact that became increasingly apparent: as Northern industry expanded, the North's political weight grew correspondingly. Its population and industry were concentrated, whereas that of Southern plantation agriculture was dispersed. Because the House of Representatives was weighted on the basis of population, the envisioned economic reciprocity between industry and agriculture would concentrate political power in the North. The South therefore had a clear political reason for preferring foreign markets to Northern ones: export markets did not entail a corresponding growth of Northern political power in Congress.

An additional consideration was the economic fact that while a growing urban demand for agricultural produce might be of some benefit to the South, it also would tend to increase the price of Western provisions as Northern capitalists bid against Southern planters. This would increase the latter's food expenditures at the same time that it increased their home market. To be sure, these views did not rise to the forefront of Southern consciousness until the mid-1840's, but a wary attitude towards Northern prosperity existed from the outset.

The very first act passed by the American Congress was the tariff of 1789, which levied quite moderate duties of $5\frac{1}{4}$ per cent to $7\frac{1}{2}$ per cent *ad valorem* (with 10 per cent on glass, the most highly protected item of this period) and

---

[46] Quoted *ibid.*, p. 27.
[47] Alexander Hamilton, *Report on the Subject of Manufactures* [1791], in Frank Taussig, ed., *State Papers and Speeches on the Tariff* (Cambridge, Mass., 1893), p. 58.

specific duties for spirits, sugar and coffee. The official words of the act cited these duties as being "necessary for the support of the government, for the discharge of the debts of the United States, and the encouragement and protection of manufactures." During the next fifteen years tariff rates were nearly tripled on many articles, in a series of five steps generally of $2\frac{1}{2}$ per cent each: in 1790 to meet the growing national debt; in 1792 "for the protection of the frontiers and other purposes"; in 1794 and 1797 to finance rising federal expenditures; and in 1804 to provide funds for the government to patrol its waters against pirates. By the latter year tariffs had come to average some $17\frac{1}{2}$ per cent to 20 per cent on most of the major dutiable imports. The principle of protectionism was voiced in the presidential messages and published letters of the presidents, although the immediate cause of tariff increases was the government's pressing need for revenue.

In December 1807 an embargo was declared against all trade with England in an attempt to end her practice of boarding and searching American vessels and impressing into her own navy naturalized Americans who once had been British citizens or simply had no papers to prove otherwise. The Embargo reduced U.S. imports by nearly 60 per cent, and was followed in 1809 by the Non-Intercourse Law, which for a year forbade any trade with France as well as with England. Hostility toward England grew, led in the House of Representatives by Clay and Calhoun, and in 1812 erupted into naval war, whereupon all tariffs were doubled to finance U.S. military operations. It was therefore natural that the presidential messages of Jefferson and Madison should endorse the ideal of American industrial independence from England.

The Treaty of Ghent, which brought peace with England and restored normal commercial relations between the two countries, ushered in an era of economic warfare that was soon reflected in domestic U.S. politics. The treaty was drawn up on December 14, 1814, and was ratified by Congress on February 17, 1815, ending the economic isolation that had nurtured America's industrial growth during the foregoing seven years. Imports jumped more than tenfold, from $13 million in fiscal 1814 to $147 million by 1816. This great influx of low-priced British manufactures threatened to extinguish American industrial capital, and thereby to restore American industrial dependence on England, leaving it prone in the event of future warfare.

Agitation for higher protective tariffs soon followed the treaty, with the strongest pleas for national industrial self-sufficiency being made at first by two non-Northerners: Calhoun of North Carolina and Henry Clay of Kentucky. The result was the Tariff of 1816, in which the principle of protectionism was explicitly acknowledged by law for the first time since 1789. According to the U.S. Tariff Commission's official history of the tariff, "protection for the first time ceased to be incidental and became a direct object of the tariff," supported by all parts of the country.[48] The new tariff introduced a schedule of minimum duties, a forerunner of the "American Selling Price" system of import evaluation for tariff purposes.

The tariff was not yet a political issue capable of dividing the nation into sectional camps. First of all, the South did not yet feel an economic antagonism toward Northern industry. Venting their hostility mainly toward England, the Jeffersonians believed that domestic industry was necessary to secure American economic independence, even though this might shift the nation's economic weight in favor of the more industrialized sections of the North. Jefferson acknowledged the evolving state of affairs in his much-publicized 1816 letter to Benjamin Austin: In contrast to the laissez-faire sentiments that he earlier had held largely on grounds of political philosophy, Jefferson now stated that "we have experienced what we did not then believe, that there exist both profligacy and power enough to exclude us from the field of exchanges with other nations; that to be independent for the comforts of life, we must fabricate them ourselves. We must now place our manufactures by the side of the agriculturist. The former question [of the political philosophy of free trade] is now suppressed, or rather assumes a new form. The grand inquiry now is, Shall we make our own comforts, or go without them at the will of a foreign nation? He, therefore, who is now against domestic manufactures must be for reducing us either to a dependence on that nation, or to be clothed in skins, and live like beasts in dens and caverns … Experience has taught me that manufactures are now as necessary to our independence and our comfort."

Advocates of industrialization, realizing the *de facto* protection being laid by revenue tariffs, wisely did not emphasize this effect, or even claim it as the leading motive behind the increased rates, although the annual messages of all the presidents consistently upheld the principle of protectionism. As Stanwood describes these developments: "The Republicans were now the national party, the upholders of the majesty of the Union, the champions of a bold and progressive policy … Jefferson himself began unconsciously an approach to the Federalist position, but did not proceed far on the road. Madison, and still more completely Monroe, passed over and occupied the enemy's camp. In the early days of the government there was no actual party division on the tariff question; but unquestionably the Federalists, with Hamilton at their head, were more zealous for the cause of manufactures than were the Republicans. All this had changed long before the year 1816. A Republican Congress ordered the reprinting of Hamilton's 'Report on Manufactures.' Republican commit-

---

[48] U.S. Tariff Commission, *The Tariff and its History* (Washington; 1934), p. 71.

tees took pains to proclaim their friendliness to the policy of protection. On the other hand, the opposition to that policy was nowhere more strongly manifested than in Massachusetts, Federalist in politics and commercial by occupation. Accordingly, although the tariff was still in no sense a party question, it is true as a broad proposition that parties had exchanged positions as much on this issue as on any other."[49]

Madison, who had early been a mild opponent of protective duties, called for tariffs in his 1815 message to Congress to produce goods that could be made from domestic raw materials and to "relieve the United States from a dependence on foreign supplies, ever subject to casual failures." Secretary of the Treasury Alexander J. Dallas submitted a protectionist report to Congress in February, 1816, contributing to the tariff enacted in April of that year.

The 1816 tariff did not prove sufficient to isolate domestic industry from foreign competition, as evidenced by the depression of 1818–19. From this date a fundamental split emerged between the free-trade standard bearers, who favored "revenue tariffs" to finance a low to moderate level of internal improvements and other activities, and the advocates of protective tariffs to be set at whatever level was necessary to protect American industry from foreign competition, with a rising level of spending on internal improvements to dispose of these funds.

By 1824 the tariff and its related issues had been propelled to the forefront of American politics. The South was coming to view industrial protection as being against its economic and political interest, and saw Britain as a much more lucrative market than the North.

North-South sectionalism emerged full-blown when the 1820 Census reapportioned the country in 1823. The Clay-Webster debate that preceded the 1824 tariff reflected the political re-alignment over the tariff issue. Speaking for the industrial interests of the Middle Atlantic states, Henry Clay coined the term "American System" to describe his three-part program of protective tariffs, internal improvements and a national bank. Webster (as would Gallatin and Walker after him) defended laissez-faire and revenue tariffs, ostensibly on grounds of national equity. He claimed that protective tariffs would benefit a particular section, the industrial North, at the expense of the common weal which he portrayed as the interest of all the nation's consumers in seeing lower prices. It was clear that the particular regions on whose behalf he spoke were the South and the Northeastern shipping region.

---

[49] Edward Stanwood, *American Tariff Controversies in the Nineteenth Century* (Boston, 1903), Vol. 1, pp. 135f.

Nowhere in the tariff controversy was this sectional division more clearly expressed than by Clay: "it is said that the South, owing to the character of a certain portion of its population, cannot engage in the business of manufacturing. The circumstances of its degradation unfits it for the manufacturing arts. The well-being of the other, and the larger part of our population, requires the introduction of those arts. What is to be done in this conflict? The gentleman [from Virginia] would have us abstain from adopting a policy called for by the interest of the greater and freer part of our population. But is that reasonable? Can it be expected that the interests of the greater part should be made to bend to the condition of the servile part of our population? That, in effect, would be to make us slaves of slaves ... What is the argument? It is, that we must continue freely to receive the produce of foreign industry, without regard to the protection of American industry, that a market may be retained for the sale abroad of the produce of the planting portion of the country." [50]

The sectionalist nature of the vote on the 1824 and subsequent tariffs is clearly revealed in Table 3: The South voted almost solidly against the tariff (although the border states of Kentucky and Missouri supported it, along with Delaware and parts of Maryland). Massachusetts, Maine and New Hampshire joined with the South in opposing the tariff, along with the New York City commercial area. But the Middle Atlantic region and upstate New York carried the day, with only a five-vote margin to spare. Stanwood observes the inherent tensions in this situation, in which the two regions that hoped to become industrial centers — the Middle Atlantic states and New England — "were ranged on opposite sides," and the two agricultural regions—the South and the West (which at that time meant the United States west of the Alleghenies)—were also separated. "New England, on the whole, believed that its industrial progress did not need a protective tariff; the Northern Middle States were sure they could not prosper without protection for iron, glass, and other things. The West was persuaded that its salvation depended upon the establishment of a steady home market for its grain. The South was still more strongly convinced that a protective tariff would limit its market for its great staple of cotton, and render more expensive all the foreign merchandise which it must of necessity import. New England was to change its attitude before the next great contest; the West, and some Northern States, were gradually to fall under the influence of the South, through political alliances; and only Pennsylvania on the one hand, and the South on the other, were to be true to the principles they held

---

[50] Henry Clay, speech in the House of Representatives, March 30–31, 1824, in Taussig, *op. cit.*, pp. 279f.

in 1824."[51] Still, the tariff was popular, and all the candidates for the presidency professed support for it, including even Crawford from the South. Andrew Jackson helped save the 1824 act from defeat on its passage to a third reading.

By 1826, Webster joined forces with Clay, citing New England's development of manufactures as having prompted his shift. The government, he maintained, had driven New England capital from shipping to industrial pursuits, and this capital had to be protected regardless of whether its origins had been well-grounded or not.

In the summer of 1827 about a hundred advocates of protection convened at Harrisburg, Pennsylvania, producing a series of memorials, recommendations and a flow of pamphlet literature. Protectionist sentiment was at its height, and in preparation for the presidential elections the following year even the Jackson men strove to appear friendly toward domestic industry. The House Committee on Manufactures was dominated by Jackson supporters, who carried out a somewhat ingenious strategy said to have been devised by Martin Van Buren. This consisted of submitting a high-tariff bill to the House, including especially high tariffs on raw materials consumed mainly in New England, in particular by its textile manufacturers (flax and wool) and commercial shipping operators (hemp and ship rope).

Many of the highest and most obnoxious duties were on articles not even produced to any great degree in the United States, such as heavy ship rope. It was hoped that this schedule of duties would prove sufficiently high to cause New England to desert the protectionist cause, so that failure to enact a protective tariff would be laid at Adams' doorstep. All attempts to debate the tariff package and modify the offensive duties were cut off by the Jackson supporters. As Frank Taussig described matters, "the Jackson men of all shades, the protectionists from the North and the free traders from the South, were to unite in preventing any amendments; that bill, and no other, was to be voted on."[52] But enough Adams men from New England voted for the bill to pass it, and after a successful trip through the Senate (where Webster supported it as the lesser of two evils) it was enacted into law as the Tariff of 1828, popularly known as the Tariff of Abominations. In 1829 official U.S. statistics showed the ratio of tariff revenue to total dutiable imports to have risen to 54 per cent, and the following year to 62 per cent, a level not approached again until the 1930s.

Stanwood makes much of the argument over the constitutionality of protective tariffs, an issue that had resurfaced in the 1890s. "The power to defeat a protective tariff either by academic argument against the soundness of the

[51] Stanwood, *op. cit.*, pp. 239f.
[52] Frank Taussig, *The Tariff History of the United States* (New York, 1888), pp. 88f.

principle of commercial restraint, or by setting off the interest of the South against that of the North, was definitely lost in the contest of 1828," he observes. "Nothing remained but to dispute the constitutional power of Congress to pass such laws," with free traders denying that the constitutional power "to regulate commerce with foreign nations" implied the power to levy imposts designed to promote one branch of industry "at the expense of" another. In this respect the 1828 bill may be viewed as laying the ground for the Nullification fight of South Carolina four years later, by which time permanent lines had become drawn to separate the slave South from the North. "For, little as the fact was recognized at the time, the tariff was but the skirmishing ground where the leaders of the conflict tried and proved the weapons that were to be used in the final campaign a generation afterward." [53]

Already in 1831 preparations were being laid for what promised to be an intensive tariff controversy for the presidential election year of 1832. The free traders held a convention at Philadelphia, and appointed Albert Gallatin to write a memorial to Congress, along with a survey of "evidence" prepared by Henry Lee. It was in answer to this meeting that the protectionists convened in New York and asked Alexander Everett to write a memorial in reply. He drew upon a number of arguments for protection that Gallatin himself had set forth in 1810, when as Secretary of the Treasury he had been asked to prepare a Report on Manufactures after the manner of Hamilton's twenty years earlier.

By this time the tariff issue had become linked inexorably with the question of internal improvements. A major motive behind the protectionist attempt to increase federal expenditures on such improvements (*e.g.*, the Cumberland Road and associated transportation projects) was to dispose of the rising tariff revenues. Free traders for their part recognized that "economy" in federal expenditures must follow from low tariffs. Hence, the Democrats now claimed that the appropriation of public money for internal improvements was as un-constitutional as the tariff, by promoting one branch of industry at the expense of others—a party plank that was repeated in every Democratic national platform until 1860.[54]

With the Tariff of 1832 the industrial North succeeded in dropping most of the "abominations" of the 1828 act, in exchange for replacing the system of minimum tariffs with simple *ad valorem* duties. A more solid protective tariff was thereby established to which New England could well adhere. But the conflicting interests between North and South had become so deep that South Carolina refused to collect duties at the port of Charleston, claiming that the tariff was "in violation of State rights, and a usurpation by Congress of powers

---

[53] Stanwood, *op. cit.*, pp. 293, 291, 295.   [54] *Ibid.*, p. 302.

not granted to it by the constitution; ... the power to protect manufactures is nowhere granted to Congress, but on the other hand, is reserved to the States; ... the interests of South Carolina are agricultural, and to cut off her foreign market, and confine her products to an inadequate home market, is to reduce her to poverty."

The other Southern states followed with protests of their own, and in November a convention held in South Carolina passed a resolution declaring the U.S. revenue laws null and void. Jackson responded by ordering the Navy to take charge of the port of Charleston and forcibly collect the duties which South Carolina refused to levy. South Carolina agreed to suspend its "nulli-fication" pending a political settlement, which came in the form of Clay's Compromise Tariff of 1833. This called for a scheduled reduction in tariff duties to a uniform *ad valorem* rate of 20 per cent by 1842.[55]

Clay and his supporters apparently hoped that a future Whig congress might restore higher tariffs. But as the Democrats remained in office through 1840, the compromise proceeded on schedule. Not until 1841 did the Whigs return to power, promptly calling for higher rates and a return to specific duties. Their 1842 tariff established somewhat higher rates, averaging about 33 per cent on dutiable imports. But destiny seemed to be conspiring against the Whigs. Although they won the 1840 and 1848 elections behind two generals—Wm. Henry Harrison in 1840, and Zachary Taylor in 1848—they had sought to consolidate the vote of the border states by nominating somewhat Democratic-leaning anti-protectionists for the vice-presidential posts: John Tyler of Virginia in 1840 ("Tippecanoe and Tyler too"), and the obnoxious Millard Fillmore in 1848. By a quirk of fate, both Harrison and Taylor died quite early in office, leaving Whig politics to be governed by men whose principles were adverse to those of the Whig stalwarts.

Increasingly, the national contest between the slave South and the industrial North took the form of controversy over the issue of Westward expansion. The South deemed this necessary to maintain its worldwide sugar and cotton monopolies. Slaves had to be fed cheaply to produce Southern staples at prices enabling Southern planters to undersell foreign producers. For this purpose new land was needed to keep pace with the growth of the slave population, as well as to extend cotton and sugar cultivation. Furthermore, the extension of these two staples would serve to bring more slave states into the union, thereby

---

[55] Duties as established by the 1832 tariff in excess of 20% were to be reduced on January 1, 1834, by an amount equal to 10% of this excess, with additional 10% cuts to be made, in 1836, 1838 and 1840. Of the remainder, half was to be removed on January 1, 1842 and the balance on July 1 of that year, by which time all maximum duties were to stand at 20%.

maintaining the congressional balance between free and slave states. From the South's vantage point, policies that retarded Northern population growth and its associated demand for Western provisions worked to reduce the cost of maintaining slaves, and therefore supported the South's relative political power. Nowhere was this sectional aspect of westwards expansion expounded more clearly than by David Christy in *Cotton is King: or, Slavery in the Light of Political Economy*:

> The opposition to the Protective Tariff, by the South, arose from two causes ... the one to secure the foreign market for its cotton, the other to obtain a bountiful supply of provisions at cheap rates ... The close proximity of the provision and cotton-growing districts in the United States, gave its planters advantages over all other portions of the world. But they could not monopolize the markets, unless they could obtain a cheap supply of food and clothing for their negroes, and raise their cotton at such reduced prices as to undersell their rivals. A manufacturing population, with its mechanical coadjutors, in the midst of the provision-growers, on a scale such as the protective policy contemplated, it was conceived, would create a permanent market for their products, and enhance the price; whereas, if this manufacturing could be prevented, and a system of free trade adopted, the South would constitute the principal provision market of the country, and the fertile lands of the North supply the cheap food demanded for its slaves.[56]

Because of the South's predominantly slave economy, an increase in America's white population would necessarily be concentrated either in the North or the West. If it could be diverted from Northern cities to Western plains, it would find itself employed at producing grain and other agricultural produce rather than constituting a part of the Northern urban population bidding against the South for these provisions and thus cutting into the profits of the slaveholders. Southern politicians therefore concluded that "we must prevent the increase of manufactories, force the surplus labor into agriculture, promote the cultivation of our unimproved western lands, until provisions are so multiplied and reduced in price, that the slave can be fed so cheaply as to enable us to grow our sugar at three cents a pound. Then, without protective duties, we can rival Cuba in the production of that staple, and drive her from our markets."

It was a Democratic writer who in 1845 coined the slogan "Manifest Destiny." And indeed, had the Civil War not occurred, continued pressure for expansion on the part of the Southern states were very likely have led to a materialization of their hope to extend the union into Cuba and even the West Indies — an eventuality some Northerners believed would lead to an offsetting northern expansion, quite likely into Canada.

---

[56] David Christy, *Cotton is King: or, Slavery in the Light of Political Economy*, 3rd ed., in E. N. Elliott, ed., *Cotton is King, and Pro-Slavery Arguments* (Augusta, 1860), p. 71.

Westward expansion was secured following the 1844 election in which Polk led the Democrats to victory over Henry Clay, who suffered defeat of his presidential aspirations for the fifth and final time. The new Secretary of the Treasury, Robert Walker, prepared a report in 1845 which integrated the Democratic Party's policy of Western expansion, ruralization of the country's population, free trade, a restrained pace of internal improvements, and continuation of the Sub-Treasury depository system for federal monies so as to prevent these funds from being added to the commercial banking system's monetary base, where they might be used to finance industrial expansion. In asserting the principle of "revenue tariffs," namely "that no more money should be collected than is necessary for the wants of the government, economically administered," Walker implicitly called for a curtailment of internal improvements. He somewhat arbitrarily suggested that "experience proves that, as a general rule, a duty of 20 per cent *ad valorem* will yield the largest revenue." He therefore recommended that all minimums and specific duties "be abolished, and *ad valorem* duties substituted in their place."

Walker further advocated the Democratic Party's long-term position that in the "interests of labor" the highest duties should be levied on luxuries rather than on goods competing with American manufactures. "If we reduce our tariff," he speculated, "the party opposed to the corn laws of England would soon prevail, and admit all our agricultural products at all times freely into her ports, in exchange for her exports.[57] (Britain's repeal of the Corn Laws did indeed occur in 1846, but was the result of domestic economic considerations and not at all the product of any negotiated reciprocity of free trade between England and America.)

Walker further asserted that a protective tariff "discriminates in favor of manufactures and against agriculture, by imposing many higher duties upon the manufactured fabric than upon the agricultural product out of which it is made." He reiterated the timeworn appeal "that the duty should be so imposed as to operate as equally as possible throughout the Union, discriminating neither for nor against any class or section." As noted above, protectionists perceived this interpretation as operating in favor of the South against the industrial North. Lack of industrial protection, they retorted, discriminated against domestic industry in favor of that of Britain. Walker himself acknowledged that free trade was intended primarily to benefit the slave states: "The cotton planting is the great exporting interest, and suffers from the tariff in the double capacity

---

[57] Robert Walker, *Report from the Secretary of the Treasury ... 1845*, in Taussig, *op. cit.*, pp. 219f., 233f.

of consumer and exporter. Cotton is the great basis of our foreign exchange, furnishing most of the means to purchase imports and supply the revenue."[58]

This report paved the way for the so-called Walker Tariff which operated from December 1846 through July 1857, and which reduced rates to about 25 per cent of dutiable imports. In 1857 tariffs were once again reduced, and averaged only 20 per cent of dutiable imports during 1859–61, the lowest for any period during the hundred years 1821–1920.

Protectionism was to triumph only in conjunction with an issue more popular, that of slavery and free soil. For the first time, the Northeast Seaboard states joined forces with the Middle Atlantic states to defeat the divided Democratic Party, and the South.

	North		South
	Middle Atlantic	Northeast Seaboard	
1810s Attitude towards England	anti	pro	anti
1820s Protective tariffs	pro	anti	anti
1830s National bank charter	pro	anti	anti
1840s Westward expansionism	anti	pro	pro
1850s Slavery	anti	anti	pro

To recap, during the war of 1812 the Middle Atlantic states had stood firmly with the South in supporting American military, political and economic independence from England. But for the next four decades the Southern and Northeastern Seaboard states joined together to dominate national policy over the tariff issue, national banking policy and Westward expansion. Only in the 1860 elections was the Southern compact with the Northeast broken as the Democratic Party itself broke into two warring factions — the Free Soil Democrats behind Douglas, and the Southern pro-slavery faction led by General Cass, paving the way for the Republican victory behind Lincoln.

The early conflict over America's attitude toward England, protective tariffs and the desirability of industrializing the nation had never actually been dropped, but had become overlayered by more domestic issues. Popular opposition to a national bank and to a strong federal government, and popular support for Westward expansion had held the balance in favor of the anti-industrial party. But as the slavery issue became more acute, the scales swung back toward the advocates of industry and free labor. The nation was forced to make a definitive choice as to which system would dominate its economic life — a rural or an urban system, agriculture or industry.

---

[58] *Ibid.*, p. 223.

In making this decision the United States was deciding whether to adopt an expansionist or an isolationist ethic, whether to concentrate its capital or disperse it, whether to create a national bank to finance internal growth or whether to oppose the system of finance-capital and paper credit. Although the moral end of the Civil War was free soil, and later abolition of slavery altogether, the economic end was protectionism and industrialization, and the ancillary policies that went with it.

UGO RABBENO'S PERSPECTIVE
ON THE AMERICAN SCHOOL

By the 1890s protectionists such as Simon Patten concentrated on integrating their economic theories with social sciences, rather than attempting to trace the origins of their theories. Many of the theoretical contributions elaborated by the early protectionists, such as the economy-of-high-wages doctrine, had for some time been abandoned to the free traders. Toward the end of the nineteenth century the American protectionists received more attention from European economists than from American writers. Eugen Dühring in Germany, Francesco Ferrara in Italy, and followers of Frederic Bastiat in France were elaborating Henry Carey's "optimistic" theory of economic growth under increasing returns with minimal reference to his tariff theories.

Ugo Rabbeno came to the United States from Italy with a view of American protectionism shaped by the writings of Friedrich List. Rabbeno endorsed protectionism as a transition policy for countries with infant industries, but decried the isolationist extreme characteristic of much American literature in the second half of the nineteenth century. This antagonism to isolationism led him to dismiss much of the idealism that characterized the American protectionists from Carey through Patten. The final section of Rabbeno's book, *American Commercial Policy: Three Historical Essays*, is an attack on these writers, drawing largely on Frank Taussig and other opponents of protectionism, including Edwin Seligman, whose extense library he used in reviewing the country's protectionist literature.

Rabbeno's initial chapters on the historical evolution of tariff policy in the United States are an exercise in delineating the "law of three stages," popularized early by Sir James Steuart and Adam Smith, and later by List. According to this theory, countries passed from the agricultural stage through the industrial stage, finally arriving at the commercial stage. By "commercial" is meant industrial exporting, as early countries in the New World were if anything more export-oriented than the more industrialized nations of Europe. This warping of colonial development to provide raw materials to their mother countries impaired their industrialization, and indeed their agricultural development for crops not amenable to the colonialist plantation and slave systems.

In many respects Rabbeno's work reflects both the biases and perceptions of his contemporary American historians. Because the only early industry in America was household handicrafts, whose output did not come onto the market, its development was not retarded by English protectionism until after about 1760. Following the Revolution the decision to industrialize was pressed by Hamilton and others as much on political as on economic grounds, although Hamilton's *Report on Manufactures* contained most of the economic rationale that characterized later American protectionism—*e.g.*, the arguments that over time protective tariffs will work to lower prices as they foster the accumulation of capital; that the prosperity of rural agriculture and urban industry are closely connected, hence the harmony of economic interests between Northern and Southern states; that the home market is more stable than the foreign market; that industrial labor is amenable to greater division and increased efficiency than agricultural labor; that raw-materials producers are obliged to pay the costs of international transport on both their exports and imports; and in general that "the importations of manufactured supplies seem invariably to drain the merely agricultural people of their wealth."[59]

Rabbeno stresses that List, like Hamilton, did not endorse protectionism as an ideal but only as a transition-stage policy—a policy that later "became more and more a 'system of isolation'" at the hands of proponents of the American System. List, like Hamilton, "admitted free trade theoretically, and as a final conclusion." This moderate free-trade sympathy leads Rabbeno to judge that, even if List "was not the originator of modern protectionism, he was certainly the first, and the only one who raised it to an organic and scientific system."[60]

This would only be true if one conceives of "system" in terms of the theory of stages of economic development, a rough generality at best. By contrast, Henry Carey, Peshine Smith and their followers refined protectionism as an overall economic system, integrating the distribution and growth of incomes of all classes with the process of technological change under conditions of increasing returns, including in agriculture. Rabbeno dismisses this intellectual achievement as being part and parcel of "capitalist protectionism," the defense of trusts and of superprofits, a far cry from the infant-industry logic of Hamilton and List. Carey, states Rabbeno, "was the first to formulate the absolute theory of protectionism, and can lay the flattering unction to his soul of having been the forerunner of the so-called 'Chinese Wall Men' ... Freedom of trade ceases to be an ideal, however remote: his ideal now is association and concentration

---

[59] Ugo Rabbeno, *The American Coinmercial Policy: Three Historical Essays*, 2nd ed. (London, 1895), pp. 300–312.

[60] *Ibid.*, pp. 304, 319, 326.

through the co-existence of industry and agriculture, and the approximation of producers to consumers ... Free trade always brings about ruin; protection general well being." [61]

This is a harsh judgment, but by the 1890s many protectionists had indeed regressed from the sophistication achieved by Carey and Peshine Smith prior to the Civil War. Trusts were indeed being built up behind tariff walls, deflation was threatening the country's farmers, and the social context of protectionism had dropped much of the nobility of its early ideals. The contrast is not really perceived by Rabbeno, nor has it been observed by most subsequent historians.

For instance, Rabbeno states that an aversion to the settlement of the Far West might have made sense in List's day (the 1820s), but not in Carey's time (the 1840s and 1850s), when "free land was far away and required considerable capital for its cultivation." [62] This overlooks the fact that the struggle against westward expansion prior to the Civil War was largely in opposition to the extension of the slave system, and expressed the faith that growth of America's internal market would be able to support the growth of the nation's economy long after the frontier had been reached and fully settled. Rabbeno barely perceives that the most important impact of the frontier in American history is in the expanding internal market, in contrast to England's primary reliance upon foreign markets. The tendency of protectionism in the United States to be much less trade-oriented than that of England was due to its thriving home market and its high wage levels.

Instead of impairing the accumulation of capital and the development of efficient production methods, these high wages led to just the reverse of what orthodox Ricardian doctrine would have anticipated. The economy of high wages doctrine could be pushed too far, however. Rabbeno held that, at a certain phase of capitalism—the high-wage phase—capitalists must lower wages to maintain profits, and therefore espouse free trade. [63] Protectionism becomes a drag on industrial development by enabling less efficient producers to remain in business longer than they would under free trade. Now that American industrialization was consolidated, protectionism was becoming merely extortionate.

The "infant industries" of List's and Carey's day had become adults. Rabbeno denied that protectionism could raise wage levels (this could be done only by banning immigrants, not goods). Nor could it any longer, under the era of trusts, lead to falling prices for consumer goods; real wages would be

---

[61] *Ibid.*, pp. 351, 370.
[62] *Ibid.*, p. 380. See pp. 173–78 for an excellent discussion of the role of Western lands.
[63] *Ibid.*, p. 245.

depressed under the trustified system of capitalist protection.[64] America was passing into the third stage of its history, in which its industry was being consolidated, the condition of the working class depressed, and protection becoming useless to the capitalists. Now that America's vacant lands were virtually all filled up, "protection nullifies the efforts of capitalism; the land rent threatens."[65]

Hardly an optimistic picture, nor an historically accurate one, but one that has been elevated to orthodoxy by the Turner school of historians and its followers.

[64] *Ibid.*, pp. 198, 210f. See also p. 171.   [65] *Ibid.*, p. 183.

II. The First Generation of Pennsylvania Protectionists

The Pennsylvania School

The evolution of American protectionism was characterized by regional differences not only in regard to the industries to be protected but also in the way the tariff issue was linked to local and social issues. Despite the passions which the tariff controversy inspired in those committed to it, protectionism was secondary to local issues in most elections. On the national level it was a quirk of fate that the only two Whig presidents—William Henry Harrison in 1840 and Zachary Taylor in 1848—died early in office and were succeeded by Democratic-leaning vice presidents who scrapped their tariff and internal improvement programs. Protectionism finally rode into office on the shoulders of the slavery issue, after the Whig Party gave way to the Republicans in the l850s.

Despite Pennsylvania's central position as the early seat of the nation's commerce, industry and banking, its politicians played a declining role in enacting national tariff legislation. Alexander Dallas, to be sure, became Secretary of the Treasury following the return to peace and authored a major protectionist argument in 1816. Andrew Stewart remained a protectionist leader in the House of Representatives for many decades, abandoning the party of Jackson for the Whigs over the tariff issue. And James Buchanan, although a Democrat, was amenable to protecting Pennsylvania's industrial interests when absolutely necessary. But the protectionist cause was hardly helped by the state leader, Simon Cameron, an opportunist whose politics vacillated according to his self-interest at any given moment.

The protectionist leader in Congress for more than a quarter-century was Henry Clay of Kentucky, whose reputation in the North was damaged by the fact that he was a slave-holder. He was joined by Daniel Webster, whose protectionism was subordinated to New England's textile, shipping and importing interests. The leading New York protectionist in Congress was William Henry Seward, who came to power as governor on the anti-Masonic ticket. New York protectionism was agrarian but anti-Southern, not having the economic links either to the cotton trade that characterized New England or to the heavy industry of Pennsylvania. Hence the distinction between "Conscience" and "Cotton" Whigs, led respectively by Seward and Webster.

As in mirrored the rest of the country, Pennsylvania's Whigs fought among themselves and permitted themselves, to be continually outmaneuvered by the

Democrats. As Eiselen emphasizes in *The Rise of Pennsylvania Protectionism*, the state's Democrats "never lost two consecutive elections during four decades of fiercely contended party strife. This remarkable record of success, in the face of Pennsylvania's admitted enthusiasm for the tariff system, would seem to require a word of explanation. A very important factor was the superior leadership enjoyed by the Democrats during the entire period of their ascendancy. Such masters of political strategy as Samuel Ingham, James Buchanan, George M. Dallas, and Simon Cameron were always at the helm, alert to seize every advantage and quick to retrieve every disaster. The only Whig with a comparable gift was Governor [William F.] Johnston."[66] The Whigs never built up a smoothly running machine of office-holders. "Finally, it should be noted that there were few elections during this period in which the tariff issue was clearly and convincingly drawn," especially during the Jacksonian era. Even when the Republicans supplanted the Whigs and came to power following the economic crisis of 1857, their state leader Cameron, the former Democrat, was bitterly hated by Henry Carey's circle and many out-of-state Republicans.

The political misalliance between Pennsylvania protectionism and the Democratic Party reflects alignments going back to the American Revolution. In the early decades of the Republic, the Democrats were anti-Federalist and largely anti-English, while the Federalists were pro-English. They also were the party of wealth, and as it increasingly endeavored to protect its industrial base it took a protectionist, and therefore anti-English position. The Democrats, originally anti-English, were obliged by their opposition to protectionism to strike the growing bond with England, especially on the part of Southern free traders. Hence the two political parties remained true to their economic base only by reversing their policies and attitudes toward England.

The Era of Good Feelings, which lasted from 1816 until the 1824 presidential elections, reflected this state of flux. Calhoun supported the 1816 tariff, as did a number of other leading Southerners. In what was virtually a one-party system, elections turned mainly on personal considerations until after 1828, when a national division split the country along North-South lines. Protectionists were pitted against free traders, and defenders of industrialization were generally against advocates of the slave system seeking to maintain America as a cotton and tobacco supplier to Europe.

Interruption of trade with England during the Napoleonic Wars and the War of 1812 fostered American industry mainly in the North. Following the Treaty of Ghent this indigenous industry—apart from household manufac-

---

[66] Malcolm Rogers Eiselen, *The Rise of Pennsylvania Protectionism: A Thesis in History*, University of Pennsylvania (Philadelphia, 1932), p. 242.

tures—was nearly overwhelmed by British imports. Military hostility between America and England gave way to commercial warfare, and the tariff controversy emerged as a national issue, with the lines now being drawn along regional self-interest. Peace was also accompanied by a worldwide banking collapse, leading to general commercial failure and economic depression during 1818–19. By 1820 protectionism was becoming a sharply sectional issue. The major protectionist pushes occurred in the presidential election years 1824, 1828 and 1832, before being laid to rest for more than a decade by the anti-protectionist impetus of Jacksonian democracy.

Pennsylvania protectionism was representative of American industrial evolution in its broad objectives, but unique in its specific political fortunes. Eiselen shows that, as might be expected, it "was the outgrowth of industrial strength rather than of industrial weakness. Almost invariably, protectionist agitation in behalf of a commodity did not appear until the domestic production was fairly well established."[67] In addition to agriculturalists hoping to broaden the country's economic base, its major proponents were established industrialists eager to consolidate and extend their home markets, especially in times of commercial depression and deflation. Their industrial base rested on iron, followed by textiles, paper, leather, brewing and publishing.

Unlike New York City, Philadelphia was the seat of vocal and entrenched protectionist interests, largely because of Mathew Carey and the protectionists who gathered around him. Carey took the lead in forming various societies to promote industrial legislation, and was aided by such friends as Charles Ingersoll. During the 1820s, the city was rivaled only by Boston in its protectionist literary efforts.

Eiselen points out that the Pennsylvania iron interest "developed its most vehement protectionism after 1840, not because of adverse economic conditions, but as a result of the introduction of the anthracite process, which meant increased output, cheaper costs of production, and a greatly improved competitive position." Its protectionism became most urgent after "the crisis of 1857 which consummated the overthrow of the Democratic Party in the Keystone State and thus dissolved the political misalliance which had so long undermined the influence of Pennsylvania protectionism at the national capital."[68] The fact that the burden of the 1857 panic fell heavily on labor, traditionally the bastion of Democratic politics in the North, turned the tide toward the Republicans.

---

[67] *Ibid.*, p. 267.   [68] *Ibid.*, pp. 268–69.

Perhaps in part because of the prominence of its Irish citizens, protectionism was more anti-British than anti-Southern. Henry Carey showed himself more willing to compromise with the South than did many other Northern protectionists.[69] In this respect Eiselen is somewhat misleading in asserting that Carey's followers were homogeneous, and indeed that protectionism itself was a homogeneous movement throughout the North. It was not, and studies of its development in individual states — of which Eiselen's alone has so far been written — will demonstrate its sectional vicissitudes and distinctions.

---

[69] For a discussion of Carey's reflection of Pennsylvania sectionalism, see George Winston Smith, *Henry C. Carey and American Sectional Conflict* (Albuquerque, New Mexico, 1951).

MATHEW CAREY, PROTECTIONIST PUBLICIST

Mathew Carey (1760–1839) was the great publicist of the first generation of American protectionists, as was his son, Henry Charles Carey, for the second generation. In his capacity as proprietor of the country's largest publishing firm, as an indefatigable pamphleteer, and as organizer and financier of protectionist literature and conventions, he established Philadelphia as the literary center of American protectionism.

Already in his Dublin childhood Carey had wished to become a publisher. "At the age of fifteen he was apprenticed to a book-seller," says his biographer, Earl Bradsher. "This was accomplished thru his own efforts; for his father, while offering him the choice of any other of the twenty-five corporations in Dublin, refused to aid him in his resolution to become a printer and bookseller."[70] Carey shortly became a writer as well, and in 1779 wrote a somewhat inflammatory pamphlet urging repeal of the penal code against Catholics. Fearing for his safety, his friends convinced him that this was an excellent moment to travel abroad. Visiting Passy, a Parisian suburb, he found employment reprinting Benjamin Franklin's dispatches from America, and then went to work for Didot, the largest European printer of the day. He also became acquainted with such men as the Marquis de Lafayette.

In 1783 Carey returned to Dublin, where his father helped him establish the *Volunteer's Journal*, in which he "defended the manufactures, commerce, and political rights of Ireland against the encroachments of Great Britain"[71]—a prelude to the struggle he subsequently was to wage on behalf of America. The following year he was imprisoned for a month in Newgate for denouncing Britain's Irish policy. Fearing the outcome of a libel suit lodged by the Irish premier, he emigrated to the United States in September 1784.

His funds exhausted, he settled in Philadelphia where, by chance, he met General Lafayette once again when the latter passed through. Before departing, the general left $400 to help tide Carey over (a sum which Carey took great pride in returning to Lafayette on the general's return visit to America forty years later). Carey used this money to establish the *Pennsylvania Herald*, the first

---

[70] Earl L. Bradsher, *Mathew Carey: Editor, Author and Publisher* (New York, 1912), p. 1. The following biography of Carey closely follows Bradsher's exposition.

[71] *Ibid.*, p. 2.

issue of which appeared on January 25, 1785. After struggling along for a few months the paper became strikingly successful by inaugurating a new departure in American journalism, reprinting the *House of Assembly* debates. This success enabled Carey to help found the *Columbian Magazine* in October 1786.

Three months later he withdrew from this venture to establish the *American Museum*, "the first really successful magazine in America." Carey's optimism, however, led him to perpetually overprint his runs, and this fact, coupled with such difficulties as having to dun subscribers for overdue funds, kept him from accumulating more than his original $400 at any one point of time. In his autobiography he describes how he was constantly obliged to run about borrowing funds during banking hours to keep his enterprise afloat.

The 1792 postal laws, which required printed matter to pay the same rate as private letters, drove his two magazines out of business. This adversity turned Carey to bookselling and printing, which proved much more profitable than his magazine activity. Book prices were then relatively high, and he grossed over $60,000 on his two biggest sellers, Guthrie's *Geography* and Goldsmith's *Animated Nature*, which were supplemented by a quarto Bible and some atlases, as well as his own *History of the Yellow Fever*.

Gradually he began to participate in American political and economic affairs. In 1810 he became one of the few vocal defenders of renewing the charter of the Bank of the United States, against the strong opposition of his fellow anti-Federalists. In defending a national bank, Carey anticipated one of the three major planks of what Henry Clay later was to term "the American System." But true to form, the bank directors made little effort to help him or to placate public opinion in any way, and the charter was denied.

During the war with England, Carey published a major pamphleteering work, *The Olive Branch*, which sold even more copies in 1815, after the return to peace, than it had during the war. *The Olive Branch* was one of the most popular political works by an American since Thomas Paine's *Common Sense*. Carey exhibited his innate philanthropism by permitting Boston printers to publish, without charge, an edition that was immediately sold out.

The return to peace brought a flood of British imports, and in 1815 Carey became part of the manufacturers' lobby in Washington seeking American industrial independence from Britain. He took the lead in organizing the Philadelphia Society for the Promotion of National Industry, which initially consisted of only ten members. He read widely in the field of political economy, and was particularly impressed by Alexander Hamilton's *Report on Manufactures* (1791). He frequently used "Hamilton" as a pseudonym, as well as the name of the French protectionist Colbert.

The products of Carey's labors began to appear in 1819 as a series of addresses to his Philadelphia group. "Before I began to write the addresses of the Philadelphia Society for the Promotion of National Industry in 1819," he wrote, "I had never devoted three days to the study of political economy."[72] But by 1832 he was able to say: "I have laboured in this great cause for above thirteen years—expended above 4000 dollars on it, for paper, printing, journeys, books, postage, etc., although I have never had any personal interest in it—neglected my business while I was in trade—lost some of my best friends and customers—gave up my enjoyments—excited deadly hostility—was subject to abuse in and out of Congress, and in newspapers, pamphlets and stump speeches—and burned in effigy in Columbia."[73]

Whereas Hamilton's report had explored why the United States should establish a thriving industry from the narrow manufacturing base in existence in 1791, Carey wrote from the vantage point of a country that already had become partially industrialized above and beyond the household manufacturing stage. It thus it was natural for him to emphasize a point not touched upon by Hamilton: Urban laborers put out of work by import competition could not shift to "collateral employments" with anywhere near the ease assumed by free-trade economists. "A man who has spent the prime of his life in making watches, cabinet ware, hats, or shoes, or weaving cloth, would be nearly as much out of his element at agricultural labor as a farmer would be in a shoemaker's or hatter's workshop … Moreover a large portion, in many cases three-fourths of the persons engaged in the cotton and woollen branches are women and children, wholly unfit for farming."[74]

A flood of British imports at that time, he concluded, would extinguish American capital and thus foreclose employment opportunities to a large portion of the nation's labor, depriving it of the means to purchase subsistence by causing a spreading depression. What, he asked, could the tanner do to shift "his various vats, buildings and tools… his hides and leather … and his outstanding debts."[75] Little except campaign for protective tariffs, he concluded. The nation could not blandly assume with Ricardo that "trade will regulate itself," as had been shown by Portugal's experience after the Methuen Treaty of 1703. Its industry was destroyed, its specie drained, and it was left prostrate, little more than a winery

---

[72] Mathew Carey, *Essays on Political Economy* … (Philadelphia, 1822), p. ix.

[73] *The Crisis, An Appeal to the good sense of the nation, against the spirit of resistance and dissolution of the Union* (Philadelphia, 1832), p. 20. See also his "Autobiography," published in Vol. 6 of the *New England Magazine*.

[74] *Addresses of the Philadelphia Society for the Promotion of National Industry*, 5th ed. (Philadelphia, 1820), p. 65. See also pp. 24f.

[75] *Ibid.*, p. 29.

for industrial England.[76] Protective tariffs, Carey concluded on a more positive note, would induce European artisans and manufacturers to immigrate to the United States. America would not be obliged to run ever further into debt to British creditors, and her banks would possess enough specie to operate on a sound basis.

The Philadelphia Society widely reprinted these essays in pamphlets of four or eight pages, in editions that sometimes ran to 1500 copies. The society also published two essays by Dr. Samuel Jackson, which form the twelfth and thirteenth of Carey's Philadelphia addresses. In March 1820, however, the society refused to contribute $80 toward the expense of printing Carey's reply to a free-trade memorial of the Agricultural Society of Fredericksburg, a reply which Carey had published under his own name. In disgust, Carey, withdrew from the society, which soon expired for lack of leadership.

Also in 1820 Carey published *The New Olive Branch*, in which he sought to reconcile the interests of farmers and industrialists by emphasizing their mutual dependence. This was the home-market argument for protective tariffs, which was soon voiced in Congress by Carey's fellow Pennsylvanian Andrew Stewart, and which was later to be greatly elaborated by Carey's son Henry. In *The New Olive Branch* Carey sought to ward off the pressures leading to the North-South conflict between urban industry and the Southern slave system that finally was to engulf the nation in civil war. This work was reprinted with the sixth edition of his Addresses to form a hybrid work, his *Essays on Political Economy: or, The Most Certain Means of Promoting the Wealth, Power, Resources, and Happiness of Nations: Applied particularly to the United States* (Philadelphia: H. C. Carey & I. Lea, 1822).

Two years later, in 1824, Carey turned over management of his firm to his two sons, Henry and Edward. He proceeded to found and edit a weekly protectionist paper, *The Political Economist*, but was obliged to abandon it after four months of intermittent publication. He continued to campaign on behalf of various political and economic projects, including an endeavor to extend to fellow immigrants, especially those from Ireland, the same helping hand he had received from Lafayette. He had helped form the Hibernian Society in 1792 to aid Irish immigrants, and served as its secretary for a number of years. In 1826 he wrote some *Reflections on the Subject of Emigration from Europe*, a handbook to prepare Europeans for what to expect and what not to expect in the United States. He emphasized the independence of American citizens, the ready availability of landed property, the low tax burden, and the freedom of religion. Two years later he helped send an agent to Ireland to help finance Irish immigration to the United States.

[76] *Ibid.*, p. 86.

Among the other causes espoused by Carey was higher wages for women. He also defended charities, denying that they encouraged idleness: He also became a partisan of the Greek Revolution and formed a committee for relief of the Greeks. He recommended that Philadelphia establish a kindergarden system and, as mentioned above, urged rechartering of the Second Bank of the United States. All told, he wrote over sixty tracts, comprising some 2500 pages, many of which were printed and distributed at his own expense. A fairly complete bibliography of his books, pamphlets and speeches can be found in Sabin's *Bibliotheca Americana*, where it occupies four full pages of notes and seven of text.

GEORGE TIBBITS, HOME-MARKET SUPPORTER

George Tibbits (1763–1849) was a prominent merchant, congressman and federalist. Born in Rhode Island and raised in Massachusetts, he moved with his parents across the state line in 1780 to Lansingburg, a suburb of Troy, New York. Four years later, at the age of twenty-one, he went into business as a local merchant. In 1797 he moved into Troy proper, where he resided for the rest of his life.

Shortly thereafter, Tibbits went into politics as a Federalist. He was elected to the State Assembly in 1800, and to Congress in 1802. While in Congress he published a number of protectionist essays in the Philadelphia *Inquirer* under the name "Cato."

His political career led him to retire from active business life in 1804, at the age of thirty-nine. He was elected State Senator in 1815, was defeated for Lieutenant-Governor behind Rufus King in 1816, and in 1820 was re-elected to the State Assembly. Four years later he was appointed one of three state prison commissioners whose 1825 report led to a general remodelling of the prison system. He followed through on this project by serving for the next five years as one of the commissioners in charge of building Sing Sing, a reform prison designed to remedy many of the penitentiary abuses of the day.

In March 1825, Tibbits read before the New York Board of Agriculture his *Memoir on the Expediency and Practicability of Improving Home Markets for the Sale of Agricultural Productions and Raw Materials, by the introduction and growth of Artizans and Manufacturers.* This speech, broadly reflecting the home-market arguments of Hamilton, Carey, Clay and Stewart, attracted wide attention, and was reprinted in Albany and Philadelphia. Tibbits hoped to turn agricultural societies into organs for disseminating protectionist doctrine, and tried to convince them that protective tariffs and industrialization would not only draw surplus labor from agriculture (thereby alleviating the existing agricultural distress and providing a more stable local urban market) but also would attract skilled artisans from other countries.

To import foreign woollens, he argued, was to import both foreign wool and the foreign foodstuffs used to feed the foreign woollen manufacturers. Once these manufacturers immigrated to the United States, or their places were taken by native American workingmen, they would become customers for U.S. farm products. What impeded the growth of American industry, he concluded, was not a lack of raw labor or capital, but of skill. For the time being, this was most easily obtainable by pursuing an active immigration policy.[77]

England's mercantilist policy had enabled her to vastly increase her taxes, "her number of people ... and her effective means, until she may well defy competition." Granting that it was difficult to transplant rural labor to urban manufactories, he contended that "manufactures, if they can find protection, will be carried on, and supplied with hands, who will come to us already learned, from the countries from which we have obtained our manufactured articles, or be made from the younger and growing population of this country." The alternative was a passive federal policy that would induce this population to emigrate from the eastern states into Canada or out West.

Tibbits noted that some English commercial traders may have objected to mercantilist policies at first, but soon found their wealth, national strength and political situation vastly improved and their land rents rising: "The population of England, must have remained vastly less, and that of Flanders, much greater, had England been content to have continued her former practice of sending her wool to Flanders, there to be worked into cloths, and the cloths sent back to England, in exchange for more wool." The principles of free trade were thus "in direct opposition to the policy which has given to the manufacturing and commercial nations of Europe, their present ascendency, and which are indispensable to the prosperity of this country."[78] "Give to manufacturers protection," he concluded, "and they will come to us from abroad. Give to artizans protection, and they will increase from our present population. Obtain the adequate number, and their consumption of agricultural produce will be immense, and much greater than any quantity which we have ever exported."[79] He closed his address with probably as eloquent a passage describing early American economic self-consciousness as can be found:

---

[77] George Tibbits, *A Memoir on the Expediency and Practicability of Improving Home Markets for the Sale of Agricultural Productions and Raw Materials, by the introduction and growth of Artizans and Manufacturers.* Read before the Board of Agriculture of the State of New York, March 8, 1825 (Albany 1825), pp. 11–13.

[78] *Ibid.*, pp. 20, 21, 23.

[79] *Ibid.*, p. 33.

The acts of England [*e.g.*, the Corn Laws protecting its domestic agriculture], in refusing to take the agricultural productions of the northern states in exchange for her manufactures, out to be considered by us in the light of friendly and paternal admonitions. These acts may reasonably be construed as saying to us, "you are of age; you have left the family; make your own clothing; your welfare demands it of us to compel you to do it; you are capacitated by God and by nature to become a great and powerful people, and to extend the language, the religion, the laws, customs and manners of England over immense regions; and even to exceed the mother country in these respects; but you never can arrive to that state, until you acquire and domesticate the mechanic arts, upon which that elevated situation is mainly dependent, Europe has millions of artizans who would flock to your shores; add to your numbers, and teach your rising population the necessary arts, if you would give them protection, until they have firmly established themselves among you. You have the history of our rise; avoid our error and unnecessary wars; exclude foreign manufactures, and you will soon have the necessary stock of artizans, and a home market for all your agricultural productions."

I should consider it a great misfortune, if England should withdraw this admonitory advice, and again admit our breadstuffs, provisions and raw materials. It would have a tendency to prevent us, for a long time, from rising to that solid and permanent elevation to which, by her policy, we are now fast approaching, and to which we may very soon attain by proper management. We want, in addition to the obstructions which she throws in the way of importations, such further obstructions raised by our government, as shall create the fullest confidence in manufacturing undertakings in this country. That done, we shall soon draw into the country a great addition to our present population, not of the description of mere ditch-diggers, but of intelligent artizans. The inducements to emigrations of this description, would probably be greater than any which the settlement of new lands has ever held out.[80]

In 1827, Tibbits added to this pamphlet a supplementary Essay on the same subject (which he had written in 1826), identifying himself simply as "an independent farmer" pleading "the cause of his brother farmers." Warning against "the syren song of purchasing cheap goods abroad," he pointed to the fact that the free-trade theories "carried into operation, in Spain, Portugal, Italy and Poland, have enfeebled and impoverished those countries, and made them tributaries, and quasi colonies of those nations which had the wisdom to repudiate and reject those theories." Britain and other nations that protected their industry had prospered, "in opposition to the general doctrines of Adam Smith, and M. Say." However, Tibbits quoted extensively from the works of Smith and Say themselves to show their arguments for industrialization and, by extension, protective tariffs for the non-industrialized countries. He cited Book IV, ch. ix of *The Wealth of Nations* to describe a vicious spiral in which low incomes (stemming from free trade policies) would induce emigration, reducing

---

[80] *Ibid.*, pp. 30f.

the home market for food and other products, lowering farm income accordingly and inducing still more emigration. The East could attract industrial artisans if it so chose, by assuring them an adequate home market. Even if England should repeal her Corn Laws, it would only be to break down American industry by accepting American grain in exchange for flooding the American market with British manufactures — a policy which would bankrupt American farmers as well as manufacturers.[81]

Adam Smith had written his book, Tibbits pointed out, "in a country, (Britain,) and at a time when the arts and manufactures had already arrived, (by the nursing care of government,) to a very high state of perfection, and were in full operation and practice, and at a time, moreover, when it might have been good policy to have withdrawn that protection and to have left them to take care of themselves; or when the necessity for protection was not as evident as it was in their infancy."[82] What was desirable for Britain at its particular stage of economic evolution was not desirable for the United States in its historical circumstances.

Like most other protectionists, Tibbits was an advocate of internal improvements. He played a major role in designing the financial plans for the Erie Canal and the Delaware and Hudson Canal, and in 1828 wrote a pamphlet on the *Finances of the Canal Fund of the State of New York Examined*. Two years later he was elected Mayor of Troy, occupying this position during 1830–36.

---

[81] *Essay on the Expediency and Practicability of Improving Home Markets ... Being an Appendix and Illustration of a Memoir on the same subject* (Philadelphia, 1829), pp. 1, 8, 10, 24, 30.
[82] *Ibid.*, p. 49.

ANDREW STEWART, PROTECTIONIST CONGRESSMAN

Andrew Stewart (1791–1872) advocated protectionist policies for nearly two decades in the House of Representatives, gaining national renown as chairman of the House Committees on the Tariff and Internal Improvements in the 1820s. Having grown up in modest conditions on his father's farm in Fayette County, Pennsylvania, he went on to become one of the originators and directors of the Chesapeake and Ohio Canal, and was also a supporter of the Cumberland Road, a local railroad and many other internal improvements.

He was elected to the Pennsylvania legislature in 1815 after graduating from Washington College, and was appointed Attorney-General for Pennsylvania by President Monroe in 1820. He then ran for the House of Representatives, where he served first as a Democrat (1820–28) and later as a Whig during 1830–34 and 1842–48. In the latter year he declined to run for Congress, in order to become a candidate for the Vice-Presidency under General Taylor, a nomination which he narrowly missed due to a bit of political intrigue by pro-Southern Whigs supporting Millard Fillmore. President Taylor offered him the cabinet post of Secretary of the Treasury, but Stewart declined for reasons of ill.

Many of Stewart's congressional speeches were reproduced in full by Whig newspapers and in pamphlets printed in editions numbering into the hundreds of thousands all told. His speeches, like those of Henry Clay and other protectionists, dealt extensively with economic doctrine. In his 82nd year, Stewart, with the assistance of one of his sons, collected his speeches on the subjects of the tariff and internal improvements that remained after his office burned in 1844, and published them in a volume entitled *The American System: Speeches on the Tariff Question, and on Internal Improvements*.

A distinguishing thread running throughout Stewart's home-market argument is the farmers' interest in protectionism, drawing upon what is now called input-output analysis. In a speech given February 1, 1827, for example, he declared:

> What is the importation of cloth, but the importation of agricultural produce? Is not cloth the product of agriculture? Analyze it; resolve it into its constituent elements, and what is it? Wool and labor. What produces the wool? Grass and grain. And what supports labor but bread and meat? ... Thus cloth is composed of the grass and grain that feed the sheep, and the bread and meat that support the laborer who converts the wool into cloth. And are we to be told that it is the policy of this country, where seven-eighths of the whole

71

population are agriculturists, thus to import annually eight or ten millions of dollars' worth of grass and grain, and bread and meat, converted into cloth, and that, too, from the starving and miserable countries of Europe, while our own are rotting on our hands?[68]

Rather than taxing the farmer and ruining agriculture, tariffs would nurture a thriving home market. The following year, in 1828, Stewart elaborated the above input-output analysis, replete with foreign-trade leakages and capital accumulation (profit) factors:

> ... it is much better for the farmer that we should import the raw material than to import the manufactured article, and for this plain reason; if wool, hemp, flax, etc., were imported raw, it would be worked up by American labor, feeding on American bread and meat; but if worked up into cloth in England, we lost this market for both. Our imports of woolen goods amounted on an average to from 8 to 10 millions of dollars a year, while our imports of wool amounted to less than half a million. The ... wool used in making a yard of cloth is equal to one-half its value, so that in $8,000,000 of cloth, there is 4,000,000 of dollars' worth of wool, and the balance of its value mostly consisted of agricultural produce, provisions, soap, tallow, wood, teazles, fuel, etc.; all these must be paid for by those who purchase and consume the cloth. A practical manufacturer [computed] the cost of the component materials of a yard of cloth, the result was, that more than three-fourths of the whole price was made up of agricultural productions. Thus, in a yard of cloth worth $4.00,
>
> | | |
> |---|---|
> | There was of wool | $2.00 |
> | Provisions, fuel, soap, tallow, etc . | $1.15 |
> | Profits, etc., etc . | $4.00[69] |

Warning of the folly of increasing American tariffs on raw materials at a time when industrial England was drastically lowering its raw-materials tariffs or abolishing them altogether, Stewart fought the 1828 Tariff of Abominations with its proposed increase in the tariff on raw wool from 15 to 150 per cent (with only a $3^{1}/_{3}$ per cent increase in the tariff on manufactured woollens), and a 71 per cent increase in hemp and flax duties (largely for products not produced in the United States) without any increase in protection to articles manufactured from these materials. "You may shut out the raw materials," he explained, "but it will answer no purpose if you still admit the manufactured article, which must always bring the raw material with it."[70] Stewart concluded that the only way to sustain high raw-materials prices for American farmers, and to reduce the long-term cost of manufactures to the American people, was to enact protective tariffs so as to enable American industrialists to catch up with and overtake their British counterparts.

---

[68] Andrew Stewart, speech of February 1, 1827, in *The American System: Speeches on The Tariff Question, and on Internal Improvements, principally delivered in The House of Representatives of the United States* (Philadelphia, 1872), pp. 134f. See also pp. 189f.

[69] Speech of April 8, 1828, in *ibid.*, pp. 158f.

[70] *Ibid.*, p. 169.

THE 1827 TARIFF DEBATE

The 1827–28 tariff debate, which culminated in the "Tariff of Abominations," saw the sectional divisions emerge which were to harden increasingly until the Civil War. Tariffs had been raised steadily since 1789, and most industries were fairly prosperous and well protected by the 1824 tariff. The Census of 1820 had shifted congressional representation in favor of the manufacturing states, giving protectionism the upper hand in American politics. All four presidential aspirants in the 1828 election endorsed protective tariffs: Adams, Jackson, Clay, and even Crawford from the South, although the latter section was coming to set itself in opposition to industrial protection and internal improvements.

Only the textile industry was in severe straits, and by 1826 about half the textile machinery in New England was idle despite the 33$\frac{1}{3}$ per cent tariff on woollens enacted in 1824.[71] English producers enjoyed lower wage costs, were much more highly mechanized, and their government had further increased their cost advantage by reducing the tariff on raw wool from sixpence to one penny per pound. This provided English manufacturers with substantially cheaper raw material than their American counterparts, to whom the price of foreign wool was increased by about 40 per cent by the time trans-Atlantic shipping charges were added to the 20 per cent U.S. tariff on raw wool. Furthermore, many English fabrics were disposed of in the United States below cost through the auction system. If American manufacturers were to compete with English imports, they would have to increase productivity by mechanizing production. But this required capital investments, which could only be made out of increased revenues supported by higher tariff protection.

The 1827 Congress saw Rollin Mallary of Vermont, a loyal protectionist, chair the Committee on Manufactures, which duly proposed a woollen bill leaving intact the 33$\frac{1}{3}$ per cent *ad valorem* tariff on woollens, but applied the "minimum" principle that had been devised in 1816 by Francis Lowell, inventor of the power loom that made the Boston Manufacturing Company the most successful textile factory in America. The Committee on Manufactures proposed three benchmark minima at $0.40, $2.50 and $4.00 per square yard.

---

[71] See for instance Edward Stanwood, *American Tariff Controversies in the Nineteenth Century,* vol. 1 (Boston, 1903), p. 253.

All imported woollens below $0.40 were to be charged a duty of $13\frac{1}{3}$¢ per yard; woollens priced between $0.41 and $2.50 were charged $83\frac{1}{3}$¢ per yard; and all woollens between $2.51 and $4.00 were charged $1.33. *Ad valorem* duties were in this manner to be converted into comparatively high specific duties.

Led by Mathew Carey of Philadelphia and Hezekiah Niles of Baltimore, the protectionists gained the lead in pamphlet and journal literature. They coordinated their efforts by arranging a five-day convention at Harrisburg, Pennsylvania, which opened on July 30, 1827 "to take into consideration the present state of the wool-growing and wool-manufacturing interests and such other manufactures as may require encouragement." Delegates from all northern states except Maine attended, including senators and industrialists, although Niles reported that a majority of the delegates were farmers. The convention proposed overtly prohibitory duties, asking for a woollen tariff of 40 per cent (rising to 50 per cent over time) with four "minimum" points set at $0.50, $2.50, $4.00, and $6.00 per square yard. Prohibitory duties on raw wool were also supported, rising from 20¢ to 50¢ per pound over time.

Belatedly, free traders throughout the country gathered their forces to wage a "campaign of education" by means of pamphlets and reprinted speeches to counter those of the protectionists. The most important of these free-trade tracts was the Boston memorial written in 1827 by Henry Lee. (Lee also wrote much of the famous 1832 free-trade memorial.) Of his work Edward Stanwood remarks: "So far as it challenges the duty of the government to protect manufactures; so far as it denies the obligation resting upon Congress to continue a policy of protection and increase duties until they become adequate to that end; so far as it disputes the proposition that protective duties result in lowering prices; so far as it seeks to show the inconsistency of Mr. Webster, Mr. [Edward] Everett, and other New England men who had opposed and now favored protection; so far as it attempts to prove that the causes of the existing depression in the woollen manufacture were not those alleged by the advocates of the woollens bill of 1827 and would not be cured by that or a similar measure;—so far, in short, as it was an argument against protection on the well-recognized lines of the classical political economy, no more powerful document was ever produced in this country."[72]

This may be somewhat of an exaggeration. The Boston memorial lacked the conciseness and scope of the protectionist works, and was longer on statistics than on theory. But because it was the first serious and comprehensive tract to address itself to the anti-protectionist cause, it was necessarily catapulted into a major position. After four printings at Boston sold out, it was reprinted in

---

[72] *Ibid.*, p. 264.

New York in an edition of two thousand copies and attracted a number of replies of which the major two were first published in Philadelphia in 1828 (*An Examination of the Report* and List's anonymous *Review of the Report*).

Lee's Boston memorial deserves some comment. He was born into an old Massachusetts family; his mother was a Cabot and his father was also prominent in the East India trade. Like other Boston aristocrats, including his two brothers, Lee graduated from Philips Andover prep school. But instead of going on to Harvard, he went directly into business for himself. He became a prominent merchant, and in 1811 sailed for India, where he remained for a number of years. After a number of unsuccessful business ventures upon his return to America, he gravitated towards more academic pursuits, particularly the analysis of commercial statistics. He contributed articles to Condy Raguet's *Free Trade Advocate* published in Philadelphia, and to a number of other Jacksonian organs.

In 1832 he wrote the *Exposition of Evidence* that formed the statistical appendix to Albert Gallatin's famous memorial commissioned by the New York free trade convention of that year. In fact, Lee's opposition to federalism was so strong that in 1832 he ran for Vice President on the Independent (*i.e.*, secession) ticket, receiving South Carolina's eleven electoral votes. Thereafter he settled down and corresponded actively with such English free traders as John Ramsey McCulloch, Thomas Tooke, William Newmarch and Richard Cobden, withdrawing from business altogether in 1840 to devote himself to reading on commercial subjects, save for one last unsuccessful run for Congress in 1850.

The Boston memorial cites the major protectionist tracts that appeared in 1827: List's *Outlines Of American Political Economy*, the Senate speeches of Clay, Webster's speech shifting into the protectionist camp, and the speeches of Rollin Mallary and Andrew Stewart in the House of Representatives, along with the writings of Henry Carey, Hezekiah Niles, George Tibbits and numerous other writers. The resulting argument and its protectionist replies synthesized the tariff debate as it then stood.

First of all, there was an argument over the history of the American textile industry as it had unfolded so far. Lee pointed out that at the time of the Revolution the United States produced three-fourths of the woollens it consumed, protected only by the 5 per cent tariff of 1789. At that time there were no complaints that tariff protection was insufficient, but now the textile manufacturers were complaining that even a $33^{1}/_{3}$ per cent tariff was not enough.[73]

The protectionists replied that America's early self-sufficiency in woollens was a natural result of its widespread household manufactures, whose home-

---

[73] [Henry Lee], *Report of a Committee of Citizens of Boston and Vicinity, opposed to a Further Increase of Duties on Importatiom* (Boston, 1827), pp. 83, 87f.

spun did not come onto the market. But household manufactures now were being phased out as "the necessary consequence of the improvement of civil society."[74] The natural course of evolution was for labor to specialize, coordinated by market pricing. However, diversification of American industry was threatened by the fact that English exporters were underselling American manufacturers, preventing less mechanized mills in particular from competing within the market system.

The country thus was obliged to over-specialize its labor in producing raw materials rather than spreading it over an economically efficient range of pursuits. If America remained agricultural, the labor power of its women and children would remain merely latent, as would the South's water power. The labor power available to a given population under industrial conditions exceeded that available under an agricultural economy. Of even greater importance was the fact that machine power was available almost exclusively to manufacturing populations. (Mechanization of crop production lay far in the future.) The textile manufacturers' complaints of inadequate protection thus were being voiced at a time when economic conditions were radically transformed from those which had existed a half-century earlier.

Protectionists also claimed that free trade resulted in a chronic U.S. payments deficit with England and other countries, draining its capital and impairing its industrialization in a vicious circle. England's economy possessed the funds to enable its manufacturers to dump their output at a loss for a time in order (to use Lord Brougham's famous words) "to stifle American manufactures in their cradle." This need not even be a deliberate strategy; it occurred naturally. As the United States and other countries began to develop their industry, England's export markets began to be foreclosed. This caused a crisis and overproduction in England, which dumped goods in foreign markets under distress conditions. English depression thus became worldwide, but England's great concentration of capital enabled it to gain an upper hand by bailing out its own producers. Over time, as England's highly protected industrial and agricultural economy ran a growing trade surplus with the rest of the world, it drained the money and capital resources of other countries to give its own producers a growing advantage in producing capital-intensive goods—an advantage that could be offset by less industrialized, less capital-rich countries only through tariff protection.

America had to finance its trade deficit either by running up a growing debt to England or by exporting American gold "and thus, by decreasing the fund on which labour must depend, lessen the demand for American labour,

---

[74] *An Examination of the Report of a Committee of Citizens of Boston and Vicinity ... by a Pennsylvanian* (Philadelphia, 1828), p. 18. (Hereafter referred to simply as *Examination*.)

and consequently the consumption of agricultural products."[75] Lee replied that America's foreign debt was incurred mainly to pay for the Louisiana and Florida territories. In fact, he claimed, the balance-of-trade doctrine was an exploded mercantilist fallacy. By definition, no overall payments deficit was possible, because to import any given class of goods was simultaneously to induce the exportation of others "to provide the means of paying for what we buy … as we import more foreign goods, we shall create by the importation a new demand for agricultural produce."[76]

Even if this reciprocal balance were not the result of an automatic economic mechanism, Lee claimed, it would be maintained by deliberate policy on the part of England: If America would not take English manufactures, England could not afford to buy foreign crops and raw materials wherever they were cheapest, but "must necessarily resort to the Brazils, Egypt, and the East Indies, where this staple [cotton] can be had in exchange for her produce and manufactures." Indeed, England lacked the gold to pay in cash for even one year's importation of cotton, and therefore had to pay in manufactures. Given the premise that Anglo-American trade was, in effect, a barter operation, it followed that "foreign trade … differs only in extent, not in its effects" from domestic trade and "the truth is … that there is no such thing as a balance of trade against one nation, in its dealings with another … The balance is in favour of every country."[77] To cease importing from England not only would reduce American crop exports, it would deprive the country of the gains from trade that commerce afforded.

Protectionists had their own view of the circular flow between the United States and England: "a single bale of fine cloth which weighs only eighty pounds, contains in it the price not only of eighty pounds of wool, but also of several thousand pounds weight of grain, the maintenance of the working people that produced it."[78] To an increasing degree, this grain to feed English workingmen

---

[75] Quoted in Lee, *Report*, p. 22. See also *Examination*, p. 73.

[76] Lee, *Report*, pp. 103, 109, 141. Today, of course, economists would point out three fallacies in this thesis. First of all, England and the United States were not the only two countries in the world. Thus England could spend in third countries the proceeds of its trade surplus with America. Furthermore, the marginal propensity of Englishmen to consume American agricultural products (in contrast to English domestic goods or imports from other countries) was by no means 100 per cent. Finally, England could use its gold inflows for non-trade options such as the purchase of American capital assets, railways, Western lands, etc.

[77] *Ibid.*, pp. 150, 155f., 111.

[78] *Examination*, p. 20. See also p. 54. This was implicitly an early formulation of input-output analysis, replete with foreign-trade qualifications.

came either from the United States or other suppliers. The problem was that the exportation of American grain and other raw materials, to be worked up into manufactured goods abroad and re-imported in finished form, must necessarily occur on declining terms of trade. Henry Clay reasoned that America's annual population growth was four times as fast as Europe's. Assuming American exports to increase in proportion to its population growth, much more agricultural produce would be thrown onto world markets than Europe's less rapidly growing population could absorb—except under declining terms of trade. (This need not be true if Europe's industrial export surplus outstripped its population growth, thanks to productivity or other factors. But this prospect was not acknowledged by Clay.)

As the *Examination* argued, "such is the state of the demand for some of the most important articles of our own production, that an increase in the production itself, affords no addition to our means of payment: the fall in prices deprives us of all advantage from the increase of production."[79] The more Americans exported, the less they would earn! Nor were matters helped by the fact that foreign markets were inherently unstable, as Americans occupied only the position of residual suppliers. The best hope for balanced and equitable markets between agriculturalists and industrialists was for the North and South to enter into mutual relations.

This did not convince Southerners and most other free traders, who by this time had become convinced that prospects for selling cotton, tobacco and other plantation products were much greater in England than in the North. As for the Northern and Western farmers who would represent the swing factor in state and national elections for many years to come, Lee argued that foreign markets were more prosperous, if not more stable, if one took into account the boom conditions that developed when crops failed abroad. Was war not an "ordinary relation of the nations of the world," making unlikely another interruption of trade such as had occurred during the Napoleonic Wars.[80]

Each side sought to isolate the other as holding the "most narrow sectional views." Protectionists accused free traders of being witting or unwitting tools of Southern ambition and British cupidity. Mathew Carey pointed out that even if an overall trade balance existed between America and England, "the great increase of the produce or export of cotton, or tobacco, or sugar, or any other Southern staple, has no favourable effect on the welfare of the farming

---

[79] *Ibid.*, p. 24. A similar logic has guided the Arab oil-producing countries in recent years.
[80] Lee, *Report*, pp. 132–38, 117f.

interest."[81] American exports were mainly Southern plantation exports, not Northern exports. Furthermore, the commercial depressions following periodically from America's trade deficits — the effect of its unbalanced agrarian economy — caused widespread farm bankruptcy. As long as England maintained its Corn Laws, "any hope of finding an increased foreign demand for our bread stuffs will be delusive."[82] This was part of the famous home market argument for protectionism. Increased industrialization would draw surplus labor from agriculture, increase the home market for farm produce, and thereby sustain high farm prices and incomes.

Lee replied weakly that this might occur to an extent, but market costs to farmers also would rise as higher tariffs pushed up prices for the protected articles. Protective tariffs would "tax the many for the benefit of the few." Lee thus denied the thesis upon which the infant industry argument for protection rested: namely, that tariff protection spurred falling prices over time. Woollen prices had fallen, but this was in no way the result of past tariff protection. Lee argued as if America were already producing, marketing and consuming all that it could. Under this static assumption, higher tariffs could only increase prices and transfer income from unprotected to protected occupations.[83] In this respect free traders generally viewed the tariff problem only in terms of its Ricardian context of distribution theory within a fixed productive economy, not as a productivity issue. The sectionalist argument thus acquired a class basis as free traders counterpoised the consumer's wage and buying interests to the employer's monopolistic profit drives.

The tariff debate turned ultimately on the question of whether America should take deliberate steps to industrialize or passively remain an agricultural, raw-materials exporter. Lee claimed that "manufactures are forced upon England by her circumstances. She has a limited territory and a population so dense, that they must be employed in that way or perish. Do we envy her condition in that respect? ... low wages, a spirit of competition, which nothing can bring forth but necessity." Success in industrial competition connoted a victory of nations with low living standards over more prosperous agrarian countries like the United States. Lee approved fully of Benjamin Franklin's

---

[81] Mathew Carey, *The Boston Report and Mercantile Memorial* (Philadelphia, 1828), quoted in [Friedrich List], *Review of the Report* ... (Philadelphia, 1828), p. 51. (Hereafter referred to simply as *Review*.) List also wrote a "Lecture on the Boston Report, and Particularly on its Principles Respecting the Landed Interest in Pennsylvania" for the *National Gazette*.

[82] *Examination*, p. 25.

[83] Lee, *Report*, pp. 124, 86f., 23, 28.

pessimistic pre-Malthusian statement that "great establishments of manufacture, require great numbers of the poor to do the work for small wages; those poor are to be found in Europe, but will not be found in America, till the lands are all taken up and cultivated, and the excess of the people who cannot get land, want employment."[84] America would industrialize naturally enough once its vacant lands were filled up and its wage levels began to decline with further population growth.

Protectionists pointed out that England's early industrialization had been the result of a deliberate, highly protectionist strategy. In the absence of British mercantilism, Holland or France would "naturally" have become the industrial center of Europe. They urged America not to repeat the unfortunate fate of Portugal in 1706 and France in 1786 after their free-trade treaties with England. Better to prepare for the day when the nation's lands would be filled up, by putting in place an industrial capital base now. Protection was no tax at all: Increased industrial income would enable manufacturers to mechanize and thus reduce costs. Friedrich List contended that "there is a vast surplus of productive power in the world; and in such a state of things, the home market is of greatest importance ..."[85]

The major productive power to be tapped was that of machinery, which could multiply America's manual labor power by one or two hundredfold, greatly reducing the cost of productive work effort. List placed in a dynamic context Ricardo's famous wine-cloth example of gains from trade, demonstrating how free trade might foreclose productivity gains in nonindustrialized countries: "Wine is as much an agricultural production as flour ... The art of making wine may have been improved by the modern improvements in chemistry, but we believe it will not be pretended, that any labor saving machinery has been introduced into the process ... Let us state the case, adapting it to the woollens, instead of the wine ... up to 1817, (and there have been many improvements in machinery since) ... one single person could produce as much cotton yarn as 200 persons could before machinery was used ... The whole labouring population ... including the agricultural, is ... on the authority of Mr. Owen and others, believed to be multiplied one hundred fold." Even if the contribution of machinery were only half as large as estimated by Owen, each doubling of capital investment would multiply England's effective population power by fifty-fold, "and consequently the whole country would benefit of this great acquisition of productive power." A given amount of machine-aided

---

[84] *Ibid.*, pp. *27, 93.*
[85] *Review*, pp. 84, 54. See also *Examination*, pp. 89, 102.

industrial labor thus would exchange for a growing amount of agricultural labor, turning the factoral terms of trade in favor of industrial nations that substituted machinery for manual labor.[86]

By modern standards of judgment, the protectionists carried the debate on the historical argument, the balance-of-payments argument and the attempt to ground international trade theory in dynamic productivity analysis rather than static distribution theory. They also carried the day politically, leaving free traders with only a constitutional argument against Congressional power to levy protective tariffs, except as an incidental result of federal revenue needs. As early as 1820 a Philadelphia memorial conjured up the menace that, "once admit, that Congress may use the power of taxing imports ad-libitum, for any other purpose but that of revenue, and you give them in reality, the power to say to the citizens of these United States, you must devote yourselves to agriculture, commerce or manufactures, not as you may happen to be inclined, but according to our sovereign will and pleasure."[87] Protectionists had little trouble pointing out that the principle of protectionism had not been questioned until nearly a half-century after the Constitution had been ratified.

If protectionism could not be defeated either by academic reasoning or by constitutional arguments, it would be opposed by political maneuvering. A foretaste of the Tariff of Abominations was revealed in Lee's attempt to press protectionism to an absurd and divisive length, by claiming that "to equalise the advantages of the 'American System' to all parts of the Union, Congress should grant bounties to all the other great branches of industry; for instance, a bounty of 20 cents a bushel on wheat, 20 dollars a hogshead on tobacco, and 3 cents a pound on cotton ..." The 1828 Committee on Manufactures, five of whose seven members were anti-protectionists, supported (to quote Stanwood) "every proposition to carry protectionism to an extreme with regard to articles which the advocates of the system did not regard as needing a change in the tariff, opposing every suggestion which those advocates deemed necessary to remedy defects in the tariff as it existed." Thus, although the committee's report "contains not a word hostile to the protective policy," its intended effect was to be counter-effective: "Iron, hemp, flax, molasses, spirits, printed cottons, — and wool, were granted adequate, perhaps more than ample, protection. The plan of the Harrisburg convention, with respect to woollen goods, was rejected. The demand of the protectionists was denied at the most essential point ... The free traders and the politicians who were posing as protectionists in order to

---

[86] *Review*, pp. 44f. See also pp. 10, 14f., 17f., 20.
[87] Quoted in Lee, *Report*, p. 125.

defeat protection or to make it as obnoxious as possible advocated and endeavored to retain in the bill high duties for which the real protectionists cared nothing, and to prevent the adoption of any amendment to give them that which they desired much."[88]

The final bill was enacted into law on May 19, 1828, and was denounced by most of the leading protectionists. As John Randolph concluded, "the bill referred to manufactures of no sort or kind except the manufacture of a President of the United States," as it enabled Andrew Jackson and his followers to pose for a time as friends rather than as enemies of American industrialization. This mask was soon dropped as the sectional divisions grew ever stronger over the tariff issue, culminating in the nullification struggle of 1832.

[88] Stanwood, *American Tariff Controversies*, pp. 269–71.

FRIEDRICH LIST, CODIFIER OF THE FIRST GENERATION OF PROTECTIONISTS

Friedrich List's *National System of Political Economy*, first published in Germany in 1841 and translated into English in 1856, is by reputation the epitome of protectionist doctrine. List first developed his theories in the United States, to which he came in 1825. Here he remained for six years, settling in Pennsylvania, where he edited a German-American newspaper in Reading and sought to develop railroad and mining interests. Through his friend General Lafayette, upon whose urging he had first decided to come to the United States, List soon made the acquaintance of most of the country's political leaders.

He immediately became friends with Mathew Carey, an emigre also indebted to Lafayette, and espoused the protectionist cause. Carey and his associates directed List's attention to the static assumptions and unwarranted generalities that characterized British laissez-faire orthodoxy. In 1827 he published his *Outlines of American Political Economy*, based on his pamphleteering work for the Harrisburg Convention of that year and containing his later protectionist views in clear embryonic form.[89] Four years later List returned to Germany, where he transplanted the American economic philosophy and doctrine to lead the agitation for a German customs union — the Zollverein of 1834, which paved the way for subsequent German integration — and to become an intellectual forefather of the German Historical School of national economists.

The major influences on List's thinking were Daniel Raymond (and through him, Lauderdale), Alexander Hamilton and Mathew Carey. Given the time at which he wrote, his books reflected the views held by the first generation of American protectionists. A new generation was to be initiated in 1848 with publication of Henry Carey's *The Past, the Present, and the Future*. Henry Carey and his followers developed a more broadly-based doctrine of economic development comprising full-blown systemic analysis rather than the doctrine of exceptions that List and his contemporaries had put forth. In this respect List's writings do not reflect the most mature achievements of American protectionism. It was only after his work that protectionism became elevated from the status of institutionalism, claiming merely national application, to a doctrine

---

[89] For a detailed review of this period of List's life, see William Notz, "Frederick List in America," *American Economic Review* 16 (June 1926).

of universal scope, controverting the tenets of British laissez-faire as they applied to England's own development as well as to that of the less industrialized countries of continental Europe and America.

The tariff debate did not become a prominent and divisive issue in American politics until after the Treaty of Ghent (December 1814) which restored normal trade relations between the United States and England, lead to economic stagnation in its wake that developed into the crisis of 1819–20. Tariff agitation soon developed both in continental Europe and the United States. Advocates of free trade found a ready defense of their position in the doctrines of Adam Smith and David Ricardo. But no such pre-existing theoretical defense of protectionism was available, save for a few concessions made by Adam Smith himself praising the benefits of home trade in contrast to foreign trade, and in the United States by Hamilton's *Report on Manufactures* (1791), which contained most of the theoretical observations held by the first generation of protectionists. Neither continental Europeans nor Americans ever sought to return to the arguments of eighteenth-century British mercantilism, although in many respects their doctrine of productive powers was related to that earlier body of theory.

The early American protectionists replied to free-trade doctrine mainly by citing the visible evidence as to the adverse effects of free trade on American industry. Developing a growing prejudice against systematic and abstract reasoning as such, in large part because of the excesses to which it was pushed by doctrinaire free traders, these early protectionists insisted that the scope of political economy was necessarily time-bound and geographically limited merely to national application. This enabled them to dissociate the policy conclusions of British economic thought from relevance to the American tariff controversy, but it also placed limits on the scope of any alternative theories which they might enunciate.

Even before the tariff debate broke out in full force, American writers denied that any doctrine could be universally descriptive of the economic development of all nations. In 1809, Loammi Baldwin entered a plea for a separate system of political economy to describe American conditions. In circumstances such as those in which the United States found itself, he concluded, "every thing relative to political economy must be original ... we cannot be too cautious how we assume for correct maxims, those which are found in European works on political economy."[90] Subsequent protectionists greatly elaborated this attitude. Each nation's growth, they claimed, was determined by its own distinct set of social institutions.

---

[90] Loammi Baldwin, *Thoughts on the Study of Political Economy in connection with the Population, Industry, and Paper Currency of the United States* (Cambridge, Mass., 1809), p. 67.

From this thesis it was but a short step to contend that every nation was an exception to broadly stated economic laws. It followed that political economy was, by nature, ircapable of enunciating universal truths and universally optimal policies. Early protectionists granted that the doctrines of Adam Smith and Ricardo provided a valid interpretation of British historical experience. But political economy, they stressed, was a product largely of national institutions rather than a science of universal scope. Thus, List stressed that "every nation has its particular economy," adding that

> American national economy, according to the different conditions of the nations, is quite different from English national economy ... It has for its object to supply its own wants by its own materials and its own industry; to people an unsettled country; to attract foreign population for capital and skill; to increase its power and its means of defence in order to secure the independence and the future growth of the nation.[91]

Because of America's distinct institutions and historical problems, List argued, the analysis of its economic development called for an entirely different set of rules and precepts from those of British political economy. This attitude was reflected by the very titles of such representative works as Alexander Everett's *America* (1827), List's *Outlines of American Political Economy* (1827) and his American-inspired *National System of Political Economy* (1841), Calvin Colton's *Public Economy for the United States* (1848), Willard Phillips' *Manual of Political Economy, with Particular Reference to the Institutions, Resources, and Condition of the United States* (1828), and Francis Bowen's similarly entitled *Principles of Political Economy, Applied to the Condition, the Resources, and the Institutions of the American People* (1856). This emphasis on national economic conditions, coupled with an espousal of inductive reasoning from "facts" and "unique historical experience," enabled the early protectionists to reject the deductive, *a priori* method of British political economy.

A form of inductive institutionalism replaced the "cosmopolitical" point of reference which characterized British economic thought. In this vein John Rae, who believed that political economy was rightly "a science of experiment, a branch of the inductive philosophy," was soon using the very word "system" in a derogatory manner. Lord Bacon, he stated,

> affirms that there always have been, and must be, two sorts of philosophy—the popular, and the inductive; or, as they might perhaps be denominated, the philosophy of system, and of science. In the one, the mind explains natural phenomena according to its preconceived notions, in the other, it traces out, by a careful interpretation, the real connexions between them.

---

[91] Friedrich List, *Outlines of American Political Economy* [1827], reprinted in Margaret Hirst, *Life of Friedrich List and Selections from his Writings* (New York, 1965), pp. 203, 167. See also pp. 204–210. Pagination of all subsequent quotations from List's *Outlines* will be from this edition.

In keeping with this dichotomy, Rae remarked of Adam Smith that "if we ... view his work as an attempt to establish the science of wealth, on the principles of the experimental or inductive philosophy, it is exposed to the censure of transgressing every rule of that philosophy."[92]

In a similar vein List appealed to "common sense" to oppose the "scholastic" reasoning of British economists. He asserted that "Mr. Say likes no facts; he is almost an enemy of facts; he banishes them to a particular literary apartment called statistics, not to be troubled by them, and with the few he alleges he is tolerably unfortunate."[93]

This emphasis upon "facts" rather than theory is indicative of how the impulse to a new doctrine preceded its actual development. List reminisced on how it was only after he had arrived at protectionist convictions by direct observation that he began to rationalize his views.[94] This empiricist attitude led many of the first generation of protectionists to apologize for whatever theoretical reasoning they were able to muster. Daniel Webster, for instance, remarked in 1830 that, "though I like the investigation of particular questions, I give up what is called the 'Science of Political Economy.' There is no such science. There are no rules on these subjects so fixed and invariable as that their aggregate constitutes a science. I believe that I have recently run over twenty volumes, from Adam Smith to Professor Dew, of Virginia, and from the whole, if I were to pick out with one hand all the mere truisms, and, with the other, all the doubtful propositions, little would be left."[95]

Tending to bolster this somewhat immature impulse was the fact that political economy in Britain was itself becoming an increasingly disparate body of thought. By the 1840s dissension had arisen as to its most fundamental concepts. Of all the disciplines pretending to scientific formulation, its postulates appeared least universal in scope and application. To many observers, not only in America but also in Europe, political economy seemed not a mature science at all, but still in its infancy. In this vein Comte remarked of political economists that, "looking with an impartial eye upon their disputes on the most elementary ideas of value, utility, production, etc., we might imagine ourselves present at the strangest conferences of the scholiasts of the Middle Ages

---

[92] John Rae, *New Principles of Political Economy* (Boston, 1834), pp. 328, 329, 337.

[93] See List's speech of November 3, 1827 before the Pennsylvania Society for the Encouragement of Manufactures, Hirst, *Life of List and Selections*, pp. 274, 276. See also his *Outlines*, p. 149.

[94] *Outlines*, p. 175.

[95] From a letter by Mr. Webster to Mr. Dutton dated May 9, 1830, quoted in William Elder, *Questions of the Day: Economic and Social* (Philadelphia, 1871), p. 191. See also Alexander Everett's 1831 "Memorial to Congress," p. 168.

about the attributes of their metaphysical entities; which indeed economical conceptions resemble more and more, in proportion as they are dogmatized and refined upon."[96] Like Rae, he proposed the inductive method of logical reasoning, an analytic method hitherto associated mainly with the natural sciences.

England's attempt to impose her free trade and Malthusian doctrines on other nations, under the unwarranted claim that the precepts of these doctrines were universally applicable (and this in the face of her own disputes), represented to American protectionists more of a colonialist strategy than disinterested scientific thought. They therefore pounced upon John Stuart Mill's assertion that many of the methodological problems of political economy arose from its tendency to generalize from a faulty base, reasoning from the historical experience of a single nation—England—that is, from a set of facts and institutions that were not and could not be universal in nature. But if Mill's American readers endorsed his criticism, they scoffed at his proposed solution that it become an even more abstract science, and a branch of moral philosophy at that. Colton derided Mill's praise of abstract hypothesizing, and Peshine Smith seized upon Mill's somewhat bald statement:

> In the definition which we have attempted to frame of the science of Political Economy, we have characterized it as essentially an abstract science, and its method as the method *a priori* ... Political Economy, therefore, reasons from assumed premises—from premises which might be totally without foundation in fact, and which are not pretended to be universally in accordance with it. The conclusions of Political Economy, consequently, like those of geometry, are only true, as the common phrase is, in the abstract; that is, they are only true under certain suppositions, in which none but general causes—causes common to the whole class of cases under consideration—are taken into account.[97]

The hypothetical character of British reasoning induced writers such as Colton to swing to the opposite extreme and define political economy as a purely empirical science, based on inductive investigation on a nation-by-nation basis. In a manner reminiscent of List he asserted in 1848 that, because of each nation's distinct historical experience, "a Science can not be made out of the Laws of Public Economy, except for one Nation, each by itself." Claiming "that public economy has never been reduced to a science, and that all the propositions of which it is composed, down to this time, are empirical laws,"

---

[96] *The Positive Philosophy of Auguste Comte*, translated by Harriet Martineau, 2 (New York, 1868), p. 62. List also derided the "scholastic" tendency of British laissez-faire.

[97] John Stuart Mill, Essay 5: "On the Definition of Political Economy; and on the Method of Investigation Proper to it," *Essays on Some Unsettled Questions of Political Economy* (London, 1844), pp. 143–45. Italics in original.

he added that these laws, while perhaps applicable to European nations, were "entirely inapplicable" to the United States.[98] Colton therefore defined the object of political economy to be not the discovery of universal truths, but rather "the application of knowledge derived from experience to a given position, to given interests, and to given institutions of an independent state or nation, for the increase of public and private wealth."[99]

In a similar vein List remarked that "*National economy* teaches by what means a certain nation, in her particular situation, may direct and regulate the economy of individuals, and restrict the economy of mankind, either to prevent foreign restrictions and foreign power, or to increase the productive powers within herself..." His *National System* asserted that although J. B. Say recognized "the existence of a national economy or political economy, under the name 'économie publique,' ... he nowhere treats of the latter in his works; secondly ... he attributes the name *political* economy to a doctrine which is evidently of a *cosmopolitical* nature; and ... in this doctrine he invariably merely speaks of an economy which has for its sole object the interests of the whole human society, without regard to the separate interests of distinct nations."[100] List in fact did not recommend protection for tropical nations, but only for nations of temperate climates such as Europe and the United States. Furthermore, he endorsed protectionism only as a transition phase to ultimate free trade throughout the world, once all nations had achieved equality in their productive powers.

Attacking the "cosmopolitan communism of free trade," the Boston protectionist Willard Phillips believed that even Colton had gone too far in his willingness "to adopt the doctrine of the free-trade economists in the sense that a nation should observe rules of economy no less than an individual; but this is not their sense."[101] Economic rules, he contended, existed not for nations at all, but solely for individuals.

---

[98] Calvin Colton, *Public Economy for the United States* (New York, 1848), subheading for chap. 2, pp. 38, 18. It was for this reason that Colton substituted the term "public economy" for that of political economy, on the ground that the latter term had fallen into disrepute (p. 23).

[99] *Ibid.*, pp. 26f.

[100] *Outlines*, p. 155, and *National System of Political Economy* (London, 1885), p. 121.

[101] Willard Phillips, *Propositions Concerning Protection and Free Trade* (Boston, 1850), pp. 27, 24n. Phillips here refers specifically to Colton's statement (*Public Economy*, p. 58) that "there cannot be two kinds of economy, one for private, and one for public purposes, any more than two kinds of morality. We maintain, that public economy differs from private, not in principle, but only in comprehensiveness ..."

Colton's definition of political economy as an empirical doctrine, based upon each nation's historical experience, precluded its formulation as an abstract science possessing universal principles. As Colton quoted Mill:

> The property which philosophers usually consider as characteristic of empirical laws, is that of being unfit to be relied upon beyond the limits of time, place, and circumstances, in which the *observations have been made* ... Until a uniformity can be taken out of the class of empirical laws, and brought either into that of causation, or of the demonstrated [scientific] results of the laws of causation, it can not with any assurance be pronounced true *beyond the local and other limits within which it has been found so by actual observation.*[102]

Colton and his contemporaries satisfied themselves with asserting that America, because of its distinct historical and social attributes, formed an exception to the rule of British doctrine. These protectionists therefore represent the ancestors of the institutionalist (historical) school of economists that flourished in America during the final decades of the nineteenth century. The line runs from the protectionist circle centered around Mathew Carey and Daniel Raymond, through Friedrich List to Germany and from there, via Roscher's circle, to American students like Patten and Ely studying at German universities. But while this institutionalist attitude did help establish ideological pressure to develop a new set of concepts more applicable to American experience, it afforded no new theory as such to pit against that of the British school. Colton and his contemporaries did identify particular and distinct tendencies at work in America, and established what was to remain a protectionist emphasis on the physical conditions of production and distribution, on labor skills and education as a major element of the nation's capital, on the concept of latent capital in general, and on the rent of location. But these points were not integrated into a general doctrine.

The shortcoming of this generation of protectionists lay in the constraint inherent in its approach to economic reasoning, a self-imposed constraint that produced a doctrine of exceptions to rules rather than a new set of rules. These writers did not pursue the logical truth that there are no exceptions to the rules, but rather (again in the words of J. S. Mill), that "what is thought to be an exception to a principle is always some other and distinct principle cutting into the former: some other force which impinges against the first force, and deflects it from its direction. There are not a law and an *exception to* that law, the law acting in ninety-nine cases, and the exception in one. There are two laws ..."[103]

---

[102] Colton, *Public Economy*, p. 39, quoting from J. S. Mill's *Logic*. Italics and brackets added by Colton.

[103] Mill, *op. cit.*, p. 162.

Had the early protectionists perceived more clearly this concept of "exception," they would have recognized that they were implicitly calling for a new set of rules to describe American economic development. In fact, List's own somewhat ill thought-out concept of "exception" was indicated in his *Outlines,* in which he stated that Adam Smith's "error consists in not adding to those general principles the modifications caused by the fractions of the human race into national bodies, and in not adding to the rules the exceptions, or to the extremities the medium member."[104]

This is not to say that the first generation of protectionists made no theoretical contribution. Their first concern was to distinguish between the interests of the few and those of the many. Thus List observed in his *Outlines:*

> In consequence of my research, I found the component parts of political economy to be (1) individual economy; (2) national economy; (3) economy of mankind. Adam Smith ... teaches how an individual creates, increases, and consumes wealth in society with other individuals, and how the industry and wealth of mankind influence the industry and wealth of the individual. He has entirely forgotten what the title of his book, "Wealth of Nations," promised to treat.

He later reiterated that the doctrines of Adam Smith and J. B. Say regarded "wealth from the narrow point of view of an individual merchant," asserting that "this is evidently not a system of national economy, but a system of the private economy of the human race."[105]

Denying that mercantile profits played as constructive a role in economic life as those of industry and agriculture, the protectionists asserted that maximization of trading profits was at variance with the growth of America's productive powers. Willard Phillips, claiming that the free-trade theorist "forms his theorems upon the supposition that men are merely venders and purchasers, and not producers," counterpoised:

> The protectionist system considers people, in their character of producers, as substantially all of ours are. They inquire, not merely how you may make a good bargain in the exchange of what you already have, which is a very proper inquiry; but also, which is immeasurably more important, what course of policy is best calculated to put you in the way of producing something more; that is to say, to give you a chance for industry.[106]

---

[104] *Outlines,* p. 155.

[105] Mill, *Essays on Some Unsettled Questions of Political Economy,* p. 152, and *National System,* pp. 254, 170. See also pp. 356 and 137f., as well as Daniel Raymond, *Elements of Political Economy,* vol. 1, pp. 406, 139, 34 and 173; Alexander Everett, "Memorial," pp. 165f.; and Colton, *Public Economy,* pp. 33f.

[106] Phillips, *Propositions,* pp. 21, 31. On this point, see also List, *Outlines,* pp. 202, 212 and 214, and his *National System,* pp. 259f.

On these grounds American protectionists accused free traders of having elaborated only a theory of private economy that failed to acknowledge the theory of productive powers. Just as they had rejected value theory on the ground that it had become inextricably linked to the study of exchange values and the workings of the marketplace, so they renounced the term "political economy" as having become hopelessly founded upon the theory of exchange values only. In its stead they sought to develop what Colton termed "public economy" (after Say), List "national economy," and other writers simply "the American School of political economy."

Certainly the main form of economic surplus investigated by British economic thought was that of profit. Adam Smith declared that "there is one sort of labour which adds to the value of the subject upon which it is bestowed: there is another which has no such effect. The former, as it produces a [market] value, may be called productive; the latter, unproductive labour."[107] Productive labor was that which created a profit for its employer, irrespective of its contribution to society's real economic surplus. Thus, List observed:

> ... Adam Smith has merely taken the word capital in that sense in which it is necessarily taken by rentiers or merchants in their bookkeeping and their balance sheets, namely as the grand total of their values of exchange in contradistinction to the income accruing therefrom ... He has forgotten that the ability of the whole nation to increase the sum of its material capital consists mainly in the possibility of converting unused natural powers into material capital, into valuable and income-producing instruments, and that in the case of the merely agricultural nation a mass of natural powers lies idle or dead which can be quickened into activity only by manufactures.[108]

There were many forms of capital that created a physical surplus without a financial profit, headed by internal improvements and other "national" forms of capital. Daniel Raymond listed among the nation's capital such institutions as "the nature of the government ... the climate and soil of the country ... the extent of the territory in proportion to the number of inhabitants ... the denseness of population ... the equal or unequal division of property ... the state of cultivation and improvement ... the degree of perfection to which the arts and sciences have been carried ... the nation's advantageous situation for commerce ... the industrious habits of the people."[109]

---

[107] *The Wealth of Nations*, bk. 2, chap. 3.

[108] *National System*, pp. 227f. In a similar vein List ridiculed Adam Smith's definition of productive labor: "The man who rears pigs is thus productive, the man who teaches men is an unproductive member of society. He who prepares bagpipes or jews-harps for sale is a producer, the greatest virtuosos are non-productive, because the harmonies they evoke cannot be brought to market." (*ibid.*, p. 127).

[109] Daniel Raymond, *Elements of Political Economy*, vol. 1, p. 48.

The growth of productive powers, protectionists concluded, tended to exceed the growth in private profits out of which capital was formed. Neither profits nor the increase in money income was the mainspring of economic growth, but the progress of technology and invention, and the increasing productivity of the nation's labor, capital and land. In this respect it would be erroneous to view American protectionist thought primarily as a doctrine of international trade. It was rather a theory of the means by which a nation could most rapidly increase production by augmenting both the number and the productive powers of its population. Raymond and Rae, List and Carey set forth their basic principles independently of direct reference to the issue of protective tariffs. As J. Shield Nicholson wrote in his introduction to the 1885 edition of List's *National Economy:* "On List's view there is no real opposition between free trade and protection, because neither is an end in itself, but simply a means to achieve a certain end, namely, the greatest development of productive power." [110]

The task of constructing a universal set of rules detailing the growth of productive powers was undertaken only by the second generation of American protectionists, which clustered around Henry Carey as the first generation had grouped around his father. Carey fils was more than just an organizer; he was a theoretician in his own right who inverted the Ricardian theory of cultivation and the Malthusian theory of population. In view of his achievement and that of his followers such as E. Peshine Smith, the view taken by List's biographer Margaret Hirst is ill-taken. List, she believed, "stands on firmer ground than Carey; he founds himself on his doctrine of nationality and productive power, while Carey's protectionism is inextricably mingled with his theory of value and wages, and his belief in economic harmony and in the importance of association for industrial progress." [111] Henry Carey's son saw this to be precisely his father's strong point, observing that "[Henry] Carey had but a poor opinion of List's 'National System of Political Economy,' for the very good reason that it lacked just what he had aimed to present in his own books ... broad, deep and enduring fundamental principles, interlocked and interwoven into one grand and harmonious whole, like Carey's own great and noble 'Principles of Social Science.'" [112]

Carey's follower Peshine Smith, also was disappointed by List's work, on the ground that "his book is empirical ... it builds an argument so much upon the accumulation of particular instances ... He has certainly contributed little to

---

[110] Introduction to List's *National System* (London, 1885), p. xxi.

[111] Hirst, *Life of List and Selections*, p. 121.

[112] Henry Carey-Baird, "Carey and Two of his Recent Critics," *Proceedings of the American Philosophical Society* 29 (1891), quoted in Hirst, *Life of List and Selections*, p. 120.

the abstract principles of political economy."[113] It was all he could do to muster a favorable review of List's book for the *New York Tribune* (April 12, 1856), which is appended to this introduction. Later, in England, T. E. Cliffe Leslie took an indirect jab at List in summarizing the contribution of more sophisticated American protectionists: "instead of taking sulk at political economy and turning his back on it, as the English protectionist did, the shrewder American sought a political economy on his own side, advocating a development of all the natural resources; and authors and lecturers were soon forthcoming to supply the demand for economic science of this sort."[114] List did not formulate such a doctrine, but he played a major role in paving the way for it, both through his criticism of the limitations inherent in British laissez-faire, and in grounding his analysis on the doctrine of productive powers.

Peshine Smith's Review of List's "National System"

In this book Americans have a national interest. Dr. List, the author, was invited by Lafayette to visit this country in 1824, and accompanied him on his triumphal progress. He settled in Pennsylvania, discovered the Tamaqua Coal Mines, and made the more important discovery that the system of Political Economy which he had studied in the Old World was visionary and unfruitful. "There only" said he, in his preface to this work, of the United States, "have I obtained a clear idea of the gradual development of the economy of a people." He returned to Europe in 1830, and began the agitation for the suppression of Customs on the interior boundaries of the German States, and the establishment of a uniform tariff on the exterior frontiers, which resulted in the Zollverein or German Customs Union, now embracing thirty-one millions of people. This was the transplanting in Europe of our own system—that of sustaining and alimenting absolute, unrestricted freedom of domestic commerce by a common Protective League for its defense against interference by the commercial policy of foreign nations—securing free trade to *producers* between themselves, and thus increasing production by defending them all against being made the spoil of the men who fetch and carry. Under that system the Zollverein States—which thirty years ago exported wool and imported cloth from England—have doubled their domestic production of wool, manufacture the whole of it, import more and manufacture that, export the cloth and undersell the British manufacturer in foreign markets. They have wholly ceased to import cotton goods from England, and purchase cotton in the wool instead of the thread. In short, they have achieved, by English confession, signal progress in all protected branches of industry; wages have increased thirty per cent in the face of the cheapened production, and consumption in all kinds has increased so immensely as to furnish conclusive proof that the benefits of the system have inured not to the capitalists merely, but to all classes, and most of all to the laborers. The largest increase of consumption

---

[113] Smith's review appeared in the *New York Tribune*, April 12, 1856. For a more disparaging view of List see his letter to Carey, April 3, 1856, where he thinks the book not even worth the price.

[114] T. E. Cliffe Leslie, "Political Economy in the United States," *Fortnightly Review* 28 (October 1880), reprinted in his *Essays in Political Economy* (Dublin and London, 1888), p. 142.

is always found in the class whose consumption was nearest the minimum and whose number is the largest. The poor and the *people* are synonymous in the Old World. But the highest evidence of the power these States have obtained is in the persevering effort of both parties to engage them in the Eastern War, and their successful resistance. It is their strength that has enabled them to save their strength and augment it.

Dr. List may be truly said to have founded the Zollverein. It has rarely if ever been given to any one man to effect so great and beneficent a result. This book develops the philosophy which led him to his noble task, and by which he won the German mind. That which has ac-complished — much is certainly worthy of study. The fact that his book is empirical — that it builds an argument so much upon the accumulation of particular instances, is perhaps no abatement of its popular untility. He has certainly contributed little to the abstract principles of economy. In this direction nearly all he has done is to substitute the "Theory of Productive Force" for that of Values. He shows that the European Economists overlook the truth that "the power of creating wealth is vastly more important than wealth itself; it secures not only the possession and the increase of property already acquired, but even the replacing of that which is lost." Their system ignores what may be called *virtual* or latent wealth, and treats nations as if they were actually exerting the whole productive power of which they are capable; and the only question was how their forces should be directed. The moment this idea is introduced, their theory explodes. It is as if the philosopher found himself dealing with expansive steam when he had reckoned only on the dead weight of water. He begins to comprehend then how protection from external pressure may be the essential condition of the development of latent force—how the iron environment, which is itself constrained, may be instrumental to the highest activity.

Dr. List's book is rendered interesting from its being so largely historical. The translator, Professor Matile, a colleague of Agassiz and Guyot in Switzerland, is now resident in Phila-delphia, and, we hope, may find a hearty greeting for his contribution to our literature. A valuable preliminary Essay, giving a critical estimate of the chief European Economists and exposure of the shortcomings of their system in its relations to humanity and religion, has been supplied by Mr. Stephen Colwell, who has also added frequent notes to the text — often of more than equal import.

III. The Boston Protectionists

WILLIAM C. JARVIS, PROTECTIONIST NATIONALIST

William Charles Jarvis (d. 1836) was born into a Boston family that had emigrated from Wales in 1668. He was a nephew of Dr. Charles Jarvis (a delegate to the Constitutional Convention of 1788 and a member of the state legislature) and a cousin of William Jarvis (1770–1855), a fellow protectionist who, as U.S. consul-general at Lisbon in Jefferson's administration, was largely responsible for introducing merino sheep to America.

Jarvis was admitted to the Suffolk County bar in 1811. Four years later he moved to Pittsfield, representing that town in the state legislature during 1821–24. He was elected State Senator from Essex County, and Speaker of the Massachusetts House of Representatives three times—twice from Pittsfield and once from Woburn, where he moved in the mid-1820s to become director of the state prison. He also becameone of the customs house officers until Andrew Jackson's election in 1828.

The Republican was published in 1820, the same year that Daniel Raymond published his *Thoughts on Political Economy*. Like Raymond, Jarvis established his take-off point on the thesis that mercantile interests are not necessarily those of the nation as a whole, and that the private riches of individuals are not necessarily "an addition to the aggregate wealth of a country." Most basic to a nation's well-being was a thriving agriculture, for which Jarvis recommended direct support, stressing in particular the popularization of modern farm technology and management. He also held that "a well regulated commerce" should aim at achieving self-sufficiency by displacing foreign sources of supply. He thus sharply qualified Adam Smith's maxim that citizens should buy in the cheapest markets. "The judicious master of a family, in this country," he asserted, "sees the folly of purchasing that which he can procure by the labor of his own family. And instead of pursuing such a course, he takes measures to bring into operation the greatest quantity of the productive labor of his household; and in this way he clothes himself and his family … and saves the surplus of his beef, pork, corn, and wheat, for an addition to his capital stock. That then, (to retort the conclusion of Dr. Smith,) which is prudent in the conduct of every well regulated family, can scarcely be folly, in the conduct of a great nation."[115]

---

[115] William C. Jarvis, *The Republican; or, a Series of Essays on the Principles and Policy of Free States. Having a Particular Reference to the United States of America and the Individual States* (Pittsfield, 1820), pp. 209, 200, 216, 220.

America's commercial ties to Britain were undermining her long-term independence: "Intimate commercial connections, of all things, are the most efficacious, in creating dangerous partialities: and where the interest of a great portion of a people, are inseparable from an unrestrained intercourse with a foreign power, it will be difficult to make them acquiesce in the disruption to the tie. It is therefore a serious question in politics, whether it be not one of the duties of a wise and provident government, to guard a nation by skilful expedients, against an influence which may be so dangerous and embarrassing," particularly where this influence "is unproductive to the nation, and in hostility to its manufactures." Better that each interest "contribute to the support of the others, and thus co-operate to advance the general welfare," even where it was necessary to exert "private sacrifices which may be incident to such an effort." For "though some channels of mercantile enterprize may be narrowed, others will be widened, and new ones eventually opened."[116]

Jarvis hoped that America might become an exporting power. Like Huskisson and other strategists of English industrialization, he advocated abolition of tariffs on raw materials, including wool. He suggested deflation as a means to promote exports. Paper-money inflation had worked to price American manufactures out of their domestic market, but could be counteracted by a hard money policy such as Napoleon had pursued in France.[117] For the interim, Jarvis suggested that America emulate England in enacting protective tariffs on industrial manufactures. However, in his essay on taxation he indicated a preference for taxing luxuries so that the tariff burden would fall mainly on the rich.

The problem with this strategy was that it was the more prosaic manufacturers that needed protection. This was to be the great problem dividing protectionists and free traders during the 1820s, leading to a general political realignment by 1828, in which Jarvis sided with Clay and subsequently with the Whig Party.

Jarvis' work is somewhat rambling, a common symptom of early American attempts to place protectionist sympathies in a general setting. He was seeking a basically political context, and this was his difficulty. It was men like Mathew Carey, Daniel Raymond and Friedrich List who succeeded more in establishing protectionism as an economic doctrine in its own right.

---

[116] *Ibid.*, pp. 128, 130f., 183.
[117] *Ibid.*, pp. 228f. See also p. 218.

ALEXANDER EVERETT, BOSTON PROTECTIONIST

Alexander Hill Everett was born in 1790 into one of the oldest Boston families. He grew up in the village of Dorchester, adjoining Boston, to which his father had moved upon retiring from the ministry two years after Alexander's birth. Everett attended public school locally and was apparently a precocious student, for at the age of twelve he entered Cambridge College (now Harvard) as its youngest member, and graduated at the head of his class four years later, in 1806.[118]

At the age of seventeen, after working for a year as an instructor at Phillips Exeter Academy in New Hampshire, Everett returned to Boston to study law through the offices of John Quincy Adams. When the latter was appointed Minister Plenipotentiary to Russia in 1809, he offered Everett and two other unpaid prodigies the opportunity to accompany him. Everett was formally attached to the American legation at St. Petersburg for two years, living as a member of the Adams household. He returned to Boston in 1812, opening his own law office and entering politics soon after the outbreak of war with England. After supporting the war in a series of articles for the Boston *Patriot* he ran unsuccessfully for State Senator from Suffolk County.

Early in 1815, shortly after the Treaty of Ghent ended the war with England, Governor Eustis of Massachusetts was appointed Minister to the Netherlands. Upon his recommendation Everett was appointed legal secretary to the legation, a post which he occupied for two years. In 1818 he succeeded Eustis as Charge d'Affaires at the Hague, serving in this capacity for nearly six years. After the election of Adams to the presidency in 1824 he was appointed ambassador to Spain. In this position he was charged to manage the affairs with Spain not only of the United States but also of Spain's recently liberated colonies in Latin America, inasmuch as the United States was as yet the only nation that had acknowledged the independence of the new Latin American countries.

Following Andrew Jackson's victory in the 1828 elections, Everett returned to the United States to pursue literary activity, purchasing Jared Sparks' interest in the *North American Review* in 1829. During the next six years he turned this

---

[118] For biographical information see Edward Everett Hale, *Sketches of the Lives of the Brothers Everett* (Boston, 1878), and E. F. Everett, *Descendants of Richard Everett of Dedham, Massachusets* (Boston, 1902).

quarterly into a leading protectionist organ.[119] In 1830 he ran once again for the State Senate from Suffolk County. This time he won, and was re-elected annually for the next five years. In December 1831 he attended the National Republican presidential nominating convention at Baltimore as a Massachusetts delegate, becoming chairman of a committee that nominated Henry Clay in opposition to Jackson. During the election year of 1832 he wrote a vituperative series of editorials against Jackson for *The Boston Daily Advertiser and Patriot*, which received wide circulation as a pamphlet under the title "The Conduct of the Administration."

Despite these sympathies Everett adhered to the Democrats following Clay's defeat and formation of the Whig Party in 1832. This about-face was largely the result of his opposition to a national bank. Although he remained a Democrat for the remainder of his life, he also remained protectionist in sympathy. As such he became somewhat of a political anomaly: a defender of protective tariffs within a party dedicated to free trade, an advocate of domestic industry in a party whose policies were designed to prevent the growth of this industry, and an advocate of population concentration in a party dedicated to westward expansion and Manifest Destiny whose aim was to disperse and ruralize the nation's population.

Meanwhile, the *North American Review* imposed a substantial operating loss on Everett, and late in 1835 he sold his interest to his younger brother Edward, who was on his way to achieving somewhat greater political renown. Moving from Boston to neighboring Roxbury, Alexander Everett ran unsuccessfully for Congress in the 1838 and 1840 elections, despite the fact that Norfolk County was less strongly Whig than Boston's Suffolk County. Indeed, his Democratic leanings were blamed for his brother's defeat as a Whig, and the fact that each brother's political views seemed to be held against the other may have been partially responsible for Alexander's decision to leave Massachusetts. In June 1841 he accepted the presidency of Jefferson College in Louisiana, although somewhat poor health prevented his taking an active role in the college administration and he resigned the position a year later.

---

[119] In addition to editing the review he wrote most of its articles on political economy, including "British Opinions on the Protecting System" (1830); "The American System," "Phillips' Manual of Political Economy," "Life of Henry Clay" and "The Laws of Population and Wages" (1831); "Hamilton's Men and Manners in America" and "The Progress and Limits of Social Improvement" (1834); and "Rae's Political Economy" and "Immigration" (1835). For a full bibliography of Everett's articles in the *North American Review* see William Cushing, *Index to the North American Review, Vols. I.-CXXV, 1815–1877* (Cambridge, 1878).

In 1845 the incoming Democratic President Polk appointed him U.S. Commissioner to China, the first U.S. representative under the treaty negotiated by Caleb Cushing, Everett's fellow-Bostonian, protectionist and Democrat. In the process of leaving for China, Everett opened a debate over Malthusianism with the Virginia economist George Tucker, in an exchange of letters in the *Democratic Review* that continued until Everett's death in China in 1847.

Like many of his contemporaries, Everett came to political economy by way of moral philosophy and history. His early anti-Malthusianism followed mainly from his optimistic desire to reconcile the long-term growth of America's and Europe's population with the prospects of continued democracy and increasing prosperity. This stood in contrast to the doctrine of diminishing returns, impoverishment and ultimate overthrow of the institutions of private property and political freedom which his more pessimistic contemporaries were forecasting, especially in Britain. From his earliest writings he held that population growth tended to bring increasing prosperity rather than pressing upon the limits of society's limited productive powers. The freer and more equitable society's institutions, the greater would this prosperity be, as a rising level of prosperity was correlated with the degree of political freedom.

This optimistic view of social evolution was apparent in Everett's first book *Europe: or a General Survey of the Political Situation of the Principal Powers, with Conjectures on their future Prospects: by a Citizen of the United States* (Boston and London, 1821, translated into German in 1823 and Spanish in 1828). The discovery of America had provided the impetus for a revolution in Europe's economic and social development, he asserted. The American colonies generated a demand for European manufactures that had set in motion a train of commerce and industry, bringing about an extension of prosperity and property ownership.[120] So strong had Europe's impetus for social progress become that it could be halted neither by the vestigial feudal institutions that still weighed upon it, nor by possible Russian military conquest. "As the cause of political improvement is identical with that of civilization and general prosperity," Everett concluded, "every measure that has a tendency to produce these effects ... tends also to the promotion of liberal institutions ..." A return to the old feudal aristocratic forms could come only by striking "at the root of the general prosperity of a country in all its branches. To prohibit or discourage agriculture, commerce, and manufactures is the only certain way of checking political improvement."[121]

---

[120] *Europe* (Boston, 1821), pp. 423, 37, 265–67. See also Everett's later companion volume, *America* (Philadelphia, 1826), pp. 334f., 99–101.
[121] *Europe*, pp. 10, 450, 30f. See also America, p. 337.

Everett attacked Malthus for fearing that the Code of Napoleon, which replaced the ancient law of primogeniture with an equal division of land among the bequeather's heirs, would bring about a myriad of uneconomic microfundia and a return to feudal poverty and the forms of militaristic dictatorship associated with it. The Code of Napoleon was neither adverse to liberty nor "inconsistent with the best possible improvement of the soil." Variations in human ingenuity would lead to property holdings of various sizes, with the average farm size for France's agricultural population tending to stabilize at a point "just sufficient to support an industrious family." The rural population would exert moral prudence to keep its families (and farm sizes) stable and self-supporting. Those who were unresponsive to this moral check and who multiplied beyond the ability to care for their progeny would find that "the check of disease and poverty would present itself."[122]

This check of disease and poverty was scarcely at odds with Malthus, although Everett did give greater weight to man's prudence at regulating his numbers. He believed that the extreme point at which the check of disease and poverty would be brought into play would not generally be reached.

Increases in farm population beyond the optimum number that could work the land would migrate to the cities or emigrate abroad. In either case the result would be an increase in international trade and a growing importation of food into Europe. That continent's growing urban population would find employment manufacturing industrial goods to export to its colonies and ex-colonies in exchange for their surplus foodstuffs, while those who emigrated to the New World would devote themselves mainly to producing food and other raw materials to exchange for Europe's manufactures.

So far, Everett's views were quite laissez-faire. "The time will doubtless come," he acknowledged, "when manufactures will be established in all parts of America, amply sufficient to supply the wants of the inhabitants; and when they will cease to come to Europe for anything but the products, that are peculiar to the soil and climate. But this period is still remote ..." He assumed that agricultural countries could provide a food surplus sufficient to feed the industrial nations "for a long time to come," and that world commerce would "produce a progressive increase of wealth and population, and a regular tendency towards improvement in the social and political condition of society."[123]

In 1823, Everett published *New Ideas on Population, with Remarks on the Theories of Godwin and Malthus.* The leading new idea was "that the increase of population is a cause of abundance, and not of scarcity; since it augments

---

[122] *Ibid.*, pp. 41–43.　　　　　　[123] *Ibid.*, pp. 434–36.

the supply of labor in precisely the same proportion with the demand for its products, and developes at the same time the new element of skill, by means of which the same quantity of labor is applied with greater effect, and becomes more productive than before." Malthus, he accused, treated men solely in their capacity as consumers without acknowledging their role as producers. "It is sufficiently notorious," he asserted, "that an increase of population on a given territory is followed immediately by a division of labor; which produces in its turn the invention of new machines, an improvement of methods in all the departments of industry, and a rapid progress in the various branches of art and science."[124]

Everett believed that labor productivity might increase at a rate as much as ten times that of population density, although he assumed for argument's sake that it would increase just in proportion to population density. A doubling of population would thus double its per capita productive powers, thereby increasing its output by fourfold. This was the same model he was to put forth two decades later in his debate with Tucker.

Everett concluded that Europe's poverty was the result of vicious political institutions rather than any niggardliness of nature. Elaborating on the theme developed in his earlier book, he asserted that Europe must extend its realm of property ownership in order to maximize the productive powers of its labor. This democratization of property was a precondition for the optimizing principle of the "invisible hand" of private enterprise to be set in motion, as it had been in the United States where "almost every citizen possesses political rights; and takes a part, in one form or another, in the government of the country. These circumstances naturally give to the individual a sense of his own dignity and value; and tend to produce, in the first place, attention to his own interest, or habits of foresight and industry, and, secondly, intelligence, or the capacity of promoting his own interest, and that of his family and connexions."[125]

[124] *New Ideas on Population, with Remarks on the Theories of Godwin and Malthus* (Boston and London, 1823, pp. 120, 21, 26f., 38. A second edition was published in Boston in 1824, and the work was translated into French in 1826. Everett also contributed articles to the *North American Review* during his residence in the Netherlands, although these were on literary subjects rather than on political economy. In his *New Ideas*, Everett did not discuss scientific innovation as an independent factor in economic growth, but only as a dependent function of increasing population density. In this he differed from most other American protectionists.

[125] *Ibid.*, p. 90.

Everett put forth a multi-stage theory of economic development that harkened back to Sir James Steuart and Adam Smith (and later was appropriated by Friedrich List) to describe the relationship between population and its means of subsistence. Young nations such as the United States, which possessed ample "unsettled" lands or which were still in the pre-agricultural age of barbarism, generally found increasing population density to be accompanied by growing productive powers of labor in agriculture, as well as in industry and commerce. Even for nations whose soil was already "fully occupied," increasing population density tended for a time to augment productivity in agriculture. Beyond a point, however, increasing population density brought about diminishing returns in agriculture, so that the increase in productivity deriving from population growth accrued solely to commerce and industry. Food output, Everett believed, ultimately was limited by land area, and therefore was limited for each nation by its natural boundaries. As a result, "if we suppose the number of inhabitants of such a territory to be regularly increasing for an indefinite length of time, and if we also suppose that they are obliged to subsist upon the direct products of the soil which they occupy, it will of course follow that there must be sooner or later an excess of population and a deficiency of food." But this "perfectly obvious proposition" was "of very little practical importance." For "it is not true that the inhabitants of a given tract of territory must necessarily subsist upon the direct products of the soil they occupy." Industrial food-deficit nations could exchange their manufactures for the foodstuffs of less developed countries. Just as the productive potential of non-agricultural labor was "unbounded and incalculable," so the room for population growth in Europe's colonies and other agricultural nations was so great as to be virtually unlimited—and from this population growth would follow a rising supply of foodstuffs in exchange for European manufactures.[126]

Despite the fact that Everett imagined himself to be anti-Malthusian, he added no new dimension to population doctrine. His argument portrayed Malthus as nothing more than a straw man. He did not succeed in tackling the latter's analytic system of checks, nor his theory as to man's tendency to respond to rising incomes by increasing the rate of population growth, *e.g.*, Malthus's rudimentary statement of the so-called Iron Law of Wages. Everett's statement that men were producers as well as consumers did not dispute the key issue of diminishing returns in agriculture—the idea that mature nations' ability to produce subsistence increased less rapidly than the bodily needs of their popu-

---

[126] *Ibid.*, pp. 37–40, 44, 46, 82. The acceptance of diminishing returns in agriculture was common to almost all American protectionists prior to 1848.

lations. He virtually granted the Malthusian framework of analysis in asserting that Malthus had "not even attempted to calculate the real rate at which population increases under the operation of all the natural checks," and in concluding that "it is not true that the human race possess a rapid and infinite power of increase, under the checks to which the progress of population is subject."[127]

Everett's argument thus consisted merely of focusing attention on the medium run in which Europe could draw upon the food surpluses of still sparsely populated, less developed countries. He did not touch on the long run in which the then-agricultural countries, among them the United States, might possibly industrialize, experience population pressures of their own and become in their turn food-deficit nations—a pattern of evolution that Everett implicitly endorsed by granting the assumption of diminishing returns in agriculture.

Within three years he was to turn his attention to the time when the United States should itself cease to be a food-surplus country. While serving as U.S. ambassador to Spain he published a companion volume to his earlier book on Europe, entitled *America: or a General Survey of the Political Situation of the Several Powers of the Western Continent, with Conjectures on their Future Prospects: by a Citizen of the United States* (1826, translated into Spanish and German in 1828). Everett showed himself to be no friend of Spain, scorning that nation's "notorious decrepitude and wretched imbecility."[128] The liberation of Spanish America completed the freeing of the New World from the yoke of Europe, and Everett urged Spain to recognize the independence of its former South American colonies. Nonetheless, the inequitable forms of property ownership in South America, its heritage from Spanish land grants, would retard the development of true democracy there. Spanish America could not expect to achieve the rapid social and economic strides made by the United States until it had passed through yet another revolution that would redistribute its land and transform its institutions of property ownership.[129] In this observation the modern reader will recognize exceptional foresight.

Cuba was still far from winning its independence from Spain. In fact, Britain contemplated taking the island in the event of war with Spain. Even the French and Mexicans harbored designs on the island. The United States viewed Cuba as falling within its sphere of influence, already envisaging future

---

[127] *Ibid.*, pp. 48f., 55, 46. Everett believed that the earth's population had remained constant for some millennia.
[128] *America*, p. 172.　　　　　[129] *Ibid.*, pp. 343f.

statehood for it (especially on the part of the slave states). Certainly it had no intention of permitting Cuba to fall into the hands of any power stronger than Spain, in keeping with the Monroe Doctrine. It was in these circumstances that Everett suggested to the Spanish Secretary of State that Spain seek a loan of $15 to $20 million from the United States, with Cuba as collateral, and on the condition that U.S. troops would occupy the island to defend it against potential British designs. Everett clearly expected Spain's finances to be mishandled in such a way as to pose "the probability of the eventual acquisition of the entire sovereignty."[130]

Still, he held a narrow view of the role of government in directing economic and social reform. Even where clear inequities existed as in Spanish America, the proper function of government was merely to adapt itself to society as it existed, not to transform it. To be sure, Everett anticipated that a subsequent revolution would sweep away the remnants of feudal property rights in Spain's ex-colonies. Nonetheless, he did not deem this transformation to be the task of their governments, and in this respect he adhered to his traditional liberalism. Governments did not initiate social and economic change, but were changed (not necessarily violently) in response to society's economic and social transformations. Implicitly, political evolution lagged behind economic development.[131]

The chapters on Spanish America deal mainly with political and moral philosophy. Of greater interest is Everett's defense of protective tariffs for the United States, which he based in large part on his population and agricultural theory. He deserves credit for introducing population theory into the American tariff controversy, at least on the protectionist side. Earlier protectionists like Daniel Raymond had expressed their antipathy towards Malthusianism, but did not directly relate population theory to their tariff argument. Everett defended protective tariffs for America on grounds akin to those used by the Ricardians to defend free trade in Britain's Corn Law debate, although he viewed the Ricardian thesis from the vantage point of the United States. The Ricardians had argued that because of diminishing returns in agriculture beyond a point, England could avoid the rising prices of foodstuffs only by importing its food. Similarly for America, Everett reasoned, if diminishing

---

[130] Everett to John Quincy Adams, Madrid, November 30, 1825, Adams MSS, quoted in Samuel Flagg Bemis, *John Quincy Adams and the Foundations of American Foreign Policy* (New York: 1949), p. 542n. There is no record of a reply to this suggestion. For other activities of Everett in Spain see *American State Papers* VI, pp. 1006–14. In 1841 Everett acted as Confidential Agent of the government of Cuba (see *The Everett Letters on Cuba* [1897]).

[131] *America*, pp. 187–81. See also "Hamilton's 'Men and Manners in America,'" *North American Review* 38 (January 1834), p. 258.

returns in agriculture occurred not long after the nation came to be fully settled, it followed that when this "natural" geographic limit was reached, America must itself become a food importer. Given increasing returns in industry resulting from growing population density, and assuming that the terms of trade would evolve "wholly to the advantage of the manufacturing, and at the expense of the agricultural community,"[132] the result would be that America could import ever-increasing quantities of food to nourish its growing industrial population.

This assumption that the terms of trade (as measured in terms of comparable labor effort, or what is today termed the factoral terms of trade) would turn to the advantage of industrial exporters was fundamental to Everett's argument. He believed that increased industrial productivity would not be accompanied by falling export prices for manufactures (although domestic sales prices would fall in keeping with increased productivity, because of domestic competition). Export prices were held to be determined by the opportunity-cost that the less efficient, non-industrial nations would have to sustain to produce similar goods, not by the actual costs in the industrial exporting nations. (Everett did not explain any political-economic mechanism to insure this development.) In Ricardian terms, rather than the terms of trade settling at some equitable midpoint between average production costs in the industrial and agricultural nations for their respective commodities, international prices would reflect comparative costs in the agricultural countries, not those of the industrial nations. The latter nations thus would benefit strongly as their industrial productivity increased steadily, while their export prices held constant.

Food prices also were presumed to remain constant over time, and no constraints were recognized as limiting the world's supply of arable land at optimum cultivation levels, although diminishing returns would occur as countries urbanized. According to this theory, foreign trade was implicitly exploitative in nature. A given amount of labor devoted to producing industrial manufactures in the advanced industrial nations would command ever-increasing amounts of agricultural labor in the less developed countries. Everett thus wished to see the United States evolve from an exploited food exporter to an exploiting industrial exporter, imitating Britain's pattern of what might be called terms-of-trade imperialism.

This view led Everett to abandon his earlier liberalism and opposition to government intervention in economic activity. Only by enacting protective tariffs could America prepare its domestic industry for the day when its soil, having become fully occupied, no longer could increase its food output in

---

[132] *America*, p. 143.

proportion to its population growth, obliging the nation to obtain its food from abroad. Protective tariffs constituted the single valid exception to the rule of laissez-faire, and even then only to undo the harm that earlier governmental regulations had done.

Under normal historical circumstances, industrial growth would have developed naturally for the United States and protective tariffs would not have been necessary. However, in America's case, protection was required to overcome the special historical factors that had impaired its industrial development. Britain had prohibited domestic manufactures during the colonial period, and industrial depression followed the Napoleonic Wars after normal trade with England resumed. As a result, Everett concluded, "it is here, if anywhere, that the remedial legislation on economical subjects ... might be resorted to with profit." For "if the absence of domestic manufactures be owing in a great measure, as I have supposed, to political causes and the habits generated by them, it comes within the regular province of government to apply a remedy." [133]

Everett's defense of protectionism contained a number of arguments already characteristic of protectionist writers. Perhaps the most common was the idea that fluctuation of foreign markets, often war-induced, subjected the U.S. economy to disturbing exogenous shocks. "The home market is, in general, fixed and certain," Everett maintained. "Foreign commerce, on the contrary, is a sort of game in which fortune exercises at least as much influence as prudence and skill." [134]

The main and most original impact of Everett's argument, however, dealt with the uneconomic effects of rural population dispersion, and with the social overhead imposed by commerce conducted over large distances. Along with his quasi-Ricardian views, this formed the second area in which he used population theory to bolster his protectionist conclusions.

Foreign trade had the adverse social effect of diverting labor from the task of production to that of distribution. "The first and most obvious of the inconveniences alluded to, is the waste of commercial labour, produced by carrying across an ocean three thousand miles wide, the bulky agricultural products, that must be given in exchange for the manufactures we import, and bringing back the latter in turn from the same distance." This treatment of commerce as a social overhead cost held significance for the optimum geographic distribution of America's population. Whereas Malthusian theory portrayed the

[133] *Ibid.*, pp. 135–36, 165, 126.
[134] *Ibid.*, p. 149. Everett elaborated this point in "British Opinion on the Protecting System," *North American Review* 30 (January 1830), p. 186, as well as in his 1832 "Memorial to Congress," pp. 144–46.

country's great land spaces as a major (albeit transitory) economic advantage, Everett viewed the population dispersion associated with these spaces as entailing a great social overhead, primarily in the form of transport costs. The country's advantage did not lie, he argued, "as the above-mentioned [Malthusian] theory supposes, in the facility afforded by the great extent of the territory, taken in connexion with the original scantiness of the population, for obtaining by labour an abundant supply of the means of subsistence. Labour will furnish this any where, and is in general more productive in proportion to the density of population, because more skillfully applied."[135] Population therefore should not disperse itself over the land to engage in agricultural pursuits, but should remain in the Eastern industrial centers where it would benefit from economies of scale.

Excess population dispersion and its associated lack of industrial self-sufficiency in the agricultural hinterland served to break the circular flow of goods between farm and town. "The cultivator feeds the manufacturer, who supplies him in turn with articles of use and comfort. But this exchange can never take place to any great extent, excepting where the two classes are situated in the neighbourhood of each other, and belong to the same political society. Provisions are too bulky, and in most cases too perishable, to bear transportation from one quarter of the globe to the other. If not consumed on the spot where they are raised, they cannot be consumed at all ... What then follows? Our cultivators have in most parts of the country, and in the usual state of commerce, nothing to offer in exchange for foreign manufactures, and of course no means whatever of obtaining them."[136]

This evil could be corrected only by establishing domestic manufactures in the vicinity of the farming regions, even at the expense of initially higher costs. "If a cultivator in the western country obtains from his neighbours in exchange for a part of his grain, good clothes and furniture, and a good education for his children, of what consequence is it to him, whether he gives for these comforts and blessings more or less grain than they cost in Europe. He cannot send his grain to England to buy clothes and furniture, nor his children to be educated. His wants must be supplied by his neighbours, who will consume his provisions in exchange for what they give him, or not at all ... Every article of use and comfort which he can get at home for his surplus products, is therefore so much clear profit to him, although it cost him twice

---

135 *Ibid.*, pp. 148, 340.
136 *Ibid.*, p. 153. This passage is reminiscent of Jefferson's well-publicized admonition that America "place the manufacturer by the side of the agriculturist" in his letter to Benjamin Austin of January 1816.

as much as a similar one is worth in England, France, or China."[137] Everett thus controverted the implicit assumption of full employment that marked the classical theory of comparative advantage.

Everett incidentally praised the moral benefits which accrued from a compact population. Manufactures, he asserted, "check at once, all emigration to distant parts. The family circles remain unbroken, and the happiness and virtue of the people unimpaired. Every succeeding generation obtains, with an equal amount of labour, a more abundant supply of the means of subsistence than the preceding one, and life is of course growing constantly easier and easier to all from year to year." There was thus little validity in "the vulgar error, that manufactures are of an immoral tendency."[138]

In this praise of population density Everett anticipated Henry Carey's "principle of association" upon which the latter based his Philosophy of Concentration. Indeed, Everett's ideas foreshadowed numerous thoughts of Carey, not insignificant in view of the fact that it was Carey's publishing house that published *America*. Not only did Everett's optimism as to the steady secular decline in the labor-cost of producing commodities anticipate Carey's emphasis on technological progress that underlay his theory of value, but Everett's observations as to the economic and social benefits of population density were to reappear, in a greatly elaborated sytem, in Carey's *The Past, the Present, and the Future* (1848).

Society's ability to support its population, Everett claimed, was "determined in every country by the extent of the territory, taken in conjunction with the political institutions and the state of civilization."[139] Primary among these institutions for the United States were the widespread ownership of property that helped maximize its citizens' wealth-creating powers, and protective tariffs which, by nurturing industry, enabled it to prepare for the day when it would have to import its foodstuffs from abroad. Nonetheless, Everett continued to attribute increasing productivity potential directly to

---

[137] *Ibid.*, p. 155. Peshine Smith and Henry Carey later elaborated further upon the advantages of localized balanced growth between agriculture and industry.

[138] *Ibid.*, pp. 158f. See also "The American System," *North American Review* 32 (January 1831), p. 128: "The political and moral advantages that result from them [*i.e.*, manufactures] are not less apparent. By retaining the rising generations of the people in the neighborhood of their homes, and within the domestic circles to which they belong, they keep them under the influence of the strongest natural motives to virtue. By substituting the cultivation of the arts of social life, and the tastes, manners, and habits that result from it for those of the roving emigrant, or the solitary settler in the wilderness, they improve the character of the people, and elevate the standard of civilization."

[139] *Ibid.*, p. 144.

economies of scale and the division of labor following from increased population density. "Now what produces the division of labour?" he asked: "not, as some fantastically suppose, an instinctive disposition in the human mind *to truck, barter, and exchange,* the reality of which it would be difficult to establish, but the increase of population which, by increasing the number of labourers in proportion to the work actually in hand, enables each to devote himself to a particular department; and thus augments at once the quantity and quality of the products of the labour of all."

He did not cite the evolution of social institutions except as this followed from increasing prosperity. Nor did he remark upon the revolution in industrial productivity brought about by the introduction of steam power, but attributed technological progress exclusively to increasing population density and the economies of scale deriving therefrom. He did not distinguish between capital in the form of tools wielded by manual labor and the steam-powered capital that was visibly displacing manual labor. Nor did he discuss the spread of education and the acquisition of labor skills by the working class. In these respects his argument remained strongly colored by his anti-Malthusian but basically Ricardian views formulated in Europe's intellectual environment, overlayered by his desire not to see America develop into a raw-materials supplier for Europe. American optimism, he perceived, must take a protectionist form different from the liberal views he held vis-à-vis Europe. But he did not base his protectionist doctrine upon technological grounds as did most of his contemporaries, a tendency that by the 1840s led them to envision a prosperous autarchic America.

Everett's essays on political economy in the *North American Review* sought to reconcile protective tariffs with a long-term philosophy of laissez-faire. "The very maxim upon which the British writers found their reasoning against the protecting system," he asserted, "is, that every man understands his own interest best, and will take better care of himself than any body else can take care of him. But is not this principle, the general correctness of which we readily admit, as true of communities as it is of individuals?"[140] Protection was by its very nature only a transitional policy toward ultimate free trade. Manufactures "in their infant state … require the aid of protecting duties, and without it, they can rarely, if ever, take deep root—obtain consistency, or ultimately flourish. Afford them the protection they want, and they soon outgrow the

[140] "British Opinions on the Protecting System" (Boston, 1830), reprinted from the *North American Review* 30 (January 1831), p. 165.

necessity for it."[141] Adam Smith, he concluded, went too far in reacting against the governmental restrictions which existed in his day.[142]

Everett soon rejected laissez-faire altogether, as a guiding rule, asserting in 1831 that "the principle that an individual, if left to himself, will always give his labor the direction most likely to promote his own interest, will not bear the slightest examination. It is infinitely more important to the interest of an individual, not to give his labor the direction of forging bank notes, or robbing on the highway ... The arguments which are habitually urged against legislative protection of domestic industry, apply with precisely the same force against the legislative protection of our property and persons from the arm of the pickpocket and the assassin ... In short, the principle in question, when pursued into its consequences, strikes at the root of society..."[143] The ultimate effect of laissez-faire was anarchy, which had been defended in the late eighteenth century by Godwin and Rousseau on the ground that man was innately good but corrupted by social institutions. "And yet it is simply on the basis of this wholly untenable theoretical proposition," Everett concluded, "that Adam Smith and his followers rest their doctrine of the impolicy of affording a legislative protection to domestic industry."

Here then was a new and fundamental qualification of his social optimism: Men needed society's guidance to realize their full concerted productive potential.

Other protectionists were developing the basis for a different line of argument against laissez-faire economics, grounding their opposition in large part on the distinctions drawn by Lauderdale between physical wealth and financial riches, between use value and exchange value. The principle of the Invisible Hand, they argued, served to maximize private riches as measured in the marketplace, not the nation's future potential productive capacity. Not only did Everett avoid this line of reasoning, but he failed to distinguish between wealth and riches, and sometimes was guilty of using the two concepts interchangeably. (In his debate with Tucker, for instance, he implied that a physical increase in export volume signified a corresponding rise in the dollar value of these exports.)

Nor did he join with his fellow protectionists in investigating the role of production inputs which were not reduceable to labor-equivalents and which did not even necessarily involve a direct cost. His review of John Rae's *New*

[141] "The American System," *North American Review* 32 (January 1831), p. 133.
[142] See "Philips' 'Manual of Political Economy,'" *North American Review* 32 (January 1831), p. 229, as well as Everett's 1832 "Memorial to Congress," pp. 165–66.
[143] *Ibid.*, p. 232.

Principles of Political Economy (1834) did not elaborate upon that author's emphasis upon invention and innovation as the major force in increasing a nation's wealth. Everett tended to endorse a concept of capital simply as accumulated or embodied labor, implicitly tangible and material. He regretted Willard Phillips' suggestion "that in estimating the wealth of a nation, we are to consider not merely the accumulated produce of labor which it may possess, but the natural advantages of soil and climate that belong to it, and even its political condition, and intellectual and moral character; every thing, in short, which influences production." On the contrary, Everett asserted, "the wealthiest nation is not the one which possesses the purest air—the clearest sky—the richest soil—the most abundant supply of water—the best political constitution—or the highest intellectual or moral qualities; but the one which possesses the greatest amount of the accumulated products of labor; that is cultivated fields anid gardens houses and workshops ships, carriages, furniture, machinery of all descriptions, and finally, money, which is the representative for the purpose of exchange of all other articles." [144] True, Everett used the term "dormant capital" in his 1832 "Memorial to Congress." He also described how protective tariffs would accelerate America's physical wealth-creating capacities by economizing on its transport overhead and by holding population in the East, where it could benefit from the division of labor in production. Nonetheless, he did not emphasize the concept of latent wealth to the degree that his contemporaries did.

His 1832 protectionist meniorial was written in response to a request of the "Friends of Domestic Industry" that convened in New York in October 1831. It was a reply to Albert Gallatin's free-trade memorial prepared for the anti-tariff convention held earlier in Philadelphia. This exchange of tariff conventions and memorials was akin to that of 1827–28, and both sides used much the same arguments as they had earlier. Everett's memorial drew heavily on the fourth chapter of his book on *America*. The relative absence of American manufactures did not stem from natural causes but from historical ones, specifically Britain's prohibition on the development of local industry. Domestic trade would set in motion "exactly twice the amount of domestic industry and capital which is put in motion by [foreign trade]." Protection would not merely "transfer the capital already existing from one employment to another," it would employ labor and capital which would otherwise lie dormant: "a certain portion of the capital and labor of almost every community, is at all times either unemployed, or not employed so as to yield the ordinary returns. A circumstance which renders practicable the introduction of a new branch of industry that did not

---

[144] *Ibid.*, pp. 220–22.

exist before, by stimulating enterprise, has a tendency to bring this dormant capital into activity ... an act of legislation which counteracts the danger of foreign competition, is precisely one of those circumstances that multiply the channels of industry ... The capital which is put in motion by the establishment of manufactures, is therefore not withdrawn from other employments, but is furnished by the increase that regularly takes place in every flourishing community. That his increase, if not taken up by manufactures, *might be* employed in some other way, is a mere baseless assumption."[145]

Protectionism did not imply a national loss. It led to falling prices over time and set more domestic labor and capital in motion. It provided a steadier home market, hence fewer failures and bankruptcies of existing capital. It set in motion a local exchange of products between town and countryside, especially for perishable provisions that could not be exported in any event. It provided national independence from foreign suppliers in case of future wars. And it concentrated the nation's population in the East, affording greater opportunities for the division of labor. The tariffs collected would go directly to the government, which would spend them on internal improvements and public works that were social capital whose benefits accrued to all classes.

Finally, Everett closed with one of the earliest pleas for outright American isolationism. The United States possessed the vast territory, the population and the inexhaustible richness and variety of natural resources to maintain "a self-subsisting and really independent position in the world." Protective tariffs aimed "to render us a world within ourselves, deriving, from a friendly intercourse with foreign nations, all the advantages which we now do, but exempt from the continual shocks which our industry has heretofore sustained from a too close connection with that of Europe."[146]

Everett follwed this memorial with a highly effective pamphlet on *The Conduct of the Administration* (1832), reprinted from *The Boston Daily Advertiser and Patriot*. He likened Jackson to Oliver Cromwell as a military chieftain seeking to undermine America's democratic institutions, with the aid of shifty Martin Van Buren working in alliance with the South. Following Jackson's reelection in 1832, however, Everett adhered to the Democratic Party (over the currency issue), and thereby gave up the position of prominence he had attained as one of the leading protectionist spokesmen among the supporters of Henry Clay and his American System.

[145] "Memorial of the New York Convention, to the Congress of the United States," presented March 26, 1832, and referred to the Committee on Manufactures, in *Journal of the Proceedings of the Friends of Domestic Industry, in general Convention met at the city of New York, October 26, 1831* (Baltimore, 1832), pp. 133, 137–40.
[146] *Ibid.*, p. 167.

No review of Everett's writings would be complete without citing his 1844–45 debate with Prof. George Tucker of the University of Virginia, ostensibly over the Malthusian theory. In this debate Everett repeated his earlier theories of population and its implications for trade policy. The *cul-de-sac* into which his reasoning had led him became apparent. Actually, the debate did not entail controversy between the two theorists as to population theory as such. Only Tucker discussed the rate of population growth, optimistically differing with Malthus in anticipating that "prudential restraint … in an enlightened and well regulated community, will always keep down population to the point which admits of substantial comfort." Everett did not hestiate to concede the tendency of population to increase steadily without upper limit.[147]

Nor did the debate concern the relative evolution of productivity in industry and agriculture. Tucker was willing to grant for argument's sake that industrial productivity might increase in keeping with the growth of population density, and Everett conceded that population growth beyond a point was accompanied by diminishing returns in agriculture. Tucker perceived that this latter assumption of diminishing returns in agriculture implied an upper limit to the earth's potential food output. Because "all human subsistence is derived from the earth," and because the earth itself had natural limits, it followed "that the quantity of food thus furnished has natural limits, which cannot be exceeded, whether it be equal to the support of 200 to the square mile, or of twice or thrice that number." Everett was clearly inconsistent in failing to recognize that, under the assumption of diminishing returns for every nation, population growth abroad must entail diminishing returns for the world as a whole.[148] In other words, both debaters viewed food as essentially the embodiment of land area — the sense in which Ricardo had viewed it — rather than of soil's chemical constituents which could be augmented readily through the use of artificial fertilizers (an argument that came into prominence only in the 1840s).

Foreign trade for Everett represented a permanent solution to diminishing returns in the agriculture of mature nations, whereas for Tucker it was only an intermediate-term palliative. Sooner or later, Tucker concluded, all nations must become mature. Thus, whereas Everett believed "that the happiness of mankind will be indefinitely increased by his multiplying propensity," bringing proportional gains in labor's productivity in manufactures and increasing this

---

[147] "The Malthusian Theory — Discussed in a Correspondence between Alex. H. Everett and Professor George Tucker, of the University of Virginia," *The United States Magazine and Democratic Review* 17, pp. 297–310 (October 1845), 379–91 (November 1845), and 438–44 (December 1845), and "The Condition of China," *ibid.* 21 (November 1847), pp. 397–410. For the population views cited, see pp. 386, 388, 302, 304.

[148] *Ibid.*, pp. 298, 382, 305.

labor's command over food produced by the lessindustrialized nations, "I think it is best promoted by the moral part of his [man's] nature, and by subjecting that propensity to the control of his reasoning and foresight."[149]

America could not simply hope to emulate England's industrial strategy and exploit foreign countries indefinitely as it had been exploited by England. Diminishing returns ultimately must push up food prices, obliging America to exchange an increasing amount of industrial exports for its food imports once its population passed a given level of density.

Tucker won points on all actual issues of contention. The major issue was that of international price relationships between industrial and agricultural producers. Everett asserted that industrial productivity in the United States would increase in keeping with population density (once its lands came to be fully occupied). Domestic prices would decline in keeping with reduced production costs, but international export prices for manufactures would remain unchanged. Less advanced non-industrial countries therefore would not share in the benefits of productivity gains in the advanced nations. The relative command of labor in industrial nations over that in agricultural countries would increase steadily. This increase in industrial labor's purchasing power over foreign food (and food-producing labor) would increase in proportion to the productivity gains of this labor—assuming labor productivity in agricultural countries to remain unchanged, and assuming that the supply of food from these countries would increase *ad infinitum* to meet the demand of the industrial nations. Thus, with every doubling of America's population, labor productivity in manufacturing would double, and the nation could import twice the quantity of food per industrial worker.

The terms of trade between industrial and agricultural counties would be set not by marginal costs in the industrial nations, but by relative costs in the agricultural countries. This would deprive them of gaining the benefits of world technological advance, much as Everett felt that the United States had failed to benefit from England's improved productive techniques in the form of improved terms of trade. To this argument Tucker replied that, "As soon as the improvement [in industrial productivity] has lost its temporary character of monopoly, and becomes diffused, the article produced falls in price according to the amount of that saving, and it will take a proportionately greater amount of it to purchase the same quantity of raw produce."[150]

---

[149] *Ibid.*, pp. 379, 388, 301.

[150] *Ibid.*, p. 381. Were this not to occur immediately, Tucker continued, the fact that foreign trade would produce a higher profit than domestic commerce would lead producers to compete with one another so that export prices would soon be brought into line with domestic prices, "yielding always the same average profit." See also p. 384.

Everett could not reply to this assumption of normal international competition, and conceded that "after an improvement has taken place in the productiveness of manufacturing labor, the price of the product gradually falls abroad as well as at home." But this price decline at least would widen the market for manufactures, so that a deficiency of food in the industrial nations "of course corrects itself, so far as this can be done by the regular operation of the laws of trade; and there is no apparent reason why provisions, if deficient, may not be introduced by sea or land, to any extent, at any point where they are wanted, excepting the cost of the operation or a deficiency in the supply abroad."[151]

However, Everett was reluctant to acknowledge what was implicit in the Malthus-Ricardo argument: Economic evolution would create towns and manufactures in the agricultural countries themselves, "by means of which a demand would be afforded at home for all the food they could raise," curtailing the available international food surplus.[152] This pattern of evolution was precisely what he anticipated for the United States.

Tucker suggested that limitations on international transport facilities must at some point limit the international flow of food. Rising transport costs would have to be added to the increasing costs of cultivation, so that although foreign trade might work for a time to stave off the impoverishing effects of diminishing returns in agriculture and rising food costs, "*such counteraction cannot be permanent.*"[153] Thus, his argument was explicitly couched in terms of the long run, whereas Everett's was essentially medium-term in scope. Everett shared Tucker's conviction that "fully settled" nations would be unable to provide for their own food needs, and it followed from this that the then-underpopulated areas of the world which were exporting foodstuffs must evolve into food-deficit countries themselves. In this sense it was Tucker who remained the anti-Malthusian, and Everett who ultimately was Malthusian.

Everett's contribution to the American discussion of population theory lay mainly in his analysis of the economic effects of population density. His shortcoming lay in his failure to controvert the theory of diminishing returns as a long-term tendency of agricultural production. This was a common feature of the first generation of American protectionists, and was to be controverted by the second generation which followed the isolationist doctrines of Henry Carey. This second generation of American protectionists based its doctrines mainly on anti-Ricardianism. In 1848 Henry Carey changed the entire complexion of

---

[151] *Ibid.*, pp. 441, 443.
[152] *Ibid.*, p. 382.
[153] *Ibid.*, pp. 383, 389, 301, 458, 384.

the population and tariff controversy by postulating a natural historical tendency to increasing returns in agriculture in his *Past, Present, and Future.* Not only did the secular progress of technology increase the productiveness of agricultural labor on all lands, he asserted, but population growth generally proceeded in each nation from the least to the most fertile soils. Meanwhile, increasing population density worked at the intensive margin of cultivation to reduce society's food-distribution charges, as the sparsely populated agricultural hinterland, over which crops had been expensively and laboriously transported, was transformed into an integrated urban-rural entity.

Thus, Carey's protectionism rested on an anti-Ricardian base, whereas Everett's had rested upon a Ricardian one. Whereas Everett concluded that rising industrial exports offered the sole means for America to escape from Malthusian-Ricardian poverty, Carey defended isolationism. Denouncing the Malthus-Ricardo formulation, he found foreign trade not only unnecessary to the United States, but undesirable. The result was that by the 1850s Everett's position became vestigial, and increasingly sectionalist as it was appropriated *in toto* by Francis Bowen, his successor as editor of the *North American Review* and spokesman for the Boston protectionists.

FRANCIS BOWEN, MALTHUSIAN PROTECTIONIST

As the most conservative of the American protectionists, Francis Bowen (1811–90) was the least willing to set aside the moral-philosophical approach of Adam Smith, Malthus, and Ricardo for the natural-scientific approach of the American School. Indeed, at a time when most protectionists were following Henry Carey in grasping the doctrines of Auguste Comte and seeking to ground economic theory on a broad technological basis, Bowen sought to expel any student from Harvard caught reading Comte.[154] His reluctance to question the doctrines of production underlying the Ricardo-Malthus system led other protectionists to condemn him. The fact that he became the most established academic protectionist, teaching at Harvard for over thirty years, was due mainly to the highly sectionalist nature of his protectionism, and to his underlying conservatism.

Bowen's education and early career ran parallel to that of the earlier Boston protectionist Alexander Everett. Like Everett he graduated from Harvard at the head of his class (in 1833). And like Everett he taught a few years at Phillips Exeter Academy (mathematics, from 1833 to 1835). He then became an instructor at Harvard for four years, teaching the course in Natural, Mental and Moral Philosophy.[155] He always remained a moral philosopher, asking primarily what "should be" rather than becoming an objective economist seeking to analyze actual facts. Indeed, he was an enemy of the new scientific discoveries so eagerly grasped by other Americans. Denouncing Darwin's views as "monstrous" because they threatened the doctrine of divine revelation, he condemned all sorts of progressives as red republicans.

Again like Everett, he purchased control of the *North American Review* (in 1843) and remained its editor through 1854, writing about one-quarter of its articles. During 1843–47 he also edited the *American Almanac* and *Repository of Useful Knowledge* and then, during 1848–49, lectured at the Lowell Institute on the application of metaphysical and ethical science to the evidences of religion.

---

[154] Joseph Dorfman, *The Economic Mind in American Civilization: 1606–1865*, Vol. 11 (New York, 1946), pp. 836, 700.

[155] The first course in political economy given by Harvard, then a strictly Unitarian clerical college, indicated its point of reference: it was entitled "Paley's moral and political philosophy — political economy." From Michael J. L. O'Connor, *Origins of Academic Economics in the United States* (New York, 1944), p. 113.

He returned to Harvard in 1850 to become McLean Professor of Ancient and Modern History—which included the class in political economy—but before the university overseers could confirm his appointment he published an article in the *North American Review* rejoicing at the overthrow of Kossuth's revolutionary government in Hungary. This was a cause widely espoused in America, and the overseers refused to confirm his appointment. Bowen therefore left Harvard after teaching only one semester and went back to the Lowell Institute to lecture on political economy. But in 1853 he was invited to return to Harvard as Alford Professor of Natural Religion, Moral Philosophy and Civil Polity. This time the overseers almost unanimously confirmed his appointment, and he remained at Harvard until 1889, becoming known as the "Old Roman" for his conservatism.

Bowen began his teaching by replacing Wayland's clerical textbook, *Elements Of Political Economy*, with McCulloch's edition of Adam Smith's *Wealth of Nations*. He then collected into a makeshift textbook most of the articles on economic subjects he had earlier published in the *North American Review*. The result was his *Principles of Political Economy, applied to the Condition, the Resources, and the Institutions of the American People* (1856), which he dedicated to his sponsor at Harvard, one of the "merchant princes of Boston," the Cotton Whig Nathan Appleton.

Although O'Connor considers Bowen's *Principles of Political Economy* to be "the first outstanding nationalist treatise for colleges,"[156] which it may have been by default, it received a devastating review by Peshine Smith in Greeley's New York *Tribune*. The fact that the 546-page book was a "heterogeneous and superficial" jumbling together of published articles, said Smith, deprived it of compactness and unity. Smith deplored Bowen's view of economics as merely a theory of exchange and as a moral-psychological theory rather than an analysis of production having its basis in natural science and technology. "Our Cambridge professor," he accused, had

> the superlative impudence to declare that ... he has 'endeavored to lay the foundation of an American system of Political Economy'—coolly ignoring the fact that there is an American school whose distinction it is to have pursued the opposite method; to have started from facts, and not from assumptions; to have made Europe ring with the consequent explosion of dogmas long undoubtingly accepted by its leading economists. There is not a word in this book to show that he ever heard of Carey ... Is this affectation or ignorance? Whichever it may be, the result is a blank failure to produce an American system; and, in its stead, a patchwork adaptation of the European system to American circumstances—by a little paring in one place and a little elongation in another; by

[156] *Ibid.*, p. 60.

qualifications timidly reaching toward a doubt, seldom or never amounting to a denial. It is … the familiar effort of trimmers and compromisers to serve God upon such principles and in such fashion as to give the Devil no solid ground for offense.[157]

Peshine Smith criticized John Stuart Mill, Bowen's favorite contemporary economist, and thereby indirectly Bowen himself for turning his back deliberately on "Bacon, Whewell, Herschel and Comte, and abjur[ing] the canons of investigation upon which the positive sciences have made their way …" Smith was upset by the fact that Bowen's nominal claim to be inductive rather than deductive and his opposition to the doctrines of Malthus and Ricardo while retaining their pessimistic underlying assumptions. This, Peshine Smith felt, diverted attention from the actual distinction between American and British economic thought.

Bowen was reflecting the views of his predecessor Everett when he asserted that "the limit of population in any country whatever is not the number of people which the soil of that country alone will supply with food, but the number which the surface of the whole earth is capable of feeding; and it is a matter of demonstration, that this limit cannot even be approached for centuries … London taxes all the counties of England for sustenance; England taxes all the countries of the earth for sustenance."[158] It followed "that the practical or actual limit to the growth of population in every case is the limit to the increase and distribution, not of food, but of wealth … It makes no difference whether the mass of the people are engaged in hammering iron, spinning cotton, or raising wheat; for the product in each of these cases either is food, or is exchangeable for food, which amounts to precisely the same thing."

Peshine Smith recognized that "this is a mere dodging of the question, for Malthusianism has anticipated and answered the pretended refutation. As to the first 'great fact,' it is apparent that the ability of England to draw sustenance from any country depends on the ability of that country to raise a surplus after feeding its own people. That surplus either dwindles with the increase of population in the food-producing country, or its population is kept down by the increasing difficulty, present or prospective, of obtaining food, or by sickness,

---

[157] [E. Peshine Smith], "Bowen's Political Economy," *New York Tribune*, April 5, 1856. For Bowen's definition of political economy to which Peshine Smith objected, see *Principles of Political Economy, applied to the Condition, the Resources, and the Institutions of the American People* (Boston, 1856), pp. 2, 17.

[158] Bowen, *Principles of Political Economy*, p. 148. See also Alexander Everett, *New Ideas on Population, with Remarks on the Theories of Godwin and Malthus* (Boston, 1823), p. 46. Everett reiterated this view in "The Malthusian Theory—Discussed in a Correspondence between Alex. H. Everett and Professor George Tucker, of the University of Virginia," *The United States Magazine and Democratic Review*, Vol. 17 (1845).

war, 'moral restraint' or some other of the Malthusian checks. Upon either hypothesis the validity of Malthus's doctrine is intact." The problem of a country exporting industrial goods to pay for its imports was the fact that, under diminishing returns in agriculture, (which Bowen did not attempt to contro-vert), the terms of trade must steadily decline for industrial exporters, so that "the more people hammer iron and spin cotton the more cotton and iron must they offer for a given quantity of food. The proportion of their labor expended directly or indirectly in supplying the primary necessity increases." Bowen's argument was, Peshine Smith concluded, "a humiliating example of the shifts to which a man is driven by the sham of rejecting a theory while adhering to the mode of reasoning and the most vital consequences which attend it."

Bowen's underlying Malthusianism also led him to endorse the Iron Law of Wages, which hardly led to optimistic views of the future for America's democratic economic and political institutions. "So long as land continues abundant and cheap," Bowen held (in common with most self-satisfied British aristocratic observers), "and the wages of labor high, so long as the population will continue to increase with great rapidity, barbarous tribes will die out before its advancing wave, and the desert will be peopled. But as the country fills up, and the wages of labor fall, it will become more difficult to rise from one class to another, and the rate of increase will diminish."[159] Peshine Smith countered by claiming that "the facts of history abundantly repel it as an empirical con-clusion, and the real American system of Political Economy, which Mr. Bowen has never heard of, establishes a law directly the contrary. It proves from incon-trovertible laws of vegetable chemistry and physiology that increasing density of population promotes the relative increase, not only of wealth generally, but specifically of food and raw materials; and it also proves that not only does production in the normal course of nature grow more rapidly than population, but that of the increased mass of products—as it would be if they were equally divided—an increasing proportion is won by the laborer for wages."

Bowen also differed from the Carey school of protectionists in urging a dis-persion of America's population to the West, more in keeping with Democratic than Republican policy. He based his argument on his own counterpart to Ricardo's theory of diminishing returns, that of increasing rent-of-location over time. Assuming that since "the population, as it increases, remains station-ary, or on the same spot, so that the grain must be brought to it at a price enhanced by the cost of transportation," it followed that "the increase of population is an evil because the community are obliged to send farther and

---

[159] Bowen, *Principles of Political Economy*, p. 160.

farther off for their supplies."[160] He suggested migration of labor as the solution to this problem, hence a justification of the country's westward expansion.

Both Peshine Smith and Frank Taussig considered the book's best chapter to be that in which Bowen applied Mill's theory of international prices to the American tariff argument.[161] However, this theory was not really linked with the theories of population, rent, money and banking in the systematic manner attempted by more sophisticated American protectionists. Nonetheless, it was adopted as a text at the University of Pennsylvania in 1859 and at Episcopalian Trinity College after Calvin Colton died in 1855. In 1870 Bowen prepared a new edition, retitled *American Political Economy; including strictures on the Management of the Currency and the Finances since 1861.*

It is indicative of the Boston intellectual climate that Bowen's slightly progressive monetary views, lauding the decline in the price of gold while urging the dollar's gold content to remain unchanged—an inflationary policy at that time—led Harvard to shift him away from teaching economic subjects in favor of Dunbar.[162] Bowen gravitated towards more philosophical topics, publishing a review of *Modern Philosophy, from Descartes to Schopenhauer and Hartmann* in 1877, and finally his autobiography, *Gleanings from a Literary Life, 1838–1880.*

---

[160] *Ibid.*, p. 180.

[161] Frank W. Taussig, "Francis Bowen," in Palgrave's *Dictionary of Political Economy*, ed. Henry Higgs (London, 1926), p. 175.

[162] Dorfman, *Economic Mind in American Civilization*, pp. 841–43.

Erastus B. Bigelow, Protectionist Entrepreneur

Erastus Brigham Bigelow (1814–79) was a self-made inventor and entrepreneur, and founder of the Bigelow Carpet Company ("A title on the door rates a Bigelow on the floor"). Bigelow grew up in quite modest circumstances on his father's farm near West Boylston, Massachusetts. His father supplemented the family income by working as a wheelwright and chair maker, and later set up a small cotton factory. Young Bigelow worked on a neighbor's farm and played the violin for dancing parties and for a church orchestra to earn funds to get a better education. At an early age he began to invent hand looms for weaving suspender webbing and piping cord, the earliest of what were to become more than fifty patents for weaving machinery. By the age of sixteen he had saved enough money to enroll at the Leicester Academy, but at his father's urging — and having exhausted his savings — he did not proceed to Harvard as he had hoped. Instead of returning to the cotton mill, however, he chose to work at a Boston dry-goods store. Here he taught himself stenography, and in 1831 wrote a twenty-five-page booklet on the subject *(The Self-Taught Stenographer)* which sold so well during the first two weeks following publication ($75 gross) that he proceeded to publish and market his own edition. This proved to be a mistake, and the eighteen-year-old author ended up $400 in debt.

Bigelow then went into a business partnership, but did not do very well until he set out by himself to start his own cotton and twine factory. With this modest success behind him he moved to New York, where he invented a power loom capable of weaving knotted counterpanes. He licensed this invention to a Boston firm in exchange for one-quarter of the profits, but the firm soon went insolvent and his earnings amounted to nil. Still, this Horatio Alger story was to have a happy ending. Bigelow invented many other types of power looms, his first really major invention being a loom to weave coach lace (1837), and shortly thereafter a more important carpet-weaving loom. In 1841 he and his brother formed a quilt and carpet company that grew quite rapidly after 1846, winning a prize at the 1851 Crystal Palace Exhibition in London. This was the forerunner of the Hartford-Bigelow Carpet Company, which soon became the major rug-making firm in the country.

Bigelow was one of the founders and first president of the National Association of Wool Manufacturers. Despite his protectionist views, he ran (unsuccessfully) for Congress as a Democrat in the 1860 elections. The following year he became a leading member of the twenty-one-man committee that designed the Massachusetts Institute of Technology to implement progressive principles of scientific education. He began to publish articles on the tariff, reading widely in American and British literature and compiling a lengthy statistical tome, *The Tariff Question, considered in regard to the policy of England and the interests of the United States* (Boston: 1862). This was republished without the 242 pages of statistical tables in 1877 as *The Tariff Policy of England and of the United States Contrasted*.

Bigelow viewed his book's most important contribution to be its statistical summaries, and it is without doubt the most statistically illustrated protectionist work up to this time. Government reports on American commerce had been compiled and edited by Democratic administrations, *e.g.*, by free-traders hardly interested in presenting their statistics with anything resembling a protectionist focal point. Bigelow analyzed the changing pattern of American foreign trade, demonstrating the nation's shift in export markets away from England toward the Western Hemisphere countries, whose demand for American provisions and other exports was much more stable than that of England, to which America was only a residual supplier. The West was a major supplier and exporter of breadstuffs, but America's grain exports had been declining rapidly since the country opted for the free-trade Walker Tariff of 1846. Thus, free trade and increased industrial imports from England did not automatically increase American farm exports as free-trade advocates often argued.

Bingelow concluded that because the West itself probably would desire to begin manufacturing as it found its foreign grain markets limited (especially those of Europe), its self-interest lay in supporting protectionism. In the Northeast, the region's commercial and navigation interests would find that the domestic industry growing up behind tariff walls would bestow "a corresponding benefit on trade, not only by multiplying the commodities to be distributed, but by increasing the ability of the country to buy." Nearly one-third of America's imports and exports were carried in foreign vessels anyway, Bigelow pointed out, adding that "nearly sixty-five per cent of *all* our imports, and more than eighty per cent of our imported *dry goods*, come to the port of New York. The latter branch of business is well known to be largely in the hands of foreigners, or of those connected with foreign houses."[163] It followed that if the

---

[163] Erastus B. Bigelow, *The Tariff Policy of England and of the United States Contrasted* (Boston, 1877), pp. 89–96.

nation must gear itself to developing and retaining export markets, it should focus its attention on the neighboring Western Hemisphere countries, which had grown so rapidly since the 1840s that they had overtaken the entire rest of the world as a steady market for American provisions.

Like most other protectionists, Bigelow rejected the utopian cosmopolitanism underlying British laissez-faire theory: "There is something highly pleasing and plausible in the thought of an unfettered and universal commerce. It chimes in with our best aspirations; for it suggests the welcome idea of peace among nations,—of permanent peace; for in no other condition of things is free trade possible." However, he warned, "let us not expect to find in collective humanity the disinterested goodness which is so rarely exhibited by the individual members. Let us rather assume that other nations will act, in the main, on selfish principles." It was insufficient for free-trade advocates to argue merely that gains from trade could be achieved by the world as a whole, if these gains were monopolized as a matter of course by the industrial lead nations such as England. Furthermore, "war is an evil to which we are always liable … it is obvious that the doctrine of free trade … ignores the probability, if not, indeed, the possibility of war." Most important of all, whatever the abstract theorists might argue, "to all theories and reasoning against protection stands opposed the unmanageable fact, that experience has been always and everywhere in its favor," with Great Britain itself being the major protectionist nation since the Renaissance and demonstrating to all practical observers the gains which could be reaped from proper mercantilist policies.[164] England had first become rich by following protectionist policies, and the time had come for America to do the same.

On this point Bigelow drew upon the speeches and writings of Peel, Gladstone, and other participants in Britain's parliamentary debates over the Corn Laws and trade policy. England's government could be depended upon to work continually to extend the nation's industrial power. At one time the most efficient device to achieve this end was the system of protective tariffs and navigation acts, including those which had governed the colonial United States. Since 1848 the objective of consolidating British industrial supremacy was best served by free trade.

The major purpose of any government directing an economy was to enhance its technology, Bigelow argued. This required above all the securing of adequate capital resources, a precondition for financing industrial undertakings. "Although capital employed in this direction could do nothing without skill, it is certain that skill would be all but powerless without capital."[165]

---

[164] *Ibid.*, pp. 71, 62f., 59.   [165] *Ibid.*, p. 63.

Among nations as among individual companies, capital was the ultimate deciding factor in competition. He quoted McCulloch's *Commercial Dictionary* to explain the growing industrial advantage of capital-rich nations:

> The immense accumulation of capital that has taken place since the close of the American War has been at once a cause and a consequence of our increased trade and manufactures. Those who reflect on the advantages which an increase of capital confers on its possessors can have no difficulty in perceiving how it operates to extend trade. It enables them to buy cheaper, because they buy larger quantities of goods, and pay ready money; and, on the other hand, it gives them a decided superiority in foreign markets where capital is scarce, and credit an object of primary importance with the native dealers. To the manufacturer, an increase of capital is of equal importance, by giving him the means of constructing his works in the best manner, and of carrying on the business on such a scale as to admit of the most proper distribution of whatever has to be done among different individuals. These effects have been strikingly evinced in the commercial history of Great Britain during the last half-century, and thus it is, that capital, originally accumulated by means of trade, gives it, in turn, nourishment, vigor, and enlarged growth.[166]

Capital-intensive nations thus tended to reap the benefits of diverging international productive powers and incomes. First of all, industrial exporters were in a position to secure for themselves most of the world's money and capital resources. The abundance of capital that followed from their trade surpluses tended to lower interest rates, giving them a cost advantage in manufactured goods produced largely by capital, especially heavy manufactures. This capital advantage enabled them to augment their industrial exports still further, attracting more money from abroad and financing their industrialization in an upward spiral. Thus, the nations that concentrated skill and technology within their own borders would earn the lion's share of the world's gold.

Bigelow used a form of break-even analysis to divide England's imports into those raw materials which were later re-exported in the form of finished manufactures, and those which were consumed at home for domestic use (*e.g.*, tea, coffee, and raw materials to produce manufactures consumed within England itself). "To sustain her present position," he argued, "England must have an annual foreign demand for her manufactures of at least $650,000,000" in order to secure the foreign-exchange to finance her autonomous imports. In drawing this distinction Bigelow anticipated the "structural" analysis of international trade and payments reformulated by Keynes and Moulton in the 1920s. England's textile industry employed one-fifth of its entire population,

---

[166] John Ramsey McCulloch, *Commercial Dictionary* (London, 1859), p. 720, quoted in *ibid.*, p. 67.

if one included those engaged in procuring iron to build and coal to fuel the machinery which powered its industry. This employment was centralized around Britain's export opportunities, affording a vast political base to insure government support of that nation's export promotion.[167]

Although Bigelow emphasized technology as an increasingly inexpensive substitute for other factors of production, he claimed that America could not compete with England in foreign markets or at home until its cost structure was generally equalized with that of England: "to compete with a foreign country on equal terms in our own market, certain conditions must be the same, substantially, in both communities ... the two countries should be nearly alike in the possession of skill and capital, in the price of labor, in the enjoyment of an established business, and in the extent of their business operations and connections."

This clearly was not the case. First of all, England had a twenty to thirty per cent cost advantage in the price of its labor, especially among unskilled workers. On the other hand, its cost of land was higher than in the United States because of its high population/land ratio. This left the balance to be made up largely of the cost of capital. It was here that England's abundant and inexpensive credit, available to its industrial entrepreneurs at much lower rates than that available to their American counterparts, threw industrial advantage in its favor. Furthermore, "neither the laws nor the condition of the United States can be considered favorable to great accumulations of capital," making loans scarce because of their high-risk element as well as the paucity of monetary resources. "How," asked Bigelow, "is it possible that the American producer, paying from ten to thirty per cent more for his labor, with money which costs him nine per cent (and is generally hard to get at that), should successfully contend with his British rival, who easily obtains at four per cent all the capital he wants?"[168] Because American manufacturers could not match England's low labor and capital costs, they required higher prices—supported by higher tariffs—in order to support themselves while an urban industrial base putting in place. Inasmuch as the government had to be supported by some kind of revenues, it was best for these to take the form of industrial tariffs. Given proper tariff protection, the nation could mature into a worthy rival of England.

[167] Bigelow, *Tariff Policy*, pp. 27–29.
[168] *Ibid.*, pp. 65–70.

IV. FROM BORDER-STATE PROTECTIONISM TO THE EMERGING NEW YORK MAINSTREAM

Henry Clay, Formulator of the American System

It is unnecessary here to give a political biography of Henry Clay (1777–1852), presidential candidate in 1824, 1828, 1832, 1836 and 1844, frequent Secretary of State, author of the Missouri Compromise of 1821, the Tariff Compromise of 1833–42 and the 1850 Compromise, and the great Whig exponent of what he termed the American System of protective tariffs, internal improvements and a national bank. Clay played a major role in advancing protectionist doctrine at a time when there were virtually no political economists as such and the subject was elaborated mainly by journalists and politicians. In this respect he succeeded Alexander Hamilton as a political leader who sought to systematize an argument and popular program for industrialization.

One of the threads which he picked up, and which deserves especial comment here, was that of natural energy entering into the industrial process, just as the Physiocrats had perceived it entering into agriculture. Hamilton earlier had voiced this view, and Thomas Jefferson came to espouse it by 1817, when he wrote to William Simpson that "I was once a doubter whether the labor of the cultivator, aided by the creative power of the earth itself, could not produce more than that of the manufacturer, alone and unassisted by the dead subject on which he acted; in other words, whether the more we could bring into action of the energies of our boundless territory in addition to the labor of our citizens, the more would be our gain. But the inventions of the later times, by labor-saving machines, do now as much for the manufacturer as the earth for the cultivator. Experience, too, has proved that mine was but half the question: the other half is, whether dollars and cents are to be weighed in the scale against real independence. The question is then solved, at least as far as respects our wants." Clay, elaborated this argument: as Colton describes his views,

> Mr. Clay had occasion to notice, as long ago as 1824, that some British authorities estimated the machine power of Great Britain as equal to two hundred millions of men. The number of operatives to apply this machinery has never amounted to one million. Here, then, is a nation, with a population of some twenty-five millions, with a producing power of two hundred millions. Its capabilities of producing wealth by artificial means, is so great, that its natural power is scarcely worthy of being brought into the account ... One man at home did the work of two hundred, less or more ... Science, which makes one

133

man as powerful as two hundred, or a thousand, left to their natural powers, will and must prevail against numbers. That nation which cultivates the useful, mechanic, and manufacturing arts, all of which have their foundation in science, and which excels in them, other things being equal, will excel in strength, and maintain a superiority.[169]

Clay also developed a sophisticated theory of how the terms of trade would turn against the sparsely populated, raw-materials exporting countries:

> The more rapid increase of population in the United States, than in European countries, and the consequent multiplication of producing power, come into the scale, and demand employment, which other countries will not give to it; foreign consumption of the products of American labor and the American soil, instead of increasing, and keeping pace with the ratio of increase of producing power, had fallen off, with the exception of cotton; it was therefore necessary to create a home market; the foreign demand for American produce, in terms of peace, must continue to decrease, in relation to the ratio of the increase of population, here and elsewhere...
>
> Let us suppose, that half a million persons are now employed abroad in fabricating, for our consumption, those articles, of which, by the operation of this [protective tariff] bill, a supply is intended to be provided within ourselves; that half a million persons are, in effect, subsisted by us; but their actual means of subsistence are drawn from foreign agriculture. If we could transport them to this country, and incorporate them into the mass of our own population, there would instantly arise a demand for an amount of provisions equal to that which would be requisite for their subsistence throughout the whole year ... But if, instead of these five hundred thousand artisans emigrating from abroad, we give by this bill employment to an equal number of our own citizens, now engaged in unprofitable agriculture, or idle, from the want of business, the beneficial effect upon the productions of our farming labor would be nearly doubled. The quantity would be diminished by a subtraction of the produce from the labor of all those who should be diverted from its pursuits to manufacturing industry, and the value of the residue would be enhanced, both by that diminution and the creation of the home mrket, to the extent supposed.[170]

In other words, under an international specialization of labor, countries with the fastest growing populations (those with the highest wage rates, and most sparse population) tended to increase their exports more rapidly than did the slower growing European industrial nations. Assuming that growth in exports was proportional to population growth as per capita surplus — creating powers and productivity were presumed constant — there must ensue an oversupply of raw materials on world markets. The price of food, cotton, and other raw-materials would fall, lowering wage costs for England and other food-importing countries, while reducing revenues to U.S. crop exporters. This deterioration in farm earnings could be offset only by nurturing domestic

---

[169] Calvin Colton, *Life and Times of Henry Clay* (New York, 1846), Vol. 2, pp. 159f..
[170] *Ibid.*, pp. 156–58. See also pp. 315f.

industry, so as to transfer existing farm labor (and channel new immigration) into urban industrial pursuits, creating a home market for farm output. This was basically a supply-and-demand analysis based on population theory, taking productive powers as much for granted as did the Ricardian doctrine against which Clay argued. If the productive power of machines increased from a manpower-equivalent of two hundred to that of a thousand, as suggested by Clay, it would follow that the economic (hence exportable) surplus would increase fivefold even without any population growth. In this respect the arguments voiced by Clay were echoed in the debate between Alexander Everett and George Tucker in the 1840s on the foreign trade implications of population growth.

Colton's *Life and Times of Henry Clay* is much more than a simple chronological presentation of Clay's life and thinking. It is organized according to subject lines so as to form an integrated argument for Clay's three planks of the American System. Among its most valuable chapters are the historical ones which give the authoritative Whig version of Jackson's campaign to crush the Second Bank of the United States and the subsequent formation of the Sub-Treasury system under Van Buren. In addition to serving as an anti-Jacksonian tract the work afforded a compendium of arguments demonstrating the interest of the nation's farmers and laborers in protective tariffs.

CALVIN COLTON, ECONOMIC THEORETICIAN FOR HENRY CLAY

Rev. Calvin Colton (1789–1857) was a leading Whig journalist of the 1840s, the official biographer of Henry Clay and editor of his works, and one of the two major pre-Civil War protectionists to occupy a chair of political economy (the other was Francis Bowen of Harvard). His *Public Economy for the United States* (1848) provided an elaborate defense of the inductive "historical" method of political economy that characterized the first generation of American protectionists.

Colton was born in 1789 in the Longmeadow section of Springfield, Massachusetts. He was a fifth-generation descendant of Quartermaster George Colton, one of the founders of Longmeadow, who had emigrated from England sometime before 1644. George Colton's descendants played an important role over the years in the municipal, religious and military life of Longmeadow, and were especially active in Protestant church affairs. One of the many preachers in the family line later commented that "we are born to be deacons. True, indeed, the people have a voice in putting Coltons or others into this office. But a Colton is a deacon anyway, vote or no vote."[171] In addition to serving as preachers the Colton descendants distinguished themselves as fighters: George's son, Captain Thomas Colton, gained renown as an Indian fighter, and Calvin Colton's father, Major Luther Colton, served in Major Andrew Colton's company of Minute Men in the American Revolution.

Colton's ambition and fiery personal characteristics seem to have destined him to become a preacher. After graduating from Yale College in 1812 he studied divinity at Andover Theological Seminary. He was ordained in 1815, and after serving as a missionary in western New York was appointed to the Presbyterian pastorate at Batavia. Failure of his voice in 1826, however, coupled with the death of his wife, led him to retire from the ministry. He embarked on a series of travels, the first of which he described in his *Tour of*

---

[171] Quoted in George W. Colton's family history of *Quartermaster George Colton and his Descendants, 1641–1911* (Lancaster, Pa., 1912) p. 463. Useful biographical information on Calvin Colton also is contained in an anonymous article on "Rev. Calvin Colton" in the *International Monthly Magazine of Literature, Art and Science* 4 (August 1851), pp. 1–3.

the American Lakes, and among the Indians of the North-West Territory, in 1830: Disclosing the Character and Prospects of the Indian Race (London, 1833). From the outset he was a defender of Indian rights (he believed the American Indians to represent the lost ten tribes of Israel and therefore to be essentially Judeo-Christians). Like many of his fellow New Englanders, however, he readily accepted the institution of Negro slavery.

During 1831–1835 he traveled in England, where he served as correspondent for the New York *Observer* and wrote travel narratives and sundry books on popular and religious subjects. Works published in London include his *History and Character of American Revivals of Religion* (1832), *Manual for Emigrants to America* (1832), *The Americans* (1833), the *Tour of the American Lakes* cited above, and *Church and State in America* (1833). Colton's observations on his British experience were set forth in his *Four Years in Great Britain* (New York, 1836). His later Anglophobia was not yet apparent, although a strong sense of his American identity was.

Upon returning to America he took orders in the Episcopal Church, writing a number of books asserting its comparative virtues[172] and serving as rector of the Church of the Messiah in New York City during 1837–1838. His earliest political writings date from these years, as he expressed his opposition to the abolitionist movement in two pamphlets, *Abolition a Sedition* and *Colonization and Abolition Contrasted*. In the first pamphlet he contended that the subject of slavery was a matter of state's rights and therefore lay beyond the limits of action by the national government. As a result, he concluded, there was no justification for the discussion of abolition except in those states where slavery was established. In his second tract he endorsed the colonization movement, which already was shipping American Negroes to Liberia as an alternative to abolition.

In 1839 he wrote *A Voice from America to England*, contending that while the American government was republican rather than democratic in form, the force of public opinion had made it a democracy in fact. A rapid flow of political pamphlets followed, including *A Reply to Webster, One Presidential Term, The Crisis of the Country*, and its sequel, *American Jacobinism*. As editor of the *True Whig* in Washington during 1842–1843 and author of the highly popular *Junius Tracts* that appeared during 1843–1844, Colton gained national renown as a Whig pamphleteer, although his position on slavery placed him in the by-then waning Clay wing of the party.

---

[172] Colton's *Protestant Jesuitism* was published anonymously in 1836, followed in the same year by *Thoughts on the Religious State of the Country, and Reasons for preferring Episcopacy*. In 1855 he published *The Genius and Mission of the Protestant Episcopal Church in the United States*.

Following Clay's defeat in the 1844 elections, Colton traveled to Ashland, Kentucky, where Clay provided all his correspondence and personal documents for Colton to use in compiling his biography and the collected edition of his works. The first product of this enterprise was his two-volume *Life and Times of Henry Clay*, which appeared in 1846. Rather than being a simple chronological presentation of Clay's life and thinking, it was organized according to subject lines to form a partisan argument, much of whose logic was supplied by Colton himself. Among its most valuable chapters are the historical ones that give the authoritative Whig version of Jackson's campaign to crush the Second Bank of the United States and the subsequent formation of the Sub-Treasury system under Van Buren. In addition to serving as an anti-Jacksonian tract, the work afforded a compendium of arguments demonstrating the interest of the nation's farmers and laborers in protective tariffs. It obtained a wide audience, with the first printing of five thousand copies sold out within six months of publication.

Also in 1846, Colton published his pamphlet on *The Rights of Labor*, which is in many ways an embryonic exposition of his *Public Economy*. His leading assertion was that labor was capital, above all in the sense that free labor supplied mental faculties as well as physical effort to the productive process. Slave labor, however, supplied only physical effort, and thus "occupies the position of a power simply, as horse power, or any other productive agency, that is the property of its owner [*i.e.*, the slaveholder, not the slave], and subject to its will. Slave labor has no political rights in itself, and when the rights of labor are spoken of in this work, the labor of slaves does not come into consideration, any more than that of horses. This is not said to disparage a slave as a human being, but simply to determine the position of his labor in political science … The object is to make the same distinction in science, which actually exists, between free and slave labor." [173]

No opposition need exist between slavery and protectionism, Colton continued: "Georgia is becoming a manufacturing state, and feels the need of protection. North Carolina decidedly, and Virginia probably, is in favor of the protective policy." This was a vain hope, of course, and simply established Colton as a member of the "cotton" wing of the Whigs.

American urban labor was independent, he claimed, by virtue of its ever-present alternative of migrating to the back-woods and producing its own subsistence. Europe's labor possessed no such alternative, and therefore was merely "the *Agent of Power*," the tool of its employer. The source of difference

[173] *The Rights of Labor*, pp. 5f.

between American and European wage levels was thus "a *political* cause,"[174] deriving from the comparative economic freedom of the American laborer. Colton's isolationism also appeared in this pamphlet: "This country has come to be a world in itself,"[175] he asserted, adding that it was best left that way to develop its free institutions without laying itself open to the impoverishing effects of having to compete with foreign pauper labor.

Two years later, in 1848, he published his *Public Economy* (reprinted in 1849 and 1856). Coincidentally his voice returned and he began to preach again, this time in French (which he had taught himself) as well as in English. Shortly thereafter he was offered the specially-created chair of Public Economy at Trinity College in Hartford, Connecticut, which he occupied from 1852 until his death in 1857. His tenure was spent in teaching political economy, preaching, and completing his edition of Clay's works.

Public Economy is in many respects a pamphlet rather than a theoretical work, especially in the vituperativeness of its argument against free trade and its nationalism vis-a-vis England. The ultimate question of free trade, Colton asserted, was whether America, which had won its nominal political independence from England, should be once again reduced to a condition of economic dependence. The very purpose of the American Revolution had been essentially to establish a protective system against England and thereby gain freedom in fact as well as nominally (ch. VIII). Free trade was merely "a license for depredation on the rights of others" (ch. IV), so that Europe with its cheap pauper labor could break down the high value of free American labor. America, he believed, could *never* afford free trade, even when its industry had become as sophisticated as that of rival nations. Trade with countries that possessed lower production costs in any respect, be it in wage rates or interest rates, would impair the return to its labor and capital. "The great aim of British statesmen," he asserted, "is to bring American labor down to the same level with the European, which can only be accomplished by a system of free trade."[176]

Colton's views on the scope and method of political economy represent the most significant aspect of his book. The differences in social and economic structure between the United States and Europe had not "been duly weighed as an element of public economy," he believed. However appropriate the precepts of British political economy might be for the aggrandizement of that nation's power, they were not universal in scope. Claiming "that public economy has never been reduced to a science, and that all the propositions of

---

[174] *Ibid.*, p. 8. Colton did not assert that American labor's high wages followed from its superior productive powers, as was soon to be argued by such protectionists as Peshine Smith.
[175] *Ibid.*, p. 94.   [176] *Public Economy*, pp. 56, 98.

which it is composed, down to this time, are *empirical* laws," he added that these laws, while perhaps applicable to European nations, were "entirely in-applicable" to the United States. Every nation, because of its distinct historical experience and institutions, was an exception to any set of broad economic generalities, so that "a Science can not be made out of the Laws of Public Economy, except for one Nation, each by itself."[177] Colton defined the object of political economy to be not the discovery of allegedly universal truths, but rather "the application of knowledge derived from experience to a given position, to given interests, and to given institutions of an independent state or nation, for the increase of public and private wealth."[178] His theories thus applied only to the United States: "We do not profess to write for any other country."[179]

In view of this comparatively narrow scope of political economy, England's attempt to foist her free-trade doctrines and her pessimistic Malthusianism on other nations, under the unwarranted claim that the precepts of these doctrines were universally applicable, represented little more than a colonialist strategy of exploitation rather than disinterested scientific thought. It also was hypocritical: Save for repealing her Corn Laws, Britain had never granted free trade. Even her repeal of the Corn Laws was designed mainly to strengthen the empire by reducing the cost of food (and with it British wage costs) so that her manufacturing system could more easily thwart the attempts of other nations to develop their own industry. "And how should it happen," Colton asked, "that nearly all British writers on the subject ... should have become one solid phalanx of Free Trade advocates, while the British government has produced nothing but protection?"[180] The answer was that the Free Traders were no more than British apologists.

American economic growth was best stimulated, Colton believed, by a business-oriented banking system whose monetary reserves were nurtured by a protectionist policy aimed at accumulating precious metals in the United States as a basis for its commercial credit structure. "We want, then, a system of public economy, which shall not only tend to keep in the country what is commonly reckoned enough of money, to carry on its trade and commerce; but we want a system that shall tend to increase that amount, as far as may be, in a degree, commensurate with the development of the means for its profitable

[177] *Ibid.*, pp. 46, 38, 18, and subheading for Chapter II.
[178] *Ibid.*, pp. 26f. See also p. 62. In a similar vein List had remarked in his *Outlines of American Political Economy* (1827) that "National economy teaches by what means a certain nation, in her particular situation, may direct and regulate the economy of individuals, and restrict the economy of mankind, either to prevent foreign restrictions and foreign power, or to increase the productive powers within herself ..." (p. 155).
[179] *Ibid.*, p. 57.   [180] *Ibid.*, p. 93.

use."[181] In addition to enacting protective tariffs so as to terminate the exportation of monetary metals to settle trade deficits with Europe, the nation should abolish the Sub-Treasury system, by which government revenues periodically contributed to business recession by draining the specie backing of the nation's bank currency into the vaults of the Sub-Treasuries.

Money, Colton contended, was an institution serving as the nation's "Tools of Trade" as well as a measure of value. The precious metals were indeed commodities, and had been used as such long before their development as "money." As an institution, however, money was more than a mere collection of precious metal. It played a role as a tool of commerce just as machinery served as a tool of industry. "M. Say, and all of his school, hold ... that it makes no difference whether a nation parts with cash in trade, or with other commodities ..." This was the same as saying that it made no difference whether a farmer sold his corn or his plough. To be sure, the precious metals were the only sound basis for banking. Nonetheless, "The American banking system was not established solely, nor chiefly, for economy in the machinery of the circulating medium—which is the reason assigned to it by Adam Smith—but its main design is to supply a defect of that medium."[182] Later protectionists such as Stephen Colwell were to reason from this premise that a state theory of money was needed.

Another of the leading grounds on which Colton defended protective tariffs was "that a protective system is the great power that sustains, and the only cause that can secure, general and popular education in the United States." As one of the new points of his book he asserted that the concept of labor as capital "has never before been introduced into a system of public economy as an essential element."[183] He devoted an entire chapter of his book to the

---

[181] *Ibid.*, p. 227. Colton had argued in his *Life and Times of Clay* (II, p. 482) "that CURRENCY is a part of policy necessarily connected with protection; that the very existence of a sound currency depends on an adequate protective system."

[182] *Ibid.*, pp. 211, 249.

[183] *Ibid.*, pp. 177, 45. The thought that labor's educational attributes represented a tangible form of capital was of course not new to American protectionist literature. Friedrich List had noted in 1827 what he termed the "capital of mind," and proceeded to enunciate a rough description of investment in productive working skills (*Outlines of American Political Economy*, pp. 196–199). The following year Willard Phillips observed that the "expense of education may justly be considered as an investment of capital on which the party instructed is entitled to a profit by a corresponding enhancement of his wages" (*Manual of Political Economy* [Boston, 1828] p. 133). Colton was overly nationalistic, of course, in asserting (p. 302) that "European economists have never invested labor with the attributes ... of capital." British writers such as Cantillon, Adam Smith and McCulloch had refined to a comparatively sophisticated degree the concept of labor's working skills as earning a special premium.

subject of "Education as an Element of Public Economy in the United States," treating labor's educational and working skills as "capital, and capital of the most productive kind."[184]

Colton did not assert that America's high industrial wages were the result of superior productive powers, either of the laborer himself or of the industrial capital which he operated. Instead, he put forth the somewhat Malthusian explanation of American wage rates he had given in his pamphlet on *The Rights of Labor,* attributing them simply to the relative scarcity of labor resulting from the fact that the American workingman possessed the alternative of migrating to western lands and providing a livelihood for himself there. "The time has never yet been in the history of the United States as an independent nation, when labor was not in this sense an *independent agent*—when it could not reject an unsatisfactory offer, and yet live ... it has always had an *alternative.* As a last resort the American laborer can at any time go to the back-woods ... This wide back-woods field for American labor, is a security for its independence for ages to come, if not for ever ...[185]

Were this argument valid, of course, then the "pauper labor" argument for protective tariffs would be irrelevant to the American wage-earner, inasmuch as the worst that could happen to him from cheap imports and business recession would be the necessity to move from urban to rural employments—the "last resort" to which Colton referred. Indeed, Colton's "permanent back-woods" theory of high wage rates was inconsistent with his "pauper labor" argument against free trade, according to which protective tariffs were in the workingman's interest because they alone protected his high wages from competition from lesser-paid European labor. "It is manifest," Colton argued, "that when the products of American ... labor are brought into the free and open market with the products of European and other foreign labor of the same kind, the labor itself is in the same market; and that the tendency is to reduce the price of American labor to that of foreign labor."[186]

International prices thus were portrayed as being a direct function of wage differentials *unadjusted* for differences in labor productivity. According to this theory, low foreign wages resulted in low production (and import) prices, which reduced the ability of American manufacturers to employ urban labor profitably. The result of free trade under these conditions would be that the demand for domestic labor would gradually fall until its wages had sunk to Europe's "pauper labor" level.

---

[184] *Ibid.*, p. 171.   [185] *Ibid.*, p. 285.   [186] *Ibid.*, pp. 429f. See also pp. 178f.

This early protectionist argument was soon to be controverted by other protectionists. Colton himself, indeed, had earlier noted the falsity of the assumption underlying this theory, namely, that internationally traded commodities were produced by identical processes (that is, by equal amounts of labor and capital, each possessing equal productive powers and equal capital costs). In his *Life and Times of Henry Clay* he had explicitly noted the greater degree to which Britain's labor was aided by the powers of capital: "Here, then, is a nation, with a population of some twenty-five millions, with a producing power of two hundred millions. Its capabilities of producing wealth by artificial means, is so great, that its natural power is scarcely worthy of being brought into the account."[187] It thus was British capital rather than British labor which threatened American industry. As British prices fell, America's industrial sales prices would also be forced down under free trade, with the ability of domestic industry to employ labor suffering accordingly.

This was of especial concern to the industrial slaveholder (a somewhat rare breed, to be sure), inasmuch as slave labor was less efficient than free labor and therefore more costly to its employer. "Slave-labor invariably demands protection, much more than free labor, in all its work that is common to free labor, because the former is not only more expensive for a given amount of its products, but because a free man works for himself, while a slave works for a master ... It can not subsist permanently without protection, as it would in the end eat up itself, and expire of its own *vis inertiae*. There never was a greater mistake than for slaveholders in the United States to go for Free Trade."[188] Colton believed that manufacturing enterprise held out a prospect for Southern slaveowners, an idea few of them shared. The only effect of his attempt to win the South to the cause of protection was to alienate Northern readers.

Colton cannot be said to have enunciated a sophisticated concept of capital or wages. The "theory of productive powers" that played such a great role in the theorizing of many of his protectionist contemporaries is virtually absent from his work. He was primarily an attacker of theories rather than a formulator of new doctrines. His argument against free trade emphasized more its exploitative and detrimental effects on America than the virtues of protection and industrial growth in nurturing the country's productive powers. In this respect his arguments were somewhat unsophisticated even for the first generation of protectionists.

---

[187] *Life and Times of Henry Clay*, II, p. 159.
[188] *Public Economy*, pp. 420f. Colton added that "We are not the advocates of slavery. We speak as an economist."

Colton's shortcomings and internal contradictions were soon criticized among the protectionists themselves. Francis Bowen reflected that Colton's "ponderous volume ... is not likely to make many converts to his reasoning in favor of a protective tariff," on the grounds that "The author is not so happy in founding his doctrines upon abstract principles, as in fortifying and illustrating them with statistical details. His figures prove that the conclusions are sound, but they are often deduced by a summary process in logic from very doubtful premises."[189]

In fact, the year in which Colton's *Public Economy* appeared, 1848, was pivotal in the evolution of American economic thought. In Colton's work it received what was in many respects the culminating defense of the first generation's historical and nationalist method. In Carey's *The Post, the Present and the Future* it received the outlines of a theory of economic growth that was to inspire a new generation of protectionists—one that approached political economy as a discipline of much more universal scope than earlier protectionists had acknowledged. It might well have been with Colton's disparate argument for protectionism in mind that Peshine Smith wrote just two years later that "young men cannot well have a [protectionist] faith made up of shreds and patches. It must be a consistent whole."[190]

Colton had observed that the "rules" of British political economy were inadequate to explain America's economic problems but did not really set forth a new set of rules. He opposed Malthusianism, asserting that it was merely an apology for the inequities of British society, but did not controvert its leading assumptions. "The high prices of labor and capital in this country are the results of a cheap social organization; or cheap government,"[191] he asserted, stressing that America had no parasitic and warring aristocracy to support as had European labor—as if high costs of social overhead could reduce Europe's production costs. He advocated high wages for American labor yet did not relate wage rates to labor productivity, holding instead a crude theory of international wages and prices and apparently believing that America would be priced out of world markets so long as its living standards remained high. His greatest shortcoming thus lay in his attempt to formulate a merely nationalist and historical argument for protectionism rather than developing an economic theory focusing on the superior wealth-creating capacities of industrial development.

[189] "Colton's *Public Economy*," *North American Review* 73 (July 1851), p. 91.
[190] "Political Economists: Henry C. Carey," *American Whig Review* 12 (October, 1850) p. 377.
[191] *Public Economy*, pp. 159, 283, 302, 64.

Yet this nationalism was the most popular aspect of his book. As a pamphleteering work it mobilized the anglophobia which existed among many Americans against British economic hegemony. Colton in his nationalism pushed to their limit the narrow concepts of Friedrich List and Alexander Everett as to the scope of political economy, attacking the universality claimed by Ricardian doctrine. It was only subsequent protectionists who were to formulate an economic argument more universal in scope, which portrayed Britain rather than the United States as a "special case" and extended the inductive method which Colton and his contemporaries praised so highly into a new and higher realm of theorizing.

HORACE GREELEY, PROTECTIONIST PUBLISHER AND PAMPHLETEER

Horace Greeley (1811–72) was perhaps the most popular newspaper editor in American history. His New York *Tribune*, particularly in its form as a weekly news summary mailed to out-of-town subscribers, exerted an unparalleled influence on American political life during 1841–72, and earned Greeley the presidential nomination on the Democratic ticket in 1872. In addition Greeley compiled numerous books popularizing protectionism, abolition, land reform and labor issues.

Greeley began as a Whig journalist, going into business for himself at the age of twenty-three to publish the *New Yorker* (1834–41) with $1,500 he had saved while working as a printer. Setting his own type and working virtually alone, he built up sales of the 14-page weekly to 4,500 by the end of its first year and doubled this circulation within two more years. In 1838 he began commuting to Albany to edit a companion weekly, *The Jeffersonian*, official organ of the New York State Whig Central Committee. The paper reprinted Whig speeches sprinkled with Greeley's editorials, for which he was paid $1,000 by the Whig editor and political manager, Thurlow Weed.

It was through Weed that Greeley met William Henry Seward, the party's rising light who in 1838 became the first non-Democratic governor of New York in forty years. Following Seward's election there was little further need for a campaign paper, and Greeley turned to writing for space rates in Weed's *Albany Evening Journal* and other papers to supplement his modest income from the *New Yorker*. He had hoped to be rewarded by Weed and Seward in the form of patronage as State Printer (which probably would have given him a net income of $20,000 annually), but was thrown no plum by the new regime.

Strains in fact existed between Greeley and Seward from the outset. Greeley was a great admirer of Henry Clay, but Weed felt that the Whigs needed a less controversial candidate for president in the 1840 elections, pushing General William Harrison, who avoided dividing the party and its electorate by saying almost nothing on any political topic. A Democratic paper wrote snidely that Harrison would be happiest in a log cabin with plenty of hard cider, and this epithet caught on in reverse, as the Whigs campaigned victoriously on the plank of "Liberty in Log Cabins rather than Slavery in Palaces."[192] Weed suggested that Greeley edit a Whig campaign paper called, appropriately, *The Log Cabin*. The periodical's weekly circulation grew rapidly to 60,000 copies.

Nonetheless, following the Whig victory in 1840 Seward once again neglected to reward Greeley with the postmastership of New York or some other post. Greeley's finances were depleted, aggravated by $9,000 in unpaid subscribers' bills for the *New Yorker* and an even greater sum for the *Log Cabin*. In the words of his biographer William Harlan Hale: "The fading *New Yorker* was consuming most of what he had earned during the campaign, and the surviving *Log Cabin* was but a shadow of its former self. In ready cash he had little more than $1,000 in hand with which to launch the *New York Tribune*—most of which starting capital was lent him by a Whig political friend, James Coggeshall."

The *Tribune* was announced as "a New Morning Journal of Politics, Literature, and General Intelligence ... to advance the interests of the People, and to promote their Moral, Social, and Political well-being." It rapidly caught on, thanks to Greeley's policy of including news items about local people, giving advice and muckraking—a strategy foreshadowing that of the Hearst tabloids a half-century later. The paper finally got adequate financing from Thomas McElrath, who invested $2,000 to become a full partner with Greeley and was responsible for merging the *New Yorker* and *Log Cabin* into a weekly *Tribune* edition, picking up stories and editorials from the daily. This "salvaged Greeley's sprawling properties and cheaply projected the *Tribune* far beyond the city's boundaries—into that western area, in fact, where Greeley's heart and understanding lay. It was this new far-flung weekly *Tribune*, far more than the local daily, that was to make Greeley famous and McElrath rich."[193]

Meanwhile, Greeley's status as a Whig was somewhat idiosyncratic: On the one hand he advocated protective tariffs, industrialization and the accumulation of capital, and on the other he was drawn to socialistic theories such as those of Albert Brisbane, whose *Social Destiny of Man* (1839) converted Greeley to Fourierism, and whose plan to create a utopian community, *Association; Or, Principles of a True Organization of Society* was serialized in Greeley's *Tribune* in 1842 (for which space Greeley was apparently paid $500 by Brisbane). Greeley invested most of his *Tribune* profits for 1843 into a plan to build a Sylvania Phalanx in northern Pennsylvania, although this colony survived no better than other Fourierist communities. Greeley continued his socialist advocacy

---

[192] William Harlan Hale, *Horace Greeley: Voice of the People* (New York, 1950), p. 57.
[193] *Ibid.*, pp. 65, 70.

by serving in 1845 as a delegate to the first meeting of the New England Work-ingman's Association, and employed two leading Fourierites on the *Tribune* staff—Charles A. Dana as city editor, and Stephen Pearl Andrews as Washing-ton Correspondent.

Rather than feeling an intrinsic conflict to exist between labor and capital, Greeley believed that protection for American industrial capital was in the interests of labor. In 1843 he published in twelve monthly issues a periodical entitled *The American Laborer, devoted to the cause of Protection to Home Industry, embracing the Arguments, Reports and Speeches of the ablest civilians of the United States in favor of the Policy of Protection to American Labor.* The inevitable effect of free trade, he argued, was to "increase the predominance of any particular nation which had obtained an ascendency in any branch of business," and thus to reinforce England's industrial monopoly. "Free Trade makes Alabama a Cotton Plantation; Jamaica a coffee-field; Sicily a wheat-field; Sheffield a pin factory, &c. &c.—But this policy does not develope men; it does not inform them; neither does it feed them. A largely exporting country is always a poor country; much of its labor is unemployed and unproductive; and very much of the product is consumed in transportation, exchanges, &c. &c. There will be rich merchants and factors in Egypt, Sicily, England, the West Indies, the Planting States, &c. but the Laboring mass will be poor and degraded so long as they do not produce the great bulk of their own necessaries of life." [194]

This publication emerged out of the four-day National Home Industry Convention held in New York City in April 1842, whose proceedings and reports were reproduced in Greeley's magazine, with Greeley himself serving on the Committee to consider the General Interest of Manufactures and American Labor, and the necessity of Protection. Just as the state must protect its citizens against swindlers, he argued, so it must act to insure prosperity and harmony for all. Only the tariff could provide this, along with protecting the nation against foreign commercial warfare. "We seek to build no policy like that of Great Britain, to make our own Country the Rialto of Nations, the maker, and refiner, and trafficker and carrier for all other Countries. We do not want other Nations constrained by policy or craft to bring their bread to be baked in our ovens, any more than to carry our loaves to theirs." He further reflected that, "in looking back to the history of our country since the Declaration of

---

[194] Horace Greeley, ed., *The American Laborer, devoted to the cause of Protection to Home Industry, embracing the Arguments, Reports and Speeches of the ablest civilians of the United States in favor of the Policy of Protection to American Labor* (New York, 1843), pp. 30f. (Also in 1843 Greeley published and wrote a lengthy introduction to William Atkinson's *Principles of Political Economy* supporting protection to capital and labor, including protection of labor unions.)

Independence, this strange anomaly presents itself—that we have been uniformly more prosperous under the most adverse circumstances, than we have been under those that were most favorable."[195]

During wars the value of farmlands rose in keeping with the output of home industry, only to be crushed upon return to peace and resumption of free trade. Hence Greeley's support for Clay in 1844, a year in which he published *Protection and Free Trade: The Question Stated and Considered*, as well as a book of *Whig Songs for 1844*. After Clay's defeat Greeley turned once again to labor topics, conducting a debate with a former employee, Henry Raymond (future editor of the *New York Times*) on the subject of *Association Discussed: Or, the Socialism of the Tribune Examined* (1847). As Greeley later explained his political views he "aspired to be a mediator, an interpreter, a reconciler, between Conservatism and Radicalism—to bring the two into such connection and relation that the good in each may obey the law of chemical affinity," and "to elucidate what is just and practical in the demands of our time for a social Renovation ..."[196]

In 1848, Weed and Seward once again succeeded in nominating a popular general—Zachary Taylor—for President on the Whig ticket. This led Greeley, who had hoped to see Clay renominated, to walk out of the Philadelphia National Convention. Seward ran for Senator of New York, inspiring Greeley to ask Weed if he might be nominated for Governor, or at least Lieutenant Governor or, failing that, for Congress, where a New York City seat had just been vacated. Greeley ran and won the congressional race, and spent a turbulent ninety days in the House of Representatives apparently offending everyone by muckraking congressional abuses, trying to abolish the issue of grog in the Navy (he was the author of a number of anti-alcohol tracts), proposing that the United States change its name to "Columbia," and urging a reform of the Homestead Bill "providing for the granting of 160-acre tracts on the public domain to *bona fide* settlers, with no immediate payment whatever to be required of them, the provision reading that after seven years of occupancy they could take formal title to the land at the nominal government price of $1.25 an acre." Although the House buried this proposal, Greeley made the most of it in the *Tribune*. Meanwhile, Seward wrote Weed that Greeley "won't let them adjourn until three o'clock, and martyrizes himself five or six times a day by voting against the whole House. I am sorry, but who can

---

[195] *Ibid.*, pp. 49, 142.

[196] *Hints toward Reforms* (New York, 1850), preface. On Greeley's land reform views see Charles Sotheran, *Horace Greeley and Other Pioneers of American Socialism* (New York, 1892).

reason with him?"[197] After Taylor's victory in the fall presidential elections Greeley hinted to Weed that although he wanted no spoils, it might be appropriate to name him Postmaster General or perhaps an ambassador. But he had antagonized too many vested interests to rank very high on the patronage list. Yet he still felt close to Seward and Weed, writing to one politician that if Seward could "only maintain that position" which he adopted in his "higher law" speech against extension of slavery, then "he is our home for 1856." However, when Seward arbitrated a libel suit against the *Tribune*, Greeley was greatly disappointed in the outcome. His relations with Seward and Weed reached a final breaking point following establishment of the *New York Times* in 1851, when Henry Raymond supplanted Greeley in the triumvirate relationship. The *Tribune* lost its unique source of inside news information and its advance texts of speeches delivered by Seward and other Whig leaders. Most important, there was a law requiring New York City banks to insert each week in one city paper a paid announcement summarizing their week's transactions, and this lucrative plum went to the *Times* via an investor in the paper who also happened to be state banking superintendent, empowered to select the lucky paper.

Greeley finally began to push Weed in earnest for some compensation for his years of service, preferably the nomination for Governor in 1854. Instead, Weed threw the nomination for Lieutenant Governor to Raymond. After the election—won by the Whigs—Greeley wrote a long letter to Seward complaining of the lack of support he had received for his political ambitions announcing that "it seems to me a fitting time to announce to you the dissolution of the political firm of Seward, Weed, and Greeley, by the withdrawal of the junior partner."[198]

In 1854 the Republican Party was formed, led by an old anti-rent friend of Greeley, Alvan E. Bovay, who had settled in Ripon, Wisconsin. Greeley moved quickly to join the new coalition, and criticized Seward for adhering to "the vacant shell of Whiggery," the party having lost its free-soil section and most of its pro-labor progressives by its refusal to enunciate a party program. Greeley hoped to influence the Republicans to widen their political base to include the non-slave South, as well as to defend protective tariffs. His hope was to split the Democratic Party into a non-slave faction (led by Stephen Douglas) and a Southern pro-slavery camp, gradually winning the former over to the new party.

[197] Quoted in Hale, *op. cit.*, pp. 131f. For a discussion of Greeley's activities in Congress see James Parton, *The Life of Horace Greeley* (New York, 1855), pp. 288–318.
[198] *Ibid.*, p. 166.

The Republicans, he believed, needed someone not identified with radical abolitionist appeals, preferably a non-Easterner. He thus adopted Weed's general attitude just at a time when Seward and his associates had developed a strong ideological basis for their Republicanism. But he was a poor judge of the political currents around him. He wrote in January 1860: "I *know* the country is not *Anti-Slavery*. It will only swallow a little Anti-Slavery in a great deal of sweetening. An Anti-Slavery man *per se* cannot be elected; but a Tariff, River-and-Harbor, Pacific-Railroad, Free-Homestead man, *may* succeed *although* he is Anti-Slavery; so I'll try to get a candidate who will fairly and readily unite votes to win."[199]

As matters turned out, the tariff issue was downplayed as much as possible in the election: It had failed to swing the balance in the 1830s and 1840s, and opposition to the spread of slavery seemed to be the peg upon which to hang protectionism, not the other way around. Greeley campaigned against Seward, insisting that the latter could not win the presidency if nominated because of the antagonism his views had created in New Jersey, Pennsylvania, Indiana and Iowa. At the Chicago nominating convention he was almost single-handedly responsible for defeating Seward in favor of the then unknown, politically gray character of Abraham Lincoln. The chairman of the Indiana delegation said that "Greeley has slaughtered Seward, but has saved the Republican Party."[200] Greeley had been long in coming over to Lincoln's support, but after early backing Bates he finally did so as the last means of stopping Seward.

Despite his normally pacifist views, Greeley was a hawk in the Civil War. He continued to press Lincoln, and later Andrew Johnson, for political favors or appointments, but was not highly admired by either and merely was given some embarrassing tasks by Lincoln during the Civil War. Upon the return to peace he wrote a two-volume review, *The American Conflict: a History of the Great Rebellion in the United States of America, 1860–1864* (Hartford, Conn., 1864–66), followed in 1868 by his autobiography, *Recollections of a Busy Life.*

Greeley continued to write in defense of protectionism and to defend the harmony of interests between labor and capital. In 1869 he published his *Essays designed to elucidate the Science of Political Economy, while serving to explain and defend the policy of Protection to Home Industry, as a System of National Cooperation for the Elevation of Labor*, which he dedicated to his old hero Henry Clay. "Protection," he argued, "is another name for Labor-Saving through Co-operation, by bringing producer and consumer nearer each other ... instead

---

[199] *Ibid.*, pp. 165, 215. See Jeter Allen Isely, *Horace Greeley and the Republican Party, 1853–1861* (Princeton, 1947).
[200] *Ibid.*, p. 223.

of circuitously, through several intermediates, and at great cost. In thus reducing the proportion of exchangers and increasing that of producers in a community, it inevitably increases the aggregate product of human effort, and thus enhances the recompense of Labor. As Canals and Railroads have increased production and wealth by reducing the cost of transportation, so Protection achieves the same end by shortening the distances for which transportation is required."[201] This was basically a restatement of Henry Carey's "Principle of Association" and of the views set forth by E. Peshine Smith who exerted influence over both Carey and Seward, and whose articles and book reviews had been published by Greeley and Dana in the *Tribune*.

Dependency on agricultural exports, Greeley warned, would render American farmers dependent on distant and uncertain markets, would divert productive labor to sustain the unproductive transport overhead, and would restrict farmers to producing two or three great staples, concentration upon which would deplete the soil of its minerals and essential fertilizing elements. Greeley pointed to Europe's beet sugar industry to show what protection could achieve. He hoped that tea might be grown in America inasmuch as the country's climate and latitude paralleled that of China, Japan and India.

Greeley also employed a form of input-output analysis to demonstrate that iron-making was allied with many subsidiary occupations, including the manufacture of capital goods, fuel, transport, feeding the labor employed, and so forth. "A people who have but a single source of profit are uniformly poor," he argued, "not because that vocation is necessarily ill-chosen, but because no single calling can employ and reward the varied capacities of male and female, young and old, robust and feeble. ... A diversity of pursuits is indispensable to general activity and enduring prosperity. ... In Massachusetts, half the women and nearly half the children add by their daily labor to the aggregate of realized wealth; in North Carolina and Indiana, little wealth is produced save by the labor of men, including boys of fifteen or upward. ... the chief end of a true political economy is the conversion *of idlers and useless exchangers or traffickers into habitual, effective producers of wealth.*"[202]

He thus analyzed the productive process in terms of technical relationships, ignoring the class relations emphasized so strongly by Marx and other European socialists. It may thus seem somewhat ironic that Greeley employed Karl Marx during the 1850s and 1860s as foreign correspondent for the *Tribune*, but this

---

[201] *Essays designed to elucidate the Science of Political Economy, while serving to explain and defend the policy of Protection to Home Industry, as a System of National Cooperation for the Elevation of Labor* (Philadelphia, 1869), pp. 341f.

[202] *Ibid.*, pp. 137, 188, 30, 322, 19, 29.

was fully in keeping with Greeley's and Dana's international political views and many of their domestic views as well. In fact, many of Marx's reports were lifted wholesale by Dana and published as Tribune editorials.

Late in Grant's administration Greeley joined the Republican revolt against the corruptions that had come to characterize Grant's appointees. The insurgent Liberal Republicans held a convention in Cincinnati in May 1872, and Greeley announced his willingness to run for President so long as the rump party adhered firmly to protectionism. He secured the nomination over his nearest rival, Charles Francis Adams (supported by Carl Schurz), and this virtually obliged the Democrats to nominate him too in order to avoid splitting the anti-Grant vote — even at the cost of endorsing the Cincinnati platform "with its demands for equal Negro rights, for amnesty in the South, for civil-service reform, for 'sound' currency, and for an end 'to all further grants of lands to railroads or other corporations.'"[203] Greeley was somewhat anomalous as a Democrat, and even more out of place as a serious political figure. Just before the elections his wife died and Greeley followed her a month later, after losing the election in a particularly grueling campaign.

---

[203] Hale, *op. cit.*, pp. 330, 338.

E. Peshine Smith, Synthesizer of the Second Generation of the American School

Erasmus Peshine Smith (1814–82), the most sophisticated of the pre-Civil War economists, was the major intellectual influence on his fellow protectionist and mentor, Henry Carey (1793–1879)—a fact recognized by Carey himself, though by few others. Smith sought to develop political economy as a quantitative engineering science, "to construct a skeleton of Political Economy upon the basis of purely physical laws, and thus to obtain for its conclusions that absolute certainty which belongs to the positive sciences." [204] More specifically, he sought to transform protectionist economic thinking from a body of disparate and often self-contradictory parts into an integrated doctrine of economic growth. Indeed, the *Manual*'s organization, patterned after that of Ricardo's *Principles of Political Economy*, indicates Smith's intent to formulate a theory of economic development which could be counterposed to Ricardian laissez-faire economics. This represented a sharp break from the first generation of protectionists, the embryonic historical school which had sought to develop little more than a theory of exceptions to Ricardian political economy.

Peshine Smith recognized that the earlier protectionists had often "struggled to maintain sound positions by unsound arguments, and brought weakness instead of strength to the cause they labored to serve." Although there had been a time, he continued,

> when it might do for us, whigs and protectionists, to rely upon the instinctive detection by our people of the errors in fact, and fallacies in reasoning, which are involved in the defence of the Foreign Trade policy, which calls itself Free Trade ... that time, we apprehend, has passed. The time never was, when we could rely upon contemptuous sneers at theorists ... young men cannot well have a faith made up of shreds and patches. It must be a consistent whole. [205]

In his endeavor to formulate the required integral doctrine, Peshine Smith attributed economic growth mainly to man's growing command over energy, portraying industrial capital as the mainspring of national wealth. This

---

[204] *A Manual of Political Economy* (New York, 1853), pp. iii.
[205] "Political Economists: Henry C. Carey," *American Whig Review* 12, p. 377.

depiction of economic activity in terms of energetics represents the doctrinal embodiment of a tendency which a generation of protectionist writers had sought to explicate, and which has remained a distinct feature of American thought extending through Brooks and Henry Adams in the 1890's to the Technocrats of our present century. Nature's resources, especially her energy resources, were viewed as infinite in potential, in sharp contrast to the pessimistic "scarcity" economics of British Ricardian orthodoxy.

Peshine Smith was born in New York City on March 2, 1814, nine months before the Treaty of Ghent ended the war between the United States and Britain and ushered in an era of economic competition between the two nations, in which he was to play a featured role. Shortly thereafter the family moved to Rochester, the political center of western New York, where Peshine Smith spent his childhood and most of his life.

Smith returned to New York City to attend Columbia College, from which he graduated in 1832. He seems to have adopted protectionist sentiments by this time, for he later commented that his student years at Columbia had taught him "just enough to see that the grounds upon which the friends of Protection generally based the defense of their policy was unsound." The following year be took a degree from the Harvard Law School and returned to Rochester, where he practiced law for sixteen years, joining the legal firm of William Henry Seward early in his career. This association led to a long friendship between the two men that was to determine much of the course of Smith's life. His fortunes were to follow those of Seward through the latter's terms as Governor of New York, as U.S. Senator, as acknowledged leader of the Republicans in their early years, and as Secretary of State under Lincoln and Johnson. In fact, Peshine Smith's *Manual*, published in 1853, one year before the Republican Party was founded, provided a doctrinal basis for the new party's program of protective tariffs, industrialization, internal improvements, and abolition — all policies that were enacted during the Civil War in Reconstruction periods.

Smith's life as an active writer on economic and political subjects dates from 1849, when he withdrew from legal practice to become editor of the Buffalo *Commercial Advertiser*. The following year, at the age of 36, he entered into what was to become a lifelong friendship with Henry Carey, in the process of writing an article for the *Whig Review* on the latter's economic theories. In the initial letter of a correspondence spanning nearly thirty years, he described Carey's *The Past, the Present, and the Future* as having come to him "as welcome as a torch to a man groping in darkness; I saw by its light, that the path I desired to follow was demonstrably safe and sure. Safe and sure I had before felt it, but could not find the system of the logic by which I could prove the truth to myself or to others."[206]

What Carey had done was to controvert the Ricardian theory of diminishing returns in agriculture and to portray man's economic evolution with unbounded optimism. Man did not progress from the best to the worst soils, Carey claimed, but from the worst soils—those on the mountaintops, which settlers were obliged to occupy in new regions for security reasons—to the superior soils of the valleys below. Once having occupied these soils, however, it was man's duty to maintain their fertility through wise agricultural practices, otherwise they would become depleted. This entailed the creation of a localized economic balance between town and country, in which the manufacturer was placed side by side with the farmer, Hence the harmony of interests between the agriculturalist and industrialist.

Peshine Smith interpreted this as more than simply a historical law. He recognized that it formed the basis for constructing a doctrine of political economy upon the basis of the physical sciences generally, a doctrine which would focus on man's technological potential as compared to his realized stage of production. Given the technological promise of society's existing economic state, what degree of this potential could and would be realized? The great question was what constraints prevented any given nation from realizing its full technological potential. Peshine Smith found that America's trade with England prevented it from accumulating industrial capital and led to soil-depleting modes of farm cultivation, thereby preventing the country from achieving its full potential productive powers. This afforded a new and much more scientific defense of protectionism than had hitherto been enunciated.

Referring to himself as "in the situation of a clergyman waiting for a call," he enlisted Carey's support in his attempt to spread protectionist thinking. In the summer of 1850 Carey rejected an offer of the chair of political economy at New York University, recommending Peshine Smith in his stead. Smith replied that he would not accept this post at any price, the reason apparently being the Democratic Party's domination of New York City politics. The following winter Carey recommended him to Nathan Appleton as the "one man in the country that knows how to teach it [political economy] as it should be taught," and suggested that he fill Francis Bowen's vacant McLean Chair of Ancient and Modern History at Harvard, a position more attractive to

---

[206] To Carey, April 14, 1850, from the Carey collection at the Philadelphia Historical Society. For more biographical information on Peshine Smith, see my dissertation *E. Peshine Smith: A Study in Protectionist Growth Theory and American Sectionalism* (New York University, October 1968).

Smith but which failed to materialize.[207] Smith in fact maintained a lifelong antipathy towards universities, as did most of his fellow protectionists. He wrote to Carey: "I regard it as eminently desirable that the office of instruction should as far as practicable get out of the hands of the men of the cloister and into those, who have been in the world for which they undertake to prepare youth."[208] That same day he wrote to Thurlow Weed, Seward's political manager, that he was "not above teaching boys, though I think that teaching men from the Professor's chair of a daily journal is the only University worth mentioning in these latter days."[209]

But there were few editorial posts open to protectionist writers, and that autumn Smith chose to fill an exigency as Acting Professor of Mathematics and Natural Philosophy at the newly founded University of Rochester rather than accept the political appointments which Weed offered him in Washington. He remained at the university for two years, during which period he read widely in the natural sciences, grasping eagerly the application to economic doctrine of the increasing use of steam technology, of Liebig's experiments and writings on organic chemistry and physiology, and of the concept of conservation of energy just then beginning to be widely applied by Joule and his colleagues.

It was at the University of Rochester that Peshine Smith wrote the *Manual*, which found its genesis in a series of articles written for *Hunt's Merchants' Magazine* during 1851–52. Carey's investigations, Smith recognized, provided merely a take-off point. For when the theories of Malthus and Ricardo "have been merely *negatived*," he later remarked, "without the supplanting the false by a true law, reaching back into and grafting itself upon *physical* science, no progress has been made."[210] Like Ricardo, he sought to formulate general economic laws in precise mathematical terms. The problem with Ricardo, he believed, was that he deduced his system with his eyes closed, ignoring the physical, technological, and economic reality around him. It was for this reason that, except for a two-chapter prefatory discussion of soil fertility, the *Manual*'s organization was modeled on Ricardo's *Principles*. In its third chapter are introduced the concepts of value and utility which find their counterparts in Ricardo's first chapter. Rent, wages, profits, and foreign trade are then introduced in the same sequence as that used by Ricardo.

---

[207] See Carey to Nathan Appleton, Feb. 10, 1851 (in the N. Appleton Collection at the Massachusetts Historical Society, Boston, Massachusetts).

[208] To Carey, October 2, 1850. On his anti-academic feelings, representative of the American protectionists, see also the *Manual*, p. 174.

[209] To Weed, October 2, 1850, from the collection of Weed and Seward letters at the University of Rochester.

[210] To Carey, July 17, 1858.

Like other Americans of his century, including John W. Draper, Henry and Brooks Adams, Simon Patten, and others, Peshine Smith sought to develop a theory of historical and social development on the basis of natural laws. The common complaint of American economists and historians was that Europeans, following the lead of Britain, insisted on interpreting all subjects in terms of moral philosophy and political prejudice. The result of this approach was similar to the constraining influence which religion had exerted on the development of science: man's analytic powers were turned inward to develop deductive systems, not towards the world to analyze the natural development of societies. John Stuart Mill had defined political economy as "the science which treats of the production and distribution of wealth, so far as they depend upon the laws of human nature," and as "the science relating to the moral and psychological laws of the production and distribution of wealth."[211] As against this approach, Peshine Smith asserted that political economy must not only introduce to the study of society the same mode of investigation that characterized the natural sciences, it must take as its very subject matter the relevant knowledge of its predecessor physical sciences:

> The question is, then, if we desire to construct a science in a field of investigation lapping upon physics on the one hand, which is altogether scientific, and upon human nature on the other, which as yet cannot be included within the scientific category, at which end are we to begin? At the known, the measurable and ponderable external nature? or at the unknown, the invisible, the mysterious, the fluctuating internal nature?

There was, he claimed, "an American school whose distinction it is to have pursued the opposite method [from that of British economists]; to have started from *facts*, and not from assumptions."[212] "I cannot undertake to say what social science will be," he wrote to Carey, "but it seems to me it cannot be constructed until Political Economy, giving the laws of human progress in respect to its material basis, the increased command over matter, is first tolerably perfected."[213]

Nowhere was Peshine Smith's grounding of economic thought in the physical sciences and social technology more clear than in the doctrine of land and its rent. Ricardo had erroneously viewed soil as possessing "original and indestructible powers." In fact, no such powers existed, an observation especially apparent in the United States, whose lands were rapidly being depleted from one-crop farming, a practice termed "mining the soil." Peshine Smith attrib-

---

[211] John Stuart Mill, *Essays on Some Unsettled Questions of Political Economy* (London, 1844), p. 133.

[212] Review of Bowen's "Principles of Political Economy," New York *Tribune*, April 5, 1856. See also *Manual*, pp. 3, 21.

[213] To Carey, April 3, 1859.

uted this soil exhaustion to the country's pattern of foreign trade: so long as it continued to be a net crop exporter, the soil would be depleted of its phosphates, nitrates, trace minerals and other essential fertilizing elements, as had been analyzed by Justus Liebig and other agricultural chemists of the 1840's, a decade which saw a virtual revolution in agronomy. Peshine Smith was thus led to treat soil as essentially a converter like all other forms of capital, in its particular case, transforming chemical matter—the soil's composition, supplemented by the gases of the atmosphere—into crop output. The soil's fertilizing elements could be either withdrawn from the soil or added to it. However, only when a local rural-urban balance was established between farmers and industrial town-dwellers, could adequate crop rotation policies and other scientific agricultural practices be implemented. If the United States continued to adhere to the theory of comparative advantage, it would find its agricultural productivity diminishing steadily as its lands were exhausted—an eventuality not recognized by Ricardo. On the other hand, Smith believed that soil productivity could be augmented indefinitely, so long as the farmer found it economically remunerative to apply fertilizer to the soil. A nation's farm output was thus much more a function of soil quality than of mere land area. Fertility was a product of man-made capital investment and was subject to increasing returns as population density increased and society's distribution-overhead was reduced.

Peshine Smith also broke from British tradition in his concept of labor. Ricardo had viewed the work performance of labor as a fixed productive entity, an inherent ability independent of nutritional and related consumption standards. Implicit in this view was the conclusion that pauper labor, fed and clothed at a minimum subsistence level, was capable of contributing as great an output of work effort as labor which enjoyed superior living standards. It followed to Ricardo that high profits were incompatible with high wage levels. Peshine Smith, by contrast, found them complementary: not only was highly-paid manual labor superior in strength and exertions to poorly-paid manual labor, but, as society's productive powers increased over time, capitalists introduced increasingly sophisticated forms of capital, which in turn required increasingly skilled labor to operate it. The American system of political economy, he wrote in 1852, "rests upon the belief, that in order to make labor cheap, the laborer must be well-fed, well-clothed, well-lodged, well-instructed, not only in the details of his handicraft, but in all general knowledge that can in any way be made subsidiary to it. All these cost money to the employer and repay it with interest."[214] In the *Manual* he reiterated that "high proportional

---

[214] "The Law of Progress in the Relations of Capital and Labor," *Hunt's Merchants' Magazine* 26 (January 1852), p. 42.

wages are the index of cheap production."[215] Highly paid labor on a per diem basis thus turned out to be cheap labor on a unit-cost basis, enabling well-fed and well-educated American labor to out-perform Europe's pauper labor.

Wage payments were therefore a function of labor's productive powers, not of the supply and demand for labor. The industrial workingman in America was not well-paid simply because the large expanse of vacant lands held out an alternative mode of employment and diminished the supply of industrial labor at any wage less than that which the laborer and his family could eke out by migrating to vacant lands. A precondition for high wages was a productive power of industry high enough to defray these real-wage costs. Labor, working in conjunction with energy-mobilizing capital, afforded a great economic surplus out of which both the workingman and capitalist could share in rising incomes. Wages were thus a residual income remaining after payment to the capitalist of normal interest plus profit, and wages and incomes could rise together—a doctrine at odds with that of Ricardo and with the wages-fund doctrine then prevalent among British economists. This productivity-theory of wage rates afforded a powerful argument to win the votes of labor to the cause of industrial protection.

Peshine Smith's greatest break with the Ricardians occurred in his analysis of capital and the evolution of its productive powers. The British economists had viewed capital mainly as an adjunct to their value theory, and hence as a form of embodied labor. The examples of capital chosen by Adam Smith and Ricardo in their discussions of value were not energy-generating substitutes for labor—*e.g.*, independent producers of work effort such as the steam-engine —but were simple tools to supplement labor. According to this treatment of capital, the hand-fed loom and the steam-powered loom, the pencil and the steam-engine, were homogeneous forms of capital. Peshine Smith viewed capital as something much more than embodied labor: he attributed economic growth mainly to man's growing command over nature's energy resources, primarily through fuel-powered, energy-intensive capital. The result was a depiction of steam-powered industry as the mainspring in man's economic development, a powerful argument for nurturing and protecting domestic manufactures.

Smith in fact portrayed capital in a role similar to that which the Physiocrats had attributed to land a century earlier, namely, as the unique factor which tapped nature's productive powers. It was nature, not labor, that was the exploited factor responsible in the final analysis for society's growing energy surplus—a doctrine which Peshine Smith hoped would help reconcile the views of labor and capital as to their mutual interest in cooperating to exploit nature through steam-driven production.

[215] *Manual, p. 104.*

In primitive societies human labor provided the major source of productive energy. The maximum potential output of such societies was therefore constrained by the size of their population, multiplied by the modest energy-surplus which man could generate over and above his own subsistence needs. Only with the accumulation of energy-intensive capital such as the waterwheel, the steam engine, and other energy-transforming devices, did man begin to accelerate his economic growth, by supplementing manual effort with the latent energies freely existing in nature, energies "which cooperate with him gratuitously, through the intervention of the machinery devised for giving play and direction to their activity."[216]

Energy-intensive capital was at first utilized merely to supplement manual labor, but it gradually came to supplant it. This tended to transform the nature of labor itself: the workingman's status was elevated from that of providing merely manual effort—that is, of converting food into work energy on a par with the ox and other beasts of burden—to that of a trained engineer whose contribution to production consisted in applying technical skills to operate society's industrial capital. This evolution necessarily resulted in profound social improvement.

What Peshine Smith termed the "Law of Endless Circulation in Matter and Force" was simply the law of conservation of energy in its application to economic phenomena. Believing all economic laws to have their counterparts in those of the natural sciences, he characterized the reproduction of wealth as a vast energy transfer system within nature's overall equilibrium, the only question being the extent to which man would proceed to exploit nature's latent wealth. "The entire universe then is motion," he wrote to Carey, "and the only point is how much of the universal and ceaseless motion shall we utilize and how much shall we permit to be working against us."[217] The answer would be determined by man's "wit and will" the wit to extend the frontiers of his technological ability, and the will of society to provide an adequate inducement to invest in this technological potential. For America this entailed the enactment of industrial protection.

Instead of representing social output in terms of "human satisfaction" or other utilitarian measures, Peshine Smith developed an energy-measure proxy for society's economic surplus. In Ricardian value theory the capture of surplus energy, existing freely in nature, entailed no corresponding human labor cost, and was therefore dismissed as being merely a "free" economic service. It was precisely this ratio of industrial energy to human labor effort—or kilowatt-

---

[216] "Money," *New York Tribune*, January 9, 1853.
[217] To Carey, February 21, 1857. See also letter of December 28, 1854.

hours per capita, as we would measure this ratio today—that represented the key to society's wealth-producing power, Peshine Smith declared. Economic growth consisted of the per capita increase in society's expenditure (harnessing) of energy. The *Manual* defined utility as "the *aid* which nature renders" in supplementing manual labor effort. This energy was gratuitous, *e.g.*, cost-free, in that it entered the productive process without entailing a corresponding expenditure of human effort. Thus, man's ability to harness "the gratuitous co-operation of the forces of Nature adds immensely to the capital of a nation, without adding to its value."[218]

Although the *Manual*'s definition of utility was not yet rigorously conceived in terms of energy input, Peshine Smith already revealed his desire to co-measure utility with value so as to provide a measure of energy surplus: "The difference between [utility and value]—between the gross amount of service, in the satisfaction of wants, that the possession of a thing will bestow, and the gross amount of labour which must be undertaken to secure it—is the sum of the effects produced by the gratuitous operation of the forces of Nature."[219] Not until three years after the *Manual*'s publication, however, did he refine his concept of non-human energy input (utility) as being strictly co-measurable with human labor-effort (value) expended directly in production:

> I had, I think, in my book substantially hit upon a half of it—see page 70—in speaking of Value as the sum of the obstacles to the attainment of a given article or service. It measures the *resistance* which nature opposes to man. The truth becomes much more striking by the apposition of the other half of it, that Utility measures the *aid* which nature renders. You make the water float a log downstream for you. The velocity of the current measures its Utility. You tow the same stick *up against the current*, its velocity measures the Value of the work—the labour it requires. There must be a better illustration somewhere, in the action of positive and negative electricity—or the magnet with its one pole attractive (Utility): the other repellent, Value.[220]

This concept was later stated with even greater clarity in Peshine Smith's notes for a never-published review of Carey's *Principles of Social Science:*

> Production & Consumption are mere transformations of substance—alterations of matter in its quality without increase or diminution of its quantity.
>
> In every transition of matter from one condition to another, *force* is employed, i.e., *consumed*: and *force* is also evolved that is Produced.
>
> When we regard any commodity as an Object, the Forces necessary for its Production are summed up & measured by Value.
>
> When we regard it as an Instrument, the Forces capable of being generated—*set free* is the expression—by its Consumption, are summed & measured by Utility. ...

[218] *Manual*, p. 142.
[219] *Ibid.*, p. 70.
[220] To Carey, November 5, 1856. Italics in original.

> The force required to produce a ton of coal = its value, & the force exerted by it in a steam engine = its utility, are only formulae which express, after the manner of physical science, a truth which every spoken language implicitly recognizes.[221]

The productivity of capital in Smith's model consisted of the amount of energy harnessed by it, relative to its value in terms of the human labor costs necessary to reproduce that portion of capital used up in production, to provide its fuel and associated operating expenses, and to acquire the relevant skills necessary to operate this capital. Whereas pre-industrial mercantilism had believed nations to be powerful simply in proportion to their population (as a rough proxy of their power to create a national economic surplus), Peshine Smith found national power proportional to a nation's population plus the manpower equivalent of its capital.

This interpretation of economic development and national power in terms of changing factor productivity led Peshine Smith to analyze foreign trade not only as the result *of* existing variations in productivity among nations, but as an influence *on* the evolution of productive powers. The result was a more dynamic treatment of foreign trade and economic development than had characterized his *laissez-faire* opponents. He denounced free trade specifically for its adverse effects on the development of society's productive powers. First, the importation of low-priced manufactures discouraged domestic industrialists from investing in capital, thereby cutting off the nation's greatest source of potential productivity growth. Second, by reducing industrial activity and the growth of urban employment, it slowed the growth of urban wage rates, thereby preventing the country's laborers from making the investment in education and working skills that was a precondition for increasing their productivity. Free trade thus retarded productivity growth for labor and capital, and actually reduced that of land. The *Manual* argued that America's export surplus in agricultural produce was interrupting the natural cycle in which the mineral constituents removed from the soil in the form of crops were returned to it in the form of local urban refuse. Under free trade, America disturbed the natural rural/urban balance.

Treating technology as a subject rightly belonging to the realm of political economy was a distinctly American trait. As early as 1823, Daniel Raymond had written, in his *Elements of Political Economy,* that political economy "is not only the most important, but the most comprehensive science. It not only comprehends a knowledge of the influence of agriculture, commerce, and manufactures on public wealth; but the administration of justice, civil liberty,

---

[221] To Carey, August 16, 1858. See also letter of October 11, 1855.

public morals, and even the arts and sciences themselves are but branches of this science, inasmuch as they all have their influence in promoting national wealth."[222] As List had put matters, "the point in question is not … that of immediately increasing … *the values of exchange* in the nation, but of increasing *the amount of its productive powers*."[223] This tendency of thought, which Peshine Smith pressed to a much further degree than earlier writers, was alien to European economic and historical analysts. Courcelle-Seneuil, who reviewed the *Manual* in France, admitted that Peshine Smith's definition of political economy proved too original and "specifically American" for him to understand, and added that "in order to found his theory on purely physical laws, Peshine Smith has simply left the realm of economic science." The *Manual*'s emphasis on the effect of international trade upon productivity in agriculture, he added, entailed propositions "in truth, more agricultural than economic."[224] Similarly in Germany, Böhm-Bawerk dismissed this approach to economic analysis as an "indirect productivity theory" which lay outside the mainstream of British and Austrian value theory.

It is somewhat ironic that Peshine Smith's logical method, and that of so many of his fellow Americans, was closely akin to that of Auguste Comte, whose works Peshine Smith did not read until the *Manual* was completed. Comte had portrayed all sciences as branches of a single trunk of knowledge, along which scientific investigation evolved, beginning with mathematics and progressing successively through astronomy, physics, chemistry, and biology, to arrive at political economy and, ultimately, sociology, as the most general social science. "Now," Comte wrote, "it is clear that the action of man upon nature depends chiefly on his knowledge of the laws of inorganic phenomena, though biological phenomena must also find a place in it. We must bear in mind, too, that physics, and yet more chemistry, form the basis of human power. … Here we have another ground on which to exhibit the impossibility of any rational study of social development otherwise than by combining sociological speculations with the whole of the doctrines of inorganic philosophy."[225]

---

[222] Daniel Raymond, *The Elements of Political Economy*, 2nd ed. (Baltimore, 1823), Vol. 1, p. 10.

[223] Friedrich List, *National System of Political Economy* (London, 1885), p. 170. See also Willard Phillips, *Manual of Political Economy* (Boston, 1828), pp. 12–14.

[224] Courcelle-Seneuil, "Comte rendu du 'Manuel d'economie politique' de M. Peshine Smith," *Journal des Economists*, first series, 38 (August-December, 1853), pp. 239, 242.

[225] *The Positive Philosophy of Auguste Comte*, translated by Harriet Martineau, Vol. 2 (New York, 1868), p. 118.

Comte himself, however, never implemented this approach in his own writings on economic subjects, but remained trapped within the moral-philosophical system of reasoning that emanated from British writers. It was left exclusively for American writers to fulfil the task of constructing a theory of economic and historical development on a materialist technological basis. Smith urged Carey to take as given "Comte's doctrine of proceeding and shew that all the economists as well as himself have abjured it in practice, by trying to speculate on what according to principles of *human nature* man would like, instead of looking to physical nature to find its power over him and his power in respect to it. It is a question of *forces*, not of *wishes*."[226]

Upon completion of the *Manual* early in 1853, Peshine Smith had become Deputy State Superintendent of Public Instruction at Albany, a position he occupied for more than three years. This period was the most active in the development of his economic thought and in his correspondence with Carey, despite the fact that he continued to maintain his home in Rochester, fulfilling his six-day working week in five days so as to spend weekends at home — a practice which meant a weekly round-trip of 460 miles. Smith also remained active in Rochester literary society, and, as one of the founders of the Pundit Club in 1854, he delivered the group's first lecture (on the subject of Carey's financial theories) at the home of his soon-to-be-famous neighbor, Lewis Henry Morgan.

Late in 1856 Smith learned of an opening as Reporter of the Court of Appeals at Albany, a position he accepted the following June, anticipating that it would leave him considerably more time in which to write. But the reporter-ship left him with "little time outside and little disposition to do anything," and his economic theorizing virtually came to a halt.

Meanwhile, Seward's political career seemed to be carrying him towards the presidency. He had been the leader of the "Conscience" or abolitionist Whigs, so-named to distinguish them from the Webster (or "Cotton") Whigs. This abolitionist wing became the core of the Republican Party in 1854, which two years later held its first national convention, nominating Fremont as its presidential candidate and saving Seward for what it anticipated would be a much stronger showing in the 1860 elections. "Four years hence," Smith wrote to Carey, "I think the people will want a man who has *always* been right, on the tariff as well as on slavery — the one because of the other." In fact, Smith was an uncompromising opponent of slavery who felt that the anti-slavery issue was the only bandwagon that could carry protectionist doctrines to power.

---

[226] To Carey, March 10, 1856. See also letter of January 22, 1854.

"I look on everybody who is fighting the Southern domination as fighting our battle [*i.e.*, that of protectionism] whether he means it or not. If he thinks he is not, I do not care to undeceive him till the fight is won."[227]

Like most of Seward's friends and supporters, Smith was bitterly disappointed in 1860 by the former's failure to obtain the Republican presidential nomination. This occurred because, as the acknowledged leader of the Republicans, Seward's firm beliefs had made enemies of many moderates and Know Nothings—just as Lincoln's victory at the Chicago nominating convention has been widely attributed to his comparative anonymity at that time. Despite Smith's pain at having to see Seward settle for the post of Secretary of State, upon completion of his reportership he proceeded to join Seward in the State Department. An early aim of the Republican administration was to encourage a more rapid flow of immigration to America, and towards this end, a new Immigration Act had been passed in 1864. One of its most ardent proponents was Henry Carey, who as early as 1862 had proposed Peshine Smith for the post of Commissioner of Immigration—largely in recognition, no doubt, of the *Manual*'s theory of population growth and its economic benefits. And, despite the continued pressures on Smith's time as Court Reporter, his reply to Carey's initial proposal was that "it is no affectation that induces me to say that I fail to recognize in myself any such special qualification for the service of promoting immigration as you attribute to me. I have no desire to take the duty upon myself; on the contrary I would undertake it only as a war service, such as a man is not at liberty to decline, if it shall be thought that I owe it to the country."[228]

In 1865, however, apparently with the understanding that he was to become Commissioner of Immigration, Smith joined the State Department, where his legal background was temporarily put to use in advising Seward on matters of international law. His salary of $5,000 per year ranked him as third in the department, after Seward's first Assistant Secretary of State (his son). As matters turned out, by the time Smith's appointment as Commissioner was approved by the Senate, on March 21, 1866, it had become apparent that the department's workload of legal cases had grown large enough to require the

[227] To Carey, November 14, 1856. On the saving of Seward for 1860, see also his letter to Carey of July 13, 1855. Smith had resigned as editor of the *Commercial Advertiser* when the editor attacked Seward for his anti-slavery speech in 1850 (see letter to Carey, April 14, 1850). Smith later wrote to Carey that he would not take the oath of office as Commissioner of Immigration if President Johnson vetoed the Civil Rights bill (to Carey, April 18, 1866).
[228] To Carey, September 2, 1862.

services of a full-time legal expert with high responsibility. Thus it came about that on the very day that his appointment as Commissioner of Immigration was being approved in the Senate, his name was being proposed in the House of Representatives for the position of Solicitor of the State Department. In July he left the immigration section to return to his earlier advisory position in international law as Examiner of Claims (the official title eventually decided upon). This position he occupied until 1871.

Seward remained Secretary of State until the termination of Johnson's administration in 1868. For the next two years he traveled around the world, and was greeted with particular friendship in Japan. His meeting with the Mikado may have been partially responsible for Japan's request in 1871 for an American adviser to the Mikado in international law. Seward's successor as Secretary of State and fellow upstate New Yorker, Hamilton Fish, recommended Peshine Smith for the position. The Meiji Restoration had taken place in 1867, signalling the resurgence of Japanese nationalism. Until 1871, the British ambassador, Sir Harry Parkes, had successfully countered this trend, but when he returned to England for a vacation in April 1871, Foreign Minister Fukushima seized the opportunity to reorganize the diplomatic corps. It was this reorganization that led to Smith's being invited to Japan later that year, starting a forty-year tradition of having the advisor of the foreign office be an American.

"I dread to sever myself from my family and country," Smith wrote to Carey, "and yet I dread to decline. It is an opportunity for useful and honourable service such as is seldom presented to a mortal. Any of the great powers of Europe would pay largely to put their man in my place. Next July Japan revises its treaties with all the Western powers, having reserved that right in existing treaties. ... But as one of my best friends says, 'it is a great calling before the importance of which all question of pay, comfort, danger and all that sort of thing, are insignificant'."[229] Following an interview with Japanese representatives Kido and Fukuchi he accepted the position, becoming the first American to serve the Japanese government in an official capacity.

"I am quite satisfied with my situation," he wrote after becoming settled in Yedo, the diplomatic suburb of Yokahama, "and am encouraged to hope that I may be—am already—very useful. The Japanese statesmen appear to have sound notions upon the policy of encouraging the protection of native industry and I think the revised Treaties will be most unacceptable to the Christian powers in this particular. We mean to utterly reject commercial trammels unless

---

[229] To Carey, September 2, 1871. Smith is referring here to the Ansei Treaty.

we get some distinct consideration for submitting to them. I trust also to get rid
of the 'most favored nation' clause so that we can retaliate upon those who
treat us in a supercilious and unfriendly way, without the necessity of physical
warfare."[230]

Smith soon went native, and has been credited by Japanese scholars with
the founding of shirt-sleeve diplomacy in Japan. He adopted the kimono, wore
a double sword, and took a Japanese mistress.[231] After swords were banned as
weapons he affected a small wooden one when he went out. These exploits
appear to have put him in good stead with Foreign Minister Fukushima, and
in 1874, the Japanese government renewed his two-year contract for three
more years. Following this renewal his wife joined him from Rochester.

Especially gratifying to Smith was the egalitarian quality of Japanese
society. Finding it devoid of servility and flunkyism, he wrote happily to Carey
that the nation had *"never had a slave."*[232] There was still a coolie trade between
the Western nations and China, however, which he seized an opportunity to
end shortly after his arrival. On June 5, 1872 the Peruvian ship *Maria Luz* was
shipwrecked off the coast of Yokohama with a cargo of 230 Chinese coolies.
Although the American ambassador to Japan had been instructed to represent
the interest of Peru should any conflict arise, Smith advised the Japanese government to detain the coolies. The captain of the Peruvian ship protested officially
and Peru nearly declared war on Japan. The case was submitted for arbitration
to the Russian Emperor, Alexander II, who at Ems in May 1875 ruled the
seizure lawful. The coolies were returned to China and the trade war was
declared illegal and soon disbanded.

Smith left Japan in 1877, by which time "the American System of protectionist economic theory had become generally common thinking among
[Japanese] statesmen, government officials and philosophers."[233] Prior to his
departure, at his wife's request, he left $5,000 towards the construction of an
Episcopal church. Upon his return to Rochester he wrote to Carey in search
of a journal receptive to protectionist articles, but found none. He also proposed to write a short manual for use in secondary schools, but again did not
follow this up. He died in Rochester in 1882, at the age of 68.

[230] To Carey, March 25, 1872. In 1875 Japan announced its protectionist policies.
[231] See Kiyoshi Tamobashi, *Meiji Diplomatic History* (Iwanami Koza, *Course in Japanese History*), p. 16. See also Yasushi Yedonami, "Protective Trade Policy in the early Meiji Era and the arrival of E. P. Smith in Japan," *Kyoto University Academic Journal* 33 (1938), 2nd part [in Japanese].
[232] To Carey, March 25, 1872.
[233] Yedonami, *op. cit.*, section 6.

With a life and literary output like this, the question arises as to why Peshine Smith remains virtually unrecognized in the annals of economic thought. He is cited neither by Schumpeter nor by Gide and Rist in their histories. Those who do cite him but usually relegate him to a footnote as one of Henry Carey's followers. John Turner, for instance, dismissed Peshine Smith in a single sentence, asserting that he was "a devoted disciple (of Carey) whose *Manual of Political Economy* ... is only an exposition of Carey's thought in small compass."[234] What he did not observe was that Peshine Smith's anti-Ricardianism, in particular his application of Liebig's theories of agricultural chemistry and physiology to rent and wage theory, was formulated before Carey published his *Principles of Social Science,* and that Carey acknowledged his indebtedness to Smith for the "Law of Endless Circulation in Matter and Force" upon which he based his doctrine of balanced and localized growth between agriculture and industry. The influence of Peshine Smith on Carey has rarely been recognized, although over ten per cent of the *Manual* is quoted verbatim in the latter's *Principles of Social Science* and a voluminous correspondence from Smith to Carey has been preserved. Carey mailed to Peshine Smith for criticism and suggestions the preliminary drafts of each chapter of his *Principles of Social Science,* as well as later articles.

Even more misleading about the relationship between Peshine Smith and Carey is Dorfman's description of the *Manual* as "Carey's *The Past, the Present, and the Future* in a third of the space and far more readable."[235] Carey had merely inverted the Ricardian theory as it applied to the historical progress of cultivation, without tackling either the static concept of soil which underlay Ricardo's theory of differential rent, or Ricardian value and wage theory. Peshine Smith proposed to supplant Ricardian thought with a fundamentally different conceptual system, based not only on a more scientific concept of soil but also on broader concepts of utility, productivity, and capital. While deeply impressed with Carey's integration of the ideas of population density, soil fertility and foreign trade, he developed a quite original line of thought, one that went far beyond Carey. Peshine Smith's energy-theory of capital and the accompanying energy-concepts of value and utility were never pursued by

[234] John W. Turner, *The Ricardian Rent Theory in Early American Economics* (New York, 1921), pp. 141–42.
[235] Joseph Dorfman, *The Economic Mind of American Civilization*, Vol. 11 (New York, 1946), p. 807. This description is all the more curious in view of the fact that the *Manual* is by word count a full 79 per cent of the length of Carey's book. Dorfman quotes (inaccurately) only a minor passage from the *Manual*, dealing with the undesirability of labor unions, and leaves its significant theoretical contributions untouched.

Carey. It was to be eight decades after the *Manual*'s publication before the Technocrats, unaware of the concept's earlier formulation, revived the explanation of the reproduction of wealth in terms of the expenditure and conversion of energy.

A major reason for Peshine Smith's neglect is undoubtedly the fact that the *Manual* represents merely the half-way point in the development of his concepts of capital and productivity. Because he never found himself able to revise this work, these concepts were refined solely in his correspondence with Henry Carey during the five years following the *Manual*'s publication. Finding the doors of the academic community shut to his ideas, and dependent upon earning a livelihood, he accepted employment which robbed him of the leisure necessary to further refine his doctrines. Throughout his life he grieved to Carey about his frustrated desire to incorporate his ideas into a new book. "I shall go crazy with thinking," he wrote in 1871, "unless I rewrite my book or write a new one or have my head taken off and thus be saved all the trouble." [236] When a major review article which Smith had submitted to the *North American Review* on Carey's *Principles of Social Science* was rejected, he seems to have become discouraged from writing further essays. He later lamented that "it is a great disadvantage not to be able to command space in a Review where people are forced to see your article, but the Reviews will have none of us." [237] He felt the tragic conflict of his life was that he could not devote all his energies to the pursuit of theoretical inquiry and at the same time fulfil the duties of his political appointments.

And yet despite the fact that he was a highly political man, Peshine Smith was not a political apologist. His theories explained economic phenomena as he saw them. He portrayed the economic waste created by pauper labor and slavery, the depletion of America's soil resources caused by its international trade patterns as they then existed, and the vast opportunities for economic growth afforded by industrial capital, as well as the economic benefits which he foresaw would accrue to the United States from increasing population density and market size.

While by no means unaware of institutional factors and particular historical circumstances in economic growth, Peshine Smith restricted the scope of his analysis to that which was universal among nations. This approach was sharply at odds with the historicism enunciated by the first generation of protectionist writers in the United States who clustered around Mathew Carey in the 1820's through the 1840's. Peshine Smith's generation clustered around

---

[236] To Carey, October 22, 1871.   [237] To Carey, March 1, 1879.

Henry Carey, inspired by the latter's search to defend pro-industrial growth and tariff policies, not simply on the ground that America represented an exception to the British rule, but because a new set of rules existed altogether which had been ignored by British political economists. It was this generation that came to power in 1861 and whose doctrines guided the nation's economic development over the remainder of the century.

Economic Writings of E. Peshine Smith

1. "Political Economists: Henry C. Carey," *American Whig Review* 12 (October 1850), pp. 376–87.
2. "The Study of Political Economy," *Hunt's Merchants' Magazine* 25 (July 1851), pp. 64–76.
3. "The Law of Progress in the Relations of Capital and Labor," *Ibid.* 25 (November 1851), pp. 531–45; 26 (January 1852), pp. 31–44, (August 1852), pp. 178–87.
4. *A Manual of Political Economy.* New York: George P. Putnam, 1853.
5. "Money," New York *Tribune*, January 9, 1855, p. 4.
6. "Bowen's 'Principles of Political Economy ...,'" New York *Tribune*, April 5, 1856.
7. "List's 'National System of Political Economy,'" New York *Tribune*, April 12, 1856.
8. "Henry C. Carey," biographical note in S. Austin Allibone (ed.), *A Critical Dictionary of English Literature and British and American Authors, Living and Dead.* Philadelphia: J. S. Lippincott, 1858.

A French translation of the Manual was published in 1854 which included some pages and notes added to the original. This translation marks Peshine Smith as the second American political economist to be translated into that language (the first being Alexander Everett, whose *New Ideas on Population* was translated into French in 1826). In 1855 Ferrara published an Italian translation, and a German one followed in 1878, published in F. Stöpel's *Bibliothek der Volkswirtschaftslehre und Gesellschaftswissenschaften* (Berlin; xvi+398 pp.) that is said by Böhm-Bawerk to have obtained a wide circulation.

The *Manual* was adopted as a textbook at Princeton in 1858, and was used there at least through 1861. Meanwhile, Carey's praise for the book and his numerous lengthy quotations from it in his *Principles of Social Science* promoted its reputation, and new printings appeared in 1858, 1859, 1860 and 1868. Cornell University adopted it as a text in 1871 in keeping with its policy of teaching two contrasting courses in political economy, and it was also used at Hobart College in Geneva, New York. Carey's son, H. C. Baird, reprinted the *Manual* in 1872, 1873, 1877 and 1897 as part of his series of the protectionist writings of his father's associates. Finally, A. M. Kelley reprinted the work in 1966.

V. Henry Carey's Generation after the Civil War

WILLIAM ELDER, FOLLOWER OF CAREY

William Elder (1806–85) was a popularist of anti-slavery and protectionist views. After brief careers in medicine and law and a foray into politics, he decided that his major interest and talent lay in writing on political and economic topics. In 1845 he gave up his legal practice in Pittsburgh and moved to Philadelphia, where in 1847 he was put in charge of the anti-slavery *Liberty Herald,* and in 1848 wrote most of *The Republic,* a Free Soil campaign paper. The brief essays which he contributed to these and other newspapers were collected in 1854 into his first book, *Periscopies.*

As a protectionist, Elder was naturally drawn into Henry Carey's circle. This contributed to his being invited to the Treasury Department as statistician following the outbreak of the Civil War. He wrote a widely-circulated pamphlet on the *Debt and Resources of the United States* in 1863, and two years later a pamphlet on *How the National Debt Can be Paid,* which was distributed by the financier Jay Cooke as part of his campaign to sell government securities. Soon after the war Elder returned to Philadelphia, where in 1871 he wrote his most popular book, *Questions of the Day: Economic and Social,* a popularization of Carey's protectionist and related economic views. Two years later he returned to Washington as clerk in the Comptroller's Office of the Treasury Department, remaining twelve years at this post. It was here that he wrote his *Conversations on the Principal Subjects of Political Economy* (1882), his final work.

RICHARD W. THOMPSON, SELF-MADE PROTECTIONIST

Richard Wigginton Thompson (1809–1900) was a self-made man who rose to become Secretary of the Navy in the Hayes Administration. In his early teens he left his home in Culpeper County, Virginia, and found employment as a storekeeper's clerk in Louisville, Kentucky. He soon moved on to Indiana, where he taught school, worked in a store, and studied law at night, gaining admittance to the Indiana bar in 1834. During the next four years he served in both houses of the Indiana legislature, acting for short periods as president pro tem of the State Senate and as acting Lieutenant Governor. In 1840 he was voted to the Electoral College behind Harrison on the Whig ticket, and in 1841–43 served in the House of Representatives. During the Democratic administration of Polk he was elected once again to the Indiana State Senate, and returned to Congress during 1847–49. He then withdrew from politics until 1867, when he was given a judgeship in Indiana's circuit court. He attended the Republican Conventions in 1868, 1876, and 1892, nominating Benjamin Harrison in the latter convention.

The peak of his career came when he was appointed Secretary of the Navy in President Hayes' cabinet. This has been called by Hayes' biographer the only major appointment "dictated entirely by political considerations and it was the only bad one." The problem was that Thompson saw no conflict of interest in becoming chairman of the American Committee of the Panama Canal Company at a salary of $25,000 per year in 1881 while still holding his cabinet post. Upon hearing of this commercial employment, President Hayes notified Thompson "that his resignation (unoffered) had been accepted."[238] Thompson was in fact criticized frequently on ethical grounds during his career, often by his own friends.

In addition to writing on the tariff, Thompson wrote a number of anti-Catholic books warning of papal intrusion into American politics: in 1876 he published *The Papacy and Civil Power,* and in 1898, *The Footprints of the Jesuits.* Meanwhile, he compiled his *History of the Protective Tariff Laws* in 1888, followed by his *Recollections of Sixteen Presidents* in 1894.

---

[238] Eckenrode, *Rutherford B. Hayes* (New York: 1930), pp. 242, 303.

ROBERT ELLIS THOMPSON, PROTECTIONIST EDUCATOR

It was natural that the least academic resistance to protectionist doctrines in the United States would be at the University of Pennsylvania. Economically, the state was the seat of protectionist doctrine, thanks to its coal, iron, and related heavy-industrial interests, coupled with the presence of Mathew and Henry Carey. Intellectually, the University itself traced its origins back to Benjamin Franklin's 1751 Philadelphia Academy, which in colonial days had made the first serious moves away from religious sectarianism. Franklin's *Proposals for a Complete Education of Youth* (1749) had suggested "a course of instruction which, although dealing primarily with history," presented history in a predominantly economic setting. "He proposed that information be given in the curriculum on the history of commerce, on the invention of the arts, on the rise of manufactures, on the progress of trade, and the change of its seats together with the reasons and causes therefore."[239] It is therefore somewhat surprising that the University apparently did not introduce a course explicitly in political economy until 1855, when it was taught by the free-trader Henry Vethake. Following the latter's departure in 1859 the subject was appropriated by protectionists (using Bowen's *Principles of Political Economy* as their textbook). Finally, Henry Carey's supporters won dominant sway in 1869 when the political economy course was replaced by "Social Science," the new title alluding to Carey's compendious synthesis of protectionist doctrine, *Principles of Social Science* (1858–60), which was required reading for the course. Robert Ellis Thompson (1844–1924) was appointed the professor for the new subject, which was part of the "English" requirement for the University's B.A. degree until 1878, when it was continued separately as part of the senior requirement.

Thompson was born in Ireland of Scotch-Irish descent, on a three-hundred-acre farm twenty miles southwest of Belfast. At the age of thirteen he emigrated to the United States with his family. His Irish background, encom-

---

[239] Michael J. L. O'Connor, *Origins of Academic Economics in the United States* (New York, 1944), p. 66. See also Thomas H. Montgomery, *A History of the University of Pennsylvania from Its Foundation to A.D. 1770* (Philadelphia, 1900), and Edwin R. A. Seligman, "The Early Teaching of Economics in the United States," in J.H. Hollander, ed., *Economic Essays in Honor of John Bates Clark* (New York, 1927), p. 289.

passing the years of the terrible potato famine (1844–47), may have contributed to his strong dislike for England, a characteristic common to Carey's isolationist associates. Rabbeno called Thompson "an exaggerated protectionist," emphasizing that he typified how "the main motive of the petitions for industrial protection was the desire of becoming completely independent of England."[240] Cliffe Leslie described him in 1880 as "the chief living expositor of Carey's ideas,"[241] and Thompson, having become one of the University's best-liked and most popular teachers, did indeed seem to be an ideal teacher of Carey's theories.

Thompson graduated from the University of Pennsylvania in 1865 with the highest honors, delivering the Greek salutatory at the commencement exercises. After graduating from the Reformed Presbyterian Seminary two years later (he was ordained in 1874), Thompson went on to take his M.A. from the University of Pennsylvania in 1868, delivering the Master's oration at the commencement. Choosing to teach rather than to pursue a predominantly religious career, he joined the University faculty as an instructor in mathematics and Latin. The following year, in 1869, he began to teach the Social Science course to which he devoted his full teaching schedule from 1871 onwards. From this time on he was also an active writer and editor: during 1870–81 he edited the *Penn Monthly*, a University-sponsored magazine for which he wrote many articles over the years, and from 1881–92 he edited an offshoot of this magazine, *The American*, a weekly paper dealing with current events and literature.

Thompson's textbook on *Social Science and National Economy* was published in 1875, with editions subsequent to being retitled *Elements of Political Economy, with Special Reference to the Industrial History of Nations*. This supplanted Carey's three-volume work as the text for the Social Science course. Following Carey and Comte, Thompson viewed political economy as "a subdivision of the science of Sociology ... which itself is a subdivision of the greater science of Anthropology, the science of man." It was a science because it pointed to tangible laws in accordance with which men must live to bring about desired and predictable economic and social effects. There thus existed for society "an economic 'constitution and course of nature;' the nation that complies with its laws attains to material wellbeing or wealth, and the nation that disobeys them inflicts poverty upon itself as a whole, or upon the mass of its people."

[240] Ugo Rabbeno, *The American Commercial Policy: Three Historical Essays*, 2nd ed. (London, 1895), p. 125.

[241] T. E. Cliffe Leslie, "Political Economy in the United States" [1880], in *Essays in Political Economy*, 2nd ed. (London, 1888), p. 145. For biographical summaries of Thompson see *The Barnwell Bulletin*, Vol. 12 (October 1934), and James H. S. Bossard, "Robert Ellis Thompson—Pioneer Professor in Social Science," *American Journal of Sociology* 35 (September 1929).

Man must be studied "in society," not in isolation. "The old lawyers and political philosophers talked of a state of nature, a condition of savage isolation, out of which men emerged by a social contract, through which society was first constituted. But no one else has any news from that country; everywhere men exist in more or less perfectly organized society." Political economy must thus join with the study of history, as well as drawing upon the applied scientific discoveries that have given society the arts of agriculture, dyeing, cooking, and other applications of chemistry, physics, and other sciences. Just as the discovery of chemical and physical laws has improved industrial technology, "so the discovery of the economic laws that govern the advance of society in wealth, has greatly changed for the better the economic methods of the nations." [242]

If true political economy in its social context did not deal with microeconomic man in his desert-island abstraction, neither did it place him in the equally abstract cosmopolitical world context. The real world was divided into nations, a fact that Adam Smith and his followers ignored. "Smith writes as if the world were all under one government, with no boundary lines to restrain the movement of labor and capital,—no inequalities of national civilization and industrial status. ... Sharing in the reaction of the Physiocrats against the excessively political drift of the Mercantile school, he also goes to the other extreme, and gives us, not a science of national or political economy, but of cosmopolitical economy, which is not adapted to the actual historical state of the world, but only to a state of things which has not, nor ever will have, any existence." [243] Smith's cosmopolitanism was completed and systematized by J. B. Say, whose "very first title-page dropped the awkward words 'of nations,' and from this time the abstract conception of wealth, its production, distribution, and consumption, became the themes of what was still called 'political economy.' ... He was the first to announce that commodities are always paid for in commodities, and that therefore to check the amount of imports is to limit in equal measure the power of export." Empirically, however, trade was never in balance: it was associated with gold flows which were not in the nature of commodity transfers and whose monetary effect was just the opposite from that envisioned by free-traders:

> The drain of money away from a country does not make it as some have said—"a good place to buy in but a bad place to sell in,"—just the reverse. It makes it a bad place in which to buy anything but special products of its soil or climate, because although labor is cheap, the commodities produced by labor are dear through its inefficiency. It makes it, therefore,

---

[242] Robert Ellis Thompson, *Elements of Political Economy, with Special Reference to the Industrial History of Nations*, 3rd ed. (Philadelphia, 1882), pp. 12–15.

[243] *Ibid.*, pp. 19f.

a good place for the sale of the merchandise of countries more happily situated. "To him that hath shall be given." Money tends to where money is ... because the presence of great accumulations of capital in England, have made English labor productive to a degree that outweighs all other considerations.

In this respect Thompson harkened back to the arguments of Josiah Tucker and other writers associated with British mercantilism, postulating income- and productivity-divergence mechanisms as characterizing world trade and payments. "Money flows naturally to the places where it is most abundant, just as water tends to run down hill; but as it is often the chief problem in hydraulics to overcome that natural law, so also it is a chief problem of national economy to bring the power of capital to bear upon the less developed and less wealthy districts of the country."[244]

Under the influence of Malthus and Ricardo, political economy had become a study more of the poverty of nations than their wealth. Malthus saw the cause of poverty to lie with man's procreative tendencies, and Ricardo found it to lie in the artificial monopoly of land tenure, not with government policy. Their theories were thus "a godsend to the cosmopolitical school" by distracting public attention from the positive or negative role played by public policy. However, Thompson stressed, the correct approach was not to be found in the writings of the German Historical School, *i.e.*, the "socialists of the chair" (a dig at his fellow Wharton professor, Simon Patten), for these writers were subject to all the errors of the cosmopolitan school.[245]

England owed her industrial and commercial development to her steady pursuit of a nationalist economic policy, *e.g.*, that of mercantilism. Thompson cited Bishop Berkeley as being a forerunner of Carey's school of economics, particularly in his positive ideas about the beneficial effects of monetary inflows stemming from a trade surplus. In the United States, Hamilton, List, and Mathew Carey had sought to develop anew the doctrine of national growth, a doctrine refined by Henry Carey, who first enunciated systematically "the laws of human nature, and of that external nature, in harmony with which man was created."[246]

Thompson began the main body of his book by tracing the evolution of nations as "moral personalities," from the family through the tribe, city and city-state. He then placed this political evolution against the backdrop of man's growing command over nature: first, his relationship with the soil, then the growth of population, society's evolution through different forms of land tenure, the development of industries, the fortunes of labor during this pattern

---

[244] *Ibid.*, pp. 151f., 178.   [245] *Ibid.*, pp. 25f.   [246] *Ibid.*, pp. 275, 29.

of evolution, and the development of commerce and money. In adopting this expository pattern Thompson was closely indebted to E. Peshine Smith, as was Carey himself. He traced how the functions of labor, land and capital were increasingly differentiated as society evolved, just as in the case of animal and vegetable evolution from lower to higher forms.

International trade warped the evolution of these forms, being undesirable on a number of counts not recognized by free-trade theory. First of all, "exchanges are not, as this theory assumes, effected on the basis of labor expended, but on money-price, which is quite another matter. We might be able to produce iron at a far less expenditure of labor in Pennsylvania than in England, and yet not be able to sell it so cheap in the world's markets as England does." Differences in money-cost arose from differences in "the extent and the method of taxation, the cost of capital, the rate of wages, the differences in the purchasing power of money, and the like." Secondly, the orthodox free-trade theory "assumes that the chief end of national as of individual economy is to save labor, whereas the great problem is how to employ it productively. If buying in the cheapest market reduce the amount of employment, it will be for the nation that does it the dearest of all buying. A farmer who spends his idle hours in making a sled might have got one at the factory for the price of wheat that cost him less labour; but he may have been wiser in making than in buying, because these idle hours would otherwise have been wasted." Adopting the passive policy of free trade would not be part of the natural order of things, but would violate the principle of nationality. In practice, the ideal of free trade was "the exchange of the raw materials of some countries for the manufactured productions of others. It is therefore an unfair exchange" in that the main costs of international transport fell on the raw-materials exporter, who also had to bear most of the risks, inasmuch as his prosperity depended "upon a thousand contingencies for his success, of which other producers know nothing."[247]

Finally, Thompson made the point that supporters of free trade throughout the world were generally those who opposed free speech and supported either slavery or ecclesiastical domination, whereas those supporting protectionism tended also to support domestic freedom of speech, thought, and political association. Thus, free-trade was a misnomer, and was in fact associated with slavery in more ways than one: it was a mask for political and social as well as economic oppression, and for entrenchment of an inequitable status quo. True protection would not destroy international commerce but would transform it and make it more equitable.

[247] *Ibid.*, pp. 210–14.

In 1881 the Philadelphia iron manufacturer Joseph Wharton, seeking to found a school that would teach explicitly protectionist doctrines, donated $100,000 to found the Wharton School of Finance and Economics as part of the University of Pennsylvania. (His endowment rose to $500,000 by the time of his death in 1902.) Thompson was named dean of the new school—the country's first business school, soon to be emulated by the Universities of California and Chicago—which opened its doors in 1882. He lectured to the senior class on "Political Economy, American Politics, Money, Credit, International Trade, Monetary Issues, the Stock and Bond Market, Taxation, Relations of Wars and Military Systems to National Industry, Public Debts, Wages, Labor, Strikes, and Lectures on Living Issues—Land, Labor, Socialism and Communism, Free Trade and Protectionism, Popular and Industrial Education." Meanwhile, he maintained his close ties with the University of Pennsylvania proper, continuing to teach its Social Science course, becoming its librarian in 1882 and its chaplain a few years later. In 1883 he resigned his deanship at the Wharton School (but continued his teaching there) to become the University's John Welsh Centennial Professor of History and English Literature. By this time his reputation was spreading. In 1884–85 he took a leave of absence to lecture at Harvard on protectionism (publishing his lectures as a separate book on *Protection to Home Industry*), and during the following academic year lectured at Yale on the same subject.

Meanwhile, basic changes were occurring in the temper of American protectionism. In 1883, shortly after the Wharton School opened, Edmund James was appointed senior professor. James had been trained in Germany along the principles of the historical school, the *Kathedersozialisten* that Thompson had attacked in his textbook. Thompson thought James and the rising post-Carey generation of historical economists leaned dangerously towards socialism. Tension between Thompson and James was aggravated by the latter's appointment of his close friend and fellow student at Halle University, Simon Patten, as professor of economics in 1887. The previous year Thompson had published a disparaging article on "Laveleye and the *Kathedersozialisten*" in the *Penn Monthly*, and was soon to complain directly to Wharton that James, Patten, Ely, and their fellow Americans trained in Germany were obnoxious socialists.[248]

James for his part did not find the views of Carey and his followers sophisticated enough to serve as the basis for graduate economic study, and sought to emulate Johns Hopkins University as an example of the proper study of

---

[248] See Daniel M. Fox, *The Discovery of Abundance: Simon N. Patten and the Transformation of Social Theory* (Ithaca, 1967), pp. 41–42.

historical method. In 1888 he and Patten inaugurated the series of University of Pennsylvania Publications in Political and Social Science modeled after Schmoller's *Jahrbücher* and other publications of the German historical school, and in 1889 he helped found the American Academy of Political and Social Science, elbowing Thompson aside in school affairs, and forcing him out of the school altogether in 1891 in an affair which developed into a public controversy. Apparently the problem was that James and Patten wanted to model the school after the pattern of German universities, "which meant a faculty composed of highly-trained specialists, and an opportunity for students to select the teachers and the courses they preferred, instead of following a curriculum made up largely of prescribed studies. Professor Thompson earnestly insisted that this was a mistaken and impossible theory of education, because the American college was not the counterpart of the German university, but of the German *Gymnasium*, therefore the student entering the American college was not fitted to take up university work as it was understood in Germany. Such a training, he insisted, would not be an education, but specialization."[249] This was an attitude that was becoming rapidly obsolete in the nation's higher education, and at the age of fifty-seven Thompson faced the problem of deciding upon his future career.

In 1891 he had given the Stone Lecture Series at Princeton Theological Seminary on the divine order of human society. These lectures were quite favorably received and the Princeton faculty offered to recommend him for a new professorship of Christian Sociology, but Thompson declined in order to remain in Philadelphia. For a decade he taught at the Wagner Free Institute of Science there, and became a contributor to the *Sunday School Times* and other publications. Then, in 1894, he became president of Philadelphia's Central High School, a post which he held through 1922. In addition to his administrative duties he lectured to the senior class on political economy, and also taught the course on ethics, which he continued to give throughout his twenty-six-year term. During this period he also wrote a history of the American Presbyterian Church, and a number of other books on religious subjects.

Thompson's problems at the Wharton School typified the strains developing between American industrialists and the new "philosophers of protectionism." Like many other followers of Carey, Thompson found himself becoming an advocate for industrialists at a time when American industry had moved far beyond the infant stage to that of trusts. Protectionist writings of the Carey school were becoming more and more conservative. Under Mathew Carey and his contemporaries they had often been pro-labor, supporting charities and the

---

[249] *The Barnwell Bulletin*, Vol. 12 (October 1934), p. 37.

working classes at a time when American industry itself was often a small system led by master mechanics—men such as Rep. William ("Pig-Iron") Kelley and others who had been absent from protectionist ranks before the war—were becoming vested interests in their own right. American consumers were finding that protectionism did not lead to declining prices so long as trusts had their way, protected by high tariff walls.

The new historical school of protectionists, typified by men such as Patten, advocated protectionism and government direction of economic activity on idealistic grounds more akin to the early American protectionists. They viewed industrial profit as a means to elevate the status of society generally, not merely to augment the capital controlled by industrialists personally. This may partially explain why, four years after Thompson was forced out of the University of Pennsylvania, James himself was fired, and Patten later was eased out in 1917 when he supported the retention of the socialist professor Scott Nearing, following his own early opposition to American entry into World War I.

By this time protectionism and economic nationalism had lost most of its idealism and was neither a minority statement nor a sectional issue, but part of the doctrine of an economically victorious nation. Indeed, precisely because of America's world economic supremacy following the War, its industrialists were less and less interested in continuing to attack laissez-faire doctrines. America was beginning to emulate England's espousal of free-trade doctrines, having already succeeded in emulating England's industrial protectionism. Protectionist philosophy had governed American economic policy since the Civil War and had now outlived its usefulness. American economic orthodoxy therefore joined that of Britain in espousing laissez-faire, in fact surpassing Britain in its new cosmopolitanism as a euphemism for commercial and industrial domination.

Van Buren Denslow, Chicago Protectionist

Van Buren Denslow (1834–1902) of Chicago was the last major follower of Henry Carey. His *Economic Philosophy of Society, Government and Industry* (1888) defends Carey, not only as the founder of American economics as a distinct school, but as the first economist to apply Auguste Comte's scientific method to the study of society. This method stood in opposition to that of British laissez-faire economics, which was riddled with *a priori* political and moral preconceptions, and above all with an unwarranted pessimism regarding man's ability to exploit nature.

In 1880 Denslow reviewed the leading social thinkers, praising Comte and Herschel (the astronomer) in particular for their logical methodology. It was Comte, he subsequently stated, who sought to ground the principles of social science—and thus political economy—in the study of man's progressing technology. Comte "regards the sciences as standing in a complete logical order, beginning with mathematics, which involves the fewest elements and the most certainty, and proceeding from thence through astronomy, physics, chemistry and physiology to sociology, which is the last, highest, and most complex of the sciences, involving the most elements and the least certitude. … Mathematics involves only the three elements of expansion, duration and number, or space, time, and quantity … Astronomy adds to these three elements that of motion. Physics supplies all the qualities of matter. Biology adds life. Sociology combines man in society." [250]

Man's social organization was originally dictated mainly by his natural surroundings. The development of civilization enabled him to free himself from the constraints of nature, and to channel its powers increasingly to serve his own needs. As this occurred, the structure of his society and the patterns of trade that developed among regions and nations became less a function of pre-existing qualities and more a function of manmade capital being substituted for the virgin qualities of soil, manual labor, and other pre-existing productive qualities. This historical-materialist approach had permeated American protectionist literature from the outset, and was the counterpart to Marxian analysis in Europe. Denslow, who wrote with a strong pro-industrialist class

---

[250] Van Buren Denslow, *Principles of the Economic Philosophy of Society, Government and Industry* (New York, 1888), pp. 6f.

bias, detested Marx and misrepresented him, but his analysis was nonetheless parallel on many points. "The Political State," he wrote at the outset of his *Economic Philosophy*, "is shown to be the apparel of which the Industrial Life of the People is the wearer." [251] It was the American School's optimism that distinguished it from the Marxian doctrine of class conflict, not its materialist methodology.

This view of society as an evolving form, based ultimately on technological principles, implied that British proponents of laissez-faire were somewhat primitive in their concept of "natural" trade patterns among nations:

> The word nature came into the English language with a religious meaning, as distinguishing what a man is at birth in contrast with what he becomes by grace or divine *(supra-mundane)* influence. From this it passed to mean the constitution which all things have under law, as distinguished from changes they may take on supernaturally. In both these old senses man is a put of nature, and in the first of them nature is the whole of man.
>
> Gradually nature, which at first had meant what man was at birth, (from *natus*, born) came to be used by some as meaning the world exterior to man, to which the root meaning of the word nature, viz., birth, has no application. Whatever there be in man, which obtains command of the forces of exterior nature, must of course be put of man's nature. It is not, therefore, a contest between man and nature, but between nature in man and nature exterior to man. The forces which wealth aids man to control are, perhaps, "the great forces of nature." But the forces, in man, which do the controlling, must be still greater forces in man's nature, or they would not control. [252]

Man and nature were thus not two distinct entities but were intimately associated, in a way which Comte's positivist method could make clear. Savage and poor life necessarily connoted social poverty, stemming from man's inability to tap the forces of nature. "The jurist sees in it a feebler development of law, the theologian regards it as an erroneous manifestation of faith, or debasing consequence of superstition, the moralist recognizes its essential identity and parity with vice and crime as they appear in civilization ... but the economist recognizes all savagery as arising from the utter and complete absence of wealth or capital, and consequent lack of organization of an industrial or working society." Even for the modern man, "stripped of his clothing, the virtue of decency becomes impossible. Take away his bread, and to a starving man, the law even excuses theft, because it knows that nothing else remains." [253] Denslow criticized British economic thinking specifically for its moralistic foundation, which was necessarily arbitrary and time-bound. Indeed, moral impulses might all too easily have disastrous consequences: "It is the very best men that lead in the work of mischief, if mischief it is to be called. The per-

---

[251] *Ibid.*, p. xv.   [252] *Ibid.*, pp. 43f.   [253] *Ibid.*, pp. 47f.

secutions of the Christians by the Roman Emperors, the tendency of dying persons to bequeath their lands and goods to the church, and to overestimate the virtue of charity as compared with industry, led into the middle or dark ages. The exaggerated value which men, during several centuries, attached to the work of bringing the whole world under one religious government—a fanaticism which had its outcome in a sacrifice of industry to monasticism and in a waste of European life and energy upon the crusades—in religious persecutions, and in the prosecution and burning of witches, and the religious wars, all threatened to quench civilization in Europe wholly. There is little doubt that these veritable cyclones of human hate, black with all the destructive possibilities of reviving barbarism, were led on by the very best, purest, and noblest minds, the most spiritual and self-sacrificing, as they were judged at the time, in the world's best circles. There is equally little doubt that it was the substitution of the spirit of gain, of industry, and of business, caused by the revival of trade in Europe under the stimulus of the discovery of the Indies and of America, which rescued the world from the darkness into which it was ever more deeply plunging, by bringing back the thoughts of mankind to their secular and material interests."[254]

So far he remains on familiar ground, with Adam Smith's "Invisible Hand" guiding man to achieve the greatest good through the impulse of his own self-interest. However, whereas the British economists simply stopped here, Denslow was adamant on the need for the state to shape the channels along which man's self-interest would operate, so as to prevent it from being directed in ways adverse to the growth of productive powers. Political economy, he insisted, was not simply a science of sales, it embraced the art of statecraft:

> However political economists may seek to dodge it by their definitions, Political Economy is a criticism upon statesmanship, so long as it continues to be any thing. They may say it is a "science of sales" only, and that there is nothing of a political nature about it; that it has been wrongly named; that it should be called Catallactics, or Plutology, or the like. But to this the statesman may reply: "Why, then, do you bore us with it? We have no time to do more than acquaint ourselves with those sciences and arts which have a bearing upon government. You say yours has not. If your science is that of selling and exchanging, go on with your didactical exposition of swapping and trading. It has no more to do with us than a treatise on weaving or spinning."
>
> In fact the men who define Political Economy as a "science of sales" mean thereby that it is a science which teaches that the right of individuals to make sales is superior to the right of government to affect any manner by legislation the nature or quality of the sales they shall make. ... Hence their definition of Political Economy is annulled by the

---

[254] *Ibid.*, p. 446. Denslow's freemasonry shows through alongside his Comtianism in passages such as these.

quality of the thing they put forth as being Political Economy. ... If it were scientific in its quality, it would not be a science of sales, but a science of the relations which government sustains to sales. This restores the name "Political" to their "Economy."[255]

Asserting that academic economists were deteriorating into "a sect antagonizing the statesmen," he claimed that the essence of statecraft was to regulate trade. Commerce supplied the money necessary to fuel domestic economic life, and established the pricerelationships that determined the relative profitability of occupations, hence the direction which capital investment would take in each country. It was precisely this aspect of matters upon which the British mercantilists once had concentrated, but which contemporary British economists ignored. "Of late political economy has tended [more] to become social economy than international economy. It has been occupied more in studying the relation of classes to each other, such as in England ..."[256] This shift of economic theory towards distribution analysis within a static economy, rather than focusing on the nature and strategy of economic growth among nations, made it all too easy for economists to presume that nations were essentially similar in their economic qualities and objectives. A fundamental concept of Denslow's book was that "nations are collective persons, having each its individuality and its career to pursue ... and hence that any given economic expedient ... must be studied in the light of the antecedent career of the nation adopting it. ... It will obey the inner law of its constitution, be its career long or brief."[257]

International trade was divided into two classes of commodities. First were those in which natural conditions rendered certain commodities truly natural products of a given country, such as the cultivation of tea in China or coffee in Arabia and Brazil. In such cases "protectionists say: 'Off with all duties'— let these articles be free."[258] The second class of international trade was in manufactured goods, in which comparative cost-advantage was acquired historically, through a nation's political policies and social nature rather than through some pre-existing climatic or geological destiny. Nations seeking to develop their industrial capacity must place the political principle of nationhood paramount so as to coordinate the development of their productive powers.

The free-trader Perry had queried in his popular textbook as follows: "The south end of Vermont trades freely and advantageously with its neighbors across the line in Massachusetts; is there any good reason why the north end of Vermont should not trade just as freely and advantageously with its neigh-

---

[255] *Ibid.*, p. xii. This passage is strongly reminiscent of Peshine Smith's *Manual of Political Economy* (New York, 1863), p. 21. Although Denslow's views on soil derived from Peshine Smith by way of Carey, he nowhere cites Smith.
[256] *Ibid.*, p. 65.   [257] *Ibid.*, pp. xiiif. See also pp. 65, 575f.   [258] *Ibid.*, p. 573.

bors across the line in Canada?"[259] There were a number of reasons, replied Denslow, headed by the fact that residents of Vermont paid much higher taxes than Canadians, for the purpose of developing their state and supporting its educational infrastructure. These taxes were necessarily added to the cost of Vermont commodities. Hence a tariff was necessary to equalize these differing tax rates, otherwise Vermont producers would find themselves priced out of the market; their sales and payment of taxes would fall off; and Vermont would be deprived of revenue which could further develop the state. "When a man has married a wife," he drew an analogy, "and becomes the head of a family of his own, the closer relationship which thus binds him to his wife and daughters precludes the dignity and propriety of his receiving services from, and rendering attentions to, the wives and daughters of his neighbors, merely on the ground that, in a single transaction, it might be shown to be cheaper."

Just as the state of Vermont needed to protect its tax base in order to undertake internal improvements, so American labor as a whole required sufficiently high wage rates—and consequently high selling prices for its products—to enable it to educate itself and sustain relatively high living standards. "If the 'diversity' on which a competitor depends for his ability to undersell us, is a disinherited and pauperized proletariat of starved workmen, undergoing eviction from their homes and exile from their country, is it not wiser in the interests of the whole human race to attract these pauperized workmen to the United States, where by one-half the expenditure of effort required in England, he can make as much iron as there, and get for himself a larger proportion of the cost of production as wages?"

A free-trader might nonetheless advocate the exchange of American grain for British steel on the ground that a given amount of labor employed in grain-growing would procure more steel for the country than could be got from trying to produce this steel within the United States itself. Underlying this free-trade attitude, however, was the bland Ricardian assumption of perpetual trade and payments equilibrium, and full employment and occupational mobility of labor. Again Denslow quotes Perry's popular textbook, which asserted that "foreign articles are certainly wrought by foreign labor; do we then by buying them employ foreign labor to the prejudice of our own laborers? We are obliged to pay for every thing we buy—are we not? In what do we pay? Clearly, in the products of our own labor. We employ our own laborers to produce the articles

[259] *Ibid.*, p. 574, quoting the 11th edition of Perry's *Elements of Political Economy*, p. 386. Denslow comments that, "as the Canadians and Vermonters both produce the same crops, they could have no motive to sell to each other: and hence, that the goods which would in fact cross the line would be English manufactures … seeking to undermine the American manufacturers in New Hampshire, Massachusetts, and Connecticut."

we exchange for foreign articles. We pay for our imports by our exports. Our exports are created by home labor … A commercial nation therefore not only does not, but it cannot, employ foreign labor. The more it buys of foreigners, the more home labor it must employ to create the articles with which it pays for what it buys," etc., etc.[260]

There were many fallacies in this statement. An economist today would point out that it assumed a 100 per cent marginal propensity to import (and on a bilateral basis, at that) on the part of foreign producers of the manufactured goods bought by the United States. It also equated the balance of trade with the entire balance of payments, and assumed equal ratios of labor to the total value of the commodities traded. Denslow pointed out Adam Smith's famous assertion that domestic demand set in motion two capitals—that of the producers of each of the commodities traded—whereas foreign trade replaced only one domestic capital. Most important of all he pointed out that if Perry's statement were true there would be no trade deficits, and hence no commercial crises, whereas in practice commercial crises were triggered by international payments. In the crisis of 1825, for instance, "the failure of returns from the foreign investments came first. Then a contraction of its accommodations by the bank of England. Then failure, in December, 1825, of about sixty country banks, besides several leading banks of London. Then long lists of factories closed, riots by discharged weavers, who in one day destroyed every power loom in Blackbourn or within six miles of it."[261] England experienced a similar crisis following repeal of its Corn Laws. Thus, concluded Denslow:

> Major Premise.—The free importation from abroad, of products which a country has the natural facilities for producing, or has produced or can conveniently produce, does not cheapen permanently or substantially the supply of the product, but displaces the domestic by the foreign product, thus tending toward a disruption of domestic industries, a drain of gold, a run on the banks, and a financial crisis.
>
> Minor Premise.—England attempted, in 1846, to get cheap breadstuffs by withdrawing protective duties from her farmers and accepting free importation from abroad, and in so doing she got no cheaper breadstuffs and no more of them, but caused a cessation in her domestic production, exactly equal to her importation, thus resulting in a disruption of her industries, a drain of gold, a run on the banks, and a commercial crisis.
>
> Conclusion, among distant economists, that the repeal of the corn laws caused the crisis of 1847.
>
> Conclusion, among English economists, that the crisis of 1847 was due to causes unknown.[262]

---

[260] *Ibid.*, p. 572, quoting Perry, *op. cit.*, pp. 396f.
[261] *Ibid.*, pp. 394, 392. See also p. 383.
[262] *Ibid.*, p. 376.

The three-cornered character of the world's international trade, Denslow continued, rendered obsolete the concept of bilateral reciprocity which underlay the two-country, two-commodity model used by free traders for didactic purposes.[263] Furthermore, American exports were bulky, and American farmers had to bear the cost of transporting them to foreign markets. Americans also had to pay the return transport costs on British manufactures, produced by labor fed with American grains. Would it not be easier to support this population at home, he asked? The market would then be brought closer to the domestic farmer, affording him a greater demand for his products at higher net prices.[264]

Finally, Denslow sought to controvert the thesis that, whereas free trade worked to integrate the world into a peaceful whole, protection was associated with nationalism and militarism. "Ten thousand Englishmen were slaughtered in 1884 in the Soudan as part of this [free-trade] programme," Denslow observed. "England has had her nose in every quarrel on the face of the earth. She is not wholly out of war one month in twenty-five … Free-trade in men and in commodities was the war-cry of our Southern Rebellion … The whole origin of our late costly war was economic error, and every fibre of its economic errors is gathered up and woven into the detestable shibboleth of England's American implements and tools—'Free Foreign Trade.' While the free trade argument has been identified with disintegration and disunion from the first, the desire to secure a national revenue through a protective tariff was the motive which welded the feebly united States of the Confederation into the present national Union." Protectionism "says to each nation, 'mind your own business.' It teaches that the best conquest it can make over its rivals is to absorb their pursuits, their arts, their populations, and their power, by active invention and peaceful immigration."[265]

Britain's bankers and traders announced to all foreign countries: "Buy where you can buy cheapest, *i.e.*, of me, or I'll conquer you." This, he concluded, "may be called for sweetness and purity's sake, free trade, but it is the protection of foreign trade by military force."[266]

Denslow followed Carey closely in describing the principles of production upon which his trade and development theory rested. In particular he followed Carey in denouncing the Ricardian doctrine of rent and Malthusian population theory. Soil had no original and indestructible powers of fertility as claimed by Ricardo. "Soil in England which once produced five bushels of wheat per acre now produce fifty-five. Some in India which once produced thirty bushels produce but seven."[267] A major cause of declining fertility was

[263] *Ibid.*, p. 600.   [264] *Ibid.*, pp. 321, 579.   [265] *Ibid.*, p. 628.
[266] *Ibid.*, pp. 316f.   [267] *Ibid.*, p. 241.

the decision by a region to specialize in producing a narrow range of export commodities. Thus no nation could be "naturally" suited to produce any single agricultural commodity:

> The wastefulness of the chief part of Southern agriculture, deserted houses standing in the midst of exhausted plantations, which were once fertile, were formerly attributed to slavery. Both it and slavery were in harmony with the waste consisting in the export of the soil in the form of cotton, molasses, and tobacco. This, by keeping the country constantly burdened by an increasing poverty and debt, made the enslavement of the laborer seem a consequent necessity, since the work was too hard and the net returns too small to enable the planter voluntarily to pay wages. He was generally eighteen months in debt for the means to feed and clothe his family and servants, and had often hardly more purchased luxuries than many mechanics at the North earning three dollars a day.[268]

The North was also wasteful in its practice of mining the soil and then abandoning it to move on to new virgin lands. The soil's fertility could be maintained only by proper croprotation, which required a diversity of home markets. The more uses to which a plot of land could be put, the greater its value would be. This led to the usual Home Market argument that the greater the diversification of American industry, the higher would be the value of its farmlands.

Denslow had earlier endorsed Carey's view of rent as payment for space, not fertility. He identified rent "with that principle of human nature which would cause a window on Broadway to rent perchance for $5.00 an hour while a pageant is passing. It is a payment for space, which is competed for actively by reason of its nearness to the societary movement. If poor land has this advantage it will be so tilled as to make it fertile. Rich land, without it, will be drained of its fertility. As MacLeod well says, 'the only original and indestructible power the earth has is that of extent.' Fertility is as variable a property in soils as health is in man."[269] Both increased over time.

British doctrine also rested on faulty doctrines of population and labor. Carey had pointed out in the 1830s, Denslow described, that "the lower the organization, whether vegetable, animal, or social, the greater the rapidity, certainty, frequency, and fecundity of its power of reproduction."[270]

Thus, as man's society grew in complexity and in productive powers, its rate of population growth tended to decline. Meanwhile, in response to the new discoveries in agronomy, wheat yields were increasing rapidly in terms of grains of wheat per ear and number of ears per stool. Industrial productivity was increasing even more rapidly, largely in response to the extension of steam power and mechanization. Thus, instead of man's population outrunning his

---

[268] *Ibid.*, p. 253.
[269] "American Economics," *North American Review* 139 (July 1884), p. 22.
[270] *Ibid.*, p. 14.

capacity to produce, the facts were just the reverse. The result was a steady growth in man's living standards.

Carey had shown, Denslow continued, how machinery supplants muscle, coal displaces wood and steam supercedes sails, so that the product of industry increases much more rapidly than the number of laborers. The starting point for economic analysis was thus man's pattern of economic development, not distribution of a fixed product. Carey's "definitions are laws of motion, not equations between commodities," Denslow concluded.[271] These laws led to differential rent occurring not primarily in agriculture as Ricardo had believed, but in industry, even though it did indeed tend to ensue from the forces of nature tapped by man:

> The first man to invent a wind-mill got, as profits, the whole difference between the cost of grinding the corn by the power previously in use, and the cost of grinding it by wind power. It was only as wind-mills were multiplied that his profits were reduced to the ordinary rates of interest on the capital invested in the mill. The gratuitousness of new natural agents is a gratuitous fallacy. The first rates of transportation by steam were graduated on those by sail. So far as steam was cheaper the engine owner made a profit. … Capital employed in using natural agents for the first time, does not at once, and while it has a monopoly, come down for its profits to current rates of interest on capital.[272]

It followed that economic rent in international trade accrued not so much to the agricultural exporters but to the industrial nations. Hence America's interest in protecting the growth of its domestic industry.

Why, Denslow asked, should man be presumed to multiply geometrically and his source of food only arithmetically? If man were viewed in his capacity of being food for other animals, would mankind appear to them to be multiplying only arithmetically while they multiplied geometrically? The truth was more that "the fruitfulness of the lower animals is as much greater than that of man, as that of plants is greater than that of the lower animals."[273] In civilized society, he quoted McCulloch as admitting, "it is only among the inferior ranks of the people that the scantiness of subsistence can set limits to the further multiplication of the human species …" The fallacies in Malthusian doctrine, Denslow elaborated, were "(1) that it is only in the savage state that the food fund, which sustains man, is supplied by nature. (2) The poor always multiply faster than the rich … Families continuously rich soon become extinct. (3) As every species of animal, including man, constitutes a part of the subsistence of other animals, the faster they all multiply, the more means of subsistence there must be. Man, by cultivating crops, grains, and grasses for the food ani-

---

[271] *Ibid.*, p. 15, citing Henry Carey, *Principles of Political Economy* (Philadelphia, 1838–40), Vol. II, p. 251.
[272] *Principles of Economic Philosophy* …, p. 289.   [273] *Ibid.*, p. 232.

mals, increases immeasurably the means of subsistence of horses, asses, mules, horned cattle, including milch cows, sheep, goats, turkeys, geese, chickens, hogs, hares, and all domesticated animals, and of many wild ones. He thus makes the excess of the activity of the procreative power, in the lower grades of life over that of man, a guarantee of the far more rapid increase in human food than man himself can possibly effect in his own numbers."[274] An increase in man's numbers viewed as consumers was simultaneously a gain in the number of producers, under conditions of increasing returns.

Controversion of the Malthusian theory of population that man's first response to higher incomes was to increase his family size—led to an anti-classical wage doctrine. Denslow essentially held a marginal productivity theory of wage rates, and endorsed Cairnes' statement that "Capitalists and laborers receive large remuneration in America because their industry produces largely."[275] It was thus the normal condition for profits and wages to increase together, in contrast to the Ricardian belief that profits and wages could only move inversely.

> The introduction of labor-saving machinery has some tendency to enhance wages, in the fact that the employer of the machinery makes at first as a profit the whole difference between the cost of performing the work by the old and by the new process, which rate of profit is only gradually reduced as other capital compete in the performance of the mine work by the new machinery. ... wherever extraordinary rates of profit are being made, there capital will forego a part of its profits in the form of increased wages, in order to increase its output rapidly and to 'make hay while the sun shines.' As the successful working on new forms of machinery nearly always involves some degree of skill, it is often better economy to enlarge the wages of those who have some degree of skill than to take on new and unskilled hands. Probably every labor-saving invention has witnessed the increase of wages to labor ... during the interval in which the former selling price of the commodity had not yet fallen to the new cost of production.[276]

Although Denslow asserted that capital in its capacity as an employer of labor would have to maintain its control over labor in order for the production process to expand at its maximum power, he claimed that physical capital had now become a laborer of sorts: "by far the largest portion of the world's work is now done by capital, not in its employing capacity, but in its capacity as a physical toiler and a displacer of human toil. Capital, in the form of engines, boilers, tracks, and other rolling stock, draws all crops to market in Western nations, leaving men to carry them on their backs only in China and parts of India. ... Almost all of what is called skilled labor now consists in the wages-worker acting as tender, feeder, or regulator to the working machine. Hence

---

[274] *Ibid.*, pp. 295f.
[275] *Ibid.*, p. 294, citing J. E. Cairnes, *Some Leading Principles of Political Economy newly Expounded* (London, 1874), p. 462.
[276] *Ibid.*, p. 299.

old-time positions are reversed. Once labor toiled physically and capital superintended. Now, in the main, capital performs the physical toil and labor superintends the machine while it does the work."[277] Capital was thus an emancipator, its greatest service for man consisting "in having abolished forcible slavery, as the means of organizing labor, and substituted for the lash the stipulated wage in money."[278]

All this implied an economy-of-high-wages doctrine such as had been held by sophisticated protectionists prior to 1860. But Denslow was confused on this point, perhaps because he was over-attentive to the immediate propaganda value of wage theory as it bore upon the tariff debate. On the one hand he stated: "If capital and labor can earn in conjunction about twice as much here as in England, because of the greater general productiveness of industry, they will have twice as much product to divide, both will get twice as much—the one in wages and the other in interest." This implied that American labor needed little protection from European producers. Denslow therefore hastened to add: "Assuming that the rates of wages in certain industries are only 21.89 per cent higher here than in England, that would render a tariff of 21.89 per cent on the importation of the product of that labor from England, necessary in order to place the producers of the same product here in a position to compete on equal terms with those in England. How much more shall we allow for difference in rates of interest on capital, and for our more burdensome taxation to pay off the public debt?"[279] On the one hand he claimed that "the skill, greater ingenuity, intelligence, and progressive capacity of American workmen are due to their higher average wage indirectly. ... while English workmen are skillful, expert, and useful, in a more automatic way, their inventive faculties since 1846 are relatively latent. What they formerly, under more favorable circumstances, contributed to improvements in machinery and fabrics, is largely lost of late to the avocations in which they have been trained."[280] Still, Americans needed tariff protection, on the tenuous assumption that both it and foreign countries had "like natural facilities of production" and "made equal use of machine power in production."[281] Under these conditions, and assuming equal labor productivity and zero transport costs, "it is obvious that wages of labor expressed in money in all countries would be equalized, those having the lowest rates being raised, and those having the highest depressed, until one common level would be obtained." He held forth the bogey of American wages becoming equal to those of India, although of course the conditions of production differed vastly between the two countries.

---

[277] *Ibid.*, p. 208. [278] *Ibid.*, p. 212. [279] *Ibid.*, p. 580.
[280] *Ibid.*, p. 597. [281] *Ibid.*, p. 595.

"If all the people in the United States could be induced to raise corn," Denslow pointed out, "corn would, of course, fall in price to, say, a cent a bushel, or almost nothing. The expenditure of effort required from each corn producer to raise it, would average four or five times as much as it now does, because we raise corn only under the most favorable conditions." [282] A free-trader would answer that this development would shift U.S. comparative advantage back to more industrial pursuits. However, Denslow pointed out, American industrial capital would have been extinguished in the interim, so that the start-up costs of re-establishing industrial production would add to America's relative industrial production costs.

More interesting was his observation on the nature of female participation in the labor force. Because many married women sought employment, and were thus not the sole means of support for their family, they were willing and able to work for less than a living wage:

> Women offer themselves in a limited number of occupations, rejecting usually the coarse, vulgar, enterprising, arduous, and dangerous. In clinging to occupations which are deemed becoming to woman as a sex, they come chiefly into competition with those women who, as members of a household can, if necessary, perform the same work, in a manner which has the effect of gratuitous competition …
> … the 360,381 women in New York, who offer to toil for hire, really offer to compete with and underbid the 1,670,988 women, or many of them, who ask no wages, and in a pinch do the same things without pay, which the toilers are trying to earn pay for doing. In domestic service, the competition is not so much between one cook and another, as a choice, by the matron of the house, whether she will hire a cook or do it herself, Hence nearly every woman works against an unpaid competitor. [283]

Perhaps the best epitaph for Denslow's work is that which he wrote with regard to Carey. The latter, he said, "supplied Bastiat with all the materials of his 'Harmonies Economiques,' except that pleasing style which is more apt to belong to the borrower than the inventor. Carey was inductive, Bastiat reductive. … Carey was profound and original, but discursive; he was a traveler with a long stride, who had the devil's own habit of constantly taking you up to the pinnacle of the temple or the top of the high mountain, and then showing you all the kingdoms of earth, as illustrations of his law." [284] Denslow was also discursive, and his book was more an example of philosophizing than an integral philosophy. He often had his eye more on the political expediency of economic doctrine than on its internal consistency, as evidenced by his wavering over wage and productivity theory. Still, his book was influential in its time as a popular updating of Carey's theories.

---

[282] *Ibid.*, p. 595. [283] *Ibid.*, pp. 325–27.
[284] "American Economists," *op. cit.*, p. 15.

Major Economic Writings of Van Buren Denslow

1. *Fremont and McClellan, Their Political and Military Careers reviewed* (Yonkers, New York, 1862).
2. *A Plea for the Introduction of Responsible Government and the Representation of Capital into the United States as safeguards against Communism and Disunion* (Springfield, Ill., 1879).
3. *Modern Thinkers principally upon Social Science: What they Think and Why ... with an introduction by Robert G. Ingersoll* (Chicago, 1880). (2nd ed.: Chicago, 1882; 3rd ed.: Chicago, 1884)
3a. *Wealth* (Chicago: 1882). (Excerpts from the above work.)
4. "Freedom in Trade. A Lecture delivered before the Philosophical Society of Chicago, Ill., April 8, 1882," reprinted from the *Bulletin of the National Association of Wool Manufacturers* (Cambridge, 1882).
5. "The Logic of Protection ... being the substance of a lecture delivered January 10, 1883 before the Revenue Reform Club of Brooklyn, New York."
6. "American Economics," *North American Review* 139 (July 1884).
7. *Thomas A. Edison and Samuel F.B. Morse* (with Jane Marsh Parker). (London, 1887).
8. *Principles of the Economic Philosophy of Society, Government and Industry* (New York, 1888).

Non-Economic Works

1. *Manhatta; a legend of the Hudson* (New York, 1856). (Poetry)
2. *Owned and Disowned; or, The chattel child. A tale of Southern Life* (New York, 1857) (2nd ed., 1860).
3. *The Pyramid of Giseh. The Relation of Ancient Egyptian Civilization to the Hebrew Narrative in Genesis and Exodus, and the relative claim of Moses and the pyramid to inspiration considered* (New York, 188-).
4. *The 'Why I Am's'* (New York, 1890).

DAVID RICE, PROTECTIONIST PUBLICIST

David Rice followed Carey's school of American protectionists in seeking to win the country's farmers and laborers to the cause of protectionism and, at an extreme, isolationism. His *Protectionist Philosophy* was published in 1890 to defend the McKinley Tariff against the Democratic Party's free-trade policies as embodied in the Mills Tariff bill of 1888. All governments, he asserted, required some source of revenue for their operation. Historically, these revenues had taken the form of tariffs and excise taxes: the government of Great Britain, the bastion of free-trade doctrine, was collecting over $100 million each year in customs duties. The tariff debate thus turned actually on the issue of what kind of tariffs nations should have.

Because free-trade tariffs sought to leave existing production patterns and cost-ratios unchanged among nations, they were levied on articles which the nation did not "and cannot produce," such as tropical agricultural commodities and certain raw materials. Rice advocated that tariffs be placed on industrial commodities, whose production they would stimulate under conditions of declining cost over time in the United States. The aim of protective tariffs was thus to transform the international division of labor and production, leading the nation to maximize its productive powers and to secure within its own borders the world's highest-productivity industries. Citing the fact that the price of nails in the United States had declined some 72 per cent between 1865 and 1889, as had the prices of other articles protected by rising import duties, he concluded that tariffs should be levied only "upon such commodities (besides mere luxuries) as we are capable of producing in economy and quantity to regulate prices in the home market." [285]

Domestic production costs, Rice declared, could be minimized only by guaranteeing adequate returns and continuous production for a steady home market. "Modern production must be at wholesale and conducted by vast capital, a perfectly organized and managed plant, and with a skilled corps of workmen, to be economical, but it must be more than this. *It must be substantially continuous and to the full capacity of the establishment.* It is only thus, that the vast modern development of steam and machinery can be economically utilized." The ensuing economy of production would "far exceed the petty

---

[285] David Rice, *Protectionist Philosophy* (New York, 1890), pp. 5, 177f., 85, 32, 15.

199

savings of free-trade tariff methods, in crude materials and inferior wages. ... Large capital commands cheap credit, of which, under stress of domestic competition, the consumer gets the benefit." Protective tariffs would not, like free-trade tariffs, add to the final selling price of commodities over time, but would lead to falling prices so long as industrial capital remained competitive. [286]

Bastiat's "Petition of the Candle-Makers to Shut out the Sunlight" misrepresented the protectionists. Because there was no way that candles could furnish light less expensively than the sun, they would not qualify for protective tariffs. The example was a crude parody tilting at wooden men. The function of protectionism, according to Rice, was not to achieve absolute isolation from foreign commodities at any price, but rather to assemble "vast instruments of capital in great manufacturing establishments, and thus [to] cheapen production, by insuring to domestic competition a home market, certain and increasing." [287] A free-trader would have said that any tariff which sought to transform world production patterns would deny to the protected economy the Ricardian gains from trade. This might be so at an instant of time, Rice replied, but it was not so over time: domestic industry followed a learning curve and steadily increased its productive powers behind protective tariff walls. He chided free-traders for assuming that all commodities are made only by the current expenditure of labor, neglecting the economics of capital-intensive production. "Free-trade tariff reform insists upon the tacit assumption that capital and industry are in the position of one hundred years ago, when the aggregation of the single workman with his kit of tools for capital was the all-sufficient factor for industrial production." This logic, he analyzed

> ... might all be true if men made cloth in the same way that men did in New York one hundred years ago, but how is it under modern conditions? It requires an investment of one hundred to five hundred thousand dollars in the mill and equipments, let us say, before the first yard of cloth can be made cheap enough to afford to sell it for the price of one bushel of wheat. Every manufacturer knows that it requires a certain size of mill and equipment to make cloth cheaply, and that a mill costing less cannot make it. But even the building of this expensive mill and equipping it in the best manner will not produce the cloth. It will require, let us say, from three to five hundred skilled hands to run this expensive mill. Now this skill is a matter of education. It takes time ... Is it then true, as [Sumner] says, that "as soon as there was unemployed labor and capital" in New York "some one" would make the cloth?
>
> It is perfectly evident, therefore, that if a million of men were out of employment in New York, "some one" would not make the cloth "as soon as" they were unemployed ... even if the capital were provided, simply because that labor was utterly useless for making cloth.[288]

[286] *Ibid.*, pp. 66, 73,189, 215, 175.   [287] *Ibid.*, p. 188.
[288] *Ibid.*, pp. 95, 96.

Cloth-making capital required a higher rate of return "because the commercial risk of making cloth under modern conditions is far greater than that of raising the bushel of wheat." This contradicted the usual protectionist statement that the world's raw-materials exporters were subject to much greater risks from weather and other factors than were industrial producers.

By thus emphasizing the distinct role of capital in production, Rice emphasized the fact that national planning and protectionism should not look merely at the costs of producing isolated commodities, but at the production and distribution process as a whole. American railroads might be built with tariff-protected steel rails, but they nonetheless had lower transport rates than English railroads. It was even possible that wool, yarn, and cloth each cost more to produce in the United States as individual commodities, yet "when the cloth and buttons and thread were formed into the ready-made garment, that was cheaper in the one than in the other country, under some part of the economic system of manufacture possible there, and not possible in the other nation."[289] A free-trader might reply that America should therefore purchase the textile materials abroad and concentrate on the final production stage. But this would require an international transport and distribution apparatus as an intermediary, an apparatus which was not only intrinsically wasteful, but was the precondition for foreign cartels to control the sales-price of commodities in the American market. Production prices, Rice insisted, are always to be distinguished from final sales prices by the amount taken by distributors, middlemen, and speculators. A major aim of protectionism was to cut out the middleman and speculator wherever possible, thereby lowering distribution costs and breaking the power of foreign cartels to monopolize the actual gains-from-trade.

Rice stated that free trade, not protectionism, fostered the trusts that by the 1890s had become so hated in the United States. Trusts, he analyzed, required two conditions:

> The chief and most indispensable of these conditions is, that the commodity shall be capable of being concentrated in a few hands, comparatively, either in its production or at some stage of transportation on its way to the ultimate consumer. The second condition is that it shall pass through few channels of transportation, to reach its market with the ultimate consumer. This condition may be found … to be antecedent to the first one named, since the concentration of the commodity into these few channels of transportation would appear to facilitate, if not to give its temporary control into the hands of the few.[290]

Sugar and oil represented prime examples of commodities subject to control by trusts, given their need for transport and refining. Sugar, "is brought into a very few of our seaports, and a few huge refineries employing vast capital can

---

[289] *Ibid.*, pp. 191, 104, 16.　　　　　[290] *Ibid.*, p. 150.

handle it for the whole country, for raw sugar must go through the refinery to prepare it for use, when below a certain standard." If it were produced on every plantation there could be no trust, just as there could be no grain trust. "The sugar trust only becomes possible when sugar is gathered and poured through the narrow conduits of a few refineries."

By these criteria, international trade was highly susceptible to trust-building: "the development of modern steam ocean commerce is largely responsible for the sugar trust, and, in fact, all others in either the importing or exporting nation, and for this reason: Modern steam commerce on the ocean concentrates trade, by its economy, in a few great seaports to both the exporting and importing nation. To conduct it with the maximum economy requires larger and larger steamships, sailing from only a few ports, at which goods are assembled, to only a few ports from which they are distributed. This concentrates trade into a few narrow channels."

Precisely because international trade favored distribution trusts and associated international cartels, it was a fallacy to believe "that we can determine the price at which we would be able to purchase any given commodity in foreign markets ... *if our tariff were removed*, by consulting the quoted foreign market price, while the tariff is in force and while home manufacturers supply the bulk of our wants.

Not only would foreign exporters be tempted to raise their prices—as Brazil's coffee trust had done when the United States cancelled its tariff on imported coffee—but "the removal of our tariff and the opening to foreigners of our immense domestic market for iron and steel, [for instance], would at once relieve the foreign market of the comparatively small surplus, which produces the glut, and send up the foreign price ..."[291]

Like other protectionists, Rice was especially mindful of the farmers' interest in the tariff. Under free trade the United States would remain an agricultural exporter, thereby removing from the soil the phosphorus, nitrates and other fertilizing elements that were contained in the crops. Justus Liebig had used these arguments against international trade in agricultural commodities a half-century earlier, and his reasoning had become a staple of protectionist doctrine via Daniel Lee in the U.S. Patent Office, E. Peshine Smith, Henry Carey and Simon Patten. Rice accused free-trade advocates of advising the farmer "to exhaust his soil by continually cropping it with the same cereal crops, wheat and corn, instead of diversifying his crops and recuperating his soil; wheat and corn being the only important crops salable in foreign markets. The exhaustion of the soil is a permanent national loss, as well as an immediate

[291] *Ibid.*, pp. 204f.. See also pp. 152f..

one to the farmer."[292] By contrast, diversification of employments in a given area tended to increase the value of lands, by enabling farmers to grow fruits, vegetables, and other perishable crops for local urban consumption. Under industrial protectionism farmers would no longer be obliged to sell their wheat in glutted foreign markets, but secure a more remunerative home market.

In emphasizing this latter point Rice stood firmly in the anti-imperialist center of American protectionism. He claimed that foreign markets were intrinsically unable to consume exports in keeping with America's capacity to produce. Free traders "have pointed to the millions of unclothed savages of Africa, not one in a thousand of whom has exchangeable property enough to buy even the collar of a cotton shirt, and said, 'Behold the millions waiting for the product of our factories and furnaces; behold the vast world's markets open to you.'" The truth was that Americans consumed 28 per cent of the world's sugar, 30 per cent of its coffee, 37 per cent of its iron, 33 per cent of its steel, 30 per cent of its copper, 33 per cent of its lead, 25 per cent of its cotton, 33 per cent of its wool, 33 per cent of its india rubber, and over 50 per cent of its tin and 40 per cent of its coal.[293] "In fact," Rice concluded, "it is very easy to glut the foreign market with a slight excess of food supplies over the demand, so as to make the larger crop of much less value than the smaller one. ... Therefore, when the free-trade tariff advocate says to the American farmer, 'raise more grain and sell more in Europe,' he really advises the farmer to glut that market so as to get less aggregate money for the larger amount of grain he raises ..."

This point has been made by many protectionists in the 1820s. A free-trader might reply that, if such glutting occurred, the comparative-cost curves would shift so as to adjust the pattern of American production to the new level of world prices. But, Rice argued, it would cost American producers much more to return to industrial production, once having departed from it, because of (1) the destruction of pre-existing capital caused by the free-trade interlude and its associated industrial recession, (2) the higher profit rates required by industry following a highly risky period of investment and failure, and (3) the greater economies and scale of production that would have been secured by British and other foreign industrial producers during America's free-trade interim, enabling them to export their manufacturers at low prices and thus stifle the reestablishment of American industrial production.

---

[292] *Ibid.*, p. 117.
[293] *Ibid.*, p. 124, citing figures from *The American Economist*, September 12, 1890. Rice also cites David Wells' articles in the *Princeton Review* for May and July 1883 indicating that American agricultural and industrial producers must both depend mainly on growth of the home market.

In fact, other nations had already began to compete with England by enacting protective tariffs: "Austria, 1877 and 1879; Russia, 1877 and 1881; Germany, in 1879; France, in 1882; Spain, in 1877 and 1882; Greece, in 1885; and Switzerland, in 1885. Sweden and Norway followed suit in 1887–8." Furthermore, "we can hold no monopoly of our labor-saving inventions as against other nations when we have once made them public, and most of them reduce the diversity of human skill required for the manual operations in production, which they supplant."[294]

Neither Rice nor most other protectionists faced head-on the problem of industrial trusts. They claimed that free trade favored special interests such as international shippers, railroads, speculators, cartels, and various other classes of middlemen, and enabled trusts to develop in the sugar, petroleum, and related industries, but they simply ignored the fact that protectionism had nurtured an iron and steel trust and other industrial monopolies that became objects of the Sherman Anti-Trust Act of 1896. In fact, by 1890 it seemed as if protectionists were talking about one set of economic problems and free-traders about another. Each scored points, each fell into error resulting from their narrow self-interest, but for better or worse it was the protectionist philosophy and its associated isolationism that dominated the course of American foreign relations until the 1930s.

---

[294] *Ibid.*, pp. 209f., 39, 217. See also pp. 133–35, 219.

VI. Some Opponents of the Protectionists

FRANCIS LIEBER, CONSERVATIVE EDUCATOR

Francis Lieber (1800–72) was a German immigrant to the United States who achieved renown as an educator. Born in Berlin, he was a member of the Prussian army at Waterloo. Shortly after returning to Germany he was arrested for "liberalism" and imprisoned for several months. He took part in the Greek Revolution, and after a somewhat itinerant career as a tutor in various European cities he emigrated to America in 1827.

Settling in Boston, he gained employment editing the *Encyclopedia Americana* (13 volumes, 1829–33), largely a translation of a popular German encyclopedia of the day, to which Lieber added many articles of his own. In 1832 the trustees of Girard College invited him to organize an educational system, a project which led to his being offered the chair of history and political economy at the University of South Carolina. In this post he succeeded another immigrant, Thomas Cooper, whom he emulated by moving rapidly towards conservatism, especially in the case of his mild views on slavery. He held his university post for over two decades (1835–56), using J. B. Say's *Treatise on Political Economy* as his text. He opposed the South's movement towards secession, however, warning against this break as early as 1850. These sympathies led him to move north to Columbia College in 1856, teaching political science (1856–65) and ending his career as professor of political science at the Columbia Law School (1860–72). He was an active supporter of the Union cause in the Civil War, and in 1863 founded the Loyal Publication Society which published essays by Elder and other protectionists whose views he subsequently attacked.

Lieber's early impressions of the United States are contained in his book *The Stranger in America* (1835). In 1838 he wrote a *Manual of Political Ethics* which defended individual and corporate property, hence laissez-faire, and which was used as a text-book at Harvard. Other publications include *The Laws of Property: Essays on Property and Labor* (1841), and *Civil Liberty and Self-Government* (1852), which was reissued in a new edition in 1874 and used as a text at Yale.

WILLIAM GRAHAM SUMNER, SOCIAL SPENCERIAN

It is somewhat ironic that the free-trade enthusiast William Graham Sumner (1840–1910) was born in Paterson, New Jersey. The town owed its commercial prominence to the fact that in response to Alexander Hamilton's insistence that America achieve industrial independence from England, The Society for the Establishment of Useful Manufactures in 1791 established a nascent industrial center in Paterson replete with cotton mills, paper mills, and iron works. Understandably, the town attracted many Lancashire immigrants, including both of Sumner's parents.

Sumner's father and mother were apparently quite determined individualists: his father, who arrived in Paterson in the midst of the 1836 depression, so strongly opposed the custom of "store pay" (by which workers were paid in the form of credit at the company store) that he sought his fortune traveling with his newly-formed and growing family through New York, Pennsylvania, Ohio, and then back to New Jersey before finally settling down in Hartford, Connecticut, to work repairing locomotive wheels at the railroad shops of the Hartford and New Haven Railroad. It was in Hartford that Sumner attended public schools, and after delaying his high-school education for two years to work in a store, he entered Yale in 1859. Upon graduating near the top of his class, he borrowed funds from the older brother of one of his classmates to pursue a European theological education in Geneva, Göttingen and Oxford. He also borrowed funds to purchase exemption from the army draft (an exemption which then could be purchased legally by paying someone else to substitute in place of the draftee).

Another classmate induced Yale to offer Sumner a tutorship in 1866. This was at a time when tutors served as teaching assistants (generally theology students), responsible for about half the classes at Yale. There were from five to eight tutors, among whom Sumner distinguished himself by his interesting classes. He began to develop relatively progressive teaching attitudes, opposing Yale's practice of learning by rote from textbooks, as well as its overemphasis on the classics. Still, he viewed his tutorship only as an interim means of supporting himself until he could resume his theological career, and in 1869, after teaching three years, he was ordained as an Episcopalian minister. He served as assistant rector of Calvary Church in New York, and then for two years as rector of an Episcopal church in Morristown, New Jersey.

But he found his interest continually returning to political and social topics, and in 1872 he withdrew from preaching to return to Yale as the college's first professor of Political and Social Science. The newly created chair reflected the influence of Comte, Carey and others eager to press scientific methodology into the analysis of social and economic relationships. However, whereas the doctrines of Comte and Carey were associated with materialism, Sumner's religious tendencies made him seek the unifying force of society in its mores, that is, in a kind of anthropology which he called "societology" in order to distinguish his views from Comte's sociology.

Sumner soon became Yale's most popular professor and remained at the college until 1909. During his thirty-seven years at Yale he published and lectured widely. Indeed, the historian Richard Hofstadter has called Sumner "the most vigorous and influential social Darwinist in America. ... Sumner's synthesis brought together three great traditions of western capitalist culture: the Protestant ethic, the doctrine of classical economics, and Darwinian natural selection. ... he was a great Puritan preacher, an exponent of the classical pessimism of Ricardo and Malthus, and an assimilator and popularizer of evolution."[295]

These attitudes led Rev. Sumner to espouse free trade with a passion. But unlike earlier free traders, who based their views on the Ricardian theory of comparative costs and the gains from trade, Sumner based his arguments mainly on philosophical Spencerism. His argument was thus mainly political and social in nature, not economic as such. "The essential elements of political economy are only corollaries or special cases of sociological problems," he claimed[296] — and then proceeded to treat the tariff debate in terms of social analogies with biological struggles: "We see that the development of society is as regular and as natural as that of a plant, and there is no more need of human interference than there is to make a bud burst into a blossom at the proper moment." This was in direct opposition to the interpretation of Darwin by such men as John W. Draper, Lester Ward, Simon Patten and other American theoreticians who viewed human evolution as differing from that of plants and lower animals mainly in that man could become the master of his own fate. Far from endorsing state action to guide evolution purposefully, Sumner insisted that social development "cannot be hastened without injury." Evolution must thus occur passively, at a geologically slow pace. Hence, Sumner's intense opposition to all socialistic and revolutionary tendencies. He attacked protectionists specifically for their purposefulness: they were "not contented to see what the

[295] Richard Hofstadter, *Social Darwinism in American Thought* [1944], rev. ed., (1955), p. 51.
[296] Harris Elwood Starr, article on Sumner in *Palgrave's Dictionary of Political Economy*. See also Starr's biography, *William Graham Sumner* (New York, 1925) for biographical information.

natural chances of the country are and then go to work to develop them. They make up their minds first what, in their wisdom, the country ought to be, and then they set to work to force it, with nature or against nature, into that form."[297]

Early protectionists had claimed to be advocating a "natural" destiny for the United States in the sense that they were advocating policies to help it escape from the quite unnatural destiny imposed by England's colonial regulations which had warped its development prior to the Revolution. Subsequent protectionists stated that, original advantage or not, it was wise for all nations to avoid becoming raw-materials suppliers to England. Sumner could not see why the United States should be reluctant to remain an agrarian, raw-materials exporting country. He attributed its relatively high industrial wage rates specifically to its available land (and not to the high productivity of its industrial labor): "Wages are high here because men of the wages class can get all the fertile land they can till by going to it," he claimed. Indeed, while protectionists were describing how the worker's economic status was being elevated constantly as machines came to supplant manual labor, freeing this labor for higher and more intellectual tasks, Sumner argued that young America held out "grand opportunities to the man who has nothing but his manual labor to depend upon, and the protective system does, and always has taken away from the farmer, laborer and artisan, the advantages which nature offered him in the new country."[298] So much for the evolving nature of labor with society's technological progress, to say nothing about man mastering this technology to serve his own ends!

As a youngster, Sumner had been struck by Harriet Martineau's sugary *Illustrations of Political Economy* (1832–34), and in 1872 was inspired by Spencer's *Study of Sociology* to defend laissez-faire in terms of an almost theological interpretation of Spencer's survival-of-the-fittest doctrine. He embraced a kind of Horatio Alger mythology that viewed capital as being formed by abstinence and self-denial, and market competition as the ultimate means of improving man's political and economic society. "The millionaires are a product of natural selection," he held, "acting on the whole body of men to pick out those who can meet the requirement of certain work to be done." As Hofstadter has summarized his views, the millionaires "get high wages and live in luxury, but the bargain is a good one for society. There is intensest competition for their place and occupation. This assures us that all who are competent for this function will be employed in it, so that the cost of it will be reduced to the lowest terms."

---

[297] Sumner, *Lectures on the History of Protection in the United States* [1875] (New York, 1883), pp. 26, 63.

[298] *Ibid.*, p. 23.

This seemed to beg the issue of what service was performed for society by those who merely inherited their wealth, but Sumner assured his readers that "social advance depends primarily upon hereditary wealth; for wealth offers a premium to effort, and hereditary wealth assures the enterprising and industrious man that he may preserve in his children the virtues which have enabled him to enrich the community. Any assault upon hereditary wealth must begin with an attack upon the family and end by reducing men to 'swine.'"[299]

Democracy, Sumner believed, was an unattainable ideal in view of the natural differences that existed among men which would render unequal their economic power, hence their social status. As with the movements of geology or natural selection in the plant and animal worlds, society could evolve only gradually, hence Sumner's opposition to revolutionary or socialistic reforms. To interfere with competition was to endorse "survival of the unfittest … favor[ing] all its worst members." Thus Sumner opposed the Interstate Commerce Act, the free-silver movement, public charity laws, state enforcement of labor conditions, and most of all, protectionism, "The Ism that teaches that waste makes wealth" as he entitled one of his numerous articles on the subject. In these respects he reflected the views of his hero, Herbert Spencer, whose doctrines had received the adulation of such selected members of American society as Andrew Carnegie, James Hill and John D. Rockefeller.

Sumner insisted on viewing protective tariffs only on the debit side of the ledger—that is, as a tax—ignoring the credit side of the ledger, *e.g.*, the spending of tariff proceeds by the federal government for internal improvements and social programs. Taxes "are loss and waste to almost their entire extent," he stated. Society's function was not to give aid but to remove obstacles, letting the Invisible Hand of competition work its wonders. If Americans could not live without this aid, "we must have left a part of the world where life is easier for one where it is harder"—an argument which overlooked that American life might be made still easier by government activities. Protection, Sumner concluded, was "hostile to improvements. … When, therefore, competition is withdrawn or limited the incentive to improvement is lessened or destroyed."[300] It was thus the impulse of competition that brought out the best in man (never the worst, such as chicanery, dubious advertising, or the other aspects of modern wealth-earning that Veblen emphasized so devastatingly).

Sumner never did grasp the key point raised by the protectionists, namely the fact of differential productive powers among the world's labor and capital.

---

[299] Hofstadter, *op. cit.*, quoting Sumner's *The Challenge of Facts*, pp. 68, 40, 145–50, 43–44.
[300] *Lectures on … Protection*, pp. 3, 14.

He insisted that international trade was no different from inter-regional trade between the states. New York and Pennsylvania, he argued, did not exploit and impoverish Rhode Island, Alabama, and Mississippi by their trade, so why should trade between America and other nations be exploitative? A protectionist would have answered that the quality of labor and capital, taxes, and costs generally were homogeneous within the United States, but differed among nations. Sumner did not accept this, or even, apparently, the Ricardian theory of comparative costs. Nor did he allude to the Ricardian concept of international trade as being characterized by no net movement of labor or capital. Sumner thus argued that America's populations tended to move from the older states to the new ones, just the opposite of the direction that protectionists represented wealth as travelling in the world economy. A protectionist would have seized upon this analogy to analyze just why domestic trade differed from international trade, but Sumner merely let the matter drop.

At best his arguments were addressed only to the first generation of American protectionists, the institutional and historical school that had not yet developed a general doctrine of productive powers. He accused protectionists of arguing "that there is only a 'national' and not a 'political' economy, that there are no universal laws of exchange … and that [political economy] varies with national circumstances …"[301] This was hardly an apt rebuttal to the doctrines of Henry Carey, Peshine Smith, Simon Patten and their followers.

Still, Sumner is part of the distinctly American movement to extend political economy into broad social issues rather than narrowing it into a mere theory of market prices as was occurring in England under the guidance of Marshall's school. The protectionists who took the lead in forming the American Economic Association in 1885, hoping to introduce greater historical and institutional discussion into economic reasoning, had seen the association captured to an increasing degree by narrow constructionists. More and more of the socially aware economists left economics altogether to enter the realm of sociology (either through biology, as did the French followers of Comte, or through historical economics as did the followers of Patten). The American Sociological Society was formed in 1906, largely by statists, and yet Sumner became its president in 1909, the year in which he retired from Yale. This appointment was due largely to publication in 1907 of the work for which he is best known today: *Folkways: A Study of the Sociological Importance of Usages, Manners, Customs, Mores, and Morals*, in which he treated society's folkways as the major means of conveying its cohesive identity.

---

[301] *Ibid.*, p. 7.

SIMON NEWCOMB, MATHEMATICAL ASTRONOMER

Simon Newcomb (1835–1909) was a Canadian-born astronomer and economist who achieved renown in both fields. In addition to pioneering empirical studies in mathematical astronomy, and writing and editing America's most popular astronomy textbooks of the 1880s and 1890s, he was the first American to popularize and elaborate the quantity theory of money in mathematical equation form (for which reason Irving Fisher dedicated his *Purchasing Power of Money* to Newcomb's memory).

Newcomb's family was of New England descent, the first Simon Newcomb having been born six generations earlier, about the year 1666. The family moved north to Nova Scotia in 1761, where Simon's father subsequently found employment as an itinerant school teacher. Young Simon spent much of his childhood with his grandparents. He was intellectually precocious, and when he reached the age of sixteen he was apprenticed to a quack herbalist doctor, under the impression that he would become educated in modern botanic medicine. The doctor turned out to be a fraud, and urged Newcomb to adopt the philosophy that success could be achieved most readily by being a popular humbug.

Disappointed at the doctor's inability to teach him anything except showmanship, Newcomb ran away two years later, walking over a hundred miles on his way to Maine, and then proceeding to Maryland where he gained modest employment as a country school teacher and tutor. He spent much of his free time in Washington at the Smithsonian Institution and its library, where he introduced himself to Joseph Henry, a leading American scientist of the day. Henry took Newcomb in hand, and in 1857 procured for him the post of computer in the Nautical Almanac Office situated at Harvard University.

Newcomb subsequently described this appointment as removing him from the world of cold and darkness and thrusting into that of sweetness and light. It certainly marked the beginning of his life as a systematic thinker. While working under the aegis of his Cambridge astronomical colleagues he enrolled at Harvard, taking his B.S. in mathematics in 1858 and continuing graduate study for three years. In 1860 he made his reputation in a memoir "On the Secular Variations and mutual Relations of the Orbits of the Asteroids," communicated to the American Academy of Arts and Sciences, in which he sought to demonstrate that the orbits of the known asteroids had never intersected, concluding that the asteroids could not have originated from the breaking up of a planet.

In 1861 Newcomb was appointed Professor of Mathematics in the U.S. Navy and assigned to duty at the U.S. Naval Observatory in Washington. Here he began "his great work, colossal in conception and carried on with remarkable unity of purpose for more than twenty years ... 'the building up, on an absolutely homogeneous basis, of the theory and tables of the whole planetary system.'" [302] More a mathematical than an observational astronomer, Newcomb investigated the orbits of all the planets, and was awarded the Royal Astronomical Society's gold medal in 1874 for his studies of the orbits of Neptune and Uranus. He also spent many decades investigating the moon's motions and perturbations as indicated by centuries of recorded observations. The product was his classic "Investigations of Inequalities in the Motion of the Moon, Produced by the Action of the Planets" (1907).

Newcomb sometimes said that his vocation was astronomy, but his avocation economics. His first economic work was *A Critical Observation of our Financial Policy during the Southern Rebellion* (1865), published when he was thirty years of age. At the outset he sought to integrate scientific method—that of Newtonianism—with economic reasoning, claiming that political economy was an exact science in which "we can trace the effect of every intelligible cause," and referring to the "working of ... financial machinery" in clearly defined mechanistic reference. [303]

Newcomb's analysis of the economic basis of military strength was classic. "The military power of a nation is measured by the amount of industry which it can divert into the channels of war," that is, by the size of its economic surplus of war-goods over and above personal consumption. War was thus fought with armaments, not with money. "The question now is, Does money increase the amount of skill and labor which can be thus turned into the channels of war? I answer, No ... What the nation really wants is labor..." Money was neutral in its overall effects, although its use enabled taxes to be levied "in such a way that every one shall be taxed equally," as money "is the representative of labor." Without a surplus over and above consumption to transfer to the

---

[302] Raymond Clure Archibald, *Bibliography of the Life and Works of Simon Newcomb*, in *Royal Society of Canada, Proceedings and Transactions*, Series 2, 11 (1905), p. 80. For further biographical and bibliographical material on Newcomb, see his autobiography, *Reminiscences of an Astronomer* (1898); Archibald's updated memoir on *Simon Newcomb, 1835–1909* (Ottawa and Washington, 1924); William Wallace Campbell, *Bibliographical Memoir, Simon Newcomb, 1835–1909* (National Academy of Science, *Memoirs* 17), and Loretta M. Dunphy, *Simon Newcomb: His Contribution to Economic Thought* (1954).

[303] Newcomb, *A Critical Observation of our Financial Policy during the Southern Rebellion* (New York, 1865), pp. 19f.

government and armed services, however, "no amount of money, paper or metallic, would enable us to wage war ... If all our labor is exhausted in the production of food, clothing, and other necessities, we cannot make war at all." Thus, "the source of military strength may be concentrated into one word, Frugality. It is the frugal man who consumes less than he produces."[304] This analysis is similar to that of the gross national product theory developed during World War II to allocate income and output.

The problem of financing the war by issuing bonds rather than taxation lay in the economic and political strains conveyed to posterity. Newcomb was quite clear that a bond issue could not transfer the war's cost onto future generations. "The generation that wages the war must be the one to shed its blood, feed its armies, and cast the shot and shell which its armies are to use. Food, clothing, shot and shell are the real expenses of war. In running to debt for these articles, we do indeed bequeath to posterity the work of raising the money to pay for them. But posterity not only raises the money, but also receives the pay, so that we may as logically say that posterity gets paid for the war as to say that it pays for it." Still, financing the war by loans had serious political implications for future income distribution, "by causing an antagonism of interests between the East and the West." Because about 80 per cent of the debt would be held in the Eastern states, "while more than half the taxes will have to be paid by the States which own the other fifth," it followed that "different sections may have entirely different pecuniary interests."[305] The West would advocate agrarian and populist economic policies to relieve itself of the tax-burden necessary to pay off the debts, while the East would seek deflation. Newcomb, a hard-money man throughout his life, urged that the government guarantee the gold value of all bonds which it issued, in order to prevent the success of populism.

There was an alternative to taxation or bond issues as means to finance the war: the government could simply print money to finance its purchase of war material and pay its troops. Indeed, the entire government debt could be extinguished overnight by stamping each bond "legal-tender money." But this would not be equitable on moral grounds, as it would erode the purchasing power of patriots (those who chose to accept government money and purchase bonds) while favoring unpatriotic doubters of the government's fiscal responsibility, who turned their money over rapidly and refused to invest in government loans. In short, Newcomb concluded, "a system of paper money may be described, in general, as *a convenient device for throwing the entire burden of an extraordinary expense upon that class of the community who have most faith in the paper money*."[306]

---

[304] *Ibid.*, pp. 37–40, 43f. [305] *Ibid.*, pp. 66–68. [306] *Ibid.*, p. 114.

Francis Bowen, writing in the *North American Review,* praised Newcomb's "remarkable talent for the systematic evolution of his subject ... carry[ing] back the investigation of each point to first principles ..."[307] Bowen argued that the government had no choice but to suspend specie payments and issue greenbacks in their stead. In opposition to Newcomb's extreme hard-money policy he cited the Bank of England's successful suspension of specie payments for over twenty years, during the first seven or eight of which the currency did not depreciate more than six or seven per cent. The problem, Bowen recognized, lay in the government issuing greenbacks in excessive amounts, not the substitution of paper for gold as an event in itself.

Bowen was evidently attracted by Newcomb's writing, and at the end of the Civil War he suggested that Newcomb update his views on the currency question and evaluate those of Henry Carey. Newcomb recognized that "at present we regulate the currency only by contracting or changing the form of debts; and in future its regulation must be affected by the mode of paying the debt." He urged a rapid discharge of the national debt, through a policy of direct taxation based on "each man's accumulated wealth, income, and profession," suggesting "two annual direct taxes of five hundred millions each, provided that government indebtedness of every form should be received in payment of the tax." For more normal and ongoing categories of government expenditure, he suggested an excise tax on consumer goods.

Carey argued against a return to specie payments on the ground that this would injure the nation's industrial interests, which tended to be net borrowers. He warned that labor and capital would be unemployed for lack of sufficient money to establish the "societary circulation." Newcomb, despite his political observations on the role of debt, believed in what is now called the "neutrality of money": he asserted that "the amount of each man's labor is regulated by a law which is wholly independent of money. He will labor as long as the wealth which he produces compensates him for the irksomeness of the labor, and no longer." Products of labor are exchanged for other products of labor in accordance with a labor-barter theory of value, "without reference to the circulating medium ... Money has no 'power' to effect exchanges. It is only the instrument, not the cause, of the exchange ... The community will always have enough of the medium of exchange, because any transportable commodity can be used as such ... The first effect of the temporary diminution in the demand for goods would be, that every one would offer his products a little cheaper." The "societary circulation" would thus "go on at its natural rate. The fifty-cent note will perform all the exchanges formerly performed by the dollar note."

[307] Francis Bowen, "Newcomb's Financial Policy," *North American Review* 100 (1865), p. 605.

In passages such as these Newcomb ignored the impact of pre-existing debt on the financial mechanism under conditions of inflation or deflation. On behavioral gounds he favored deflationary policies over inflationary ones (although supporting absolute price stability as the best alternative of all). When gold rose in value, he observed, "or the value of the dollar falls, those who owe money are enriched at the expense of their creditors, while in the opposite case the creditors are enriched at the expense of the debtors. Hence every change in the value of the dollar is an evil. But it is less injurious to national wealth when the creditor is benefited at the expense of the debtor, than is the opposite case, because, as a general rule, the creditor class are disposed to save their money, and the debtor class to spend it ... Frugality being the foundation of all national wealth and strength, the habits which conduce to wealth and strength are encouraged by an appreciation of the currency ... Eras of depreciating paper money have always been those of luxury, extravagance, and waste of wealth." Conversely, "when men in general contemplate the future of government credit and the national currency with confidence, instead of paying out their money as fast as they receive it, they will save it up for the purpose of investing in government bonds, or in the hope that prices will fall."[308] Falling prices thus spurred saving, *e.g.*, the economic surplus over and above current consumption (presuming full employment). In this observation Newcomb introduced the concept of the velocity or turnover of money, pointing out that in periods of rising prices every one was "anxious to pass off all the money he receives as soon as possible."

Newcomb's next article for the *North American Review* criticized Carey's *Principles of Social Science,* and gave him an opportunity to distinguish his own classical economic method from that of the American protectionists. "A very popular mode of philosophizing on social subjects is that well described by Mr. Mill as the Chemical Method," he wrote. "In Greece and Italy where they adopted policy A, the good effects E, F, G resulted, while in France and Russia, where they adopt policy B, the evils I, K, and L prevail. Therefore, if you would enjoy these good effects, you must adopt policy A, and avoid policy B ... The natural effect of this method is to make man the creature of society ... We do know a great deal about individual men and their motives. Society being made up of individuals, this knowledge may be very valuable in enabling us to discover or account for social laws. On the other hand, the forces which act in society are so diverse in different countries and ages that the chemical method

---

[308] Newcomb, "Our Financial Future," *North American Review* 102 (January 1866), pp. 100, 103, 114–16, 109–11.

can scarcely ever lead to any certain result."[309] It deteriorated to a kind of "law of averages" type of reasoning such as typified the writings of Buckle and Quetelet. Carey's historical reasoning was thus analogous to the doctrine of sympathies in the natural sciences rather than to the cause-and-effect system which characterized Newtonian mechanics. (Newcomb overlooked entirely Carey's theoretical system as a doctrine of production.)

Newcomb was to persist in this attitude throughout his life. His final article on economics, published in *Science* in 1905 (as a summary of his speech on economic topics to the American Association for the Advancement of Science) accused Spencer's term "social organism" of being too broad for economic relevance, as it included many super-economic forces. "There is a far greater degree of exactness attainable in measuring the force of economic processes than is usually assumed in the criticism based upon the assumptions of the vagueries of human nature. We may, therefore, be exact in the investigation of the action of causes," *e.g.*, in investigating such topics as "the influence of the increase of currency upon prices."[310] Newcomb praised Jevons' "application of mathematical methods or principles to the study of economics" (that is, to marginal utility theory), and Marshall's mathematical treatment of the laws of supply and demand. Newcomb reviewed numerous economic writers for the *North American Review* and other periodicals, covering the work of Peto, Baxter, Jevons, Cairnes, Bonamy Price, Shadwell, Francis A. Walker, Richard Ely, Robert Ellis Thompson and others.

Meanwhile, his reputation as an astronomer grew. In 1876 he was elected president of the American Association for the Advancement of Science. The following year he was appointed Senior Professor of Mathematics and director of the office of the *American Ephemeris and Nautical Almanac* (1877–1897), where he sought to devise "fundamental constants" to describe the planetary motions of the four inner planets, and to determine their mass by studying their influence on comets and on their own satellites. He also sought to estimate more precisely the earth's precessional constant. It was during these years that he wrote his numerous textbooks on astronomy, including *Popular Astronomy* (1878, which passed through at least seven editions and was translated into German, Russian, and Norwegian), *Astronomy for students and General Readers* (1880), *Astronomy for High Schools and Colleges* (1881, which passed through six editions), *Astronomy for Everybody* (1902), and *Sidelights on Astronomy and Kindred Fields of Popular Science* (1906).

---

[309] Newcomb, "Carey's Principles of Social Science," *North American Review* 103 (October 1866), p. 573.

[310] Newcomb, "Economics as an Exact Science," *Science* 21 (March 24, 1905), pp. 447f.

During 1884–1891, and again during 1898–1900, Newcomb taught graduate students as Professor of Mathematics and Astronomy at Johns Hopkins University. During these years he continued his activities as an economic theoretician. One of his projects was to advocate a constant tabular standard of value. As early as 1866 he had adopted an algebraic weighted-average index of price levels, and in 1879, in an article praising the resumption of gold-convertibility for greenbacks, he suggested "the well-known 'multiple standard of value' … which has never received the attention which it deserves." Referring to "absolute value" in terms of constant purchasing power, he stated that "our first problem is to find the average price of all the important products of human labor as measured in the current money for which sales are made," and then assigning a weight to each commodity used in the average. The result was what Irving Fisher subsequently termed the "compensated dollar" or "commodity dollar," the doctrine which underlay America's revaluation of gold in 1934.[311]

During 1879–80 Newcomb lectured on political economy at Harvard, and during 1891–92 at Johns Hopkins. He became president of Harvard's Political Economy Club of America in 1887, two years after the publication of his major economic work, *Principles of Political Economy* (1885), which Schumpeter has called "the outstanding performance of American general economics in the pre-Clark-Fisher-Taussig epoch," although noting that Newcomb "had not 'got on' to the Jevons-Menger-Walras level and his analysis was substantially 'classic.'"[312]

Newcomb devoted the first portion of his *Principles* to economic methodology. Six years earlier he had asserted that tariffs, banking and currency, and the standard of value were economic subjects which "must be studied in the same spirit, and, to a certain extent, by the same methods which have been so successful in advancing our knowledge of nature." Unfortunately, economic questions were generally approached with preconceived theories, leading to disparities in vocabulary and methodology. "What we want is so wide a diffusion of scientific ideas that there shall be a class of men engaged in studying economic problems for their own sake."[313] This subsequently became the

[311] "Our Financial Future," *op. cit.*, pp. 109f, and "On the Standard of Value," *North American Review* 129 (Sept. 1879), p. 225.

[312] Joseph Schumpeter, *History of Economic Analysis* (New York, 1954), p. 866.

[313] "The Relation of Scientific Method to Social Progress. An address … before the Philosophical Society of Washington … 1880," reprinted in *Sidelights on Astronomy and Kindred Fields of Popular Science* (New York, 1906), pp. 315, 317.

conservative concept of "positivism" as an economic method. According to
Newcomb's *Principles* there was indeed "a general science of economics, founded
on those characteristics of human nature and on those relations of man to his
environment which are common to all civilized people," although Newcomb
conceded to the protectionist school "that the principles of this general science
have to be specialized and modified to suit the circumstances of each people
to whom they are applied." He thus distinguished "pure economics," tested
by hypothesis, from "applied political economy" dealing with particular conditions as to time and space.[314]

Newcomb followed British practice in emphasizing "human desires" and
utility theory rather than treating economics primarily in terms of productive
powers and their social consequences. "There is," he pranted, "a wide field of
investigation included under the general term *Sociology*, or the science of
society ... But this inquiry into the origin and growth of human desires is quite
distinct from Political Economy. The latter takes the man up, ready-made as
it were, and has nothing to do with the question how he got to be what he is."
Newcomb also segregated moral science from political economy. "In other
words, having given a community of men moved by certain desires, we trace
out the laws which govern their efforts in seeking to gratify those desires. This
and this alone is the object of Political Economy as a pure science," a view
which led Newcomb to prefer the shorter term "economics" for what had been
political economy.[315]

This by no means meant that Newcomb wrote his book without specific
political conclusions. For instance, he argued that labor-saving technology did
not reduce employment. "No operation of cheapening production can cause
a diminution in the sum total of the demand for labor. Every diminution which
it may cause in one direction is compensated by an increased demand in some
other direction." He believed that labor displaced from one occupation could
always find alternative employments. Newcomb recognized the existence of
non-competing groups, but these existed mainly between three categories of
laborers, "unskilled laborers, skilled laborers, and intellectual laborers." There
was intra-class mobility, but little inter-class mobility beyond a point. Technological improvements would benefit these classes differently, according to the
nature and labor-displacing focus of the invention at hand. "It is probable that
less natural skill of a rare kind is required when goods are made by machinery.
So far as this is true, the introduction of machinery is doubly beneficial to the

[314] Newcomb, *Principles of Political Economy* (New York, 1885), pp. 539, 21.
[315] *Ibid.*, pp. 10f., 13.

day-laborer by securing him a higher order of employment and cheaper neces-saries of life at the same time. It is also true that the management of the machine may require moral characteristics—industry, sobriety, steadiness, honesty, and reliability—of a higher degree than ordinary irresponsible labor. If so, the laborer who does not possess these qualities would again be at a relative disadvantage in consequence of improvements in production. That is to say, he would lose by lower wages and gain by cheaper products, and the loss might exceed the gain. We may lay it down as a general rule that the idle, dissipated, and unreliable classes will be in about the same low state, no matter how far society advances. Even philanthropists could do nothing for them, un-less it could do away with them in the future by preventing them from being born; and perhaps there is no effective way of doing this unless by extermination."[316]

Newcomb thus showed himself extremely laissez-faire in outlook. He op-posed strikes (because they made commodities "dear and scarce" instead of "cheap and plentiful"), shorter working hours, the union shop, the formation of buying and selling cooperatives (because ordinary laborers lacked managerial ability), and also charity for the poor. As do his successors today, he represented charity as increasing the demand for beggary, and warned that the supply of beggers would respond to this demand. If there must be money set aside for the poor, he believed, the best way was to invest in rehabilitative education.

He was best known among subsequent American economists for stating the quantity theory of money in mathematical form and elaborating its implications. His version of $MV = PO$ was $K \times P = V \times R$, where K represented the industrial circulation (society's output), P the price level, V the volume of money (M in today's equation), and R the rapidity of circulation (or what is now termed V for velocity of circulation). "The absolute value of the total volume of currency circulating in a social organism," he defined, "is equal to that of the total industrial circulation of the organism during the average time that a piece of money remains in one man's hands." He was careful to acknow-ledge leakages: "to preserve the equality we must exclude from the monetary flow all such transfers as loaning money, or depositing it in a bank, because these are not balanced by reverse transfers of wealth or services." Leakages also existed as a result of bankruptcies, and repayment of debts without a new loan being made. (However, Newcomb recognized no foreign-trade leakage, adopting the classical Ricardian assumption that international trade and pay-ments were always in balance.) "When the volume of the currency fluctuates, other conditions being equal, the purchasing power of each unit of money varies

---

[316] *Ibid.*, pp. 390–94.

inversely as the whole number of units, so that the total absolute value of the whole volume of currency remains unaltered by changes in that volume."[317] This led him to warn his readers of the "money-fallacy" which confused the receipt of money with the receipt of actual purchasing power, or what today's economists call the money illusion.

The final section of Newcomb's *Principles* was devoted to an application to specific circumstances and policy considerations of the general mechanisms he had developed in his earlier chapters. Among these is a particularly well-balanced (for the time) discussion of the pros and cons of laissez-faire. Like John Stuart Mill, Newcomb feared that congressional proneness to special interests would work against the general public welfare.

Newcomb never wrote on economic statistics, nor did he attempt to quantify empirical economic phenomena. He chose only to discuss principles as they applied to economic policy. He did not use diagrams at all, and used mathematics only sparsely, although he is said to have used mathematical modes of statement in his economic lectures at Johns Hopkins University. Like other American economists, he urged that "organization" and "knowledge" be recognized as distinct economic inputs, taking their place alongside land, labor (subdivided into his three non-competing classes of relative skill), and material capital, whose formation he explained largely by Senior's abstinence theory. He weakly attempted what Marshall and others later achieved: integrating the "objective" cost-of-production approach to value theory with the "subjective" marginal-utility approach. His theory of interest recognized the role of loanable funds, time preference, and what is now called the marginal efficiency of capital.

---

[317] *Ibid.*, pp. 347, 322, 339, 344, 390–94. Marget has traced the equational statement of the quantity theory of money back to Roscher in 1854.

Bibliography of the Economic Writings of Simon Newcomb

1. *A Critical Examination of our Financial Policy during the Southern Rebellion* (New York, 1865).
2. "Our Financial Future," *North American Review* 102 (January 1866), pp. 100–35.
3. "Carey's Principles of Social Science," *North American Review* 103 (October 1866), pp. 573–80.
4. "Peto's Taxation," *North American Review* 104 (January 1867), pp. 255–61.
5. "The Let-Alone Principle," *North American Review* 110 (January 1870), pp. 1–33.
6. "The Labor Question," *North American Review* 111 (July 1870), pp. 122–25.
7. "Baxter's National Debts," *North American Review* 114 (January 1872), pp. 189–93.
8. "Jevons' Theory of Political Economy," *North American Review* 114 (April 1872), pp. 435–40.
9. "Life Insurance," *International Review* 2 (May 1875), pp. 353–70.
10. "The Method and Province of Political Economy," *North American Review* 121 (October 1875), pp. 241–70. [A review of Cairnes].
11. *ABC of Finance, or The Money and Labor Questions Familiarly Explained* (New York, 1877). [Articles taken mainly from *Harper's Weekly*.]
12. "The Silver Conference and the Silver Question," *International Review* 6 (March 1879), pp. 309–33.
13. "On the Standard of Value," *North American Review* 129 (September 1879), pp. 223–27.
14. "Our Political Dangers," *North American Review* 130 (March 1880), pp. 261–79.
15. "Principles of Taxation," *North American Review* 131 (August 1880), pp. 142–56.
16. *Principles of Taxation* (New York, 1880).
17. *The Relation of Scientific Method to Social Progress. An Address ... before the Philosophical Society of Washington ... 1880.* (Washington, 1880).
18. "Organization of Labor," *Princeton Review* 5 (1880), pp. 393–410; 6 (1881), pp. 231–46.
19. "Two Schools of Political Economy," *Princeton Review*, 2nd Ser. 14 (November 1884), p. 291. [On Robert Ellis Thompson.]
20. *Principles of Political Economy* (New York, 1885).
21. *A Plain Man's Talk on the Labor Question* (New York, 1886). [Originally published in the *Independent*, based on lectures delivered to the Knights of Labor.]
22. "Aspects of the Economic Discussion," *Science* 7 (June 18, 1886), pp. 538–42.
23. "Can Economists Agree on the Basis of Their Teachings?" *Science* 8 (July 9, 1886), pp. 25f.
24. "Soap-Bubbles in Socialism," *North American Review* 150 (May 1890), pp. 563–71.
25. "The New School of Political Economists," *Nation* 53 (July 9, 1991).
26. *The Problem of Economic Education* (Boston, 1893). [From *Quarterly Journal of Economics*, July 1893.]
27. "The Standard Gold Dollar of the U.S. Has it Appreciated?" *Journal of Political Economy* 1 (September 1893), p. 503.
28. "Ely on Political Economy," *Journal of Political Economy* 3 (December 1894), p. 106.
29. "Science and Government," *North American Review* 170 (May 1900), pp. 666–78.
30. "Economics as an Exact Science," *Science* 21 (March 24, 1905), pp. 1447–49.

JACOB SCHOENHOF AND THE ECONOMY-OF-HIGH-WAGES DOCTRINE

Most economists today assume that wage increases in any given country tend to impair its international competitiveness, by forcing up its prices in proportion to wage rates, whether through cost-push or demand-pull inflation. This view assumes that rising wage rates have no effect on labor productivity, whose increase over time is presumed to be independent of the worker's living standards. Such a hypothesis seems appropriate for today's high-consumption societies like the United States, but it is less true for economies whose labor is just emerging from minimal standards of living. The productive ability of such labor does indeed seem to increase, particularly in its early stages, as its wage levels rise, and as its nutritional, educational, and social standards generally are improved over and above subsistence levels. This correlation between wage rates and labor productivity has become known as the "economy-of-high-wages-doctrine." Jacob Schoenhof did much to elaborate and statistically illustrate this doctrine in his position of special envoy, employed by the U.S. State Department to travel around the world comparing wage rates and labor productivity.

Increasing wage rates, Schoenhof argued, tended to bring about corresponding increases in labor productivity so that prices did not rise accordingly, and indeed became a precondition for this productivity gain. In fact, wage-induced productivity gains normally exceeded the rise in wages, so that unit labor costs tended to fall over time. The mainspring of economic development was thus the steady improvement in living standards of the labor force. Productivity change was a wage-dependent variable, not an independent variable in economic development as portrayed in today's growth theory.

This economy-of-high-wages doctrine had immediate political implications for the tariff debate. If wage levels and unit labor costs tended to move inversely, as contended by Schoenhof, then high-wage countries would be able to undersell low-wage countries. American workers had nothing to fear from cheap foreign labor, and should support the Democratic Party in its program to reduce tariffs. The interest of high-wage countries like the United States lay in international free trade as a means of extending its industrial markets abroad. This was an argument which Josiah Tucker, David Hume and other British free-traders of the mid-eighteenth century had upheld when British labor was the world's most productive labor. It is only today being rediscovered.

Jacob Schoenhof (1839–1902) was born in Oppenheim, Germany, and emigrated to the United States in 1861, at the age of twenty-one. Settling in New York City, he established a wholesale lace business in which he introduced European large-scale production techniques. His experience in this trade afforded many of the examples that illustrate his subsequent writing.

While Schoenhof was setting up his commercial business in New York, the Civil War was ushering in what was to become a half century of highly protective tariffs. He appears to have familiarized himself with the writings of the major American protectionists, and to have become especially impressed with the theories of Henry Carey and his school as to the tendency of industrial development to bring about rising wage levels. But he did not share these writers' protectionist conclusions. He believed that although protective tariffs had nurtured American industry in the early stages of its development, the protectionist legacy of the Civil War had pushed tariffs to such a level that they were hindering further American economic expansion. The especially high tariffs on raw materials were pricing American exports out of world markets — markets the nation needed to maintain its high rate of industrial growth and employment. These views led Schoenhof to become a Democrat.

In 1883 he published *The Destructive Influence of the Tariff upon Manufacturing and Commerce, and the figures and facts relating thereto*, which contained all the essential elements of his later work. So-called protective tariffs, he asserted, protected neither American manufacturing industry nor the labor which it employed. True, in their initial stages they had produced a wave of new capital investment and led to declining industrial prices. "Prices, however, can never reach a true level, that of foreign competition, while raw materials are protected. Our prices may become low enough to ruin all manufacturers, and still be higher than those at which foreign manufacturers can work at a profit and export their surplus."[317] Nor were tariffs even necessary to protect American labor from the lesser-paid, but even less productive labor of Europe. "Wages are not gauged by tariff, but by general opportunities offered by the respective countries," that is, by the supply of and demand for labor. To the extent that America's tariffs impaired its competitiveness in world markets, they "circumscribed employment and reduced earnings." By increasing the prices paid by labor for its consumption goods, they reduced real wage rates, thereby impairing the souce of American labor's acknowledged superior productive powers. "The standard of living of the working class determines the rate of wages," he

---

[317] *The Destructive Influence of the Tariff* (New York, 1883), pp. 36–37.

asserted. "Where the standard of living is the highest, productive powers and invention find highest development, and production is cheapest."[318] Capitalists' self-interest thus called for higher wage rates.

The following year, during the presidential campaign of 1884, the Republican platform as usual denounced free trade for tending to "degrade our labor to the foreign standard." Underlying this assertion was the premise that international price levels under free trade were a direct function of wage differentials among nations, irrespective of whatever productivity-differentials might exist to offset this wage disparity. Andrew Stewart had provided a classic statement of this crude theory of international wages and prices in his assertion that "the tariff furnished the only security our laborer had against the degrading and leveling effects of an unrestricted competition with the pauper labor of Europe. As you reduce this wall of protection, you reduce the wages of labor."[319] Schoenhof controverted this argument in his pamphlet on *Wages and Trade in Manufacturing Industries in America and in Europe*, demonstrating that international price levels tended to vary inversely with *per diem* wage levels. Highly-paid American labor was in no manner threatened by lesser-paid foreign labor, because high wage levels resulted in high productivity and low unit labor costs. "It is not by reducing wages that America is making her conquests," he concluded, "but by her superior organization, greater efficiency of labor consequent upon the higher standard of living ruling in the country. High-priced labor means better food and better living, and these supply the American workman with that energy and nerve-power for which he is so justly celebrated. High-priced labor countries are everywhere beating 'pauper-labor' countries."[320] This pamphlet helped firmly establish the division that had developed between Democrats and Republicans as to the nature of international competitiveness.

To maintain high wage levels, Schoenhof believed, the United States must supplement its congested domestic market with foreign ones and thereby become a major export power. "I take the ground," he maintained, "that there need be no reduction of wages below that paid in 1880, that all we need is the raw material at as cheap a rate as that at which competing nations procure it,

---

[318]   *Ibid.*, p. iv.

[319]   Andrew Stewart, *The American System* (Philadelphia, 1872), p. 96 (from a speech in the House of Representatives on December 9, 1845). As late as 1928 the Republican platform was still insisting that "It is inconceivable that American labor will ever consent to the abolition of protection which would bring the American standard of living down to that in Europe ..."

[320]   *Wages and Trade in Manufacturing Industries in America and in Europe* (New York, 1884), p. 19. See also *The Economy of High Wages* (New York, 1892), p. 385.

in order to enable us to take as commanding a position in the markets of the world as sellers of manufactured goods, as we do in agricultural products."[321] Low tariffs, at least on raw materials, were thus the precondition for cheap exports, increasing employment, and continued high wage rates.

Grover Cleveland won the 1884 elections for the Democrats. The following November he appointed Schoenhof consul at Turnstall, England, and shortly thereafter confidential agent to Secretary of State Thomas F. Bayard. Prior to his departure Schoenhof elaborated his theories in *The Industrial Situation and the Question of Wages: A study in social physiology*, in which he stated "the true theory of wages to be this: 1. That the standard of living of the working classes determines the rate of wages; and, 2. That where the standard of living is highest, productive power and invention find highest development, and production is cheapest ..."[322] As in his earlier writings, he maintained that America must become an increasingly export-oriented nation if the evils of overproduction were to be avoided. "The abundance of our public lands has so far acted as a safety-valve. Without this natural blessing ... the pressure of limited markets upon our productive forces would have become unbearable."[323]

This was not the most optimistic outlook for the ability of American industrial growth to sustain rising wage rates. Schoenhof's book nonetheless expressed a basic optimism closely akin to that of Henry Carey and Peshine Smith. The results of modern industrial development, he enumerated, had been (1) to increase the productiveness of labor; (2) to reduce the proportion which labor bears to material in the price of any given product; (3) to cheapen thereby the cost of the product, and consequently to increase its accessibility to the masses; (4) to increase the money earnings of the working classes; and (5) to reduce the hours of labor.[324]

As confidential agent to Bayard, Schoenhof traveled through Europe studying the effect of technical education on production methods there—in Bayard's words, "to indicate and establish the power of education of the human hand and brain, and ... to show how 'the sweat of the brow is lessened by the conception of the brain,' and increased wages accompany increased efficiency."[325] In 1888 Schoenhof presented to Congress his report on *Technical Education in Europe, Part I: Industrial Education in France.* Four years later he published *The Economy of High Wages,* his most sophisticated work.

---

[321] *Wages and Trade*, pp. 20f.
[323] *Ibid.*, p. 150.
[325] *The Economy of High Wages*, p. v.

[322] *The Industrial Situation* (New York, 1885), p. 4.
[324] *Ibid.*, pp. 108f.

This book contains an integrated refutation of two related doctrines: the Iron Law of Wages, and the pauper labor argument for protective tariffs, which Schoenhof demonstrates to be based on the so-called Iron Law. Both theories assumed labor productivity to be unrelated to wage rates, and that ill-fed and impoverished labor was therefore as capable of exerting work effort as well-fed and well-trained labor. Only if this were true could poorly-paid labor compete in world markets on an equal footing with educated and well-maintained labor, which it would gradually pull down to its own pitiable level. Not only were minimum wages in the capitalist's interest, but the natural process of competition would keep wages down over the long run. As representative of this reasoning Schoenhof cited Ricardo's belief that increased productiveness, and consequent reductions in living costs, would soon be followed by lower money wages, so that the laborer would find himself (to use Ricardo's words) "probably, at the end of a very few years, in the possession of only a small, if any, addition to his enjoyments."[326]

Schoenhof replied that in order for the initial increase in productivity to have taken place at all, it was necessary that the laborer obtain a higher standard of living and increase his working skills. Productivity increases were thus conditional upon labor and its living standards. Even increases in capital efficiency were actually an indirect function of higher wage rates. "Indeed the law of gravitation is not more absolute than this," Schoenhof asserted, "that where, as in America, the rate of wages of labor *per diem* is a high one, the first object of the employer is to economize its employment. The result is that in no country is the organization of labor in mills and factories so complete as in the United States ... Machinery, used to the limit of its life in Europe, is cast aside in America if only partially worn, or while satisfactory in this respect, if an improvement has come out that can do the work quicker and consequently cheaper."[327] Industrialists were induced to supplement new capital for scarce labor, while this capital required in turn more highly-trained labor to operate it: "In almost every employment of an industrial nature a very great amount of training is requisite to make it effective or make it serviceable at all. Only in times of very great demand and scarcity of labor would any one employ crude labor in factories where skill is required."[328] This had far-reaching implications both for wage and employment theory and for international trade theory: it indicated that employability and remuneration of labor was a function of its working skills, and that variations in these skills and abilities divided the labor market into layers of non-competing groups.

[326] Quoted *ibid.*, p. 19.　　[327] *Ibid.*, pp. 33f.　　[328] *Ibid.*, p. 27.

American labor was thus not threatened by foreign pauper labor. The assumption was invalid "that a day's labor in any one line in one country would produce the same results as a day's labor in another country." Foreign labor not only lacked the personal capital resources possessed by American labor, but was untrained to mobilize industrial capital such as that which American labor operated. "It is a fortunate sign of the times," Schoenhof observed, "that we are at last beginning to recognize the all-important and redeeming fact, that cheap labor by no means means cheap production; that on the contrary, low cost of production and a high wage rate go hand in hand." American labor, "being machine labor, is generally cheaper than European labor, which is to a large extent hand labor or inferior machine labor or unproductive underfed labor, as compared with higher productive American labor."[329]

"Nor can the rate of wages be seriously affected by an influx of new labor," Schoenhof proceeded, "because new labor is seldom accustomed to the occupation." His ensuing theory of non-competing groups served to controvert the assumption of a homogeneous labor pool comprised of workers of equal productive abilities and tending towards an equality of wage rates, such as was being postulated by Prof. Ely, and was later to become codified by Paul Douglas, and first in his theory of marginal wage rates and wage formation, and later in the Cobb-Douglas function of economic growth. Ely had theorized "that the price of labor does not at once rise when the demand increases, as is usually the case with other commodities, for the first effect is that the unemployed receive work; and after the 'reserve army' finds employment competition among purchasers of labour raises its price." Against this theory Schoenhof replied that "the professor moves the army of the unemployed about like a condottiere, throwing it into this or into that camp which may be willing to bid for its services. The fact is not considered at all that, however large the army [may be] at any one time, those belonging to any one handicraft or employment are usually few and rather scattered ... All manufacturing industries are minutely subdivided to-day. The sewing machine operator on a Wilcox & Gibbs, would be out of place where Singer, or Wheeler & Wilson machines are in use." This multi-layered structure of the labor pool thoroughly controverted the "so-called law, promulgated by the English school of economists, that, if wages rise in one part of a country above the general rate ruling, very soon an influx will follow of labor from the lower stratum, which will soon begin to press on and reduce the rate of wages to the old standard."[330]

[329] *Ibid.*, p. 31.   [330] *Ibid.*, p. 12.

High wage rates were in the interest of the industrial employer, Schoenhof believed, because the former found himself more than repaid by increased productivity and a greater rate of work output. Europe's employers had been slow to recognize this fact. "In England, especially, the battle fought against education of the working classes was a long and bitter one." As a result, for many years in Europe "the old labor methods, going parallel with low wages, become quite ingrained with the countries where they prevail and offer sufficient grounds for their perpetuation … Conservatism becomes increasingly pronounced in proportion as the rate of wages descends to a lower and lower scale."[331] But "if anything, a loss of trade is an eye-opener," and the inroads made by German labor into British and French markets were soon recognized "to be due to a more thorough teaching in science and art schools … and the wider dissemination of knowledge among the German working classes."[332] The conclusion was clear: "The survival of the fittest is, therefore … the result of a high wage rate; and a high standard of living in industrial countries, becomes a prerequisite to a low cost of production."[333]

The association of high wage levels with high productivity and low production costs was by no means novel to American economic thought. It had been drawn early by Henry Carey, refined by Peshine Smith in the 1850s, and emphasized by Francis Amasa Walker in the 1870s. For example, Peshine Smith had asserted in 1852 that "the American system rests upon the belief, that in order to make labor cheap, the laborer must be well fed, well clothed, well lodged, well instructed, not only in the details of his handicraft, but in all general knowledge that can in any way be made subsidiary to it. All these cost money to the employer and repay it with interest."[334] Two years later, in his *Manual of Political Economy*, Smith reiterated that "high proportional wages are the index of cheap production,"[335] and emphasized the application to political economy of Liebig's analogy between the human body and the steam engine: "Looking upon the human labourer, then, just as we would upon a steam-engine, we see that the amount of force which he is capable of exerting, depends upon the amount of food supplied to him—a part of it answering the purpose of the coal which gives heat, another answering to the water that is converted into steam and generates motion. A sheet-iron jacket put around the boiler prevents the waste of heat in the one case, just as a woolen jacket

---

[331] *Ibid.*, pp. 33f.

[332] *Ibid.*, p. 67.

[333] *Ibid.*, p. 39.

[334] E. Peshine Smith, "The Law of Progress in the Relations of Capital and Labor," *Hunt's Merchants' Magazine* 26 (January, 1852), p. 42.

[335] E. Peshine Smith, *Manual of Political Economy* (New York, 1853), p. 104.

about the body of the tabourer does in the other."[336] It may have been from Peshine Smith or from Walker[337] that Schoenhof had been inspired to observe that "a half-fed or under-fed body can no more produce full results than an engine not sufficiently supplied with fuel or a horse half-starved."[338] But although he cited numerous German writers as having emphasized this point, he seems to have intentionally ignored his American predecessors.

The reason for this neglect is not hard to find. The optimistic theory of wage rates under industrial growth had been originally developed by protectionist writers, in particular by Carey and by Peshine Smith, and played a major role in their assertion that industrialization (and the protective tariffs which they deemed a necessary precondition) would benefit the industrial laborer. Protective tariffs would not strengthen the power of industrial capital relative to that of labor, Peshine Smith had claimed, because the enlightened industrialist found high wage levels to be in his own interest by virtue of their associated productivity dividends. It was thus the more sophisticated protectionists themselves that had taken the lead in controverting the crude assumptions underlying the "pauper labor" arguments of earlier advocates of protective tariffs. Increasing labor productivity tended to outstrip the rise of wages, prices declined, yet the accumulation of industrial capital was stimulated, providing an ever-growing per capita product in which the laborer might share—a residual claimant theory of wages similar to that which Walker was later to put forth.

Schoenhof thus resembles Bastiat as an optimist who, largely because of his free-trade partisanship, neglected to cite the original protectionist inspiration for his optimistic views on the evolution of wages and profits under industrial growth. What is ironic is that Republican protectionists allowed free traders to monopolize this more sophisticated theory of wages and international price-formation. That they did so is an indication of the decline in protectionist economic theorizing after the Civil War. With industrialization and protectionism firmly established as national policy, Republican platform-writers seem to have felt little need to reiterate the more intricate academic arguments for industrial growth, and easily reverted to the "pauper labor" apologeties as a crude political slogan. The desirability of industrialization was no longer a partisan issue. Thus it was as a foil to the protectionist arguments of the day that Democratic free traders took the lead in investigating the correlation between wage rates and productivity, and appropriated the early protectionist optimism on the beneficial effect of industrial growth upon wage rates, just as in Europe the optimistic movement had been preempted by free traders such as Bastiat.

---

[336] *Ibid.*, p. 107.
[337] Francis Amasa Walker, *The Wages Question* (New York, 1876), pp. 58 and 84.
[338] *The Industrial Situation*, pp. 14f.

Schoenhof nonetheless failed to attain the level of economic sophistication of such predecessors as Peshine Smith. He was not essentially a growth theorist, but occupied himself mainly with drawing the link between wage levels and labor productivity, and the consequent distinction between *per diem* labor costs and unit labor costs. Schoenhof made no novel theoretical contribution to American economic thought but simply provided a clear refutation of the crude protectionist pauper-labor apologetics (along with men like Walker and Taussig), while stressing the actual statistical data already being collected. His work complements that of such government appointees as Carroll D. Wright, U.S. Commissioner of Labor, and author of *The Industrial Evolution of the United States* (Meadville, Pennsylvania, 1895), and the numerous others who traced the influence of labor skills, mechanized production, and wage rates on labor productivity and prices. Schoenhof's achievement lay primarily in pinpointing the political distinction that had developed between Democrats and Republicans, between free traders and protectionists as to their respective theories of international wages and prices. Indeed, after the 1884 campaign the Republicans adhered to the naïve pauper-labor argument, while free-trade theoreticians adopted for themselves, without the adherence of any major protectionist, the theory that international prices were a function not so much of wage-differentials but mainly of labor productivity and the associated capital-intensiveness of production.

The Democrats returned to power behind Grover Cleveland once again in the 1892 elections. Upon his taking office in 1893, Schoenhof received the appointment of assistant appraiser at the Port of New York, a post which he held throughout Cleveland's second administration. He wrote one more major book, the *History of Money and Prices* (New York, 1896) which refuted the quantity theory of price, and supported the productivity explanation of price levels, in keeping with his earlier wage doctrines.

The only remaining questions to be asked are why the mainstream of economic theory reverted to the crude wage-differential explanation of international trade, and why this doctrine came to be put forth by free traders? The "factor endowment" analysis of international trade began to be popularized by the Swedish economist Eli Heckscher in his 1919 article, "The Effect of Foreign Trade on the Distribution of Income," and was greatly elaborated within the context of neo-Marshallian economics by Bertil Ohlin in his book *Interregional and International Trade,* published in 1933. Ohlin was a student both of Heckscher and Taussig, but gave virtually no consideration to the latter's emphasis on productivity differentials as explaining international advantage. In Heckscher's words: "If the conditions of production are the same in all countries ... each difference in the relative prices of the factors of production will make it profitable to get, by trading, any commodity which requires relatively more of the relatively scarce factor of production, for another commodity in which the relatively more abundant factor is predominant. Thus trade must continue until an *equalization of the relative scarcity of the factors of production among countries* has occurred."[339]

International price differentials were thus a function of relative scarcity of labor, capital and land, not of their productivity—a throwback to the crude "pauper labor" doctrine which had earlier been confined mainly to the protectionists. Why did this new theory rise to dominate mainstream economics? Partly because of the twentieth century's movement away from productivity analysis and partly because this analysis had demonstrated that rich, high-wage nations tended to increase their competitive advantage over low-wage countries. This was hardly a palatable doctrine to be put forth by the developed nations already coming under accusation of exploiting the world's poorer countries. Indeed, when the United States achieved industrial pre-eminence following World War I, largely through its early protectionist policies, it felt the time had come to urge the poorer countries to lower their tariffs rather than to emulate U.S. trade and development strategy. Political self-interest worked against broadcasting the productivity approach to international trade theory as elaborated by Schoenhof and his contemporaries. Thus, whereas Schoenhof originally published his books to argue against the protectionist sophisms of international trade, republication of his *Economy of High Wages* today may help dissipate the current free-trade sophisms put forth by Paul Samuelson and other followers of the Heckscher-Ohlin reaction against productivity theory.

[339] Eli Heckscher, "The effect of foreign trade on the distribution of income," in Ellis and Metzler, eds., *Readings in the Theory of International Trade*, (American Economic Association, 1949), p. 286. See also Ohlin's nearly identical statement, *Interregional and International Trade* (Cambridge, 1935), p. 15.)

Chronological Bibliography of Jacob Schoenhof's Economic Writings

1. *Über die volkswirtschaftlichen Fragen in den Vereinigten Staaten*, in *Deutsche Zeit- und Streit-Fragen*, ed. F. v. Holtzendorff, neunter Jahrgang, Vol. 130 (Berlin, 1880). (repr. New York: E. Steiger & Co., 1882).
2. *Deutsche Urtheile über Amerika*, in *ibid.*, zehnter Jahrgang, Vol. 156 (Berlin, 1881).
3. *The Tariff on Wool and Woolens*. New York: G. P. Putnam's Sons, 1883.
4. *The Destructive Influence of the Tariff upon Manufacturing and Commerce, and the figures and facts relating thereto*. New York: G.P. Putnam's Sons, 1883. (repr. 1884, 1885, 3rd ed. 1891).
5. *Wages and Trade in Manufacturing Industries in America and in Europe*. Statement before the Ways and Means Committee. New York, 1884 (repr. 1888).
6. *The Industrial Situation and the Question of Wages: A study in social physiology*. New York: G.P. Putnam's Sons, 1885.
7. *Influences Bearing on Protection*. Washington: U.S. Government Printing Office, 1888.
8. *The Economy of High Wages: An inquiry into the cause of high wages and their effect on methods and cost of production*. New York: G.P. Putnam's Sons, 1892.
9. *History of Money and Prices*. New York: G.P. Putnam's Sons, 1896.
10. "The German Tariff Proposals: whom will they affect?" *Forum* (September, 1901), pp. 105–15.

VII. The Generalists

JOHN WILLIAM DRAPER, MATERIALIST HISTORIAN

John William Draper (1811–82) was one of the pioneers of photochemistry and photography, and after the Civil War became one of the most renowned historians of western civilization's intellectual development. From the beginning he sought to integrate the physical and social sciences into a rational whole. His interests evolved, in Comtian order, from the most general and inanimate to the most highly social and political topics. As a child his major interests were astronomy and chemistry. His early publications concentrated on two branches of chemistry: first, spectroscopy and the chemical effects of sunlight, which inspired his photographic researches and speculations on the effect of the sun's light and heat on all forms of life, including man's social and intellectual development as it varied according to climate; second, the theory of capillary action and osmosis, which inspired him to pursue the parallels between the movement of sap in plants and blood in animals, and thence to seek broad analogies between physiology and the birth, evolution, and death of civilizations.

Draper spent the last half of his life in developing a materialist physiology of society, and in tracing the political implications of the natural laws which he believed governed man's social and mental development. "Why should it be thought improbable," he asked, "that the same laws which govern the inorganic world are likewise employed for the government of the world of life?" "It is no metaphor, but a reality, that the life of human societies is typified by the life of plants and animals. Throughout the whole world of organization the scheme of Nature is the same…. There are physiological laws that constrain society. There are physical boundaries beyond which society can not pass." The progress of societies "is directed in part by physical influences, and in part by the force of Ideas, but it is always determined by law."[340]

Draper was born near Liverpool, England, in 1811. His father, a Wesleyan (Methodist) clergyman, had a lively interest in science, which he seems to have imparted to Draper at an early age. Young Draper's education at Methodist schools may have helped instill a view of a rational and comprehensible order

---

[340] John W. Draper, *Scientific Memoirs, Being Experimental Contributions to a Knowledge of Radiant Energy* (New York, 1878), p. xii, and *Thoughts on the Future Civil Policy of America* (New York, 1865), pp. 239, 377. *The Influence of Physical Agents on Life: Being an Introductory Lecture to the course on Chemistry and Physiology in the University of New York* (New York, 1850), p. 7.

throughout the universe, or what was called Natural Theology. His college education at the University of London, however, was interrupted by his father's untimely death in 1829. Three years later, at the age of twenty-one, Draper emigrated with his mother and sister to a small Wesleyan community in Virginia where relatives of his mother had already settled. "The expectation of receiving a professorship in the denominational college in the vicinity was one of the strongest inducements held out to him. Repeated delays in starting, however, made the time of his arrival much later than had been anticipated; so that, when he reached Virginia, the position he had hoped for had been given to another person. He settled with his relatives at Christianville, Mecklenburg county, where he devoted himself entirely to scientific research."[341] Almost immediately he set about publishing articles and letters in American journals.

In 1835 Draper enrolled at the University of Pennsylvania's medical school, the first such school to be established in the United States. The following year, armed with an M.D., he returned to Virginia to seek a teaching post. Like most other European visitors to America he was struck by the land-extensive, soil-depleting modes of cultivation then practiced throughout the United States. It probably was at this time that he observed that American farmers and planters did not find it economic to apply the principles of agricultural chemistry and soil conservation which were commonplace in England, but to exhaust the soil in given districts and then abandon them for new Western lands. "A Virginia planter grows tobacco on his land until he has exhausted it. Of what avail to him is agricultural chemistry, with all its great discoveries? It might cost him five hundred dollars an acre to repair the mischief he has done to his estate; but he can buy virgin lands in the West at a dollar and a quarter an acre. Agricultural colleges are of no use to him. And so, for miles together in the Southern States, there are desolated and forsaken tracts — old fields, as they are called. But, if land is worth little, labor is worth much. Whoever can invent a labor-saving machine will make money. So our improvements are not in the direction of agricultural chemistry, but of agricultural mechanism." This mining of the soil, Draper recognized, was responsible for much of America's pressure for westward expansion: "That love of the homestead, so characteristic of the settled populations of Europe, can scarcely be said to exist among us. The children leave their father's hearth without reluctance, for he is perpetually anticipating leaving it himself."[342]

[341] George F. Barker, "Memoir of John William Draper: 1811–1882," *National Academy* (April 21, 1886), p. 352. For additional biographical information see Donald Fleming, *John William Draper and the Religion of Science* (New York, 1950).
[342] *Civil Policy*, pp. 168, 84f.

Draper was therefore quite responsive when followers of Edmund Ruffin, the Virginia apostle of scientific farming, sought to establish a school of mineralogy and to appoint Draper chemist and mineralogist. This project seems to have become absorbed into the neighboring Hampden Sidney College, at which Draper became Professor of Chemistry and Natural Philosophy in the fall of 1836, inaugurating what was to be a forty-five-year teaching career.

In his first lecture he exhibited his lifelong desire to create a rational comprehensive view of the world, fully in keeping with the college's theological premises: "That adaptation which we see in all parts of this mysterious frame [the world], should teach us that if it require not [God's] … constant interference to keep up such complicated changes, it is a proof of the surpassing skill with which the plan was first laid."[343] Draper's concession to theological terminology was by this time little more than rhetorical.

In 1837 a movement got underway to attach a medical school to the recently founded New York University. Pending establishment of the new school, Draper was elected Professor of Chemistry and Botany at N.Y.U. proper, but the 1837–38 depression left the university in shaky financial status, and he did not join it until 1839. He played a major role in planning and establishing the medical school, which finally opened in 1841, and he continued for many years to maintain his chemistry professorship.

During these years he pioneered in the development and technical application of photography. His early studies in the nature and effects of light apparently were triggered by his fascination as a child with "a glass containing some camphor, portions of which had been caused to condense in very beautiful crystals on the illuminated side," which induced him "to read everything I could obtain respecting the chemical and mechanical influences of light, adhesion and capillary attraction."[344] He also was interested in the photochemical reactions of chlorophyll in plants, which led him to investigate the field of photographic chemistry in general.

In 1839, soon after having moved to New York to join the university, he set out in competition with Alexander Woolcott and his N.Y.U. colleague Samuel Morse (inventor of the telegraph) to achieve a feat which Daguerre had doubted was possible: to take a portrait photographically. In October 1839, Woolcott used a concave reflector instead of a lens to take the first photographic portrait, and in July 1840, Draper produced what is apparently the first portrait photograph made directly with a lens: a study of his sister, Dorothy. Also during the winter of 1839–40, showing "perhaps an unrivaled grasp of the value of

---

[343] Quoted in Fleming, *op. cit.*, p. 13.   [344] *Scientific Memoirs*, p. xii.

photography in scientific investigation," Draper "found time to take the first known photograph of the moon, and launched, in a very modest way, the great age of astronomical photography. ... It seems that Draper was the first to take with any precision a photograph in the infrared region.... He also photographed lines in the ultraviolet at about the same time as Edmond Becquerel."

In addition, Draper seems to have invented the art of making photographic enlargements and copies from "proofs," taken "with a very minute camera; and then magnifying them subsequently up to any required size, by means of a stationary apparatus," thus anticipating both the Kodak and the enlarging process. He developed the science of spectroscopy and spectrophotometry in an attempt to analyze the chemical composition of stars from their light. Finally, he sought to introduce quantitative methods into photochemistry, inventing the "tithometer," to relate the intensity and time of the light exposure to its chemical effects. "His was an imposing achievement," concludes his biographer, Donald Fleming: "portraits, photographs of the moon, spectrographs, photomicrographs, and techniques for enlarging and multiplying. This grasp of ends which the camera might serve and of ways for increasing its use marks his real distinction rather than claims to absolute priority. But he had these as well."[345]

Draper's university teaching does not seem to have been particularly stimulating to his research, although it provided him with an impetus to formulate general laws. The university did not yet have a graduate school, and its students posed many disciplinary problems, being quite unprepared for systematic thinking and learning. Draper had to finance most of the chemistry department's equipment expenditures out of his own pocket. He "did his most important scientific work from twenty-five to thirty years before the flood tide of Ph.D.'s came in. He lacked, what might have kept him to the task, the stimulus of graduate students, with a few exceptions in his later middle age. He had therefore to content himself in great part with rubbing the illiteracy off undergraduates. Even his medical students had little interest in research."[346] Draper's best student probably was his son, who went on to achieve some renown as an astronomical photographer.

Whereas the seventeenth century lay the basis of astronomy and Newtonian mechanics, and the eighteenth century the basis of physics and chemistry, Draper observed at the outset of his *Treatise on the Forces which Produce the Organization of Plants* (1844), "it is the office of the nineteenth to discover the laws which obtain in the complicated structure of animated beings, those laws which give rise to the mysterious phenomena which we call life." There was a unity and

---

[345] Fleming, *op. cit.*, pp. 139, 23, 28, 37–41.   [346] *Ibid.*, p. 57.

universality to these laws, which governed not only plant and animal life but the evolution of societies as well. "In the history of the human race, it may be observed that epochs have occurred, which, following each other with a kind of periodicity, have stood in relationship with, or even brought about the conditions of modern civilization." Because all organized beings are composed largely of water, "it is therefore obvious that there is a very limited range of temperature in which the processes of life can be carried on. These thermometric limits are between 32° and 212° Fah. Life, therefore, is comprised within a range of 180 degrees. In this manner we might proceed to show how the existence of individuals and races is completely determined by external conditions ... we might compare the effect of climates in the torrid, the temperate, and the frigid zone ... It is within a narrow range of climate that great men have been born. In the earth's southern hemisphere, as yet, not one has appeared, and in the northern they come only within certain parallels of latitude ... The distribution of organized forms is, therefore, directly, and their very existence indirectly, determined by the distribution of heat." Just as the sun and the earth's movements through space caused the earth's climates and the alternation between night and day, so these climates governed the genesis and quality of civilizations across the globe. "THE SUN not only determines periods of awakening and sleep, of growth and decay, but ... all the movements of animated beings on the face of the globe." The Gulf Stream warms "the coasts of Europe, and spreads out in a fan-like form, the vapours that rise from it give forth their latent heat to the air, and moderate the climates of England and France. The coldness and sterility of corresponding latitudes in America is there replaced by a better temperature, and agriculture, the arts of life, science and literature have there reached their greatest perfection ... A full development of the reasoning faculty can only take place where physical circumstances conspire. It is to the climate of England and France that the human race is indebted for the intellect of Newton and Laplace."[347]

Before Darwin began to publish his theories, Draper was writing that "it is one of the greatest discoveries of the present age, that the races of animals which have inhabited our globe were of successive creation; and they constitute a series, the extreme terms of which bear no resemblance to each other; that, commencing with those of the earliest date, we are able to trace a constant progress both in intellectual and structural development." He affirmed an upward progress of evolution: "If we consider the successive races of organized

---

[347] *A Treatise on the Forces which Produce the Organization of Plants* (New York, 1844), pp. 1, 5, 8, 12.

beings, beginning from the lowest and passing to the higher tribes, it would seem as if the general idea under which Nature has been acting is, that as the more complex structures were evolved to emancipate them from the direct control of external physical forces, the vegetable kingdom, unendowed with locomotive powers, deriving its existence directly from external agents, is completely under their control. If the summer is too brilliant, or rains do not fall, a plant withers and dies. In the same manner, the lower races of animals have their existence determined by the action of physical causes; if these be favourable, they flourish; if unfavourable, they must submit to an inevitable lot. To tribes that are higher, to a certain extent, the rigour of these laws is remitted, and a certain amount of independence secured; the African lion can retire to a shade in the middle of the day; yet still he is held in a state of subjection … The sunbeam is his chain. In man alone the emancipation is complete; for into his hand Nature has committed a control of the imponderable principles [*e.g.*, heat, light and electricity. It matters not whether it be in the torrid zone or in the frigid, he tempers the seasons by his intellectual power; he resorts to every artifice of clothing, or to the warmth of fire; he dissipates the natural darkness by artificial light." Thus, whereas Marx was shortly to speak of man emancipating himself from the chains of private property and class society, Draper—in line with other American social theorists such as Henry Carey and Simon Patten—spoke of man as emancipating himself from the constraints of nature (and from sunlight in particular) to create his own technological world. "Advances in knowledge are advances in power. The civilized man of these days is a wholly different being from the man who lived a thousand years ago, and the conditions which determine his position have totally changed. With us the position both of empires and of individuals is fixed by the possession of knowledge—knowledge which is incessantly on the advance. Wherever intelligence has been given, there is a requirement to join in the advancing march. The Indian stands still, and the penalty is death."[348] But man had not yet fully freed himself from the constraints of climate, and this subject was to form the basis of Draper's subsequent social-historical theorizing, along with his views on intellectual progress in and of itself.

The main precondition for this progress was man's ability to free himself from theological belief in some "over ruling Providence … fashioning and framing each class of created forms, irrespective of external physical forces or agents, and giving birth spontaneously to unconnected tribes of animals and plants, which bear no sort of relationship to one another, and are not parts of one common plan in which there is a unity of design." Theology gave a false

---

[348] *Ibid.*, pp. 3, 13, 8.

sense of unity to the world. Only the natural sciences could provide the requisite base — a view that for centuries had faced overwhelming opposition from the Roman Catholic bureaucracy. In primitive times man had viewed the world in terms of four elements, including earth and air. But Jupiter, god of the air, had now been atomized into its component parts by Priestley's discovery of oxygen, the greatest scientific discovery since Newton's exposition of the laws of gravitation.

The theory of oxidation that provided the key to the chemical basis of animal Physiology, exploding the old theological views of Galen and his followers. If there was any arch-creator, it was the sun, not God, that was responsible for the earth's oxidation and deoxidation in the eternal plantanimal cycle. Theological reactionaries had fallen back on the exploded doctrine of Life Force (*vis viva*), supposing "that a living being is totally emancipated from the dominion of [natural] forces. But, by degrees, the rapidity with which all the great branches of knowledge, Mathematics, Mechanics, Chemistry, were advancing, caused things to be seen in their right proportions and in right positions; and men at last began to suspect that the world is not governed by many systems of laws, or one part of it cut off and isolated or even at variance with the rest, but that there is a unity of plan obtaining throughout ... This noble idea ... has been steadily and silently ... gathering strength from every new philosophical and physiological discovery ... The true peculiarity of modern Physiology, consists in its fully recognizing the relationship of an animated being to the world around; and in admitting, to the broadest extent, the control which external circumstances have over it."[349] Hence Draper's specifically American form of materialist philosophy: Evolution was a struggle by man to emancipate himself from the constraints of nature more than a struggle among men themselves.

By 1856, the year in which Draper published *Human Physiology, Statical and Dynamical; or, The Conditions and Course of the Life of Man,* he had read Comte and began to phrase his terminology in reference to the latter's theoretical schema. Asserting that physiology finally had passed from a speculative to a positive science, he sought in turn to base his social theorizing upon physiological analogies. In this respect his book — especially its second half — was as philosophical as his earlier work on *Plants.* "In Comte himself," Fleming observes, "the fascination with physiology as in some way the key to a science of society had not yet worn off. But he mostly escaped from the uncritical identification of a man's body with the body of men." But the progress then being made in physiology, particularly the links between organic and inorganic chem-

---

[349] *Ibid.*, p. 3; *An Introductory Lecture on Oxygen Gas ... 1848–49* (New York, 1848), pp. 4f., 15; and *The Influence of Physical Agents on Life,* pp. 6f.

istry being forged by Liebig in his studies of the chemistry of nutrition and body heat, and of soil chemistry, was bound to lead Draper and others to feel that the momentum of scientific law could be carried right through physiology to encompass social and political phenomena. "Wherever Draper got the notion, it is a really curious instance of physiological imperialism, the efforts of physiology to swallow up history and politics."[350]

Draper's subsequent writings dealt mainly with historical and political topics. By the end of 1856 he had virtually completed his great two-volume *History of the Intellectual Development of Europe* (which his publisher, Harper's, did not issue until 1863). In 1859 he summed up his conclusions in a speech to the newly established Cooper Union in New York, which he followed with a major address to the British Association for the Advancement of Science, "On the Intellectual Development of Europe, Considered with Reference to the Views of Mr. Darwin and Others, that the Progression of Organisms Is Determined by Law." In 1863 he lectured on "The Historical Influence of the Medical Profession," and in 1864 he gave a series of four lectures before the New York Historical Society on "The Historical Influence of Natural Causes," which he expanded the following year into his *Thoughts on the Future Civil Policy of America.* In 1867, 1868 and 1870 he published his three-volume *History of the American Civil War.* In 1870 he gave a major address to the first meeting of the short-lived American Union Academy of Literature, Science, and Art (which he took the major role in founding), and finally, in 1874, he published his *History of the Conflict between Religion and Science,* a companion volume to his *Intellectual Development of Europe.*

In his 1859 Cooper Union speech, Draper sought to ground history explicitly on the physiological principle that "nations like Individuals are born, run through an unavoidable career, and then die, some earlier, some more maturely, some at a still later date."[351] Whereas in physiology the link with physics and chemistry had been quite direct, the motive principles of society resembled those of physiology through analogy, *e.g.*, by the "sympathetic" principles which Draper himself had attacked so vigorously in his earlier writings against the quasi-medieval, theological, pseudo-scientific doctrines of "life force."

Draper's 1860 speech at the Oxford meeting of the British Association for the Advancement of Science was scheduled to be a *cause célèbre* over the intellectual struggle then raging over Darwin's epoch-making book, published the previous year, *On the Origin of Species by Means of Natural Selection, or the Preservation of Favoured Races in the Struggle for Life.* Word went out that the Bishop of

[350] Fleming, *op, cit.*, p. 59.   [351] Quoted in Fleming, *ibid.*, p. 56.

Oxford, Samuel Wilberforce, would seize the occasion to "smash Darwin," whose principles were to be supported by Thomas Huxley. Draper repeated his somewhat pre-Spenglerian generalization about the birth, life and death of societies and their component particles. True to his deductive materialist principles that were to endear him so greatly to Marxists in later years, "he showed that the advances of men are due to external and not to interior influences, and that in this respect a nation is like a seed, which can only develope when conditions are favourable, and then only in a definite way; that the time for psychical change corresponds with that for physical, and that a nation cannot advance except its material condition be touched, this having been the case throughout all Europe ...; that all organisms, and even men, are dependent for their characteristics, continuance, and life, on the physical conditions under which they live; that the existing apparent invariability presented by the world of organization is the direct consequence of the physical equilibrium; but that, if that should suffer modification, in an instant the fanciful doctrine of the immutability of species would be brought to its proper value."[352]

In the discussion which followed Draper's address, Bishop Wilberforce addressed a question to Thomas Huxley as to whether it was the latter's grandfather or his grandmother that had transmitted the line of descent from an ape. Huxley replied that he would rather descend from an ape than from a shallow rhetorician appealing to religious prejudice. A Lady Brewster fainted and had to be carried out of the meeting hall. Admiral Robert Fitzroy, captain of the *Beagle*, yelled out that he rebuked his former shipmate Darwin for running counter to the first chapter of Genesis. Draper's logic itself was largely ignored, and no one rose to make the point that Draper did not precisely relate natural selection to his postulated laws of society, but was satisfied with the statement that man could somehow understand the laws of society by analyzing its physical setting.

The worldwide impact of Draper's *Intellectual Development of Europe* cannot be overestimated. Against the light of science and the investigation of natural law he counterpoised the Roman Catholic bureaucracy, stifling freedom of thought and seeking to enslave men's minds by theological images of a supernatural God acting personally to reward virtue and punish evil. All opposition to this moral teleology, all search for causes intrinsic to nature's own logical system, met with lethal resistance on the part of the papal bureaucracy and its Inquisition, its crusades, its literal interpretation of Genesis, its doctrine of papal infallibility, and its secular political power as it substituted moral

---

[352] *Report of the British Association for the Advancement of Science*, 1860, pp. 15f., quoted by Fleming, *op. cit.*, p. 69.

exhortation for knowledge, and instruments of torture for scientific apparatus. The book was translated into nearly every European language, and had an especial impact upon Russian Marxists and intellectuals.[353] The *Westminster Review* wrote that "what Comte showed might and ought to be done for the whole world of man; what Buckle commenced for England, Scotland, France, and Spain, Draper has effected for the whole of Europe. The gigantic vastness of the task is almost paralyzing."[354]

In view of its implications for Draper's concept of America's role in the evolution of Western civilization, it is worthwhile to briefly review his *Intellectual History.* Its central theme—which is picked up again in his *Civil Policy*—is the incessant warfare between the inquiring spirit and motive force of science (typified by classical Greek culture, the Arab-Mohammedan enlightenmentand the Protestant Reformation) and the stultifying force of religion (typified by the political bureaucracy into which the Christian Church descended early in its career). As Christianity pressed towards becoming a state religion, and indeed an imperial religion, it was united with pagan faiths in country after country, while creating an intolerant monotheism so as to render the religious practices of all conquered territories subservient to Roman authority. Roman Christianity took what Draper calls the "African branch." St. Cyril's Egyptian Christianity absorbed the Isis-Horus cult and set forth the doctrine of the Trinity, while the ex-Manichaean St. Augustine introduced the obscure Oriental concepts of Original Sin, total depravity, grace and predestination, dividing mankind into the elect and the damned, the kingdom of grace and perdition, ruled respectively by God and the devil. In Northern Europe, Roman Christianity synchronized its festivals with those of the pagans, and throughout the Roman Empire the new religion adopted the idolatry typical of native Roman paganism. Wherever it ruled, the new form of Christianity exhibited a religious and intellectual intolerance unique in world religions. It soon became an enemy of science and of the scientific spirit.

Meanwhile, the geographic and social pattern of intellectual evolution was being determined largely by climate. The only historian cited by Draper in his *Intellectual Development* was the sixteenth-century French philosopher Jean Bodin, who had interpreted the evolution of nations in terms of climatic factors, and whose theories were reiterated by Montesquieu. Bodin viewed climate as

---

[353] Leon Trotsky, *Stalin* (New York, 1941), p. 35. Fleming (*op cit.*, p. 125) cites Ivan Turgenev's glowing response to Draper's work.

[354] Quoted in Barker, *op. cit.*, p. 374. For a bibliography of the book's major reviews, see Fleming.

leading to the creation of theocratic societies in the South and East, military governments in the North, and free and judicious civil societies in countries located in temperate climates. Tropical Southern climates tended to breed a character that was intellectual, moral and religious (and also melancholy, jealous and vengeful). The cold Northern climate rendered men physical in outlook, somewhat amoral and phlegmatic, while the temperate zone bred men who were judicious and rational, sanguine and choleric.

Civilization tended to originate in the South, thanks to the agricultural surplus fostered by its warmth and by its rivers (especially the Nile). This natural surplus provided Southern populations with time to contemplate and to develop the mind. Men in the North operated more under the constraint of necessity, being obliged to engage in more of a physical struggle with nature. They lacked the intellectual leisure of the South, but also the latter's theocratic tendencies and moral teleology, so that once civilization began to spread north-wards it could take a firmer scientific root.

In making these points Draper followed Bodin and Montesquieu. "The origin, existence, and death of nations depend thus on physical influences, which are themselves the result of immutable laws." But by the same token, "nations are only transitional forms of humanity," as progressive man moved constantly to transform his environment. "All over the world physical circumstances control the human race. They make the Australian a savage; incapacitate the negro, who can never invent an alphabet or an arithmetic, and whose theology never passes beyond the stage of sorcery ... Meteorology to no little extent in-fluences the morals; the instinctive propensity to drunkenness is a function of the latitude. Food, houses, clothing, bear a certain relation to the isothermal line." But "an artificial control over temperature by dwellings, warm for the winter and cool for the summer; variations of clothing to suit the season of the year, and especially the management of fire, have enabled man to maintain him-self in all climates. The invention of artificial light has extended the available term of his life ..." Gradually, as man came to manage his own environment, intellect outgrew faith, and a spirit of selfdetermination supplanted that of predestination. While remaining "under the inexorable dominion of law," man increased the relative power of his own free-will impulses. "Philosophically speaking, he is exchanging by ascending degrees his primitive doctrine of arbi-trary volition for the doctrine of law."[355]

---

[355] *History of the Intellectual Development of Europe* (revised ed.: New York, 1876), Vol. I, pp. 17, 26f., 2f.. See also pp. 6f.

Draper's *Civil Policy* continued this historical narrative, depicting the discovery of America as the culmination of the first ("Southern") European enlightenment, that of Muslim Arab, and the growth of the United States as a victory for the second ("Northern") enlightenment, that of the Protestant Reformation. What was original and positive in early Christianity, Draper narrates, was contained in the Nestorian religion, which was driven out of Egypt by the butcherous Cyril of Alexandria in the 5th century. The Nestorians migrated to Arab lands, passing on the torch of Greek and Alexandrian learning to the Arabs, and this torch was kept alive by the Mohammedans. While Christian Europe was struggling in the mental darkness imposed by the church hierarchy, the Arab-Mohammedan invasions of Spain were literally enlightening Europe.

The major Arab city in Spain was Cordova, with over a million inhabitants living in two-hundred thousand houses. "After sunset a man might walk through it in a straight line for ten miles by the light of the public lamps: seven hundred years after this time there was not so much as one public lamp in London. Its streets were solidly paved: in Paris, centuries subsequently, whoever stepped over his threshold on a rainy day, stepped up to his ankles in mud." The cream of Arab and Judaic learning was contained in the writings of the medieval philosopher Averro, who held that the earth was round, and thus contributed to the discovery of America: Columbus wrote from Haïti, in October 1498, that "Averroes is one of the writers who has made me divine the existence of the New World."[356] Although Averroes was condemned under Leo X by the Lateran Council, his maxims remained the key to European diplomacy for centuries.

Discovery of America "completed that wonderful change in Europe which had been begun by the Crusades," revolutionizing European commercial and economic relations by shifting its trade center from Venice to England, and unearthing a new land whose institutions were not impeded by the burden of Catholic barbarism. "The commercial arrangements of Europe were completely dislocated. Venice and Genoa were deprived of their mercantile supremacy; prosperity left the Italian towns; the commercial monopolies so long in the hands of the European Jews were broken down. These were the first steps of that maritime development soon exhibited by Western Europe." The centers of population, wealth and intellect shifted westward, putting Britain into the van of the new movement. Religious automony followed naturally from the commercial autonomy from Italy, and Protestantism arose to shield nations from papal influence. First wealth, then people themselves began to evacuate

[356] *Civil Policy*, pp. 190, 196.

the shell of Catholic Europe. "The crime of Spain became her punishment." The seat of the Inquisition was foresaken for lands promising greater freedom and mobility. For in Spain, as in the rest of Europe, the Arab Renaissance had not fully taken hold: "the scientific knowledge of modern Europe is the off-spring of the conquest of Spain ... To the Saracens we are indebted for the cotton manufacture," and to the Arabs for such words — and indeed, for such realities — as coffee, algebra, alcohol, cotton paper (from 1102 A.D.), Moorish linen paper, and what was retained from classical Greek knowledge and art. But despite these discoveries, Europe's development continued to be impeded by its Catholic bureaucracy and its moralistic approach. "In Europe," Draper observed, "the attempt has been made to govern communities through their morals alone. The present state of that continent, at the close of so many centuries, shows how great the failure has been. In America, on the contrary, the attempt is to govern through intelligence. It will succeed. For more than a thousand years the moral system [and its teleological interpretation of nature] has been tried in Europe. Its agent, the ecclesiastic, was animated by intentions that were good, by perseverance unwearied, by a vigorous energy. The failure is attributable, not to shortcomings in him, but to intrinsic defects in his method."[357]

It thus was in America that civilization found its path of least resistance, *e.g.*, of least theological constraint. In America "the Reformation at the present moment has farthest advanced ... It falls to the lot of the American Republic to perform the duty that was declined by Rome. Freedom of man, so far as his personal acts are concerned, is already secured; but how much still remains to be done for freedom of thought! Western Europe ... labors under the dead weight of vast ecclesiastical establishments: their influences ramify through all the ranks of society. The tendency given to them by the Byzantine sovereigns and by the Roman Papacy is unchangeable. They will ever continue to be what they have always been — the determined antagonists of science ... In those countries every onward step that science makes implies a conflict. In America, where there is no such dead weight, and where the genius of the public institutions is so different, the progress of thought ought to be free."[358]

This still left the American Civil War to be explained, and here again Draper referred to climatic factors separating the South from the North rather than concentrating on the political issues of slavery and the tariff. To place the discussion in its broad perspective he depicted the world in terms of parallel climatic bands, influencing and modifying man by heat and cold, dryness and

---

[357] *Ibid.*, pp. 95, 89, 97, 116–18, 268. See also p. 169.
[358] *Ibid.*, pp. 279f., 235f.

moisture. Southern and tropical climates were sedentary, breeding static civilizations; northern climates bred a more active man: "the climate is more equable in the South than it is in the North. The irresistible consequence of this is, that in the South the pursuits of men have a greater sameness, their interests are more identical, they think and act alike." "In the North ... summer is the season of outdoor labor, winter is spent in the dwelling. In the South labor may be continuous, though it may vary. The Northern man must do to-day that which the Southern man may put off til to-morrow. For this reason the Northern man must be industrious; the Southern may be indolent, having less foresight and a less tendency to regulated habits. The cold, bringing with it a partial cessation from labor, affords also an opportunity for forethought and reflection; and hence the Northern man acquires a habit of not acting without consideration, and is slower in the initiation of his movements. The Southern man is prone to act without reflection; he does not fairly weigh the last consequence of what he is about to do. The one is cautious, the other impulsive. Winter, with its cheerlessness and discomforts, gives to the Northern man his richest blessing." The Southern mind was more superficial, "more volatile than reflective."[359] Hence, the war between North and South then raging was as much between two different modes of civilization as it was over the slavery issue. (Hence too, Draper's inversion of Bodin's theories.)

"A nation lying east and west," Draper theorized, "will generally have less discordant interests than one the range of which is north and south. Climate varies in this latter case much more than it does in the former." Hence the greater degree of activity—and conflict—in nations spanning a range of latitudes. In this respect the United States differed from, say, China. "That social stagnation so characteristic of Asia depends primarily on the equilibrium that has been attained, in the lapse of many ages, between the strands of its population and the climate zones in which they dwell. To no insignificant extent may the same be perceived in Europe, especially among the lower, that is, among the less locomotive portion of the inhabitants. But in no part of America has that exact concordance as yet had time or opportunity to be truly established, though in the Southern States an approach has been made to it."[360] Moreover, America's climate was continually changing, because of local modifications, the spread of agriculture and internal improvements. Its population was highly mobile, largely a result of its soil-exhaustive modes of agriculture which ensued from the free availability of Western land.

---

[359] *Ibid.*, pp. 143, 43, 77, 52–54.   [360] *Ibid.*, pp. 60, 56f.

Public policy in the United States, and implicitly throughout the world, should be directed toward aiding man, through education and communication, to "neutralize those climatic differences, which, if unchecked, must transmute us into different nations." It would be "unwise to give legislative encouragement to any thing that may tend to make communities, or even families, too stationary ... In America, transportation at the lowest possible cost assumes the attitude of an affair of the highest state necessity." The free movement of population would complement freedom of thought, and would counteract the Southern tendency towards torpor and senseless antipathy towards the North. "Had the Southern States for the last ten years been pervaded by an unceasing stream of Northern travel in every direction," Draper hypothesized, "the civil war would not have occurred."[361] Here was quite a dismissal of all nonclimatic, political and economic factors, and Draper's subsequent writings, especially his history of the Civil War, elaborated his claim that the political and economic differences between North and South were layers built around their central difference in climate.

Draper's materialist interpretation of social evolution was much more technocratic than that of Marx. Like Henry Carey's followers, Simon Patten, and indeed most American theoreticians of technology during this period, he ignored class conflict. He thought of classes mainly in terms of an intellectual elite and a working class, not in terms of capitalists, landlords, farmers and wage-laborers. "To elevate or to depress a group of men, it is necessary to touch their physical condition," he wrote. "We vainly attempt the improvement of a race, intellectually or morally, by missionary exertion or by education, unless we simultaneously touch its actual physical condition." This was the task of an intellectual elite, and it was to this class that Draper ascribed the origin of the state: "In a tribe of savages each man does every thing for himself. By degrees special pursuits pass into the hands of particular individuals. The process goes on until three distinct social divisions are established—a laboring class, a trading or transferring class, an intellectual class. Political differentiation has taken place." The Republic, he continued, may "be regarded as a restrained association of free individuals, voluntarily surrendering a part of their personal independence for the common good, yet all the time conscious and jealous of that surrender. They have bartered a portion of their liberty for security."[362]

Creation of a ruling class was a function of education, which the national government should take the lead in providing: "the public prosperity is considered to depend on education ... this is a very high and noble conception.

---

[361] *Ibid.*, pp. 82, 84, 86f.   [362] *Ibid.*, pp. 158f., 254, 264.

It establishes an intrinsic difference between the people of Europe and the people of America," even though "intellectual development necessarily implies centralization." Draper averred that this was not incompatible with self govern-ment, but "in fact, it may be the logical issue of democratic principles." Machinery was elevating the status of labor from drudgery to intellectual work, breaking the economic bonds of slavery wherever it existed. The drive for wealth, subdued in ancient times, was now invigorating "experimental arrangements and mechancial contrivances … [in] expectation of gaining thereby immense wealth." "Whoever in America desires to better his fellow-men must act by influencing their intellect." American education, however, was still burdened with classical learning rather than representing the existing state of knowledge. "This evil has arisen from the circumstance that our system was imported from England … The grand depositories of human knowledge are not the ancient, but the modern tongues." American education was in any event less burdened by Catholic opposition than that abroad.

Ideas in America thus took on an impelling force rather than a resisting one. "The first act in the drama of American national life is over," Draper concluded. "There is indeed a manifest destiny before us." The United States, unburdened with Europe's theologically perverted educational system, would inaugurate a new technocratic civilization which would leave Europe and Asia far behind. "An Imperial power has come into existence before our eyes. It rivals—perhaps, indeed, it already excels—in warlike resources the ancient monarchies of Europe."[363] It would become the logical and most successful culmination of the Arab and Protestant Renaissances. A "modified man" was being created in America, unleashing a potential denied by centuries of priest-ridden intellectual barbarism in the Old World.

The Civil War had catalyzed the formation of a National Academy of Sciences, which for some reason did not cite Draper among the nation's fifty leading scientists. Visibly piqued, Draper took the lead in establishing the somewhat obscure American Union Academy of Literature, Science and Art in 1869. In Comtian fashion he sought to extend the definition of science into social fields, and urged the new organization "to throw light on all the problems of society, instead of such small issues as how to keep iron-bottom ships from corroding, shield the compass on ironclads from shock, or test whisky for puri-ty." It was, in short, to promote the science of society as well as natural science. It also was to concentrate on the development of national resources, and on the technocratic planning of American social evolution. As Fleming describes

[363] *Ibid.*, pp. 268, 30, 128, 270, 274, 240, 9.

Draper's plan, "the American Union Academy should make itself as near as might be the planning arm of the Secretary of the Interior, with his department conceived on a scale somewhat larger than life as of 1870 ... If this would afford the means for insinuating the social scientist into the democratic structure, a less alarming start could hardly have been made; and the academy petered out almost at once."[364] Finally, in 1875, the American Academy of Arts and Sciences awarded Draper its Rumford medals for his researches into radiant energy, and the following year he was elected the first president of the American Chemical Society.

Draper's views on the objective, inductive and scientific nature of American civilization were representative of a new spirit which was extending throughout the United States following the Civil War. It was during these years that Henry Charles Lea, grandson of Mathew Carey and nephew of Henry Carey, began to publish his works on the history of European Christianity, culminating in his multi-volume *History of the Inquisition.* In 1896 Andrew Dickson White, one of the founders of Cornell University, published his two-volume *History of the Warfare of Science with Theology in Christendom*, covering much the same ground as Draper. The latter himself had compiled his *History of the Conflict between Religion and Science* in 1874, and it was the most popular of all the books published by Youmans' International Scientific Library.

These views represented a distinctly American form of materialism, which was linked with social Darwinism in viewing America as emerging as a superior civilization. This would occur, its advocates believed, not on racial grounds (such as characterized the subsequent emergence of Germany and Japan) but on economic grounds, as American prosperity bred a new kind of man and a new kind of society which, through the process of natural selection, would emerge to dominate an increasingly enlightened, scientific and technocratic world of the future.

---

[364] Fleming, *op. cit.*, pp. 111f., 138.

SIMON PATTEN AND THE ECONOMY OF ABUNDANCE

Simon Nelson Patten (1852–1922) was the most original American economist of the post-Civil War generation. Like Henry Carey and his followers, he urged protection bordering on isolationism as a way for all nations to promote their economic development. It was not primarily from Carey that he derived his inspiration, however, but from the German Historical School of economists, particularly his teacher Johannes Conrad, under whom he had studied at Halle in the late 1870s.

Carey's school of protectionists had endorsed state intervention in the form of industrial tariffs (the proceeds of which would be used to finance internal improvements), but they did not sanction state regulation of industrial monopolies and trusts, or other state activities taken for granted today. They were conservative Republicans and, by the time Patten began to publish in 1885, were dangerously near to becoming apologists for the protected interests. It was thus inevitable that soon after Patten joined the University of Pennsylvania's Wharton School, in 1888, he began to feud with Carey's follower Robert Ellis Thompson, who opposed his "socialistic" collectivism. Patten had returned from Germany imbued with a faith in state action to shape economic and social development, an attitude shared by his fellow-students at Halle, Edmund James (who brought him to the Wharton School) and Richard T. Ely. These three friends played the leading role in founding the American Economic Association in 1885, hoping to develop a school of politically active economists in the United States.

Like Carey's school, Patten's first reaction against Ricardian laissez-faire economics came from his perception that its theory of production was superficial, particularly its view of soil, labor and capital as having static "original and indestructible" productive powers. Soil fertility, he recognized, depended on the principles of agricultural chemistry as they applied to crop-rotation patterns, and labor productivity depended on the worker's standard of life, education, and the technological capital at his disposal. Later, in the 1890s, Patten progressed beyond this criticism as he formulated a broad theory of national social and biological development. Ultimately, his view that the state should play an active role in setting market prices and guiding the institutional structure of society led to his being forced out of the Wharton School. By this time he had indeed evolved from a protectionist to a state socialist.

1. The Economic Basis of Protection

The Economic Basis of Protection, published in 1890, ends the first phase of Patten's attack on the static production concepts underlying Ricardian economics. The outlines of this critique had appeared in his first economic work, *The Premises of Political Economy* (1885), and were elaborated in somewhat novel form in *The Consumption of Wealth* (1889). Specialization of labor and production on a world scale, he argued, connoted a lack of variety of labor and agricultural production at the national level. If each country produced only those goods which it could sell most cheaply at a given moment of time, its soil would be depleted by one-crop farming and its labor force constrained into a narrow range of occupations. Furthermore, specialization of world labor rendered international trade more prone to cartelization, as relative production costs tended to diverge among nations following international specialization. The only alternative was for each nation or geographic region to produce a wide range of agricultural and industrial commodities, affording a suitable variety of occupations for its labor and permitting adequate crop rotation policies for its farms.

America's economic ideal, Patten concluded, "must stand in sharp contrast with the static ideal advocated by most free-traders." To follow free-traders in viewing cheapness of production as the single criterion of efficiency in trade would be valid only "if the efficiency of each laborer and the modes of production are fixed quantities." In a dynamic society, however, "we cannot accept the present efficiency of the various classes of laborers as a permanent quantity, nor can we regard in the same way the productivity of land and other natural resources." Improvement in the skill-level and intelligence of a nation's people was a better test of national efficiency. "As capital and skill are constantly displacing crude labor ... through inventions and improvements," a nation owed it to its citizens to place them in a favorable technological and social state. "National prosperity is a much larger and more complicated problem than that of the individuals who form the nation at any given time ... A progressive nation must see not merely that its present inhabitants have a profitable trade, but that the latent qualities in men and land are gradually drawn out." True, the labor force was most efficient when divided into a diversity of classes and types of individuals. But "if the labor of a nation is devoted to a few occupations," Patten asserted, "there is a bar to its development into a higher industrial stage," as it would be unable to utilize the full range of its inborn talents. "If man were as simple in his mechanism as Ricardo supposes, and had but one industrial quality developed, the social conditions which would result would harmonize fully with free-trade doctrines."[365] But man possessed a diversity of psychological impulses, and therefore required a wide range of occupations in which to apply these diverse talents.[366]

Initial lack of such diversity of labor qualities should not deter the state from promoting industry. "Every industrial quality may be acquired if the nation encourages its development. There are no marks to distinguish the English from the Italian workman but those due to the historical development of the two nations. Place the Italian nation in the social environment of the English and they would soon be as efficient. No progressive nation can accept any industrial deficiency of its people as final." Its increase in skill would soon result in a steady rise in the general wage level, creating a self-financing form of self-education.

This quite American doctrine stood in sharp contrast to that of "economic writers from Smith to Mill [who] have regarded skill among the causes determining differences in wages and not among the causes fixing the rate of wages."[367] The pattern and evolution of foreign trade was thus not determined simply by a nation's pre-existing natural conditions, but by the evolution of its technology, itself a social phenomenon. Man's destiny was to conquer nature through knowledge and determination, not remain subservient to it. To permit foreign trade to be determined by natural conditions as they existed *a priori* to man's social, technological, and economic development was to permit society to remain in a primitive state.

[365] Simon Patten, *The Economic Basis of Protection* (Philadelphia, 1890), pp. 8, 126, 133, 84, 134, 18.

[366] This was not a new argument. A century earlier, Alexander Hamilton had argued in his *Report on Manufactures* (1791) that industrialization, fostered by protective tariffs, would "open a wider field to exertions of ingenuity than agriculture," and would furnish "greater scope for the diversity of talents and dispositions which discriminate men from each other" by "affording a more ample and various field for enterprise." Agricultural labor was necessarily unemployed during most of the winter months, and women and children had only limited opportunities to labor on the land. The development of domestic manufacturing, by contrast, would afford productive employment to "persons who would otherwise be idle (and in many cases a burden on the community), either from the bias of temper, habit, infirmity of body, or some other cause, indisposing or disqualifying them from the toils of the country." Hence the aim of each nation to open as wide a field as possible to exploit the inborn diversity of character of its inhabitants. (Alexander Hamilton, *Report on the Subject of Manufactures,* reprinted in Frank W. Taussig, ed., *State Papers and Speeches on the Tariff* [Cambridge, Mass., 1893], pp. 8, 15, 19.)

[367] *Ibid.*, pp. 90, 61.

In the production of raw material we have the last part of a long struggle of man with nature. Elsewhere civilized man is now supreme and has cast off the bonds that held him to natural production. In primitive nations production is confined to localities where nature does so much that crude ignorant men can do the rest. In the production of finished commodities this influence of location is reduced to a minimum. The extensive use of capital, skill, and intelligence have freed modern nations from the primitive forms of production which confined each industry to particular regions where nature gave the most assistance. Water-power is no longer essential to national prosperity, steamboats are displacing sailing vessels, linen is no longer sent to Holland to be bleached, and railroads have given to the interior of continents the advantages formerly confined to the sea-coast.... Every new utilization of natural forces decreases our dependence upon those productive processes in which natural production is advantageous.[368]

Even tropical crops "produced under very crude conditions by the least progressive nations" could be produced under more civilized conditions in America's Southern states for one-half or one-third the price that the nation was then paying for them. Efficient American labor and production techniques, Patten believed, would more than offset a lesser original and natural advantage.

Original natural advantage could be seriously impaired if the specialization of international production was pushed to the extreme of a one- or two-crop basis. This policy had exhausted the South's cotton and tobacco lands, and stripped Michigan of its forests. "Any land," Patten asserted, "is poor land for one crop. It becomes better land through an increase in the variety of its products, and is superior land only when a suitable rotation of crops brings out all its qualities. The course of foreign trade may make the use of land for a single crop more profitable for a time, yet the gain to the owner is at the expense of the productive qualities of the land. Free-trade thus prevents a well-balanced development of the group of industries which will make the most of the land." The problem was that the free-traders "suppose that there is some land best fitted for wheat and upon which a continuous series of wheat crops can be obtained. Then other land is thought of as cotton land, and still other land as coffee land or sugar land. In this way, the whole land of the world is divided up into sections supposed to be devoted to some one purpose, just as the machines upon the market are known to be best suited for some one end." However, "there is no piece of land which can give as great a return for one crop as for a group of crops. Devote a piece of land to the continuous production of wheat and you take from the land a large share of its fertility. There will, after the first few years, be a steady diminution of the product, until at last the land

---

[368] *Ibid.*, pp. 106f.

will be exhausted and perhaps abandoned." Soil, Patten concluded, "does not have any indestructible qualities which will allow its use in any one way without serious economic advantage." Free trade, inasmuch as it led to a specialization of agricultural output among nations, was thus "not a policy which will lead to the greatest increase of the productive power of any nation."[369]

These statements had a long pedigree in American protectionist literature, reaching back to Justus Liebig, via Peshine Smith and Henry Carey. Patten's critique of Ricardo's static concept of soil and simplistic view of labor did not stem from the American protectionists, however, but from his teacher Conrad, who in 1864 had published a monograph on *Liebig's Ansicht von der Boden-erschöpfung und ihre geschichtliche, statistische und nationalökonomische Begründung,* in which he emphasized the correlation between the soil's fertility and its receipt of manure and related chemical inputs, and between labor's rate of work output and its nutritional standards. These theories Patten integrated with his own background on his father's farm in De Kalb, Illinois.

"Can the art of agriculture be based upon anything but the restitution of a disturbed equilibrium?" Liebig had queried in the 1840s, in his *Familiar Letters on Chemistry*. "Can it be imagined that any country, however rich and fertile, with a flourishing commerce, which for centuries exports its produce in the shape of grain and cattle, will maintain its fertility, if the same commerce does not restore, in some form of manure, those elements which have been removed from the soil, and which cannot be replaced by the atmosphere? Must not the same fate await every such country which has actually befallen the once prolific soil of Virginia, now in many parts no longer able to grow its former staple productions—wheat and tobacco?"[370] This argument had been seized upon by American protectionists to demonstrate that all farm districts within the United States that were net exporters of crops must, in the absence of a corresponding net importation of fertilizer, be characterized by soil-depleting modes of agriculture. This became a major element in their cry to place the consumer by the side of the producer, the farmer beside the industrial laborer to achieve a local urban-rural balance. Trade between town and country was not at all to be compared with trade between industrial and agricultural nations: the latter prevented restitution of the soil's fertility via urban wastes and proper crop rotation, the latter requiring the cultivation of perishable crops for which there could be no foreign demand.

[369] *Ibid.*, pp. 85, 29f., 57, 19.
[370] Justus Liebig, *Familiar Letters on Chemistry*, reprinted in *Complete Works on Chemistry*, tr. Lyon Playfair (Philadelphia, 1843), p. 32.

Daniel Lee gave a rough statistical estimate of the cost of America's soil-depleting modes of cultivation in his contributions to the *Report of the Commissioner of Patents. Vol. II. Agriculture* for the years 1849 and 1852. Farm income was reduced by about 10¢ per acre on 100 million of the 125 million acres of improved farmland then in cultivation, he calculated. The value of these farmlands was reduced by some $300 million per year (an average $3.00 an acre, or nearly 20 per cent of the crops' sales value) through removal of minerals from the soil by the agricultural methods then in use, "by which remark we mean that complete restitution of the elements of crops removed, such as potash, soda, lime, magnesia, chlorine, phosphoric and sulphuric acids, and ammonia, cannot be made short of an expense of three dollars an acre." Ultimately responsible for impairing the nation's soil fertility in this way, Lee asserted, was its free-trade policy: "American statesmanship has adopted a system of political economy which renders full and perfect restitution of the soil impossible so long as it shall prevail. This statesmanship, which ignores the very existence of agricultural science, and repudiates all its teachings, costs the country three hundred million dollars a year by the needless destruction of its agricultural resources."[371] To achieve a more normal pattern of economic development, America must become more self-contained.

Patten's theories were thus in line with both the American and German critiques of Ricardo's theory of rent and international trade. "The person who exports food and brings back in exchange for it certain foreign commodities makes a gain," Patten acknowledged,

> but this gain must not be regarded as a gain to the nation ... To estimate correctly the results of foreign trade two other elements must be considered. The one is the loss to the public on the food consumed at home through the higher price which results from a greater demand for exportable food, and the other the loss our agricultural classes sustain through the reduced variety of crops. The foreign market does not create a demand for the bulky agricultural products. It is merely such light, compact articles as wheat, tobacco, or cotton, that the foreign consumer wants from America.[372]

[371] Daniel Lee, "Progress of Agriculture in the United States," in *Report of the Commissioner of Patents for the year 1852. Part II: Agriculture* (Washington, 1853), pp. 7, 15, and "Statistics and Progress of Agriculture in the United States for the year 1849," in *ibid., ... 1849* (Washington, 1850), p. 25. See also *The Journal of the United States Agricultural Society* 1, no. 1 (August 1852), pp. 14–24, and *Agriculture of the United States in 1860; Compiled from the Original Returns of the Eighth Census, under the Direction of the Secretary of the Interior* (Washington, 1864), pp. iii-iv, viii, xliii-iv. This theory formed the basis for what E. Peshine Smith called "The Law of Endless Circulation in Matter and Force" in his *Manual of Political Economy* (New York, 1853).

[372] *The Economic Basis of Protection*, pp. 48f., See also pp. 41–43.

"Time again has disproved the fallacy that the best opportunities for labor were first utilitzed," Patten asserted in an argument highly reminiscent of Carey's theory of cultivation. "With each extension of the home market new uses for the land are found, and at the same time many classes of soil which were worthless while the few crops demanded by foreigners were produced, now become the more productive part of the land ... The lighter soils were first occupied because better adapted to the cultivation of wheat ... But when the growth of home markets created a demand for corn instead of wheat, these heavier lands were brought into use, and soon came to be regarded as the better land." It followed that "the law of agricultural industry is ... the opposite of manufacturing industry. The best use of land demands a variety of products, while a factory is more productive making one." [373]

Patten's criticism of the economic effects of specializing in raw-materials production is in many ways modern, especially as it applies to tropical climates and countries. "Peculiar advantages in one article," he recognized, "instead of being the cause of national prosperity, as free-traders would have us believe, are usually a hindrance to progress ... The North would be as poor as the South and its cities as small if the land of the North were used for wheat as that of the South is used for cotton. Had our nation followed the lines of relative advantage advocated by free-traders, our country would be divided into three parallel belts, used for cotton, tobacco, and wheat." There would not be much population on these lands, and the United States would resemble the South American republics:

> Cuba would be more prosperous if she were less fertile for sugar, for then Spanish misrule would not be possible. Coffee has not made Brazil or Java rich and prosperous countries. If a blight upon the grape-vine should force the people of Portugal to use their land for a variety of uses for which it is well fitted, the loss of relative advantage in grape cultivation would be a national gain. And the history of England bears testimony to the same truth. At an early period the sheep industry paid so well that the quantity of cultivated land and the demand for labor were greatly reduced, thus checking the progress of the nation. The increased number of sheep did not come from any especial advantage of the sheep industry in England. It was Continental disorder that prevented the keeping of sheep elsewhere. Thus the fact that England was far enough in advance of other nations to protect property in country districts checked the growth of population and wealth by giving a relative advantage to sheep-raising ... The advantage in various industries which might have been secured to England through its internal peace was lost because of the relative advantage of wool-growers.[374]

In fact, he claimed, existing world patterns of trade were just the reverse of those dictated by "nature": "England is especially adapted to the production

---

[373] *Ibid.*, pp. 35f., 31. See also pp. 85f.   [374] *Ibid.*, pp. 87f.

of wheat while America has the better facilities for the production of iron." America's dry, hot summers resulted in a yield of about twelve bushels an acre, as compared to more than twice this rate in England's damp climate which was good for wheat. (Patten neglected to point out that England's capital-intensive agriculture required much more labor per acre than America's soil-extensive pattern of cultivation.) Furthermore, America's iron beds were purer and thicker, and its coal beds thicker than those of England. "Yet in spite of these facts trade between the United States and England actually has a tendency to increase in America the demand for [*i.e.*, production of] wheat, ... while the same commercial conditions increase in England the demand for iron ..."[375]

Patten pressed to an unrealistic extreme, however, his thesis that "a dynamic society passes from poorer to better land by increasing the variety of its food and the diversity of its occupations." He urged that Americans must adjust their tastes "so that our pleasures and wants can be easily supplied from the material resources by which we are surrounded ... That consumption of wealth is most advantageous which creates a demand for the products of the soil in that pro-portion which will allow the best use of the soil ... our present consumption is not final ... acquired habits have created in us a liking for particular articles of food, and are accompanied by prejudices keeping us from using many articles which could now be produced with great advantage."[376] The nation should shift its tastes from whiskey to sugar, from wheat to corn, from European tastes to native American tastes generally, according to the dictates of nature (pre-cisely those dictates which he had elsewhere hoped that men and nations could overcome).

Why, Patten asked, should Americans let British consumers bid up the price of food? "The burden that oppresses the American laborer," he stated, came not so much from industrial monopolies (on which, incidentally, he was silent), but from the relatively high "price he pays for the articles we export, for those we import free of duty, and for city land. It is the price he pays for bread and meat, for tea and coffee, and for house-rent that have increased and absorb so large a part of his wages. Cuban sugar and Brazilian coffee are at monopoly prices, and not Ohio wool or Pennsylvania iron. Cotton, woollen, silk, steel, and other protected goods are sold to laborers at a lower price than ever before. In short, the laborer, as well as other consumers, has gained wherever the national policy has been active, and lost wherever it has been passive. A passive reliance on free-trade brings high prices; an active preference for home production brings cheapness. The former creates natural monopolies; the latter breaks

---

[375] *Ibid.*, pp. 32–34.
[376] *Ibid.*, pp. 114f. See also p. 103.

them down." "Free-trade may reduce the price of some commodities, but it reduces productive power so much more rapidly that the people suffer from it." [377]

This led to an isolationist position: Instead of America depending on foreign trade either as a source of imports or as an export outlet, Patten urged that foreign animals be adopted to American conditions, and tropical crops cultivated in the Southern states and in an irrigated Southwest. "Our Southern States lie in a semi-tropical region and are well fitted for all those crops which we secure from similar regions abroad … There are many portions of the South where tea can be produced with as little labor as in any part of China," given adequate instruction in tea-growing methods, an educational service which the government might sponsor. Silk could also be nurtured, as could sugar. "Florida and Cuba are under the same climatic conditions," he observed, and Florida could produce Cuban articles at perhaps half their present cost, given adequate drainage facilities. Germany's successful cultivation of the sugar beet was cited as an ideal example of adopting seemingly foreign commodities to domestic production conditions.[378]

The book's final chapter posed the question whether the ideal of American civilization should be national or cosmopolitan. Free trade, Patten insisted, tended to breed provincialism as much as it contributed to cosmopolitanism. "So firmly have free-trade notions become rooted in [economists'] modes of thinking, that they are led to suppose that the actual industries of the nation are those in which labor is most productive," because of the *ex posteriori* methods of orthodox economists, inevitably proving that all is for the best in this, the best of all possible worlds. American economic development, however, should not be determined by what was best under past types of institutions (for instance, that of slavery, which had been reinforced by free trade), but what was best looking forward in time.

> Provincialism includes a hostility to other nationalities and the desire to cling to that which has grown up within its narrow bounds. It is also a static conception, and would hold each locality to those ideas and modes of living which they have acquired from past times. Nationalism, on the contrary, is a dynamic movement, and seeks to bring each nation through a series of changes and developments that would bring a better harmony between its social conditions and its economic environment …
>
> Nationalism tends to adjust the people of a nation more closely to their environment and thus develop all its natural resources … Cosmopolitanism, however, overlooks the need of this adjustment to objective conditions and tends to adjust man more closely to a particular social condition and to cut off those portions of society lacking dominant traits. It stops differentiation and presses the nation into a fixed social state …

---

[377] *Ibid.*, pp. 68f., 135. See also pp. 49–51.
[378] *Ibid.*, pp. 99–102.

> A national ideal is not opposed to the general good of the whole world. If each nation makes the best use of its own land and of its own resources the whole world will be utilized to the fullest degree ... As long as the land of one nation is used directly to support the people of another nation only the lowest forms of commerce and the crudest material will be a part of the trade with other nations ... The value of American trade to Europe has increased just in proportion as the American people have used their land to support themselves.[379]

Patten concluded that America's "opportunities for development and progress are much more favorable than those of Europe, and we can develop into a higher civilization much more rapidly than it is possible for them to do." For America was not burdened with the social rigidities that constrained Europe's economic development. Once the nation turned inward, maximizing its own wealth-creating powers to the utmost and elevating all classes of society, "America would have little difficulty in finding imitators all over the world ... Just as English isolation from the Continent developed new industrial conditions so superior to those of the Continent that in the end other nations were forced to adopt them, so a national policy in America can develop a still higher industrial state, and thus compel other nations to make use of the same means in their development." Other protectionists were short-sighted in urging protectionism simply on the assumption that "it is good for the American people to approximate European conditions," using protective tariffs towards this end.[380] Just the opposite: America should strive to become what Europe had been unable to become: a dynamic technocratic society.

The Economic Basis of Protection was soon translated both into French and Italian. In the United States it was reviewed by Henry C. Adams, John Bates Clark, John Commons, and Frank Taussig. In England, John Bastable, who had been sympathetic to protectionism in cases where nations could force the incidence of the tariff onto the shoulders of its suppliers, declared that "Patten had merely reworked the doctrines of List and Carey."[381] This was certainly not true: Patten carried the theory of productive powers much further than had List, and elaborated the theory of soils, and especially the theory of monopolistic practices in world trade, to a higher degree than had Carey. If there is any earlier protectionist he resembles, it is E. Peshine Smith, who had devoted most of his *Manual of Political Economy* (1853) to emphasizing the adverse effect of crop exports on soil fertility. Unlike Peshine Smith and Carey, however, Patten did not discuss the growth of productive powers stemming from capital-driven machinery and other suppliers of industrial energy. The nexus of his doctrine remained largely agricultural.

---

[379] *Ibid.*, pp. 137–39.   [380] *Ibid.*, 140–42, 8.

[381] *Economic Journal* 1 (September 1891), pp. 596–99, quoted in Daniel M. Fox, *The Discovery of Abundance: Simon N. Patten and the Transformation of Social Theory* (Ithaca, 1967), p. 193.

In France, Courcelle-Seneuil, the pigeon-holer of economic theory who four decades earlier had rejected Peshine Smith's *Manual of Political Economy* as resting on propositions more agricultural and technological than "economic" (in the moral-philosophical interpretation of the term), was disturbed that Patten followed the German historical school in including political and psychological considerations in his economic theory. Gide and Rist criticized Patten's nationalistic bias. And in Italy, Luigi Cossa found Patten's argument specious, while Ugo Rabbeno attacked it at length.[382]

In the United States, Taussig granted that Patten's "arguments are very different from those commonly heard," but asserted that these arguments, even if true, were not inconsistent with the doctrine of comparative advantage:

> In countries producing raw materials, says Professor Patten, the effect of free trade is to cause the exportation of raw materials, and especially of food. The quantity produced, say in the United States, is greater than it would be without the foreign demand. Inferior soils are resorted to, the price rises, and the consumers of food are worse off than they would be in the absence of the foreign demand. Rent rises, and 'natural monopolies' have a greater share of the total production …
>
> But … the rise in the price of food and in rent does not of itself indicate that the trade of the food-exporting country with the other country is a losing one, and, moreover, that, if the trade becomes a real source of loss, it will cease of its own accord … even at the higher cost and price of food, the labor devoted to raising and exporting it may still yield a higher return in imported goods than the same labor would yield in their domestic production [at a given moment of time]; and, if it failed to do so, food would cease to be exported … The loss from the pressure of the law of diminishing returns is offset by the gain from cheaper imports.[383]

This was not Patten's major concern, however. He compared the gains-from-trade under existing conditions and productive power to the *potential* output that could be created by developing the country's labor and soil. Into the free-trade equation he added the "gains from *foresaking* trade," that is, of *not* having to invest funds at some future date to rehabilitate the soil and re-educate the labor driven out of high-skill industries by temporary cost-saving trade expedients. Taussig was erroneous in stating that "in a new country like the United States, the tendency to diminishing returns has not been felt." Nor was he able to deal with Patten's arguments concerning the ways in which international trade fostered the growth of cartels and monopolies, or to understand how "the distinction between static and dynamic societies is essentially different from that which economists have had in mind between old and young

---

[382] Fox, *ibid.*, p. *193*.

[383] Frank Taussig, "Recent Literature on Protection," *Quarterly Journal of Economics* 7 (1892), pp. 173–75. Taussig is criticizing an argument enunciated by Patten, *op. cit.*, pp. 47f., 37f., 13, 40.

countries." The distinction between old and young countries, Patten would have answered, referred essentially to their differing factor proportions, with young countries having relatively more soil than capital. His own distinction between static and dynamic societies referred to the direction of the national economy in terms of maximizing output under existing conditions and productive powers (the static case), as opposed to maximizing the productivity of labor, soil and capital over time (the dynamic case). Young societies were not necessarily dynamic, as was demonstrated by the sad experience of most South American countries.

Patten has been criticized for his optimistic belief that the Southern states could grow tea and raw silk. But such criticisms divert attention from his major points. Probably the best evaluation of his work was given by Daniel Fox in *The Discovery of Abundance: Simon N. Patten and the Transformation of Social Theory* (1967). "Patten's fellow economists praised his originality without taking account of his central idea," he wrote. "Although John Bates Clark of Columbia University declared in 1892 that Patten was providing a 'scientific basis on an optimistic faith in all of us,' he never mentioned the concept of a transition, but engaged in lengthy conflict with Patten about the definitions of cost and price ... [E.R.A.] Seligman said that Patten had 'inspired more of the younger scholars in the United States than any other individual,' but never mentioned his central thesis. ... Even his closest friends were appalled by his inability to state his theories clearly and concisely ... Few of his colleagues could spare time from their own research and teaching to unravel the theories Patten spun out in twenty-two books and a hundred and fifty articles. Moreover, despite several painful efforts, Patten was unable to bring his ideas together in a comprehensive synthesis ... His colleagues could debate his views on such problems as marginal utility, tariffs, and the theory of prices without acknowledging that they were part of an overarching conception of a transition from an age of scarcity to an age of abundance." Ultimately, Patten was to pursue his investigations beyond the confines of economics altogether as it came to be narrowed down in the early twentieth century. "The frame of reference most hospitable to Patten's ideas was that of the first generation of American sociologists. These men, most of them trained as economists in Germany or the United States, found scientific economics too constricting a discipline. They wanted the freedom to explore social change and its implications in the broadest possible manner ..." [384]

---

[384] Fox, *Discovery of Abundance*, pp. 146f., 157.

2. The Theory of Social Forces

In the 1880s and 1890s, many American proponents of laissez-faire began to shift their arguments from the classical Ricardian "gains from trade" economics to the individualistic "survival of the fittest" sociological doctrines of Herbert Spencer. Just as natural selection favored superior species in any given environment, they argued, so unregulated competition in economic society would favor the most efficient individuals, firms, and nations. Patten's *Theory of Social Forces* (1896) criticized the static view of "environment" surrounding this biological analogy, and his sequel, *The Development of English Thought* (1898), attempted to formulate an alternative view of human bio-economic competition.

Spencer had acknowledged that biology generally overlooked "the environment and its correlated phenomena ... while the organism and its correlated phenomena practically monopolize the attention." Patten replied that inasmuch as economic factors created environments, and environments influenced the selection, generation, and even the mutation of species, it followed that if "we seek in the environment for the causes of evolution ... the study lies in the field of economics ..." What was once a brutal individualistic conflict between man and beast, and later between men themselves, was now transformed into a higher, increasingly intellectual contest between man and nature. As man succeeded in improving his environment, he altered the terms upon which this contest occurred by accumulating capital and creating an active social-economic state apparatus. "A progressive evolution," Patten insisted, "depends on the power of moving from one environment to another, and thus avoiding the stress of competition." Patten thus distinguished between two kinds of progress (or, as today's economists would say, between "growth" and "development"): "Static progress increases the sum of adjustments or the average adjustment to a given environment and thus gives to an animal the power to survive in this environment ... The second kind of progress is dynamic and leads to the acquisition of new mental qualities by which adjustment to a new environment is possible ... The single aim of progressive animals is to escape from competition; the single means is to secure control of that quality which opens to its possessors a new environment."[385] In the realm of international economic policy—which Patten began to treat almost as a branch of anthropology—nations with superior educational and political systems would emerge supreme, by providing their labor and capital with superior and less conflict-ridden economic environments.

---

[385] Simon Patten, *The Theory of Social Forces* (New York, 1896), pp. 5, 7–10, 14f., quoting Spencer's *Psychology*, Vol. I, pp. 133–35.

Man's intellectual evolution was accompanied by psychological changes in his social makeup. In the beginning, when mankind first began to spread over the earth seeking the most favorable climates, "aggressive instincts which put a being in a state of opposition to his fellow creatures, are of more value to him than economic instincts which cause him to utilize more completely or to improve the conditions of his environment. Greater bodily activity and an increase in ability to experience pleasure go hand and hand ..." Later, the requisites for survival became more intellectual. "The memory is developed; the power to analyze objective phenomena into their material elements increases ... There are thus two stages of progress — the biologic and the social ... In the biologic stage ... the development of the motor powers determines who shall survive ... The social beings with superior sensory powers are thus repeatedly defeated and driven out by those whose motor development is superior ... Biologic progress is due to the struggle for existence within a given environment. Social progress is due to the necessity of breaking over from one environment to another." Patten buttressed this theory with psychological views taken mainly from William James and James Mark Baldwin: he distinguished "motor" ideas, which were products of man's genetic organism itself, from "sensory" or knowledge-producing ideas conveyed to man from his environment. Sensory ideas were higher in that they enabled man to formulate ideals to inspire political thought and action, enabling cooperative economic bonds to be formed. "Men at a very early stage of progress became conscious of the benefits of cooperation ... capital cannot be secured except by the protection of property on the one hand and by a growing desire for future welfare on the other ... The economic bonds are the effects of a more or less conscious calculus of utilities."[386] Hence Patten's belief in the harmony of interests among all sectors of economic-surplus societies, a view inspired partly by German state socialists and partly by William Morris and the Christian Socialists.

"If organisms develop it is not owing to internal conditions or to the laws of life," Patten speculated, "but to some peculiarities of the surrounding conditions."[387] New environments seemed to breed a new kind of man — a theory more Lamarckian than Darwinist. Surplus ("pleasure") economies worked to select altruistic types naturally amenable to statism, as egoistic and avaricious types succumbed to sensual overindulgence. Only in his *English Thought*, however, did Patten reconcile Newtonian model-building with the historical optimism of his Social Darwinism: he proposed an evolutionary mechanism which naturally favored state-socialist nations over individualistic economies. Hence, statism indicated the emergence of superior men rather than being a means to protect economic inferiors.

[386] *Ibid.*, pp. 50–53, 23f., 26, 85f., 90f.   [387] *Ibid.*, p. 49.

To elaborate this theory Patten suggested four character types: the Sensualists—essentially Southern, aggressive types who became priests, Military Leaders, or more often in Modern Society, Capitalists whose particular form of sensuality led them to become "lovers of power rather than of sensual indulgence"; Clingers, a submissive class of imitators; Mugwumps, a somewhat mild intellectual type; and Stalwarts, a semi-Calvinist, altruistic type of principled, socially-conscious man that appeared only in advanced economic societies. "In modern times, where social conditions are more stable, the sensualists have not been distinct races, but a class growing larger or smaller as conditions have been favorable or not." Patten's genetic views thus treated "race" as a function of character-type and economic class, and less and less as a function of national origins as such.[388]

Actually, *The Development of English Thought* was two books, quite uneven in quality. The best portion was a cultural history of British ideology, in which Patten intriguingly presented his own theories as the logical culmination of classical economics, both as to logical method (Newtonian) and to moral principles (a happy ending for the historical process). Patten divided British economics into two strands: moral philosophy as to the relationship between economic development and social welfare, and methodology as to the refinement of self-contained economic models. His concluding chapter suggested a synthesis of social optimism and Newtonian methodology based on the economic emergence of new genetic types of man.

The book's first three chapters undoubtedly put most readers off before they had a chance to discover Patten's observations on the cultural history of British economic thought, or his own resolution of its problems. Patten's biographer, Daniel Fox, calls the work "a curious combination of insight and fantasy." A contemporary reviewer praised its originality and insight, but noted its "impression of unreality, of an excursion into some scientific dreamland," and a modern observer has called it "a strange and tortured magnum opus."[389] The first chapter ("The Theory") does not state his theory (that comes only in the sixth and final chapter), but renews his discussion of man's inborn personality types. Whereas Patten's *Social Forces* claimed that these types were not hereditary, Patten now asserted that man's "motor" ideas, formed by past environments, were passed on through the genetic process.[390] Upon this pre-

---

[388] *The Development of English Thought* (New York, 1898), pp. 35 (see also pp. 101, 200f.), 27 (see also p. 186) and 9 (see also pp. 4, 41).
[389] Fox, *op. cit.*, pp. 81, 199f., citing Monroe Smith, "Patten's Study of English Thought," *Political Science Quarterly* 15 (March 1900), and David Noble, *The Paradox of Progressive Thought* (St. Paul, 1958), p. 181.
[390] *Social Forces*, p. 38.

existing set of motor responses were superimposed man's knowledge and "sensory" impulses derived from his present environment. Each physical environment was viewed as developing its own type of man, with national character being formed by hereditary personality types interacting with the current economic environment. The kinship of this Lamarckian view with twentieth-century Lysenkoism is apparent.

Patten's second chapter, nominally on the antecedents of English thought, once again does not approach the topic at hand. It collects his ruminations on the evolution of the Christian Church from Judaic religion to an increasingly secular arm of Roman power; the economic nature of the Reformation, stemming mainly from the growing commercial power of Europe's northern nations and their nationalistic desire to break away from Rome; the dietary evolution of man; the relationship between climate and woman's role in society; the bathtub's role in forming British character; and other broad-ranging topics not too completely digested. Chapter 3 deals somewhat superficially with the rise of the Lutherans and Calvinists, the contrast between Sensualists and Stalwarts, and the changing roles of town and countryside as regards sensualist pastimes. By this time the reader is two hundred pages into the book with seemingly no bearings, much as if he had come upon a history student's college notebook covering courses without too much relationship to one another.

Patten finally gets down to his task in chapters 4 and 5, dealing respectively with the Moralists and the Economists. He perceived Bernard Mandeville to be the first to insist, as a central economic tenet, that private self-interest worked for the common good even when pressed to the point of apparent immorality. This was essentially Adam Smith's concept of the "invisible hand" guiding private self-interest to serve the common weal, as well as the suggestion by Sir James Steuart and Malthus that luxurious spending by the rich was necessary to maintain the employment and well-being of the poor. However, Malthus' population theories broke this optimism, by asserting that man's passions led to overpopulation, reducing everyone's living standards a pessimistic view complemented by the Ricardian doctrine of diminishing returns in agriculture, and consequently falling profits and stagnation throughout the economy. Economic optimism was restored, Patten held, by Charles Darwin's theories, which implied that the struggle for existence — as reflected in economic competition — worked steadily to improve society by weeding out its weaker social-economic members. In this respect Darwin was elevated by Patten to the first rank of economists, standing alongside Henry Carey as representing a return to the optimistic views of economic evolution held by Mandeville and Adam Smith.

Patten then treated the attempt to make British economics a Newtonian science based on determinist mechanistic models. This tendency, first inspired by Hobbes and Locke, was elaborated by the utilitarians David Hume and Jeremy Bentham, and refined by Ricardo—all of whom oversimplified the mechanisms of man's social-economic behavior. Although Patten viewed John Stuart Mill as greatly extending the political scope of economic thought (and subsequently came to recognize Marx as representing the culmination of this Newtonian tendency), the problem, he perceived, remained the fact that mechanistic models of the marketplace—as they were then being codified by Alfred Marshall—were unable to comprehend the historical evolution of social-economic structures. They in fact represented a retreat from the models developed by Mill and Marx in that they dealt only with market prices, supply and demand, not with the complex and evolving institutional structure and direction of society.

It was Charles Darwin who deserved credit for resolving the methodological and teleological problems stumbled over by classical British moralists and political economists. Darwin, stated Patten, was "the last of the economists and the first of a new school of biologists. He is deductive as an economist, and inductive as a biologist." Patten's ensuing analysis of Darwin's theories is a landmark in the Americanization of Social Darwinism. "To show that Darwin was an economist, we must divide his doctrine into two parts as found in his first essay. The economy of food and its effects on organisms are strictly economic phenomena, and the doctrines deduced from them are legitimately a part of economic theory ... The mutability of species, however, and the conception of common ancestors are biologic and inductive ... Darwin found deductively that peculiarities in the food supply caused variations [of species]; but to complete his theory he was compelled inductively to show how present facts and the history of creation indicated that the various species had common ancestors. ... Naturally, therefore, this biological part of the investigation grew in importance at the expense of the economic. There is thus given to Darwinism a seemingly inductive character that it does not really possess."

Darwinism was closely related to the problems raised by Malthus. But experimental demonstration was necessary to show "that the steady development of breeds was possible," a fact that "had not been properly used in the discussion of human progress ... The decay of nations in ancient history seemed to sanction the belief that men were degenerated by civilization, and this belief made students blind to the steady progress of modern nations. A belief in progress and improvement was, however, common among the natural theologians, and was the main cause of their opposition to the Malthusian theory." However, some reconciliation was attempted even before Darwin. As early as 1816, Archbishop-to-be John Sumner, in his *Treatise on the Records of Creation and the Moral Attributes of the Creator*, had perceived "the bearing of the principle of population on progress, and called it the main pillar of civilization. He saw that the struggle for food was the cause of the upward tendencies in mankind ... 'The operation of this principle [of population, Sumner wrote], filling the world with competitors for support, enforces labour and encourages industry by the advantages it gives to the industrious at the expense of the indolent and extravagant.'"[391] Thus, even before Darwin, it was being argued that the struggle for existence described by Malthus was not a sign that man and nature were badly constructed. It was precisely this struggle that gave promise of man's social improvement through a necessary weeding-out process. Patten differed from the Spencerians, however, in speculating that the fittest men and nations—socially and economically—would be those which proceeded to erect an active state social-economic apparatus to aid in subduing nature to the will of man, not by struggling wastefully among themselves.

Patten viewed human evolution as occurring mainly through the weeding out of biological character types, and this conviction formed the basis of his concluding chapter. A leadership of new mental types was emerging in the superior economic societies, especially in the United States. "We are no longer cosmopolitans who wish to merge our civilization in that of the world," he concluded. "We think of ours as the civilization, and seek to impress our stand-

---

[391] *Ibid.*, pp. 343–46, quoting Sumner's *Records of Creation* (London, 1816), Vol. II, p. 172. Patten's view of Darwin as being inspired above all by deductive speculation is only today becoming generally accepted. See for instance Michael T. Ghiselin, "Darwin and Evolutionary Psychology," *Science* 179 (March 9, 1973), pp. 964–68. Darwin voiced a view quite similar to that of Patten in his unpublished notebook *M* (now housed at Cambridge University), in which he remarked that the theory of evolution "would make a man a predestinarian of a new kind, because he would tend to be an atheist," and that "the mind of man is no more perfect, than instincts of animals to all & changing contingencies, or bodies of either—descent then, is the origin of our evil passions!!—The Devil under form of Baboon is our grandfather!" (pp. 74, 122.) Ghiselin concludes that Darwin did not "confirm to the superstition that scientists must repress every impulse to apprehend the larger connection among things, and that they must keep to the 'facts.' The Darwin of the notebooks stands in stark contrast to the Darwin of his works read without attention to their implicit message. Many readers may think that Darwin was 'breaking the rules' in his flights of speculation. But the fact is that as a consequence of much thought about biogeography, esthetics, morals, economics, and various other topics he developed the theory of natural selection." Darwin was Lamarckian from the outset, treating "the organism as a material system which could be modified through interactions with his environment. But he never really resolved to his own satisfaction just what these interactions were."

ards and ideals on others." America's superior economic environment was weeding out the Sensualists and Clingers, leaving the way free for a new kind of Stalwart man. "The present epoch," Patten concluded, "is as plainly an epoch of cheapness as that [of Malthus' time] was of dearness. Then population outstripped the increase of food. The increase of food now so far surpasses the increase of population that a market for food can scarcely be found ... the farms are being deserted, and the country people are flocking to the cities in order to share in their increased prosperity." Progress "is determined by the types of men that are eliminated. Under past conditions this elimination has been mainly due to undernutrition, or, to use simpler language, starvation." This favored the most aggressive, sensualist genetic types. Now, progress by elimination was being drastically transformed in nature by man's evolution into a food-surplus, pleasure economy. "Formerly the underfed failed to survive; now it is the overfed among whom the elimination is taking place ... The plethora of food now enjoyed induces men to eat and drink more than their systems can stand ... keen appetite is plainly a disadvantage ... in the long run the evils of overnutrition will benefit the race ... Those stolid, sensual constitutions that have been so marked a characteristic of the middle class of society must gradually disappear. The dominant type will be more nervous in temperament and have an increased ability to stand the strain and the excitement of an active life."[392]

The new man would be self-controlled and efficient, yet generous and altruistic. The Protestant Ethic would evolve to an even higher degree, rendering consumption subservient to investment, egotism to prudent cooperation, and supplanting wasteful individualistic competition with a harmonious coordination of all parts of the new economic society. Thus, whereas pleasure economies had died off in the past when utility instead of pain became the supreme object of interest, America would prove able to handle its new abundance. History had shown that nations which remained Sensualist in the face of growing prosperity could not last. "No nation of North Europe goes down as the Southern nations went down one after the other," Patten later observed. In past times Europe's civilization had shifted northwards, and "a new break of similar

---

[392] *Ibid.*, pp. 381f.. On this point see also Patten's essay on "Overnutrition and its Social Consequences," *The Annals of the American Academy of Political and Social Science* 10 (July 1897). As Fox points out (*op. cit.*, p. 191) "The only American economist before Patten to deal with consumption was Amasa Walker, in *The Science of Wealth*" (1866). The Scottish economist William Smart coined the phrase "socialization of consumption" in 1892, alluding to Patten's views as expressed in *The Consumption of Wealth* (Philadelphia, 1889). On this aspect of Patten's theories see Fox, *op. cit.*, pp. 44ff.

magnitude has been made by the transference of civilization to America." New traditions must be forged, giving the state authority to direct the course of society along Stalwart principles, thereby guiding not only the progress and application of physical science and technology, but the evolution of human nature itself.[393]

America was thus on its way to becoming a new civilization physiologically as well as in its political ideals and culture and economic capability. Whereas Patten's *Economic Basis of Protection* (1890) had analyzed the sources of America's potential superiority in labor productivity and soil fertility, his *English Thought* argued that the nation's psychological fitness for the modern age would enable it to lead the entire world into an era of abundance. This reconciled the Protestant Ethic with the teachings of evolutionary theory. Sensualists would die out as "the overnutrition of women decreases their fertility ... families rapidly die out if they utilize to the full the advantages given by economic success." The remaining Stalwarts would be less prone to sensual indulgence and its associated growth in population. Meanwhile, the genetic composition of this stabilized population would be continually improved, for although the world had emerged from food-deficit status to food-surplus abundance, "there are ... many indications that progress by elimination has not ceased, but has only changed in form."[394]

Patten's *Social Forces* had claimed that, in his proposed economic-surplus commonwealth, competition no longer was to be decided simply in favor of those possessing brute atavism. Henceforth "the power to survive will be determined mainly by the industrial instincts which produce wealth or by social instincts which tend to reduce temptation and to limit the inclination to indulge in intense pleasure." The Stalwart man's civic instinct and spirit of "self-sacrifice is an essential element in all social progress." Finally, he concluded, "this feeling of social solidarity must, to be effective, be supplemented by the growth of aesthetic feelings. Crude appetites and vices are best removed by a perception of the harmony of consumption."[395]

In his *English Thought* Patten elaborated his views on the role of art in the new commonwealth, forecasting a new Stalwart art-form, utopian and socially-committed: "Sooner or later men with stalwart instincts and education will break over the line that separates economics from literature and art, and then

---

[393] "The Present Problems in the Economic Interpretation of History," in his *Essays in Economic Theory* (New York, 1924), p. 215.
[394] *English Thought*, pp. 384, 379, 382.
[395] *Social Forces*, pp. 98, 106, 108f., 126, 138, 149. See also pp. 124–26, 93, 95.

a new movement in these fields will begin that can end only in their transformation. Bold vivid ideals and visions of a future Utopia are sure finally to assume a literary form and to create pictures that can be made objective only in art. Milton and Bunyan have shown what stalwarts can do by visualizing ... The realistic and the ideal tendencies have been seldom united in the same person. This defect will be remedied if the curves of thought of the present epoch force the realist into economics and the visualizer into literature and art."[396] The new art would not be the sensualist, almost escapist fantasy of the Baroque and Romantic periods, but would praise a new form of satisfaction, that of Stalwart achievement and social consciousness, of productive rather than greedy passions.

Carey's school, Patten argued, had not succeeded in developing a science of sociology, only a science of the material conditions of production and of the tariff policy requisite to foster optimum conditions. A truly modern sociology would place much greater emphasis upon biological factors (as had been recognized by Comte, although he called his science Social Physics). In Patten's hands the new sociology became a Social Bio-Psychology, stressing the interaction between man's social psychology and man's material evolution.

A decade earlier the sociologist Lester Ward, who like Patten grew up on the Illinois prairie, had developed a two-phase analysis of man's evolution that anticipated Patten's views. As Richard Hofstadter summarizes Ward's theories, "man has been brought to his present stage of development by natural selection, of which his intellect is the supreme product; but man cannot consider himself finally superior to other animals until he supplants genetic [*e.g.*, random] with telic [*e.g.*, purposeful] progress by applying his intellect to his own environment." Telic phenomena were those governed by human will and purpose; genetic phenomena those which resulted merely from blind natural forces. Nature, Ward insisted, was fully susceptible to man's conscious control. To depict evolution as a random happening was to draw a false analogy. It was man's task to control not only nature but society itself, "in precisely the same manner as the physical forces have been utilized. It is only through the artificial control of natural phenomena that science is made to minister to human needs; and if social laws are really analogous to physical laws, there is no reason why social science may not receive practical applications such as have been given to physical science." Ward also anticipated Patten in stating that "competition actually prevents the most fit from surviving ... Witness the social waste involved in

---

[396] *English Thought*, pp. 386f., 398.

advertising, a good example of 'the modified form of animal cunning' which is the hallmark of business shrewdness ... Rational economics not only saves resources but produces superior organisms ... Hence the superior quality of fruit trees, cereals, domestic cattle." Finally, Ward argued, "Intelligence, hitherto a growth, is destined to become a manufacture."[397] Views such as these were voiced subsequently by Veblen, who also declined to equate the well-to-do with the biologically fittest. As commerce became increasingly separated from production, and wealth became a function more of advertising than workmanship, wealth accrued less from the instincts of higher man than from the application of cunning and other primitive asocial individualism.[398]

Patten hoped that America's destiny was to evolve into a new civilization, resting on a new genetic base and discouraging domination by the most power-driven, avaricious, and sensualist members of society. He urged economics to transcend the narrow utilitarianism of Benthamism, as well as its preoccupation with market costs and prices to the exclusion of the social environment in which these costs and prices were established. "We have arrived at a point in the development of the social sciences where we cannot let one another alone," he argued at the 1894 meeting of the American Economic Association. But the "cleft between the economic and sociological camps" which he described was institutionalized in 1905 when the American Sociological Society was founded at a meeting of the American Economic Association, with six of its thirty-six founders having taken their Ph.D.'s under Patten at the University of Pennsylvania."[399] His observations on society were ignored by most subsequent economists as lying outside the narrow scope of economic orthodoxy.

---

[397] Richard Hofstadter, *Social Darwinism in American Thought* [1944] (revised ed., 1955), pp. 73–76, quoting Lester Ward, *Glimpses of the Cosmos*, Vol. II, p. 352, and *Dynamic Sociology*, Vol. II, p. 539.

[398] See Hofstadter, *ibid.*, pp. 152–53.   [399] See Fox, *op. cit.*, p. 157.

3. The Theory of Prosperity

Patten's *Theory of Prosperity* (1902) is an isolated and idiosyncratic book seeking to integrate Austrian utility theory with Carey's theory of productive powers, a task that Carey's followers themselves had not bothered to attempt. The result was at once the most Austrian of Patten's books in its proccupation with utilitarian equilibrium (illustrated with incomprehensible diagrams) and also the most indebted to Carey's school for its interpretation of production and consumption in terms of the energy-transfer process involved. Patten also extended Carey's theory of increasing returns over time, covering man's utilitarian progress by analogy: "A primitive man has few wants, and these are mainly for articles that nature provides with difficulty … With progress new articles are produced that supply intenser wants, and at the same time all goods are more abundant in quantity. The appetites and passions of men are also modified, making them do and want what is more in conformity with their environing conditions."[400] So-called "absolute utilities," such as food and shelter, were not necessarily pleasure-yielding, although they were price-inelastic. As man became able to provide for higher needs, his widening range of consumption became more pleasurable (presumably in a geometric proportion).

Carey's doctrine of class harmony formed the central political focus of Patten's book. Class antagonism was not a permanent feature of economic society, but characterized only its origins, *e.g.*, the ancient tribal conflict and its associated capture of slaves which represented the most primitive kind of economic exploitation. "Most nations have been formed by conquest, and therefore start with a dominant and a subject class. The former seize the surplus, and force the latter to work for a bare minimum." Originally they seized land, the primal form of surplus capital. Gradually they became owners of capital as well. But modern economic society was no longer amenable to such form of exploitation. Partly this was because it was not labor that was responsible in the first instance for society's growth in productive powers, but capitalists and landlords, the technocrats of capitalism. "The reasoning of Carey pursued to its logical conclusion makes all income appear to be interest. Along with the return on capital goods he puts the income from land, claiming that it results from the capital sunk in improvements … Exploitation is … not a phenomenon of retrogression, but of progress … The extra income due to industrial progress … passes readily into the hands of the more progressive classes … Instead of oppression being the cause of exploitation, it is usually responsible for its de-

---

[400] *The Theory of Prosperity* (New York, 1902), p. 20.

cline."[401] The economic surplus was distributed to all members of society rather than remaining monopolized by the few, and this raised overall productivity.

This theory was similar to Schumpeter's subsequent theory of innovation: Economic rent (that is, super-profit) was created not mainly by diminishing returns as depicted in the Ricardian system, but by increasing returns and economic progress. As costs fell, thanks to technical innovation and other factors, the most efficient producers obtained cost advantages — and thus profit advantages — over less dynamic producers. Entrepreneurs themselves tended to prevent the spreading of monopoly, by constantly developing substitutes for monopolized goods and services. "Rent is constantly being created by social progress, but in any particular form it is steadily being cut down by the increase in the power of substitution ... An increased power of substitution is the only remedy for an unequal distribution of wealth."[402] Thus, progress did not cause material poverty. Patten interpreted utilitarian pleasure in terms of the energy analysis of production that Carey had adopted from Peshine Smith:

> Production is the act of putting things in motion. There is no productive process that is not resolvable into labor ... Labor is the expenditure of energy, resulting in the movement or the transformation of goods ... His energy puts objects in motion, and thus helps to create utility and value.
>
> Economists often overlook the connection between the consumption of goods and the creation of surplus energy ... Every increase of productive power adds to the quantity of goods consumed, and these if properly used augment the surplus energy of workers. They begin the day with more energy and can work longer before feeling pain ... Energy produces utility, and utility produces energy; otherwise the worker is stupid, diseased, or dissipated. From an economic standpoint dissipation includes every use of goods that does not result in the building up of the body, and thus fails to create a fund of surplus energy ... Sicknesss, the lack of sanitation, lethargy, or any form of imperfect assimilation lowers the vitality of workers even more promptly than does painful work or dissipation. Where these evils are not avoided, much of the social surplus is used up.
>
> Every healthy person starts the day with a fund of surplus energy, the expenditure of which is pleasing, and makes work pleasurable while it lasts. Pains always involve some loss in this fund of surplus energy. Cost, as it is understood in economics, is the regular endurance of fatigue due to the extension of the working day after the surplus energy of the worker is exhausted. Productive labor is that which reappears in goods; productive consumption is that which comes to sight again as energy capable of producing goods ... Goods become utilities, utilities are transformed into energy which, as work, creates new goods.[403]

[401] *Ibid.*, pp. 4, 156,162, 171. [402] *Ibid.*, pp. 139f.
[403] *Ibid.*, pp. 95, 14f., 44, 21, 30f., 41f.

Patten's version of the Economy of High Wages doctrine was thus that pleasureful consumption added to the worker's psychic and manual energy. "The theory that costs determine value rests upon the notion that labor is disagreeable," he asserted. "It cannot be said that activity or even strenuous exertion is painful so long as there are ways of exerting energy that every one highly enjoys." The English view that labor was intrinsically unpleasurable was due to snobbish prejudice against having to perform manual labor, not to the nature of labor itself. This perception paved the way for what Veblen called the Instinct of Workmanship: "Mechanical laborers are displaced, and as they disappear the standard of the laboring classes rises in an inverse ratio. Employers discover that a high class of laborers is more productive in proportion to their wages than are those of the lowest classes…"[404] Hence the harmony of interests between labor and capital in extending society's productive powers and prosperity.

[404] *Ibid.*, pp. 35, 174.

4. The Social Basis of Religion

It may seem anachronistic that social theorists like Simon Patten and other writers of the 1880s and 1890s should have troubled themselves to develop a materialistic religion suitable for the modern world. One can see why they analyzed earlier religions as being symptomatic of society's economic and social environment, but it was forcing matters to try to reconcile Christian theology with these writers' economic ideals. They nonetheless set themselves to this task, largely because of their vestigial concept of religion as the traditional means of integrating the various branches of knowledge, and indeed almost synonymous with this process of integration itself, whether on valid or invalid grounds. Patten, who grew up in a somewhat religious environment, claimed to have developed a social-economic science capable of explaining the rapid developments occurring during the late nineteenth century, and he defined religion to represent man's integrating faculty as such. Thus, by his own definition, he was developing a new religion. That this was materialist did not bother him, but merely raised the import of his contribution.

His attitude is understandable in view of developments occurring within American studies concerning the evolution of religion and superstition. What had historically been thought of as constituting religion was termed by Andrew D. White "Dogmatic Theology" in his *History of the Warfare of Science with Theology in Christendom* (1896). But after tracing the most vivid contrasts between science and theology, White nonetheless spoke of a reconciliation between the two and of an allegedly reconstructive theological force of scientific criticism. It was in this spirit that Patten wrote his *Social Basis of Religion* (1911), in which he sought to reconcile his new theology with a new kind of stalwart Protestantism. He had dealt with religion in nearly all of his writings, treating the subject as synonymous with "social psychology," a kind of increasingly rational moral adhesive to his proposed economic reforms. His *Theory of Social Forces* had suggested a "social commonwealth [which] would operate in a manner more like those of the Middle Ages than those of the present century," and whose members "would idealize society and make it the source of the desired control over nature and natural forces ... Intelligence would be idealized ... just as power is idealized in a pain economy. The God of that commonwealth would be a God of intelligence working through society and nature," not the God of power and vengeance conjured up by religions born of pain economies.[405]

---

[405] *The Theory of Social Forces* (New York, 1896), pp. 98, 106.

Patten's major theoretical work, *The Development of English Thought*, interpreted the evolution of European social and religious philosophy on economic-materialist grounds. His *Social Basis of Religion* integrated his earlier views on social psychology with an economic interpretation of man's evolving religious attitudes, proposing an ideology appropriate for man's emergence into permanent economic-surplus conditions. Such an ideology, Patten felt, was necessary to consolidate society on a Stalwart basis so that its members did not dissipate their new wealth on merely sensual forms of consumption.

Comte's three-stage schema for viewing man's intellectual evolution in and of itself—progressing from the theological (superstitious) stage, to the metaphysical (philosophic) stage, and finally emerging into the positive (scientific) stage implied a steady movement away from religious sentiment. (This did not prevent an active Comtian Church from being founded in Brazil and elsewhere.) Patten held that any three-stage evolutionary format must be social-economic rather than merely intellectual, inasmuch as all ideology rested upon an economic base. Ideas were "social impressments, due to activity carried on by men in society … The mind neither sees nor manufactures them; for ideas are social products acquired from the medium in which the thinker exists."[406] He suggested an alternative three-stage progression of intellectual superstructures resting upon man's social-economic stages of progress. First was the traditional stage, then came the skeptical (critical) revolt against tradition, and finally the pragmatic stage of social ideology. Each stage was characterized by its own religious-social psychology.

The leading criterion for evaluating the success of "pragmatic" religion—that appropriate to man's third and final social-economic stage—was its effect on man's behavior, *e.g.*, its success with economic programs (contributing to prosperity, peace, and cooperation), its physical programs (contributing to efficiency, health, and longevity) and emotional programs (instilling the motives of service, public spirit, and at its best, a new missionary zeal). "The social mission of the church," Patten concluded, "is not to make men religious, but to make men normal … Health, wealth, and efficiency are the basis of normal life." The new religion's motto would be, "Sin is misery; Misery is poverty; the Antidote to poverty is income." "Christianity needs, not preachers, but workers." "Health is thus the test of normality, and the church can safely be sponsor for social movements that improve it. On this basis must the social program of the church be built … We cannot make every one wealthy, but there is no need of poverty."[407] All this implied a rather secular religion indeed.

---

[406] *The Social Basis of Religion* (New York, 1911), pp. ix, xiv, 65. See also pp. 91, 48, 50.
[407] *Ibid.*, pp. xiii, xviii, 220–24.

The new religious fellowship looked towards man rather than towards God, preaching a gospel of social work rather than of Original Sin as in Roman Catholicism. In fact, Patten's book portrayed his Natural and Pragmatic Religions as representing the culmination of the Protestant-materialist enlightenment against the Catholic perversion of Christianity, which was destined to be swept away, just as the ancient Eastern religious and moral systems would be after "the coming of Western enterprise, education, and science ... One God will come with one economic system, one type of government, one science, and one literature," This God would be intellectual and social in nature. Thus, whereas "state religion is a result of war and want: natural religion arises out of contact with the surplus and vigor of nature; social religion is quite as clearly based on the thought of peace and plenty."[408]

Existing Christianity was in much the same anachronistic position as that of classical economics. It had been formulated to meet the social needs of a Pain Economy, and had developed as a state religion praising self-sacrifice and depicting the denigration of man. "An economy with a surplus tends to make us social; an economy of deficit arouses conflict and gives a dominance to pain reactions." Early Christianity developed within the confines of a pain economy, and its religious tenets reflected this condition. "The nations that were to shape religion lived in regions where resources were failing and disease on the increase ... Drought, disease, war, and other evils of a state of deficit being dominant in Western Asia while our religion was forming ... the lack of a clear demarcation between church and state forced religion to become a mere adjunct to patriotism and to express its needs." This forced "the emphasis of valor and self-sacrifice of virtues ... Ages of failing resources have made men feel that life is not worth living, that virtue has no reward except beyond the grave." Hence the increasing other-worldliness of primitive religion and its antagonism to nature. Sacrifice, Patten stated, "becomes a virtue only under pressure of want, and must have as a background the presence of war, famine, disease, and national disorder."

This was just the opposite of the more socially optimistic teachings of Christ, in which "the religion of service could have no better exposition." However, "it is difficult to associate Christ with a purely social religion because His teachings have been overshadowed by the striking events of His death ... If Christ's doctrines had been handed down to us by a Plato instead of a Paul, or by one who knew only of His life and not of His death, Christ to us would be

---

[408] *Ibid.*, pp. 233f., 195. Patten's three-stage view was elaborated the following year in "The Reconstruction of Economic Theory," reprinted in his *Essays in Economic Theory* (New York, 1924), p. 338.

a social leader, preaching salvation only in terms of love, cooperation, and service. Salvation through sacrifice, especially through a blood atonement, would be a repugnant doctrine from the dread of which He wished to free the world ... Yet Paul, influenced more by His death than by His life, drew from this life a meaning and gave to it a theological setting that stands in strange contrast to what must have been an earlier view of His life and teaching ... The more the tribulations, the nearer the redemption." Human evolution towards economic-surplus conditions were thus constrained by a religion more appropriate for economic-deficit conditions. Nor did Patten think much of any "religion of nature" such as was manifested by Rousseau's concept of man as Noble Savage. To bring back Rousseau's "natural man ... would be a loss, not a gain."[409] What was needed was a set of social morals which would enable man to live more in harmony with his new pleasureeconomy conditions. It was just such a Social religion, Patten believed, that would represent a return to original Christianity.

Such an evolution, he asserted, was inevitable. Bodin in the sixteenth century had looked at the geographic distribution of Europe's religious patterns and concluded that Southerners were theocratic and intellectual, Northerners much more physical. Draper had let this climatic-economic relationship drop after the opening chapters of his *Intellectual Development of Europe* (1862). He never really explained the North's emergence as intellectual, social, and economic master of Europe, save to imply that it was less fettered by theocratic prejudice than the Southern countries. Patten now spelled out what had been implicit in Draper. True, in the beginning the Northern Germanic tribes seemed as barbaric to the Romans as America's Indians seemed in Patten's time. But in the end they were Europe's salvation. "If the transference of civilization had not been accompanied by the rising missionary spirit of the early Christians, it is easy to picture what would have happened to Southern civilization. Its resources would have continued to fall off ... and war would have become increasingly brutal and destructive. A situation like that in Arab countries would ultimately have arisen and have remained permanent. The rise and decline of Mohammedanism showed what could happen to any civilization that has its base in the dry regions of the South. Under these conditions, Christianity might have created a Spain, but it could hardly have done better ... The natural obstacle to the progress of civilization lay in a doubly contradictory situation. The only place where civilization could begin its rise must fail because of the niggardliness of its economic situation; the regions where its permanence was possible lacked the cultural conditions for its rise." The Mediterranean countries

---

[409] *Ibid.*, pp. 219, 193f., 182, 196f., 199.

were able to enjoy the first great national economic surpluses, but these were necessarily meager compared to those which could, many centuries later, be yielded by Northern root crops and Northern work-oriented character. "Protestantism was a political and economic revolt from the South ... Germany and England were outside the region of drought and failing resources. With their rise a reorganization of political institutions began to conserve instead of destroy liberty, health, and capital." The religion developed under the North's rising economic conditions was destined to conquer that of the South, as "prosperity, liberty and cooperation furnish a principle more potent than the dread of want."[410]

Patten already had speculated elsewhere that, just as Northern Europe supplanted the South, so America would supplant Europe generally, thanks to its rising prosperity and relative freedom from Europe's debilitating social, political and religious systems. America would now lead the world into a new era of Social Religion, a religion of science. The Roman papacy and its state religion were thus attacked on three counts. First of all was its focus upon God rather than on Man. "It is a reversal of the order in which religious ideas developed to make religion begin with God, instead of basing it on the natural phenomena out of which it has arisen." The concept of God starts with those who would deprecate man, creating a God "to fill in the gap between man and perfection." Socially, "God is purpose, not cause; will not function. He shapes ends, not beginnings ... The social God is telic [to borrow Lester Ward's phrase], not functional." However, "society cannot become telic until our psychic powers are reshaped to meet present conditions," and man's new purpose must be understood in terms of his own self-improvement. By contrast, Roman Catholicism was based largely on the concept of a depraved and sinful man. This was its second error. But "if man is good and nature perfect, what is the cause of evil? The economist restates this problem by asking what is the cause of misery?" and concludes that poverty causes misery, and misery causes sin. "Sin, misery and poverty thus become one problem, and their antidote is income. All three can be wiped out by changes in industrial conditions ... If man is good and nature beneficent, poverty is due to specific causes that can be removed ... English misery must therefore be due to some specific cause not inherent in normal men nor in nature." Once man had succeeded in conquering nature, he had no further need for a God calling for human suffering and self-sacrifice as the leading virtues. Nor did he need to view God as supernatural, being approached only as man escaped from nature and its confines.

---

[410] *Ibid.*, pp. 202f., 189f.

Finally, man must not suppress his natural traits as called for by Catholicism: "We lose in inspiration more than we gain by the suppression of passion. The drudgery of modern industry may keep men from becoming very bad, but it likewise prevents them from reaching the loftier ends to which the free working of natural motives would lead them." If the root of sin was external to man, not intrinsic, and if external impulses were synonymous with his adverse economic conditions, then "to remove the temptation to sin means to do away with starvation, poverty, disease, overwork, and bad conditions which depress workers and turn virtue into vice."[411]

The new Social Religion must not only lead the poor into prosperity, but, once having led them there, it must aid them in adjusting their social patterns, in particular their consumption habits. Returning to his favorite theme, he claimed that "the morbidness of overnutrition shows itself in a stunted development of the higher faculties. Its cause is an arresting of the normal diversion of surplus energy from the lower to the higher organs … Disease, hysteria, and insanity are its most pronounced manifestations," and it had innumerable minor symptoms. Moderation in consumption became the new Stalwart standard of health and the social ideal.[412]

---

[411] *Ibid.*, pp. 101, 75f., 217, 40f. See also pp. 25f., 7, 38f.
[412] *Ibid.*, p. 122.

5. Theoretical Essays

Patten's books tended to lose focus, mixing perceptive observations with almost absurd system-building upon minor points. Only in his essays did he try to systematize his theories in relatively concise form. His three most important essays, "The Theory of Dynamic Economics" (1892), "The Scope of Political Economy" (1893), and "The Reconstruction of Economic Theory" (1912) are reprinted in *Essays in Economic Theory* (1924). These theories are set against the background of his articles associated with *The Development of English Thought* (1898), analyzing Malthus, Ricardo, Mill, and other English economists from the vantage point of their immediate class interest and cultural setting. "It is a weakness of economics," Patten observed, "that the social ideas upon which its theories rest have been neglected. Economic theories have been put forward as though they depended solely upon physical or objective conditions. This view obscures the relation between economic theory and the epochs in which it originated; it makes what really is of class origin appear as though it were a necessary element of human nature." The truth was that "the education, occupation, and place of residence of each person cause him to view the economic world [in a special way] influenced by his environment, and will lead him to treat each problem inductively or deductively, according to the prominence which it has in the surrounding economic conditions."[413] Thus the theories of Ricardo, Bentham, and Malthus reflected England's "pain economy" but not the "pleasure economy" conditions emerging in the United States.

Economics dealt with universals, to the extent that it dealt with the technological basis of production, *e.g.*, with the laws of the physical sciences. Once man satisfied his basic needs, however, his economic life became increasingly social and psychological in nature—or as English economists liked to say, "moral." Pain economies were governed by a physical-science approach to economics, pleasure economies by a psychological approach. "Part of economic science is based on physical nature; from it come laws of universal application which cannot be overthrown by the action of man. On the other hand, many economic laws are expressions of human nature. These are not only capable of modification, but are continually being altered. The one element, therefore, of economics is enduring, the other is temporary. By this I do not mean that human nature is easily altered, but that the features we regard as human are subject to evolutionary modification."[414]

[413] "The Background of Economic Theories" (1912), in *Essays in Economic Theory*, p. 265, and "Malthus and Ricardo" (1889), *ibid.*, p. 21.

[414] "The Economic Causes of Moral Progress,' (1893), *ibid.*, p. 164, and "The Reconstruction of Economic Theory" (1912), *ibid.*, p. 276.

The French Physiocrats, living "in an age when the physical sciences engrossed the attention of all scholars," viewed man in materialistic and mechanistic terms. Living in a pleasure-deficit economy, "their science was not a science of man, but of the conditions that limit the actions of men … In a primitive economy the physical causes of production and distribution receive the emphasis. Wealth and progress are thought to be dependent upon and conditioned upon the physical environment … Primitive men must adjust themselves to the physical world … They are mere paupers living on the bounties of nature."[415]

However, "the growing supremacy of man over physical forces reduces the importance of the purely objective world, and brings into the foreground the social mechanism through which natural agents are utilized and economized." Thus Adam Smith sought to ground economics on the basis of human psychology, but in his attempt to derive moral principles he presumed that man's psychological characteristics were universal and eternal. Bentham followed suit, in suggesting highly simplistic psychological principles more descriptive of man as he existed in pain economies than in pleasure economies. These static views of human nature were complemented by Ricardo's static view of the laws of agricultural production, *e.g.*, of the "original and inde-structible powers" of the soil, and of diminishing returns. These fallacious deductive laws were complemented by Malthus' theory on population, which broke the link between social reform and political economy that Adam Smith had tried to establish. Malthus argued that economic reforms would be unable to elevate mankind, as they would be thwarted by population pressures pre-sumably grounded in man's eternal "human nature," namely his propensity to procreate. This theory, coupled with the Ricardian doctrine of diminishing returns, rapidly "became a leading argument for those who doubted the possibility of an upward movement of all parts of society … In this way, the character of doctrines to which the name economics was given became in-tensely conservative." Economics became static in nature. What was, in effect, "dynamic economics became a part of ethics, so that economics could be made a positive science after the model of the physical sciences."[416]

The American School of political economists—those following the lead of Henry Carey—"cast a doubt upon those physical laws which the classical school used as the basis of their reasoning," and used an inductive literary mode of presentation to controvert them. Ricardo's theory that man progressed

---

[415] "The Theory of Dynamic Economics" (1892), *ibid.*, pp. 37f., 43.
[416] "The Scope of Political Economy" (1893), *ibid.*, pp. 179, 181.

from the richest to the poorest soils was historically wrong, as was his assumption of the Iron Law of Wages, according to which the level of consumption of society's members remained unchanged in the face of rising productive powers. In fact, the nature of labor was being transformed from performing unskilled manual tasks to highly skilled tasks; cost and productivity relations were in a state of constant flux; and the state was playing a growing role in improving economic life. It thus became the task of economics to pass beyond value theory to develop broad theories of economic society. "The theory of prosperity contrasts only cost with surplus, and does not need any theory of value for its discussion. The theory of cost of the earlier writers was simple, because they assumed that the laborers received none of the surplus, and that all the consumption of the laborers was in the form of food, which included clothing and shelter. The surplus was therefore the difference between the cost of food and the value of the whole produce of industry." Underlying the labor theory of value was the wheat-theory of labor, and the associated measurement of human utility solely in terms of pecks of wheat—a squalid concept of utility indeed, appropriate for pain economies but hardly for rich economic-surplus societies.[417]

The classical economics of Malthus and Ricardo were challenged from two quarters: by John Stuart Mill who sought to retain an ethical focus for its principles, and by the German historical school which also proposed a moral teleology for man's economic progress, *e.g.*, the thought that man might purposely transform his economic environment according to norms other than simple cheapness of production under existing technological conditions. Patten, trained in Germany, had early announced himself to be a disciple of Mill. However, he reflected in 1912, were he to rewrite his *Development of English Thought* he would make Mill not a terminus "but a half-way house between the dogmatic rationalism of the earlier [Ricardian-Benthamite] epoch and the rising wave of sentiment and class hatred in the new. Mill ... is a thinker becoming a socialist without seeing what the change really meant. The Nineteenth Century epoch ends not with the theories of Mill but with the more logical systems of Karl Marx and Henry George."

Such an observation was hardly popular in his day, although it is now accepted orthodoxy at the hands of Schumpeter and Marxist historians. It was Marx's role, Patten continued, to transform two leading features of English economic thought, both in keeping with Marx's German background: "The basis of English thought in natural theology must be replaced by the material

---

[417] *Essays*, pp. 34, 74, 149.

view then prevalent in Germany. Sentiment and theology were to be excluded and a social philosophy developed that would stand the test of modern criticism. This is what Marx means by scientific socialism. The second change was in the opposite direction. The early socialists had made their appeal solely to reason. They expected to convince employers that better conditions and higher wages were industrially advantageous and thus make a transition to socialism with the assent of all industrial groups. This harmony of interests Marx replaced by the theory of class struggle. Revolution was to do what the slow working of economic law had failed to accomplish."[418]

The American economists who had studied in Germany had begun to develop a new economic doctrine. The earlier American school of Carey had broken with English economics first as regards its pessimistic and erroneous physical premises—its rent and agricultural theory, its population theory, its theory of wages, and its ignoring of the productive powers of capital—and had then proceeded to follow the German historical school in establishing itself on a sociological basis. "In the first place," Patten concluded, "American thought has been made independent of European thought. We are no longer under the tutelage either of England or Germany. The second victory is that economic pluralism has won as against economic monism … If, however, there are two economies, a pain economy, based on struggle, and a pleasure economy, in which harmony prevails, neither the history of man in this pain economy nor the struggles then important are fundamental to present discussions. The approach to the social life of man must be through his present economic activities."[419] The world had entered a new phase of economic history, that of permanent economic surplus.

Under the impetus of Mill, the German historical school and its American representatives, political economy "became less physical and more subjective in its character, and instead of proceeding from nature to man, it became evident that economists must begin with the study of man and end with a study of the relation of man to nature," *e.g.*, of man as the master of nature. It was this stage in the evolution of man's economy that Patten set out to analyze in all his works. First of all he developed a theory closely akin to what is now called Engel's Law, named after the German statistician Ernst Engel who first announced it in an obscure 1857 article which was not republished until 1895 (whereas Patten formulated this theory in 1893). Engel's Law states that as income increases, *per capita* expenditure on food, rent, and clothing rise much more slowly, so that most of the growth in income goes to services and less essential items. Patten expressed this thought as a compound of two "laws."

---

[418] *Ibid.*, pp. 274, 285f.

[419] *Ibid.*, pp. 278f.

First was the Law of Necessity, which stated that men must first satisfy their basic needs for food, clothing, and shelter irrespective of the actual pleasure-giving utilities associated with these essential expenditures. "No matter how great a sum of satisfaction is sacrificed, these absolute utilities must be secured." Beyond this primal law stood his Law of Variety, which stated that, "as soon as the necessaries of life are secure, a new law of consumption asserts itself." Variety in consumption is expressed to an increasing degree. "In primitive societies, from a lack of productive power, men are compelled to choose absolute utilities, the greater part of which give but little pleasure ... The result is that in primitive societies the positive utility of the marginal increments of the commodities consumed is low — almost zero ... It has been assumed too often that we always gratify our most intense desires first ... From these premises it would follow that additional quantities of articles for consumption are sources of less pleasure than the first increments, and hence that the final degree of utility of each commodity is gradually reduced with every increase in the quantity of goods due to the increase of productive power."[420] But just the opposite was true. Thus, in the realm of utilitarian anti-Benthamite psychological laws Patten proposed an analogy to Carey's anti-Ricardian theory of cultivation. Carey had demonstrated that man historically progressed from the worst to the best soils (because of locational criteria). Patten suggested that man progressed from lower to higher utilities over time.

Man also harmonized his consumption habits as a means of maximizing his utility in consumption and his productive powers. For instance, land was being transferred from one-crop use to multi-crop rotation. "The growth of intelligence reduces the differences in land by making poor land better land, while the increase of the variety of consumption hastening this change reduces the quantity of rent due to physical causes." Thus, "the variety of consumption reduces the cost of production," reducing marginal production costs. This led in turn to Patten's somewhat obscure Law of Grouping, whereby society harmonized its output of consumable goods so as to maximize the social-economic utility of its members. The utilities of bread and butter, for instance, were greater when combined than when consumed in isolation. Hence Patten's fourth law, that the margin of consumption is raised through harmonious consumption. "The essence of social progress," he concluded, "lies not in the increase of material wealth but in a rise of the margin of consumption ... The static man is impelled to increase his material wealth as the only means of increasing his welfare, while the dynamic consumer finds a readier means of increasing his welfare in raising the margin of his consumption by rearranging his goods in

[420] *Ibid.*, pp. 34, 55, 58.

new complements." This entailed a growing socialization of consumption: "Individuals no longer adjust themselves to nature but to the society of which they are a part."[421] Hence the growth of the state's role in coordinating consumption and production among its citizens.

Patten sought to estimate the economic value of state activity. He began by criticizing Adam Smith and his followers for identifying the factors of production with the direct flow of income to labor, landlords and capitalists (in the form of wages, rent and profits). He emphasized (in the spirit of Carey's school) that there were gratuitous factors of production that received no current economic return, such as "natural forces, inherited industrial qualities, and consumption with its habits, customs and feelings. From the social point of view, these three aids to production are never elements of cost. Nature always works gratuitously for society; and although industrial qualities have been acquired by our ancestors at a large cost, we receive them as a free inheritance." Hence the growth of man's social and industrial qualities, which were transmitted from generation to generation by the state (social) apparatus, under proper technocratic leadership.

It was capitalism itself that was providing the basis for such leadership: "The earlier socialists thought the field of socialism to lie in schemes for elevating the toilers. Such schemes have failed. If they had thought of their projects as a means of socializing the capitalists, they would have been the prophets of a new epoch. The striking fact of recent industrial organization has been the socialization of the groups that control them. The system, the interests, the money power, the trusts have bad ventures, but they represent the socialization of the groups interested in particular fields. The growth of large scale capitalism has resulted in the elimination of the unsocial capitalist and the increasing control of each industry by a socialized group."

This thought was strikingly parallel to that being developed simultaneously by European Marxists. Patten spelled out its elitist technocratic implications explicitly: "With every increase in population, a better use of labor and natural forces must be made in order to supply the increased demand for food and other commodities; and, as a result, the laborers become more dependent upon the higher classes who have the industrial qualities needed to increase production as rapidly as population increases. A growing nation can continue progressive only by placing its industries more completely under the control of the intelligent classes, yet this increased control adds to the evils of distribution. The laborers now get their living, not as before directly from nature, but indirectly by supplying the wants of the higher classes ... who control and

---

[421] *Ibid.*, pp. 83, 72, 183,190, 63.

organize industrial forces." Hence the growing super-wage earned by skilled laborers and managerial ability. "Differences in nature cause rent; differences in men cause profits."[422]

All this, of course, was on the assumption that the rich earned their wealth through their productive managerial ability, not through chicanery, marketing skills, or adeptness at manipulating the stock market, such as seemed to be the case among American plutocrats of the day, as vividly portrayed by Veblen and other less idealistic American sociologists and political economists. In this respect Patten did not quite develop a theory fully descriptive of his contemporary society. He was as deductive and speculative as the British economists he attacked—a fact which he readily admitted. The new wave of American economic students returning from Germany, he observed, had been trained in inductive historical principles with which to counterpoise the deductive speculations of classical British political economy and moral philosophy. It was supposed that the Americans who founded the American Economic Association "would be historical, but no historical work has been done. The unexpected was the rise of the school of deductive theorists—the very thing the formation of the American Economic Association was designed to prevent."[423]

Patten's deductive system-building perceived that the world was moving into an era of unparalleled choice in consumption habits, of economic surplus over and above man's bare subsistence needs, and of growing state authority. His political loyalties led him to hope that this change would be gradual rather than revolutionary, and this idealism blinded him to many of the problems besetting the American economy and its society. He hoped that the state would naturally emerge on evolutionary grounds, without a socialist revolution being necessary to supplant capitalist entrepreneurs with federal technocrats. Apart from this attitude, his thought increasingly approached the views of European Marxism and materialism, the logical terminus of his own economic interpretation of history as well as of British thought.

---

[422] *Ibid.*, pp. 62, 291f., 79, 92.
[423] *Ibid.*, p. 275.

VIII. THE AMERICAN SCHOOL'S TECHNOLOGICAL OPTIMISM VERSUS THE PESSIMISM OF EMPIRE

Despite the Industrial Revolution and breakthroughs in agricultural chemistry and mechanized farming and mining, pessimistic ideas that population growth would lead to diminishing returns in agriculture and mining remained economic orthodoxy as late as the mid-19th century. The explanation for this lag of theory behind practice is to be found in the implications for trade policy. Free trade doctrine assumes that each economy produces what it is "best" at producing most cheaply under existing cost and income patterns. Absentee land ownership and plantation monocultures abroad were part of the natural economic order. To promote its position as workshop of the world, England repealed its agricultural tariffs (the Corn Laws) in 1846, seeking to negotiate free trade reciprocity with countries that agreed not to adopt industrial tariff protection or other trade barriers of their own. Its trade diplomacy aimed at convincing countries that their interest lay in supplying food and raw materials to England.

In America, Southern planters were glad to rely on Britain for industrial imports in an international division of labor that enabled English textile manufacturers and other industrialists to import cotton, minerals and other raw materials to make into products to sell back to the United States. New England shipping interests also supported free trade as opposed to national self-sufficiency. They defended this policy by treating the status quo as natural, and soil fertility as inherent and fixed (even as the South "mined the soil" by exporting soil-depleting plantation crops, while chemical fertilizers raised productivity in the North).

This was the economic doctrine taught in America's religious colleges and prestige universities—an amalgam of British moral philosophy, the economic theories of David Ricardo and Malthusian population theory. Technologically pessimistic, it forecast that population growth would force recourse to less fertile soils, increasing the marginal cost of producing food and thereby raising its price. Landlords on better soils would enjoy a rising economic rent as market prices rose above their cost of production. Rising prices for food and raw materials would squeeze profits for industrial employers, bringing capital investment and economic growth to a halt.

At best, the Ricardians argued, foreign trade could postpone this destiny by securing lower-priced food from abroad. England would remain the workshop of the world, importing raw materials from regions not yet fully settled and whose agriculture and mines had not yet succumbed to diminishing returns. This required free trade ("most favored nation" treaties) to deter these countries from enacting protective tariffs of the sort that England had legislated for centuries to secure its own industrial head start.

Although ostensibly envisioning a peaceful world free of war, this techno-logically pessimistic free-trade model inspired a renewed colonialism from the 1880s through World War I. From Africa to the Near East, European trade rivalry developed a military dimension as it sought to gain control of mineral wealth that was expected to become increasingly scarce. In America the Democratic Party had a similar expansionist belligerence—the idea of Manifest Destiny, a population pressing westward to avoid becoming a nation of crowded industrial cities with falling wage levels. Westward expansion was largely that of the Slave Power hoping to supply its plantation workers with low-priced Western grain. And despite England's ideological opposition to slavery, many of its trade strategists favored the South in the Civil War. The idea was to expand the Slave Power to appropriate western land to grow grain to feed its plantation work force. This was the program of the Democratic Party, and its geopolitical ideal was agrarian in character with roots in Jeffersonian policy and that of Andrew Jackson.

America's industrial takeoff required that British free-trade orthodoxy be rejected. The United States was still in the position of a less developed country, in a global economy whose "market forces" at the time favored British industry. Industrialization required an alternative to British free trade theory—an alternative developed by the Whigs prior to the Civil War, and Republicans after 1865. Formulated in Congressional speeches and the press, mainly by political activists and lawyers, preachers and journalists largely outside of the universities, this became the policy by which the United States built up its industrial and agricultural power after the Civil War, using its crop surplus to supply a growing and increasingly urbanized domestic industrial market rather than serving as a residual raw materials supplier, a "hewer of wood and drawer of water." To achieve industrial self-sufficiency and avoid being left behind, protectionists urged policy makers to forego the short-term gains from free trade—buying in the cheapest market.

Two models of economic development thus vied to determine national trade policy in the 19th century: free trade vs. protectionism. As technological optimists, protectionists took the lead in rejecting Malthusian population theory and Ricardian rent and free trade theory. They developed the program that enabled the United States to catch up with and even surpass England as workshop of the world, as well as becoming breadbasket and ultimately world banker. And yet despite its perception that rising living standards tend to be-come self-justifying by increasing labor productivity and thus would enable the United States to overtake England, this is not the trade and development model that is remembered today. The United States above all other countries promotes free trade theory as the only valid model through the rules laid down by the World Trade Organization, World Bank and International Monetary Fund.

If economic theory really was empirical and scientific (and based on actual historical development), the trade and productivity theories of technology and society developed by Whig and Republican writers would have become mainstream political correctness. But their protectionist views create cognitive dissonance for today's free trade orthodoxy, an embarrassment in the context of U.S. advice given to other countries today. ("Do as we say, not as we have done.")

The writers who codified U.S. industrial policy — Mathew and Henry Carey, Calvin Colton, E. Peshine Smith, Robert Ellis Thompson and Simon Patten — referred to themselves as the American School of political economy, and drafted the policies that steered the nation's rise to global industrial power. Yet their ideas remain neglected in the history of economic thought and even in surveys of American political history. The result is an intellectual black hole at the very heart of U.S. economic development as well as the evolution of economic thought. There is no hint that the nation rose to industrial supremacy by following just the opposite policy, or even that there existed a protectionist American School whose members formulated an alternative trade and development theory, more technologically realistic — and optimistic — than the free trade doctrine embraced by opponents of American industrialization. This was the body of theory that guided U.S economic development and tariff policy after the Civil War.

That war is depicted today as being waged exclusively over the slavery issue, but the division between North and South went deeper, turning on whether America should industrialize or not. This argument gained momentum after the end of the Napoleonic Wars in 1815 re-opened commerce with England, causing industrial depression in the Mid-Atlantic States and elsewhere that manufacturing had flowered during the years of wartime isolation. By the early 1850s, advocates of industrial protectionism saw that the tariff issue alone could not win over the West and Border States at the ballot box. Only by allying it with abolitionism could they forge a winning political alliance. And as matters turned out, the North's victory in the Civil War broke the South's power to block industrialization, enabling the Republican Party to inaugurate a program of protective tariffs, public infrastructure investment and a national banking system. Tariff revenue paid for internal improvements and even for the purchase of Alaska from Russia.

The American model was a full-blown alternative to that of Ricardo and Malthus. Instead of diminishing returns, it forecast rising agricultural and industrial productivity as population density increased. Instead of soil having "original and indestructible powers" as Ricardo imagined, its fertility could be chemically enhanced by fertilizer, and also by nightsoil from the cities. The westward expansion of Manifest Destiny policy would not be necessary if rising population density would bring about increasing returns.

301

Ricardo ignored the analysis of increasing returns in industry, except to argue that it need not result in mass unemployment as feared by the Luddites. But he believed that population growth would hold down wages to subsistence levels. Free traders attributed America's high wages to what families could eke out by moving to the backwoods, warning that they would fall at the point where the frontier was reached and the nation stopped expanding westward (and southward and northward too), the supply of labor on a fixed territory would drive down wages. The American School countered this simplistic supply-and-demand view by analyzing industrial wages in terms of labor productivity and profit rates, which in turn would reflect the level of tariff protection. The aim was for productivity to rise in response to higher wage levels, while tariff proceeds would finance "internal improvements" such as the Erie Canal to raise the economy's efficiency. In sum, economies would be able to feed themselves with growing ease as productivity rose with urbanization. Demographic studies of European countries showed that the higher the income of a given bracket, the lower the birth rate. The inference was that rising incomes would slow population growth, not accelerate it as Malthus believed.

Today's U.S. policy intervention in the oil-producing and highly mineralized regions of the Near East, Central Asia and Africa thus represents in many ways a throwback to the pessimistic economic theorizing that inspired the European colonialism whose rivalries culminated in World War I, and indeed that inspired America's own expansion to carve out spheres of influence across the Pacific after the Spanish-American War of 1898.

The pedigree of economic pessimism, and its argument for neocolonialism

As Malthus pointed out as spokesman for England's protectionist landlord class, Ricardo's technological pessimism with regard to diminishing returns in agriculture was at odds with reality even in his own day. His successor at the East India Company's Haileybury College, Richard Jones, argued that the progress of technology could increase agricultural productivity for a long time to come. Food costs need not rise with the growth of population, at least as long as England protected the home market for its landlords so that they could use their land rents to rationalize their farms. Justus Liebig and other agricultural chemists demonstrated how proper fertilizer and cultivation methods could increase the soil's productive powers at the intensive margin.

Unrealistic as it was, Ricardo's technological pessimism provided a logic for British industry—and Ricardo's own financial class—to repeal the Corn Laws. England would buy its grain in the cheapest markets, and its low-paid labor would provide it with a competitive advantage over less densely populated, high-wage countries, whose populations could maximize their income by exporting crops and raw materials to England. "The great augmentation of fine fertile territory, in America," wrote William Playfair, "will retard the progress of manufactures and commerce in that country, by employing the capital and attention of the inhabitants on agriculture. This may be the case for half a century, and, if England improves, the circumstances may continue to operate in favour of British manufactures for many centuries to come. ... The fertility of the soil will enable the Americans, with great ease to themselves, to make returns in produce wanted in Europe, so that we may expect a durable, a great, and an advantageous trade with them."[424] Free trade would enable England to maintain and increase its industrial productivity and learning-curve advantages over other countries.

Bernard Semmel has called this the doctrine of free-trade imperialism.[425] England would remain safe from foreign industrial competition as long as countries did not interfere with "free market" dynamics by enacting protective tariffs. To do so, Ricardo argued, would deprive the tariff-levying country of the gains from trade. Diverting labor from producing raw materials to manufacturing thus seemed to be a costly and wasteful allocation of labor and capital. The implication was that foreign countries should become economic satellites of England in their own self-interest, providing it with relatively low-priced foodstuffs and raw materials in exchange for its low-priced manufactures.

The protectionists emphasize technological potential — and ecological problems. Protectionism, by contrast, was a doctrine of how foreign countries might overtake England. Whereas classical British political economy focused on income distribution in a technologically static world, protectionists in the United States and Germany took the lead in emphasizing the evolution of productive powers in a dynamically evolving world.

It also was the protectionists who pointed to the ecological and environmental problems caused by economic growth. Today this problem receives attention primarily from "limits to growth" models, popularized since the 1970s most notably the Club of Rome. This modern-day theorizing goes even further than the Malthus-Ricardo model of secular stagnation in focusing on the depletion of raw materials, the rise of ecological pollution and the declining quality of life. But to the industrial protectionists of the mid-19th century, environmental damage caused by rising agricultural and industrial productivity

---

[424] William Playfair, *An Inquiry into the Permanent Causes of the Decline and Fall of Powerful and Wealthy Nations ... Designed to show how the Prosperity of the British Empire may be prolonged* (London: 1805), pp. 195, 268.

[425] I survey the literature in *Trade, Development and Foreign Debt: A History of Theories of Polarization v. Convergence in the World Economy* (London: Pluto Press, 1992; new edition ISLET, 2009).

was the result of a failure of market pricing to reflect what today would be called the environment's cleanup costs. The problem was worst in the sphere of plantation exports of cotton and tobacco from the South. The solution to soil exhaustion, they believed, was to apply chemical fertilizers to increase soil fertility at the intensive margin in the East rather than abandoning worn-out soils to settle further west. The policy conclusion was that while industrial tariffs would spur capital investment and rising productivity, free trade actually would reduce soil productivity—not at the extensive margin (economies bringing less fertile soils into cultivation) but at the intensive margin of soil depletion. The alternative was to increase farm productivity to feed the home market by "industrializing" agriculture.

The American School of economists (1814–1914) were the first to elaborate technological optimism into a general economic and social doctrine. Similar tendencies developed in Germany, Italy, Japan and Russia as these nations adopted protectionist policies and emerged as major industrial powers. Such optimism historically has been almost a unique product of protectionists— including the 18th-century literature of British mercantilism and even the agricultural protectionism of Malthus and Jones in England's Corn Law debate. In today's less developed countries, technological optimism is voiced mainly by nationalists and Marxists seeking greater self-sufficiency to defend against exploitation by the leading industrial and creditor nations.

There were important European exceptions, to be sure. Anti-Malthusians such as Michael Sadler pointed out that the typical response of populations to higher incomes was to slow their rate of increase, not accelerate it. And Liebig and others also demonstrated how improved diets increased the efficiency of workers' bodies as instruments of production. But these ideas did not enter the mainstream of European economic thought. Only in the United States did economic doctrine focus on the technological aspects of development in their social consequences as the central analytic issue. Marx emphasized political and financial dynamics but not technological factors to nearly the degree that American writers did.

The first generation of the emerging American School of political economists sought to develop a rationale for what Henry Clay called the American System of protective tariffs, internal improvements and a national bank. Whigs (and after 1854, the Republicans) argued that only if the U.S. economy insulated itself from that of England and other advanced industrial nations could American wage levels be protected, capital formation enhanced and the United States maintain meaningful independence from England and the rest of Europe. This body of thought had begun to gain adherents after 1815, when the return to peace following the war with England and Europe's Napoleonic Wars restored normal commercial relations between the two countries and an inundation of British manufactures helped bring on the 1817 depression. The emerging protectionist body of economic thought was refined and pursued into increasingly broad social doctrines until the outbreak of World War I in 1914, thus spanning about a century.

The American School drew on the agricultural researches of Liebig and other soil chemists to emphasize increasing returns to agricultural capital at the intensive margin (soil already under cultivation), complemented by Henry Carey's theory of increasing returns at the extensive (frontier) margin. American protectionists argued that America was far from being unsuited for manufacturing occupations as asserted by Ricardian trade theory. The doctrine of comparative costs implied that sparsely populated high-wage countries such as the United States were correspondingly high-cost industrial manufacturers. But this failed to recognize the correlation between wage levels and labor productivity. American writers developed an Economy of High Wages doctrine asserting that productivity gains tended to outstrip wage increases, thereby enabling highly paid professional labor to undersell low-wage pauper labor. In any event, steam-powered machinery was displacing manual labor, thereby driving it from lowly menial work to higher intellectual tasks. Performing these tasks required higher educational levels and social standards. Hence, higher wage rates were needed to enable workers to acquire the requisite skills and social attitudes in an upward spiral, a "virtuous circle" of positive feedback.

This growth of domestic demand was deemed capable of financing an expanding economy. Hence, the United States need not depend on foreign markets. British free trade theory, by contrast, implied a doctrine of imperialism in which England needed to exchange its manufactures for foreign raw materials, enforcing this global division of labor by force where necessary.

Finally, the American School was optimistic in its social and cultural assumptions. Instead of laborers using their wage gains to increase their numbers as Malthusian doctrine claimed, they postulated a negative response of population to increased income levels, consolidating rather than dissipating the nation's evolution into what Simon Patten (the Wharton School's first Professor of Economics) called the Economy of Abundance. These doctrines served American self-interest just as British classical thought was self-serving. But the intrinsically progressive character of American socio-economic theory renders it more appealing than the static doctrines of British free trade economics. Even as the 19th century progressed, Marshallian price theory assumed rising costs in industry as well as in agriculture so as to achieve determinate mathematical results. Business cycle analysis assumed a static technological and political environment. Upswings might be triggered by improvements in technology, but would peter out. With good reason Thomas Carlyle called economics the Dismal Science, based as it was on a Malthusian and Ricardian core.

America's about-face back to free trade rewrites history

Why has American historiography since World War I averted its eyes from its earlier economic optimism? The reason seems to lie precisely in the American System's success in developing the United States into the world's preeminent industrial, agricultural and commercial power. The shift of U.S. socio-economic ideology and trade theory parallels the nation's changing commercial self-interest as it has displaced England as the world's workshop and consolidated its role as the world's breadbasket, whose agricultural productivity has risen even more rapidly than industrial productivity.

America's evolving commercial self-interest has inspired almost an expurgation of its intellectual history. Nearly all surveys of American thought assert that there was no specifically U.S. economic theory or historiography of distinction, much less an indigenous American ideology, literary or art forms prior to World War I. To be sure, America's unique economic conditions were recognized —its broad economic expanse, its ever-moving frontier and subsequent "closing," its high wage levels and immigration, the conflict between slavery and free soil, railroad land grants and financial trusts, and the weakness of indigenous Marxian socialism. But the new body of economic theory that these conditions produced is not recognized. A century ago, in 1876, the American academic free trader C. F. Dunbar flippantly dismissed his protectionist antagonists by asserting that American writers as a whole had contributed "nothing towards developing the theory of political economy." This view has been endorsed by historians of economic thought as thorough as Joseph Schumpeter, as well as by specialists of American economic thought such as Joseph Dorfman.[426] The latter's six-volume review of *The Economic Mind of American Civilization* glosses over the protectionists and omits altogether the politicians whose speeches transformed protectionist doctrine into national policy during 1861–1931. In indulging his free-trade prejudices, Dorfman neglects the fact that to the extent that the American economic mind was original, it was highly protectionist.

---

[426] Joseph Schumpeter, *History of Economic Analysis* (New York; 1954), pp. 514, 676. There have been isolated protests against this neglect: see John B. Turner, *The Ricardian Rent Theory in Early American Economics* (1921) and Michael J. L. O'Connor, *Origins of Academic Economics in the United States* (1944). There have been some excellent studies of American political-economic thought since the Civil War, such as Richard Hofstadter, *Social Darwinism in American Thought* (1944) and Daniel Fox, *The Discovery of Abundance: Simon N. Patten and the Transformation of Social Theory* (1957). For a detailed review of the general historiography of the American School, see the introduction to my *Economics and Technology in 19th-Century American Thought: The Neglected American Economists* (New York: 1975).

Part of the problem was that the United States developed on a regional basis, each section with its distinct economic self-interest and attitudes. One can say that there was no national literature or political economy as such. Over and above the opposition between North and South, the North itself was economically, politically and even culturally divided into the northeast Seaboard, the Mid-Atlantic States and the western and border states, as well as between urban and rural areas. Regional geographic antagonism appeared among the protectionists themselves over whether industry should become export-oriented as advocated by the Boston School or isolationist as urged by Henry Carey's followers in the Mid-Atlantic States.

What has been characterized since World War I as "American" are the views centered in the prestige universities of New England and the South — the areas where American thought was least distinct from that of Europe. The social philosopher George Herbert Mead claimed in 1930 that although America's social forms differed from those of England, they were unable to produce a distinct cultural ideology: American culture "was shot through with a nostalgia for the richer and profounder spiritual experience across the Atlantic. It followed from this situation that culture in America was not an interpretation of American life. ... I believe that there is no more striking character of American consciousness than this division between the two great currents of activity, those of politics and business on the one side, and the history, literature and speculation which should interpret them on the other. ... America's native culture accepted the forms and standards of European culture, was frankly imitative. It was confessedly inferior, not different."[427]

This imitative quality of American economic philosophy included the free trade propensities of New England and the South, opposing tariff protection, internal improvements or other forms of state aid. Their universities were long under religious domination, with political economy taught more as a branch of moral philosophy than as an application of pragmatic principles. The political correctness of the day was individualism and free markets. The most prominent advocates of industrialization were political activists whose ranks rarely included industrialists themselves until after the Civil War. They were not well represented in the nation's universities, until state colleges and business schools began to be formed with an alternative economic curriculum. But Mead seems unaware of the interpretation of American industrial life as it was viewed outside of New England and the mainstream American intellectual establishment.

---

[427] George Herbert Mead, "The Philosophies of Royce, James, and Dewey in Their American Setting," *International Journal of Ethics* 40 (1930), repr. in *George Herbert Mead: Essays in His Social Philosophy* (New York: 1968), p. 114.

Underlying the tariff debate was the question of whether America should achieve self-sufficiency in manufactures or remain a primarily agricultural country dependent on plantation exports to pay for its industrial imports. This controversy between protectionism and free trade took on broad philosophic overtones beyond the tariff issue as such. Free trade advocates tended to endorse an essentially pre-industrial yeomanry reminiscent of English idealism. The prospect of industrialization loomed more as a nightmare than an ideal. The longer it could be staved off, the happier and more prosperous the nation would be. Self-sufficiency was deemed wasteful. The United States should integrate itself into the European (mainly English) economy until such time as its vacant lands filled up and its wage levels were ground down to those of Europe.

A corollary was that without an ever-expanding land area, population pressure and diminishing returns would erode U.S. living standards. The Slave Power led the expansionist campaign to appropriate more plantation land in the southwest, its slaves to be fed by grain grown by Eastern manpower moving onto Western farmland. Industrialists hoped to contain America's population in the East, not only to mitigate upward wage pressures but also to achieve economies of scale. To the extent that they promoted expansion to the Northwest, it was largely a response to Southern expansionism, aimed at maintaining political balance between slave and free states in Congress, especially in the Senate so as to prevent the South from blocking the public infrastructure investment and monetary system needed by the North to urbanize and industrialize.

Rejecting the free-trade ideal transplanted from England, the American School declared the pretended universality of British political economy invalid in a world whose national experience and social institutions differed widely. The first generation of protectionists (1814–48) tended to deny the validity of economic theory as a general body of analysis and precepts. Defending American protectionism as an exception to British free trade rules, Calvin Colton's *Public Economy for the United States* (1848) argued that this meant that economic theory itself could not claim generality of scope. After 1848, however, Henry Carey and his associates developed a full-blown alternative to British political economy, elaborating it into a doctrine replete with a broad sociological dimension after the Civil War. And having created a broader and indeed more realistic alternative to British free-trade orthodoxy, American protectionists soon were joined by writers in France, Germany, Italy, Russia and Japan. In their view the problem with British free trade doctrine was not its abstract mode of formulation but the fact that its assumptions and axioms were just plain wrong, narrow-minded and short-term.

Toward a more complex view of U.S. economic and political thought

The history of American economic controversy has been viewed largely in terms of the conflicts dominating the 1776–1815 period (Hamiltonian federalism versus Jeffersonian agrarian democracy) and the 1890–1914 Progressive Era period (Teddy Roosevelt's trust-busting, social reform and related labor-capital relations). This approach frames the economic debate in terms of the conflicts between democracy and commercial aristocracy, Jefferson and Hamilton, debtor and creditor, East and West. But the arguments between Jefferson and Hamilton had been mainly political with economic undertones. After 1815 the opposition between North and South became increasingly economic, with political overtones following suit. America's political and economic tensions shifted to a North-South axis during 1815–60. And this shift was critical in determining the course of the nation's subsequent industrial and commercial development.

Political affinities toward England or France shaped the early American policy debate. Friendly to the French reformers, Jefferson wrote to George Washington in April 1794: "my opinion of the British government is, that nothing will force them to do justice but the loud voice of their people, and that this can never be excited but by distressing their commerce." The House of Representatives passed a non-intercourse bill, but the Senate rejected it when Vice President John Adams cast the deciding vote.

But after the Treaty of Ghent (1815) the attitudes of North and South toward England and France were inverted. Threatened by normalization of trade and other economic relations with England, the American commercial and industrial aristocracy became increasingly protectionist, adopting many formerly Jeffersonian criticisms of England. Ensconced in the southern and border states, the agrarian Jeffersonians argued for free trade even though it involved dependence on England for industrial imports. "In the first of these controversies of 1794," observed Jefferson's follower George Tucker,

> the two great sections of the union were placed in an unnatural position by the undue interest which they severally felt of good or ill will towards the French and English nations, but in the last, they are influenced by a consideration of their permanent interests exclusively. The northern states being better fitted for manufactures and having a direct interest in excluding foreign rivals from the whole American market, while the southern states being almost exclusively employed in the pursuits of agriculture must look to the foreign markets for the sale of their redundant products. And so far as they are purchasers of manufactures, they are benefited by the competition between foreign and American manufactures; of course they have a direct interest in keeping the foreign markets, both for selling and buying, as free from restriction as possible.[428]

---

[428] George Tucker, *The Life of Thomas Jefferson* ... (Philadelphia: 1837), pp. 481–84, 477f. See also p. 475.

This North-South economic polarity replaced the earlier political and social orientation of America's two main political parties. Jeffersonianism became a front for the Slave Power, opposing urban industrialization. Two presidents of the University of South Carolina, Thomas Cooper and Francis Lieber, had immigrated to America and served briefly as apostles of democracy but soon became apologists for the slave system. What Northern Whigs referred to as the Jacksonian Sham Democracy used a populist rhetoric to promote its pro-Southern militaristic attitude, while Andrew Jackson's successor, Martin Van Buren, sought to create in Washington a political patronage system on the model of New York City.

Exhibiting a frank hostility toward industry, Democrats attempted to destroy the credit system through which industry was financed, highlighted by Jackson's defeat of the Second Bank of the United States and its replacement by the deflationary Sub-Treasury system. Opposing protective tariffs and internal improvements financed with import duties, they endorsed states' rights to block national government infrastructure spending. Whigs accused the Jacksonians of striving to keep America in the position of a hewer of wood and drawer of water, a rural country with a policy layered over with a veneer of military grandeur and expansionist belligerence. Indeed, Jacksonian democracy contained many of the characteristics that have come to mark today's military dictatorships in less developed countries, including their economic subservience to the then-dominant industrial power, England.

After the Civil War resolved the slavery issue, the Democratic Party retained its political base in the Solid South and strove to capture the West. It ceased opposing industry as such, building up political machines in the large commercial cities, especially New York and Boston, drawing strength from the Irish and Italian, and later Slavic and Jewish immigrants. This helped catalyze Republican anti-Catholic passions, and may have helped induce its historians to emphasize the rise of America as a secular power in contrast to theocratic Europe. Seeking to appropriate the Progressive programs of the 1880s and '90s, the Democrats aimed to replace the antebellum North-South opposition with an East-West dichotomy, culminating in the 1896 presidential campaign between William Jennings Bryan and Republican William McKinley over the soft- vs. hard-money issue.

Two sets of economic conflict emerged. On the one hand the interests of the working class and democracy were counterpoised to the drives of the plutocracy and trusts. Charles Beard's *Economic Interpretation of the Constitution* (1913) viewed the sectional conflict in terms of class conflict. On the other hand Southern and Western populism was set against the Eastern establishment, hence the work of Frederick Jackson Turner viewing class conflict in terms of sectionalism. In idealizing the frontier, he failed to acknowledge or perhaps even to see that he was expressing the Malthusian and Ricardian pessimism whose doctrines underlay expansion of slavery in the 1840s.

By the time he wrote, American "frontierism" was evolving into a higher form of Manifest Destiny. No longer was expansionism allied with the drives of the Slave Power, as in Jacksonian President James K. Polk's war with Mexico over Texas. Recast in populist terms, it was put forth as a program to rescue the American working class from poverty stemming from overproduction. A new generation of Democrats argued that American agriculture and urban industry would stagnate in the absence of foreign markets. It followed that America needed a strong military power to secure access to these markets. Inherently military, this doctrine of westward expansion was extending across the Pacific to Hawaii and the Philippines. And as in Britain's case, it called for free trade to gain entry into foreign markets, by force if necessary.

It is not surprising that most historians of the frontier tradition have been Democrats. Their neglect of the economic doctrines underlying Republican isolationism gives an impression of American history as an aggressive expansionism as claimed by New Left historians or simply the political exuberance of frontierism applauded by the more bombastic orthodoxy. Charles Beard and Richard Hofstadter have noted that this approach is pessimistic in viewing America's unique character as stemming from its open frontier—hence the implicit decline in American society after its closing.

The technological pessimism of free-trade imperialism

Two frontiers are available to an expanding economy. A focus on foreign trade and westward expansion of America into Asia led to the Spanish-American war and the Philippine trauma of 1898, which offended popular morality as radically as would Vietnam seventy years later and Iraq since 2002. The other frontier, particularly since the 1930s, has been that of government spending to promote domestic demand—once again with military overtones stemming emphasizing arms spending. Since the 1930s this government-spending frontier has become nearly as bellicose as geographic frontierism was in the 19th-century West. What John F. Kennedy called the New Frontier came in the administration of Lyndon Johnson to reflect a spirit similar to that urged by the Democratic Party under Jackson and Polk, and ground to a halt in Vietnam and Chile.

There are many kinds of frontiers—not only geographic at the extensive margin (which tends to involve military conquest), but also at the intensive margin (where soil productivity tends to rise in response to more intensive labor and capital, while site values rise as a result of rent of location when population density increases). It is most optimistic to emphasize the internal margin as promoting prosperity—the economic margin (technology and the internal market), the political margin (democratic reform) and the social margin (raise living standards and economic participation rates for the poor).

To imply that the domestic economy must stagnate in the absence of geographic expansion and empire building is to assume an inability to generate growth from within. Today, as the United States seeks to establish a new military frontier in the Near East and Central Asia, it is appropriate to contrast the ideology underlying the frontierism of military conquest with that emphasizing growth and rising living standards in the domestic economy itself. The latter is what underlay America's rise to world industrial power. It was the isolationist antithesis of geographic empire and the often militarily coercive Ricardian pessimism that served as its rationale. It was the free-trade South that initiated the Civil War, and economic pessimists in Europe that supplied the doctrine of 19th-century colonialism—an economic view of resource control and rent extraction that is still inspiring imperial belligerence today.

IX. POLITICAL ORIGINS OF THE U.S. DEPARTMENT OF AGRICULTURE

SOIL CHEMISTRY AND INTERNATIONAL TRADE THEORY 1840–62

As with most public agencies, the Department of Agriculture's official history provides an airbrushed description of the political interests shaping its origin. The myth is that politicians from agricultural states took the lead to promote helpful research into seed varieties and provide technology and marketing services. But this is not what happened. It was industrial protectionists that took the initiative. A major aim was to use the new discoveries in agricultural chemistry to demonstrate the soil-depleting character of plantation exports. The idea was to nurture an urban industrial economy in place of the slave system's practice of "mining the soil" and abandoning it for new western land.

It may seem ironic that sponsorship of the Department of Agriculture was led by Whig-Republican advocates of industrialization rather than by the Democratic agrarians pledged to maintain America as an essentially rural continent. The explanation is to be found in the implications of soil chemistry and location theory for the tariff debate. Whig (and after 1854, Republican) protectionists were eager to demonstrate the farmer's interest in a thriving home market for rural produce, and to explain that urban growth required industrial tariffs. Backing free trade, the Democratic Party sought to block discussion of soil depletion as an "externality" cost of exporting plantation crops.

The new discoveries in agricultural chemistry indicated that the way to increase farm productivity — indeed, to stem the soil depletion that was taking place throughout the United States — was to establish an urban-rural balance between industrial and agricultural employments. The idea was to substitute domestic markets for the large-scale exportation of crops. Fostering urban markets required protective tariffs. To argue these points before the nation's farmers, industrial protectionists campaigned from 1849 onward to establish a Department of Agriculture, starting under the administration of Zachary Taylor, elected in 1848. After more than a decade's campaigning, the department finally was formed in 1862. The struggle to establish it reflected the idea that America should enact protective tariffs, not rely on raw-materials exports by a rural slave-based economy to pay for British manufactures.

Democratic politicians, anti-protectionist, expansionist and basing their political power on an already solid South, were cool to such proposals. Southern slaveholders feared that the urbanization nurtured by industrial protection would force up food prices by absorbing a rising share of western grain output (the so-called "Provisions Question"), increasing the price of feeding slaves to produce cotton and other plantation crops. This threatened the South's world cotton monopoly, entailing the decay not only of its major export crops but also that slavery itself. Resenting the isolationist conclusions drawn in the 1840s by protectionists from the discoveries of Justus von Liebig

(1803–73), Albrecht Thaer (1752–1828) and John Bennet Lawes (1814–1900), the Democratic Party played down the political-economic implications of the new science of agricultural chemistry.[429]

Origins of the Dept. of Agriculture in the Patent Office's agricultural section

The forerunner of the Department of Agriculture was established in 1839 when Congress appropriated a small sum for the U.S. Patent Office to gather agricultural statistics, collect and disseminate new seed varieties, and perform various other technical functions. These routine duties were all that the agricultural section did under Democratic administrations, starting with the outgoing Polk administration (1845–48). But under Taylor's pro-tariff Whig administration (1849–52) the Commissioner of Patents used the annual agricultural reports as a forum to win America's farmers to the cause of industrial protectionism.

The first Commissioner of Patents charged with preparing an agricultural report was Henry L. Ellsworth (1836–44), a wealthy Indiana landowner and agriculturalist who advocated (especially in his 1842 report) fostering an urban home market for domestic farm produce. Ellsworth expected America's farm export surplus to grow as rising immigration and the natural growth of population would increase the supply of farm labor, while the productive powers of this labor would be augmented by the increased use of labor-saving machinery and fertilizers. Production expenses would decline, while extension of the nation's railway and road system would reduce transport costs for the farmer and open up new croplands. So rapidly might farm output grow, Ellsworth concluded, that it might considerably outstrip the growth of foreign markets, causing crop prices to fall. As an alternative he proposed to nurture a domestic market for farm products, a market composed of an urban labor force and industry employed in working up agricultural output into manufactures. This home market, he emphasized, would be considerably more stable than that of Europe. Although Britain promised to become a growing market for American grain, the virtues of a foreign market were outweighed by those of a steady and growing domestic demand.

---

[429] Liebig provided the scientific basis for chemical fertilizer by discovering the role of nitrogen as an essential plant nutrient and analyzing the effect of various additives on crops. The British chemist John Lawes established the world's first agricultural research farm. Noting the benefits of applying ground-up bones as fertilizer, in 1842 he patented a means of treating them with sulphuric acid. Its commercial success led Liebig to patent his own meat extract to restore soil fertility.

Returning to power in 1844 behind Polk, the Democrats appointed Edmund Burke Commissioner of Patents (1845–48). In keeping with the party's pro-South free trade policy, Burke portrayed America's farmers as an export-oriented interest. "In truth," he observed in his 1845 report, "our agricultural products form the basis of our immense foreign commerce, thus constituting the strongest ligaments which unite us to the great brotherhood of nations; contributing not only to our national wealth, but to the cultivation of amity and peace in our foreign relations, and to the progress of civilization at home."[430] This "brotherhood of nations" had already in 1824 been termed by Henry Clay "a tacit compact" between the Southern slave power and England, based on reciprocal markets and a common desire to thwart Northern industrial growth. The plan was for England to buy American grain and cotton, while the United States would obtain most of its manufactures from England.

Burke was as eager as his predecessor to spread knowledge of the discoveries transpiring in agricultural chemistry. In his initial report he requested a larger appropriation for agricultural research, endorsed Ellsworth's earlier request for the services of "a permanent clerk, to aid in procuring the statistical information for the agricultural report," and urged the legislatures of each state to collect agricultural statistics. In 1846, however, a Democratic Congress made no appropriation at all for the agricultural section, on the ground "that the agricultural duties of this office have been assumed without authority of law, and were therefore a grave abuse and usurpation of power." [431] No crop estimates were made for that year. Greatly disappointed, Burke defended the section by observing:

> It is not proper, perhaps, for me to vindicate the conduct of my predecessor under whose administration of the office it was introduced. It will not, however, be irrelevant to remark, that the subject had been a matter of serious consideration by the committee of the House of Representatives upon the Patent Office during the session of 1839–40, and the Commissioner was then requested, by the able chairman of that committee, to communicate to the committee "any information relative to the collection and distribution of seeds and plants; also, the practicability of obtaining agricultural statistics, with the addition of any suggestions deemed important in relation to those subjects."

Appropriations were restored the following year, and Burke devoted large sections of his 1847 and 1849 reports to the debate then underway regarding "the philosophy of fertilizer" among the followers of Thaer, Liebig and Lawes over the nature of soil fertility. These theories held vital political implications for the nation's tariff controversy.

---

[430] *Report of the Commissioner of Patents, 1845* (Washington, 1846), p. 14.
[431] *Report of the Commissioner of Patents, 1846* (Washington, 1847), p. 11.

Thaer, Liebig and Lawes showed that far from possessing "original and indestructible powers" as portrayed by David Ricardo's rent theory, soil was an instrument of variable productivity, subject to depletion or augmentation. Maintaining its fertility required continual restoration of the chemicals removed in the process of cultivation, just as industrial capital required maintenance charges—what modern national income accounts call capital consumption.

Portraying soil fertility as composed essentially of organic elements, Thaer's "humus theory" described manure, nightsoil and living plants as necessary to maintain its productive powers. Liebig's "wind and ash" theory focused on nitrogen, holding that the soil's organic constituents served mainly to help the plant derive nutriments from the atmosphere. Plants derived nourishment in the form of carbon dioxide and ammonia, which they returned through the process of vegetable putrefaction and fermentation. Fertility could be maintained by applying the dried ashes of crops, restoring the essential elements that cultivation removed from soil.

As an academic, Liebig took the lead in controverting the static Ricardian concept of land as an instrument of fixed and immutable productive powers. In 1840 he published his *Chemistry in its Relation to Agriculture and Physiology*, stating that plants resembled the human body in transforming caloric nourishment into growth (a transformation that found its expression in the form of work effort in animal bodies). Because the endless cycle of vegetable growth and decay maintained the atmosphere's supply of these elements in virtually inexhaustible quantities, it followed that no depletion of carbon or nitrogen could take place in the overall scheme of nature. But it was from the soil that plants obtained their mineral nourishment, comprised mainly of potash, soda, lime, sulfur and phosphorus. In contrast to the atmosphere's abundant provision of carbon dioxide and ammonia, the soil in any given district did not afford an endless mine of these minerals. "The principal problem for agriculture," Liebig concluded, "is how to replace those substances which have been taken from the soil, and which cannot be furnished by the atmosphere. If the manure supplies an imperfect compensation for this loss, the fertility of a field, or of a country decreases; if, on the contrary, more are given to the fields, their fertility increases." [432]

Although the soil's component elements could not be destroyed in the overall equilibrium of nature, they could be—and often were—removed from given districts. On a local basis the soil's mineral supply was determined by the rate of its crop's return (figuratively speaking) in the form of fertilizer, either as fecal waste from the towns where the food was consumed (which was prac-

---

[432] "Familiar Letters on Chemistry," in *Complete Works on Chemistry* (trans. Lyon Playfair, Philadelphia [1843], p. 40.

tical only if these towns were near-lying) or concentrated in the form of ashes, guano or special preparations. "Can the art of agriculture be based upon anything but the restitution of a disturbed equilibrium?" asked Liebig.

> Can it be imagined, that any country, however rich and fertile, with a flourishing commerce, which for centuries exports its produce in the shape of grain and cattle, will maintain its fertility, if the same commerce does not restore, in some form of manure, these elements which have been removed from the soil, and which cannot be replaced by the atmosphere? Must not the same fate await every such country which has actually befallen the once prolific soil of Virginia, now in many parts no longer able to grow its former staple productions—wheat and tobacco? [433]

In this statement Liebig established the relevance of his theories to America's tariff debate. Farm districts that were net exporters of crops must be characterized by soil-depleting modes of agriculture in the absence of a corresponding net importation or other application of fertilizer. The inference was that the nation lost the costs sunk by nature into the land—costs that did not originally need to be paid for, but which someday would have to be paid to restore the soil's fertility.

This theory gave new significance to the Whig home-market platform of "placing the consumer by the side of the producer." Before the 1840s were out, the Patent Office reports informed American farmers that according to the prevailing theories of agricultural chemistry, only the establishment of neighboring industrial towns and cities could offer hope for economically restoring to the soil the needed manure, nightsoil and other essential fertilizing elements. Barring the establishment of local urban-rural balance, America's farmland must ultimately become depleted. Urging top priority for conserving the nation's soil resources (more than half a century before Theodore Roosevelt renewed the conservation issue as a major element of the Republican platform), the Whigs advocated industrialization of America's great agricultural hinterland so as to establish this balance between town and country.

Daniel Lee's protectionist economic doctrine and agricultural science

After the Whig victory in 1848 behind Taylor, Thomas Ewbank was named Commissioner of Patents (1849–53). Taylor had hoped to establish the agricultural bureau as a distinct entity with its own finances, and to transfer it into the Department of the Interior. "This bureau," a British agriculturalist who interviewed President Taylor reported, "will hereafter present its own report to Congress, separated from extraneous matter, and embracing topics which that

---

[433] *Ibid.*, p. 32.

of the Patent Office could not overtake."[434] Beginning in 1849 the agricultural report was published as a separate volume. Following Taylor's death in office, however, the project of substantially enlarging the department and transferring it out of the Patent Office faltered, and the bureau remained as it was—with one important addition: Commissioner Ewbank appointed Daniel Lee, an upstate New York protectionist, to write the agricultural reports.

Lee had served as editor of *The Genesee Farmer*, as chairman of the New York State Assembly's committee on agriculture, and later headed the New York State Agricultural Society, at that time the most advanced such society in the nation. One of his acquaintances was E. Peshine Smith, law partner of William Henry Seward and author of the important *Manual of Political Economy* (1853) that soon would set out the Republican economic platform of protective tariffs, internal improvements and a national bank. In a letter to his fellow protectionist Henry Carey, Smith explained that "Dr Lee was in charge of the Agricultural Department of the Patent Office labouring to get an agricultural Bureau established of which he should be the head, and failing that endeavouring to worm [Commissioner of Patents] Ewbank out of office with the hope of getting his place."[435]

Lee's articles during 1849–52 are the most striking and political of all the Patent Office reports. Under his direction the Patent Office's agricultural section drew upon the available statistics to illustrate soil exhaustion and explain it as a byproduct of America's trade policy. For the year 1849, he estimated, the nation's exhaustive methods of cultivation entailed an annual loss of farm income averaging 10 cents per acre on 100 million of the 125 million acres of improved farmland then in use. This $10 million loss in annual farm income (akin to capital depreciation) was equal in magnitude to the proceeds of a capital investment of $166,666,000 at 6% annual interest. "That improved farming lands may be justly regarded as capital," Lee added,

> and a fair investment when paying six per cent. interest, and perfectly safe, no one will deny. This deterioration is not unavoidable, for thousands of skillful farmers have taken fields, poor in point of natural productiveness, and, instead of diminishing their fertility, have added ten cents an acre to their annual income, over and above all expenses. ... For all practical purposes the difference between the two systems is [$333,333,000] to the country.[436]

[434] James Finlay Wier Johnston, *Notes on North America, Agricultural, Economical, and Social* [Boston 1851], Vol. I, pp. 328f. In 1849, Eastern agriculturalists brought Prof. Johnston, of the University of Durham and one of Liebig's major followers, to the United States in Liebig's stead for a series of lectures and travels.

[435] Peshine Smith to Henry Carey, June 14, 1854, in the Carey collection at the Philadelphia Historical Society.

[436] "Statistics and Progress of Agriculture in the United States for the year 1849," in *Report of the Commissioner of Patents for the year 1849, Part II: Agriculture* (Washington, 1850), p. 25.

On the basis of the implicit value of the minerals removed from the soil, Lee's 1852 report estimated the capital loss to amount to $300 million per year —that is, $3.00 an acre, or about 17½ to 20 per cent of the crops' sales value, "by which remark we mean that complete restitution of the elements of crops removed, such as potash, soda, lime, magnesia, chlorine, phosphoric and sulphuric acids, and ammonia, cannot be made short of an expense of three dollars per acre." [437] Ultimately responsible for impairing the nation's soil fertility, Lee asserted, was the nation's free trade policy. "American statesmanship has adopted a system of political economy [that is, free trade] which renders full and perfect restitution of the soil impossible so long [as] it shall prevail. This statesmanship, which ignores the very existence of agricultural science, and repudiates all its teachings, costs the country three hundred million dollars a year by needless destruction of its agricultural resources." [438]

Soil depletion was caused in two ways. The large-scale exportation of American crops to pay for industrial imports caused the loss of the minerals embodied in these crops. And by creating a sparsely populated rural interior behind a congested Eastern seaboard, free trade rendered the return of urban wastes to the farming areas cumbersome and uneconomic. In this respect America's vast agricultural hinterland was an economic burden. "That the health of all cities, and sound farm economy, alike demand such restitution of all fecal matters, is denied by no one. But so long as indefinite millions of acres of rich virgin lands, over which no plough has ever passed, are accessible to all, few will incur the expense of making adequate restitution of the soil as a duty." [439] The soil would be mined and abandoned. This decline in soil fertility could not be halted, claimed Lee, if America continued to export the soil's crops and their mineral constituents in exchange for British manufactures. The solution to both these causes of depletion was to enact protective tariffs so as to nurture the growth of local industry.

---

[437] "Progress of Agriculture in the United States," in *Report of the Commissioner of Patents for the year 1852, Part II: Agriculture* (Washington, 1853), p. 7. For Lee's computation of the cost of these minerals as amounting to $175 to $200 out of each $1,000 of crops sold, see his 1849 report, pp. 8f. In the 1852 report he added (p. 13): "There has been enough of the elements of bread and meat, wool and cotton, drawn from the surface of the earth, sent to London, and buried in the ground or washed into the Thames, to feed and clothe the entire population of the world for a century, under a wise system of agriculture and horticulture. Down to this day, great cities have ever been the worst desolaters of the earth. ... Their inhabitants violated the laws of nature which govern the health of man, and secure the enduring productiveness of the soil."
[438] 1849 *Report*, p. 15.
[439] *Ibid.*, p. 15.

Here was an argument against the Ricardo-Malthus model that underlay Britain's free-trade doctrine and its doctrine of class warfare and social immis-eration by portraying population growth as leading to diminishing returns in agriculture. Ricardo's notion of soil having "original and indestructible powers" was unwarranted, as was his idea of diminishing returns resulting from increasing population density. Far from reflecting the laws of nature, the misery forecast by Malthus and Ricardo was at odds with the rules of well-managed nature. It was not the growing density of population that threatened America's soil productivity, but just the reverse—the fact that the free availability of land in America's sparsely populated interior led to soil-depleting modes of cultiva-tion. Diminishing returns were a violation of natural and balanced economic growth. Only as the nation filled up and population density increased would soil-conserving methods of agriculture such as were employed in Europe become profitable. Only when no virgin lands were left, when additions to the nation's population could only be channeled into non-agricultural pursuits, would the depletion of America's soil be alleviated. A balanced circular flow between town and country could be established and urban wastes systemati-cally restored to the land as fertilizer only when crops no longer were exported or their mineral constituents squandered in large congested cities such as the major ports of entry were becoming.

To achieve a more normal pattern of development, America would have to become more self-contained. Until it established self-sufficiency it would con-tinue to lose the minerals contained in its crop exports. Its population would be concentrated in a congested strip of commercial trading ports along the Eastern Seaboard while the agricultural interior would extend further and further west. Should the mining of the soil persist, Lee warned, America would be incapable of maintaining its agricultural surplus. With this logic he attempted to win Southern planters to the cause of industrial self-sufficiency:

> No cotton-grower should wish to conceal from himself or the public the fact that the soil of the South will be injured as much in the next fifteen years as it has been in the last twenty-five; ... In case no restitution is contemplated, and the present system of planting is to continue, what a humiliating and inglorious destiny must not the sunny South finally reach? Can her patriotic statesmen close their eyes against the evidence of an erroneous policy [*i.e.*, free trade] which impoverishes the soil, because full and perfect restitution appears impracticable? Our old colonial system of agriculture is defective and wrong in the extreme. Having come down to us from before the Revolution, the evils which are entailed admit of no remedy short of wise and timely legislation. [440]

---

[440] *Ibid.*, pp. 2–3. See also p. 13.

This argument shows why industrial protectionists rather than Democratic free traders took the lead in compiling soil fertility statistics. Treating land as an exhaustible and/or augmentable resource, along the lines of what Friedrich List called the "theory of productive powers," Lee urged the compilation of statistics showing trends in output per acre over time rather than merely tabulating existing crop output and its market value. The Southern free trader policy of exporting plantation crops to pay for industrial imports from what then was the cheapest market (Britain) found little appeal in statistical analyses showing that this worked to deplete the nation's soil and was exploitative inasmuch as the value of minerals consumed in the process of cultivation exceeded the market price received—an implicit indirect cost of the nation's free trade policy (what today is called an externality).

The theory of soil as a variable productive factor also served to explain the evolution of agricultural productivity in the United States. The comparative scarcity of labor in America had led not only to a more capital-intensive industrial technology than in Europe, but to an even more capital-intensive agriculture, in particular in the more industrialized Eastern states. Mechanization of agriculture under land-exploitative methods of cultivation was accelerating the deterioration of soil quality, conserving labor at the soil's expense. This had the result of depleting soil productivity while increasing that of agricultural capital. "Productiveness of crops and destructiveness of soil are two most prominent features of American agriculture."[441] However, Lee noted:

> It is only in two or three states, where State statistics aid us in our researches, that the constant deterioration of the soil is demonstrated. The object sought by those that prepared the blank schedules for the collection of agricultural statistics by United States marshals, appears not to have been to promote the interests of agriculture by improving the soil...[442]

The seeming irony that advocates of urban industrial development took the lead in promulgating the new agricultural technology—and that the Democrats, dedicated as they were to maintaining America as an agricultural nation, showed the least interest—was true on the local as well as the national level is reflected in the observation Prof. Johnston (the British visitor to America

---

[441] 1852 Patent Office report, p. 4.

[442] *Ibid.*, p. 4. Lee added: "The careful and critical study of agriculture, with a view to make it the foundation of a wise system of political economy, has never been undertaken by American statesmen. Hence, their statesmanship and political economy have been at war with the true principles of tillage and husbandry from the first settlement of this continent by Europeans. Instead of inculcating the public duty to feed the land, that both feeds and clothes all classes and all generations, they have taught doctrines and established a policy which render it wholly impracticable to supply cotton, tobacco, and grain, for home consumption, without seriously impairing the natural resources of the soil."

cited above), "that the Legislature of New York proposes to establish an agricultural college, on a scale worthy of the Empire State; and that it is the indifference of the agricultural members which has delayed it from being sooner carried into operation."[443] He added that "while the lawyers, and nearly all the other classes of men in the Legislature, are willing to vote the public money with a view to the future improvement of the staple interest of the State, many of the farmers themselves refuse to accept the grant as a gift to their class, on the ground that the knowledge to be given in the school is not required, and that its application to the soil would be of doubtful benefit."[444]

The reason for the Whigs' concern for agriculture is not difficult to understand. Like their Ricardian counterparts in Britain's Corn Law debates, they wished to see a growing industrial population fed with low-priced sustenance. In Britain this dictated repeal of its agricultural protectionism—the Corn Laws—so as to import cheaper crops by negotiating reciprocal free trade agreements. In the United States, urban industry required protective tariffs and rising soil productivity. The party of industry had as great an interest as the South in seeing low food costs, and as great a political prize in winning to its banner the swing vote of the western plains.

Refining the agricultural argument for industrial tariff protection

Upon leaving the Patent Office after the Democrats regained the presidency in 1852, Lee helped found the United States Agricultural Society, becoming its corresponding secretary and editor of the first volume of its Journal (along with Joseph C. G. Kennedy, who became superintendent of the 1860 agricultural census, and W. S. King). This politically important group was formed in June 1852 after a National Agricultural Convention in Washington was attended by most of the nation's state agricultural societies. Lee and his Whig colleagues urged the convention to memorialize Congress to establish an Agricultural Department, but were opposed by the Democratic Senator Stephen A. Douglas of Illinois and McHenry of Maryland, who argued that "it would soon become, like all the other offices of the Government, a place for politicians, and its occupants would be removable at every change of Administration." After Douglas proposed that a Department of Agriculture be attached to the

---

[443] *Notes on North America*, I, p. 471.
[444] *Ibid.*, p. 281. For a discussion of the farming class's general opposition to the establishment of land-grant agricultural colleges under the Morrill amendment see Paul W. Gates, *Agriculture and the Civil War* (New York, 1965), pp. 259–63.

Smithsonian Institution, a compromise resolution called for a nebulously defined "Board of Agriculture" (a term originally suggested by George Washington) to be "composed of distinguished characters."[445]

A passage from the Society's first issue of its Journal, evidently written by Lee, deserves rescue from oblivion here despite its length, as summarizing the economy's agricultural politics:

> It is due to our posterity and the inalienable rights of man, that a national effort be made to preserve the virgin lands of this continent from the desolation with which they are threatened; and that measures be taken to ascertain how much more of the essential elements of fertility American soil annually parts with than is restored to it again. Many millions of acres have been sadly abused, and never so much in any one year, as in that of 1852.
>
> Those that have given years to the careful investigation of the policy of American legislation, in its bearings on agriculture, believe that its tendency has long been, and still is, to foster the needless waste of all the food and raiment. If this be true, it is a truth of great moment, and one that pre-eminently deserves the consideration of legislators. That the soil in the older states has been seriously deteriorated in many districts, is not disputed; but that the policy of the Government from its foundation, has encouraged the robbing of the surface of the earth of the few things that form the staples of trade, commerce and manufactures, may not be so clear to all. … Millions of dollars have been expended by state legislators, and by Congress, to construct canals, roads and railways, improve the navigation of rivers and lakes, and facilitate the sending of the elements of crops to distant markets, never to return. While this depleting system of legislation has been steadily pursued for a century and more, what has any Legislature ever done to teach the owners of American soil the best way to restore to it as much potash as it once contained, but has now lost? This is a plain, simple question, and it deserves a candid answer.
>
> Possibly it may be said that every cubic foot of earth contains an inexhaustible amount of potash, and therefore no restitution of this, nor of any other element of crops, is necessary.
>
> It is only by false assumptions of this character that legislation against the enduring fruitfulness of the earth, and against agricultural schools and knowledge generally, can be excused, or defended. …
>
> Perhaps some gentleman, far more skilled in the natural resources of mother earth than we claim to be, may contrive ways and means fully to recuperate an acre that produces a hogshead of exported tobacco, or a bale of cotton, for a smaller sum than five dollars. We think that the United States Agricultural Society should offer liberal premiums for a series of experiments, which shall prove how much of the phosphate and sulphate of lime and magnesia, potash and soda, is removed by a year's tillage, per acre, in the cultivation of cotton, tobacco, corn and wheat, over and above what the crops contain. … Tillage is a very old art; but its chemical effects, considered in connection with sunlight and heat, rains, dews and frosts, and atmospheric gases, are still unknown. Nor is it known how much of the solids in crops is formed of elements drawn from air and water, and how much from the mould and minerals in the surface of the ground.[446]

[445] *Journal of the United States Agricultural Society*, Vol. I, no. 1 (August 1852), pp. 14–24.
[446] *Ibid.*, pp. 27ff.

The Patent Office's agricultural reports after Lee: 1853–61

During the Democratic administrations of Franklin Pierce and James Buchanan the agricultural section of the Patent Office was characterized by a series of uninspired reports of a narrow technical character. The new appointees to the Patent Office did not attempt to use its agricultural section as a forum to argue against the Whig-Republican claims that urban industry promised a much larger market, higher farm incomes and prices, and lower costs to farmers for growing and transporting their crops. Limiting themselves to the more mundane collection of agricultural statistics and distribution of seed types for which the office was originally formed, the Democratic appointees included little general reasoning beyond purely technical issues in the reports, and made no reference at all to the tariff debate. The agricultural party showed little interest in analyzing trends in soil productivity and costs.

After Lincoln's election in 1860 the Republicans moved quickly to establish a Department of Agriculture as a separate entity, which Lincoln recommended in his first message to Congress. He appointed Thomas Clemson as Super-intendent of Agricultural Affairs, still situated within the Patent Office. Despite coming from South Carolina, Clemson strongly supported formation of such a department, and observed in the Patent Office's agricultural report for the year 1860:

> How far it is accordant with the true interests of the Patent Office and with the rights of inventors to continue the administration of agricultural affairs under the aegis of that Office; how far it accords with verity to hold the commissioner of Patents to responsibility before the country and the world for the performance of duties which in the nature of things he cannot be cognizant, for the expression of opinions he cannot have matured, and for the promulgation of scientific discoveries in fields his accustomed pursuits have seldom or never permitted him to traverse, are regarded as proper and important inquiries at the present era.[447]

---

[447] *Report of the Commissioner of Patents for the year 1860. Agriculture* (Washington, 1861), p. 25. Paul Gates gives a succinct description of the political haggling surrounding the agricultural section within the Patent Office (*op. cit.*, p. 302): Agricultural leaders "disliked the subordinate position which the agricultural branch had in the Patent Office, dependent as the latter was for support on fees paid by inventors. Northern authorities felt that the agricultural branch was devoting too much of its attention to problems relating to Southern agriculture, such as replacing diseased sugar cane with disease-free cane from other countries. Southern leaders, on the other hand, were concerned at the attention given to sorghum, which might become a substitute for cane sugar and molasses."

When the Civil War broke out early in 1861, Clemson resigned to join the Confederacy, hoping in vain to establish a Confederate States Department of Agriculture. Although postponing establishment of the new department, the Civil War aided it by removing Southern opposition. [448]

The 1861 Patent Office report was written by D. P. Holloway, who announced his endorsement of Henry Carey, the most widely known protectionist economist, an indirect acknowledgement of Lee's applications of agricultural chemistry to the tariff debate. The following year, in May 1862, the Department of Agriculture finally was formed, over the opposition of senators from such agricultural states as Maine, New Hampshire, Vermont, Iowa and Kansas.

A political appointee, Isaac Newton, became the first Commissioner of Agriculture. He avoided controversial questions even pertaining to grain elevator fees, milk adulteration, railroad rates and the gouging of farmers by crop distributors. In the statistical section of his initial report, however, he reiterated the plea for soil conservation: "Whilst our national pride is gratified in contemplating such a greatly increased production," he observed, "it must occur to every reflecting mind that under our present mode of agriculture, it must be at the expense of the soil." [449] He praised the influence on farm values of an industrial home market and railroads. [450]

Joseph C. G. Kennedy made a more direct home-market argument to the nation's farmers in his report on *Agriculture of the United States in 1860; Compiled from the Original Returns of the Eighth Census, under the Direction of the Secretary of the Interior*. "In our opinion," he observed in his preface,

> the surest way in which the power of government can effectually promote agriculture, is by a steady and consistent policy adapted to encourage the arts and give confidence to the stability of our manufactures; population will then rapidly increase, commerce be promoted, internal improvements multiply, and the power of the state will augment as a natural consequence. ... That which renders the pursuit of agriculture honorable and remunerative, and therefore attractive and popular, is a certain home market ... Under such circumstances the crops seldom fail, nor do the lands grow poor; ...[451]

---

[448] As Gates aptly comments: "By withdrawing from the Union in 1861, the Southern states removed the conservative element that hd long prevented the adoption of important legislation affecting agriculture and the development of the West. In rapid succession congress enacted the Homestead Act with its free-land policy, the Pacific Railroad Act with its liberal aid for the building of a railroad to the Pacific, the act creating a Department of Agriculture, the National Bank Act, and the Morrill Act, all of which had been held up by the shrewd politics of a minority section." (*Op. cit.*, pp. 263f. See also p. 307.)

[449] *Report of the Commissioner of Agriculture for the year 1862* (Washington, 1863), p. 553.

[450] *Ibid.*, pp. 554ff.

[451] *Agriculture of the United States in 1860* (Washington, 1864), pp. iii–iv.

Sparsely populated areas tended to use exhaustive methods of agriculture. "Under such circumstances," Kennedy concluded, "it is evident that the intensive system of agriculture which is practiced in some older and more densely populated countries, where labor is abundant and the land mostly under cultivation, cannot, as a general rule, be profitably adopted at present in this country,"[452] citing an 1861 passage from the *Mark Lane Express*, a leading English agricultural journal:

> It has long been our opinion that the grain-exporting power of the United States was likely rather to diminish than to increase under the ordinary circumstances of the country. The opinion was derived from the statistical notices of the Census and of the Patent Office, and confirmed by the statements of Jay, [David] Wells, and other American writers on the subject. These authorities have warned the agriculturists that if an alteration did not take place in the mode of cultivation, the United States would, in a few years, require a large importation of wheat, instead of being able to export to Europe.

Venturing afield from merely reporting census data, Kennedy argued that industrial growth would help sustain a sufficiently high demand for crops so that farmers could pursue soil-conserving modes of agriculture.

> High farming, the systematic conservation and improvement of soil fertility during the process of cultivation has been done in individual cases with much profit, but still the great majority of farmers could not see their way clear in expending so much capital, and, indeed, it must be confessed that it is not easy to show how high farming can be made profitable with low prices. All this for the present, however, is now changed. Prices have increased to a figure never before reached in this country. Everything that the farmer can raise, is in demand at rates which are highly remunerative. This demand and high prices cannot fail to stimulate farmers to put forth every energy to increase their crops. A higher system of culture will be introduced, and, when once adopted and found profitable, will be continued, even though prices should fall to the old standard. ... It is, however, to an increased home consumption that we look for those higher prices that will give that stimulus to American agriculture it has hitherto needed.[453]

This logic provided an early justification for high farm prices, anticipating the argument for price supports in agriculture put forth some eight decades later.

Impact of the new agricultural technology on economic theory

In addition to serving as tracts to win the farmer's vote to the cause of industrial tariff protection, the Patent Office's agricultural reports entered into the population controversy then raging between the protectionists (anti-Malthusians) and free traders (Malthusians). Via this issue they bore upon protectionist growth theory in general, as their dynamic view of soil productivity was at odds

---

[452] *Ibid.*, p. viii.   [453] *Ibid.*, pp. xliii–xliv.

with the static concept of land employed by Ricardian free-trade economics and the Malthusian proponents of westward expansion and Manifest Destiny.

Already in 1848, Henry Carey's *The Past, the Present and the Future* attempted to refute Ricardo's theory of cultivation and its pessimistic implications for industrial growth. Increasing population density, he asserted, brought about increasing returns in agriculture, just as westward expansion and population dispersion (as advocated by the Democrats) tended to reduce agricultural productivity. Carey urged the enactment of protective tariffs and the fostering of industrial manufactures so as to hold the nation's growing population in the East and reap the ensuing economies of scale in agriculture and industry.

Carey's theories brought to the attention of E. Peshine Smith the relevance of the theory of cultivation to the tariff and population controversies. It was within the contours of Carey's theory of economic growth that he utilized Lee's Patent Office reports to develop his own theory, setting out in 1851

> to show, in the words of the Agricultural Report from the Patent Office, that there is a governmental policy which results in impoverishing the natural fertility of the land, which encourages the removal of all the elements of bread and meat from cultivated fields, and their speedy transportation beyond the possibility of restitution—that this is the policy which looks mainly if not exclusively to foreign trade, and, which, masking itself under the name of free trade, compels the exportation in their rudest and most cumbrous forms of the products of the earth, and with them of all the elements of fertilization and reproduction.[454]

Smith used the concept that crops were the embodiment of their chemical constituents to demonstrate that what could be taken from the soil could be restored, and that fertility could be enhanced by the application of mineral nourishment. Commercial chemical inputs, he asserted, could be substituted for intrinsic "original" fertility, making soil productivity a function of capital inputs. His *Manual of Political Economy* followed Liebig and Lee in arguing that urban wastes could convert food intake into fertilizer as nightsoil. The growth of population thus represented a corresponding increase in man's power to augment the organic powers of the soil—as long as a closed system of chemical equilibrium existed in which the earth's minerals were circulated and re-circulated between man and land. Smith termed this the "Law of Endless Circulation in Matter and Force." In the continual transformation and re-transformation of food into minerals and back into food, none of the earth's resources were consumed ("destroyed"), but merely converted. This fact, he

---

[454] "The Law of Progress in the Relations of Capital and Labor," *Hunt's Merchants' Magazine* 25 (November 1851), p. 531.

concluded, while not necessarily fatal to the theories of Ricardo, was indeed fatal to Malthusian doctrine, founded as it was

> upon the false notion, that man's consumption of food is its destruction—that having once served the purpose of supporting animal life, its capacity to contribute to that object is absolutely spent and exhausted. The failure to observe that, in the natural course of things it is returned to the earth, to be again formed into food, and resume its office in supporting animal life, is tantamount to this; and it is only in consequence of that failure, that the food-producing power of the soil can be regarded either as a fixed quantity, or as incapable of increasing in the same proportion as the food-consuming power of those who dwell upon it.[455]

Smith went much further than Lee in utilizing contemporary theories of agricultural chemistry as a take-off point to define soil as a representative form of capital. Protectionists going back to the seventeenth-century Italian economist Antonio Serra had defended industrialization on the ground that while the constraint of land area limited each nation's agricultural output beyond a point, industrial output was unlimited over the long run, and limited in the short run only by the size of the labor force. Soil productivity, Smith responded, could be augmented indefinitely just like industrial productivity. It was a function of soil quality more than raw land area as such. As a result, he argued, food output could be increased to a virtually unlimited degree just like manufactures, so long as farmers found it economically remunerative to apply fertilizer to the soil in conjunction with energy-driven equipment. Fertility was a product of man-made capital investment, subject to increasing returns as population density increased and society's distribution overhead was reduced and technological progress lowered production costs.

Carey's three-volume *Principles of Social Science* (1858–60) expounded and popularized Smith's agricultural theories, influencing Holloway's 1861 Patent Office report on agriculture and other Republican protectionists. Common to these writers was the perception that Ricardian doctrine was founded upon an erroneously static concept of soil, and that the nation's foreign trade pattern served to reduce the nation's soil fertility under existing methods of cultivation. This perception formed the basis for what Carey termed the "Philosophy of Association" between food producer and food consumer, which held as its economic ideal a closed national economy between farmers and industrialists. In this doctrine the agricultural discoveries of the 1840s were elaborated into protectionist growth theory and expounded by the Dept. of Agriculture, the Census Dept. and other government agencies.

---

[455] *Manual of Political Economy* (New York: Putnam and Sons, 1853), p. 35.

X. Obsolete Factors in the International Economy*

* First published in *Review of Social Economy*, Vol. XXX, March 1972, Number 1, presented at the Thirtieth Annual Meeting of the Association for Social Economics, New Orleans, Louisiana, December 26–28, 1971.

For over half a century, economic theory has neglected to analyze the growing international disparities in labor, land and capital productivity. Its excuse has been Heckscher and Ohlin's factor endowment theory, which attributes international cost advantage only to differing relative proportions of labor, capital and land, not do differences in relative factor productivity as in Ricardian trade theory.

The factor endowment theory rested upon four unrealistic assumptions. First of all, labor, capital and soil productivity among nations were presumed identical, so that one country's labor, capital and soil resources were each as productive as those of any other country on a per unit basis. No country's capital investment could displace that of another country because of superior technological productivity, but only because of its greater relative abundance which directly resulted in its receiving lower profit rates relative to wage and rent levels. Furthermore, no cross competition existed among the various factors of production: increased capital investment in one country could not displace, say, another country's labor. Labor, capital and soil each provided a unique service of production which other factors could not provide, and each category of commodity production was characterized by some optimum labor/capital or labor/land ratio. There was no international factor mobility, no international investment or emigration, or even trade in intermediate goods such as food, fuels or machinery. Finally, all factors in each country were presumed fully employed, except for temporary dislocations which prevented the optimum use of resources. It also was presumed that international demand conditions were such that no single category of goods produced by some specific mix of labor and capital was in chronic oversupply. On the basis of these assumptions, international advantage was held to be relative, not absolute. Every country had some advantage in producing some class of commodities. Demand for these various classes of commodities was presumed roughly proportional to their supply, so that countries tended to maximize their earning power by specializing in the production of commodity classes in which they had a comparative advantage.

The vast amount of theorizing that has been built upon these assumptions in recent decades is not deserving of the attention that has been bestowed upon it. Least deserving of all is the income theory drawn from these assumptions, which Paul Samuelson has termed the factor-price equalization theorem. This theorem purports to demonstrate how international wage levels, rents and profits tend to equalize under free trade. It advises low-income countries to dismantle their tariff barriers, and to export goods in which they have a comparative advantage at any given moment of time. Countries with much labor relative to capital, particularly if they have high rates of unemployment, should concentrate in the production of labor-intensive commodities. Countries with extensive mineral or soil resources should concentrate in primary production, maximizing the opportunity for world gains from trade. This doctrine is the mainstay of today's international economics.

There is at present no school of thought which inquires why factor returns are diverging among nations rather than converging, or why some nations are being priced out of the international marketplace for agricultural and industrial products alike. Few have inquired into the nature of economic obsolescence in the backward countries that has created dualism between their domestic and export sectors. It is therefore the purpose of this paper to investigate these problems. It is shown how capital competes increasingly with labor across national boundaries, driving lower forms of labor from the world marketplace as it has driven this labor, along with horses and other noneconomic inputs, from the marketplace in the developed nations.

Obviously, international wage levels are not equalizing. Countries whose labor forces are characterized by low-paid, obsolete manual labor are becoming poorer and poorer, and are able to compete with foreign countries in fewer and fewer product lines. The low industrial wage levels which once seemed to promise industrial advantage no longer do so, at least for regions with generally low labor skills such as Latin America, Furthermore, nations with what were originally the world's most "naturally rich" soils, those which were the first to attract foreign settlers and developers, have now become increasingly obsolete in comparison with the fertilizer-intensive agriculture of the developed nations.

Explanation for these developments is to be found in the fact that the terms of trade are moving against countries which are non-industrial or agriculturally backward not so much because of their specific commodity specialization, but because they are characterized by relatively high costs of producing industrial energy and the elements of soil fertility. They are left priced out of every market except that for scarce raw materials, which foreign capital comes in to develop. The following analysis postulates an Obsolescence Function in the international economy to explain the manner in which labor, capital and land compete with one another to produce the ultimate economic inputs of work effort (energy) and soil fertility. It then attributes the divergence in per capita national incomes which characterizes today's international economy to the divergence in productive powers and costs, which become absolute advantages for a few nations as a result of international investment and trade in capital and intermediate goods. The result is a tendency towards creating a world ghetto in the planet's economic backwaters.

Assumptions underlying the Factor-Price Equalization Theorem, and the effect of dropping them

The factor-price equalization theorem began by assuming equal labor productivity among countries, as well as equal capital and land productivity. If we drop
this assumption, and recognize that factor productivity differs among countries,
and particularly if we recognize that it tends to vary in proportion to relative
wage levels, then it is clear that countries with relatively low supplies of (say)
labor, even if it is highly paid labor, may still be highly competitive in the world
economy. For if highly paid labor is even more highly productive, it may still
undersell low-paid labor on a unit-cost basis. Similarly, one nation's capital
may be more productive than that of another nation, as technology is by no
means identical across national boundaries. We would expect factor returns
to vary directly with productivity. There would not necessarily be any tendency
for productivity to equalize among nations, and in fact every social and cultural
reason to expect that it might diverge in response to the external economies of
national development.

Matters are further complicated for today's economists when we drop the
assumption that there is no cross-competition between labor and capital in
international trade (or within the domestic economy, for that matter). It is
asserted that there is some optimum, stable ratio for employing labor, capital
and land to produce given classes of commodities. Each factor is held to supply
a unique productive service of its own. Labor services, land services and capital
services compete with other labor services, land services and capital services
respectively, but not with one another. Some textbooks, to be sure, recognize
the unrealism of this assumption. Charles P. Kindleberger acknowledges that
"there may be some ambiguity about the technological factor proportions
involved in producing a given commodity. ... in the production of many
commodities, there is a range within which one factor can be substituted for
another. Eggs can be produced by chickens roaming the range, using land, or
cooped up in batteries of nests, in which capital substitutes for land and labor.
It is impossible to say that one of these commodities is more capital intensive
or labor intensive than another until we know more about the possibilities of
factor substitution and the factor availabilities."[456] But having made this
observation, Kindleberger and other mainstream trade theorists drop it from
their analysis as if it did not exist. This is unfortunate, because pursuit of its
consequences would transform their doctrine in the direction of much greater
realism. The major productive service which labor and capital produce in

---

[456] Charles P. Kindleberger, *International Economics*, 4th ed. (Homewood: 1968), pp. 29f.

common, for instance, is work effort, a more basic unit of factor input than man-hours or raw machine-hours. It is apparent that industrial capital can produce energy much less expensively than manual labor, as the human body is a relatively inefficient energy converter at today's food and fuel costs. We would therefore expect international energy costs to be more critical in determining international industrial advantage than per diem wage rates or machine-hour costs.

Having thus cleared the air of these two unrealistic assumptions, we may turn to that of zero international factor mobility, which Viner and others take as the very definition of international economics. In Samuelson's theory and that of his contemporaries, this mobility serves to equalize incomes. But this only if we assume equal productivity among all factors moving across national boundaries. Suppose labor- and capital-productivity to be unequal among nations. Its international mobility would then convey some nations' absolute advantage across national boundaries, by virtue of its common denominator. For costs of key inputs would no longer be relative, they would be absolute. For instance, if all food were produced in one region, then human subsistence costs (net of transport differentials) would equate for all nations. If all fuel were produced in one region, and assuming there to be only one form of fuel used to produce each commodity category (*e.g.*, coal, oil or uranium), operating costs for most energy-intensive types of products would equate. If prices of capital goods are equal among nations through the process of international trade, then relative production advantages enjoyed by some countries, as a result of their superior labor or capital productivity, would become absolute cost advantages. A single great nation, such as the United States, might possess absolute advantage in both industrial and agricultural product lines, and produce a large enough surplus over and above its own domestic needs to drive from the market the labor and capital and land of many less developed countries. Capital in the world economy would tend to be employed in conjunction with the most productive, lowest unit-cost labor and fuel, irrespective of the resources of the low-paid but high unit-cost manual labor possessed by various backwaters of the world economy. This would help explain chronic unemployment or underemployment in specific areas of the world economy such as Latin America.

The Three Modes of Abstraction in Terms-of-Trade Analysis, and Their Policy Implications

During Britain's Corn Law debates in the early nineteenth century, Ricardo and Mill popularized the terms of trade between industrial and agricultural exporters, urging England to become the workshop of the world. Ricardo attributed comparative advantage among nations to different factor productivities in agricultural pursuits as opposed to those in industry, as indicated by his mathematical example of the comparative labor costs of England and Portugal producing cloth and wine. A century later, Heckscher and Ohlin shifted the emphasis of international trade theory away from productivity differentials to income differentials. They implied that countries possessed comparative advantage not so much in terms of specific commodity categories as in the relative costs of their labor, capital and land. Earlier, in the late eighteenth century, Alexander Hamilton and his followers had abstracted the nature of international competition in manufactured commodities into the single common factor input of industrial energy exerted and harnessed in production. Later, in the mid-nineteenth century, following the discoveries in agricultural chemistry made by Liebig, Thaer and Lawes, the single major factor input in agricultural and mineral production was seen to be soil fertility and "extractibility." Unlike the Heckscher-Ohlin theory, which viewed labor, land and capital as mutually non-competitive, these more technological approaches to trade theory, popularized mainly in the United States, acknowledged that work effort and primary-product extractibility might be provided by labor, capital or natural resources alike, in accordance with relative cost schedules which shifted over time and which were responsive to government policy.

In recent years Raul Prebisch has revived the commodity-oriented view of international trade popularized by Ricardo and Mill. He has captured the eye of many raw-materials exporters by postulating a secular tendency for the terms of trade to move in favor of industrial exporters, against the exporters of primary products. Given his postulated tendency (the statistical defense of which has been disputed) the solution to poverty in the low-income countries is for them to shift their production patterns away from primary production into industrial pursuits. Their problem is mainly one of producing the wrong commodities, those whose price is falling relative to the price of other internationally traded goods. Given a program to increase industrial productivity, which probably requires protective tariffs, these countries may overcome the acquired industrial advantage possessed by the more developed nations, and thereby become net beneficiaries of the shifting world terms of trade.

The Heckscher-Ohlin factor endowment theory attributes comparative advantage in given commodity lines not to relatively high factor productivity in these areas, which would seem to be the obvious explanation, but merely to international "advantage" in relative factor proportions, or more specifically, to the relative factor costs which follow from these proportions. Wages, rents and profits are assumed to be a direct and inverse function of relative factor supplies, and only of relative factor supplies. Thus, if some countries have a comparative advantage in producing agricultural commodities, it is not because their soil is richer than that of other countries, but simply because there is more of it relative to population and capital resources, so that their soil is low-priced relative to labor and capital. Other countries have been lucky enough to have been "endowed" with much more capital relative to labor and land: England found itself endowed with textile mills in the last century, and the United States with aircraft factories and mechanized farms in the 1960's. These countries' great relative supply of capital resources is responsible for the low cost of their capital in comparison with that of other factor inputs. For poorer countries, the indicated policy is to accumulate more capital if they want to shift their terms of trade to more remunerative lines, as capital seems to be the scarcest factor in the world economy. Implicitly, capital is not substitutable with labor, so that no labor-displacing tendency occurs as import capital in less developed countries.

This theory has little to say about how some countries' superior capital endowments originally came into being. (My own view is that today's developed nations were endowed above all with protective tariffs.) According to it, the less developed countries have been endowed only with labor, and although they possess a comparative advantage in the production of labor-intensive commodities, the fact that so many countries are similarly endowed tends to turn the international terms of trade against them. Still, they have a consolation prize: by definition — or more accurately, by tautology — each country has a comparative advantage in something. If it lacks capital, then it is labor-rich. Someday, if Samuelson proves correct, its wage levels and living standards may approximate those of the United States and other developed nations, thanks to natural forces at work within the international economy.

This theory says little about the terms of trade as between primary products and industrial manufactures. Some primary products are capital-intensive, particularly mineral products. Others are labor-intensive, particularly crops produced by plantation economies. The production of food crops such as grain and even chickens has become increasingly capital-intensive over the decades. All that the Heckscher-Ohlin theory states is that if nations wish to improve their terms of trade, they should increase their rate of capital accumulation, because capital is generally scarce in the international economy and its factor return is correspondingly high. There is no contradiction between this policy conclusion and that of Prebisch.

More than a century ago it was recognized that countries rich in manual labor resources and land area might still find themselves priced out of world markets both in industrial and agricultural commodity lines, as sophisticated capital and labor supplanted unskilled labor and unimproved land. International trade in industrial products was attributed to absolute advantage in the use of energy in production, with the factor contribution of labor and capital reduced to the common denominator of work effort. Similarly, trade in agricultural products found land-extensive, soil-depleting modes of agriculture competing with capital- and soil-intensive modes, with labor, land and capital being alternative technological means of producing soil fertility. This postulated competition as to the ultimate industrial factor-input, energy, and as to soil productivity in agricultural trade, attained a much higher degree of abstraction than has been matched in later international trade literature. On the basis of its policy implications, American protectionists developed national policies which helped provide the United States with world advantage in agricultural and industrial production. The nation's agriculture has substituted artificial fertilizers for virgin soil fertility with increasing success, following its earlier success in substituting steam-driven and electrically powered machinery for manual work effort. Given its surplus-producing capacity, the possibility now exists that other countries may find their unskilled labor and unimproved lands absolutely priced out of world markets. It is therefore important that we explore the theory of cross-competition between various classes of factors in international trade.

The Factor-Price Equalization (or "Pauper Labor") Argument for Protectionism in the United States

P. A. Samuelson has stated that, "Paradoxically, valid arguments for protection seem mostly to have come from free traders, not from protectionists."[457] It would be nearer the truth to state that the leading, even if invalid arguments for free trade have come mainly from protectionists.

This is particularly true of the factor-price equalization theorem. In 1848 the American protectionist Calvin Colton, official biographer and economic spokesman for Henry Clay, put forth a clear version of this theory, in order to argue why the workings of free trade later described by Samuelson would impair the high wages of American laborers, whose last wish was for their wage levels to equalize with those of Europe.

---

[457] Paul A. Samuelson, *Economics: An Introductory Analysis*, 7th ed. (New York: 1967), p. 675.

> It is manifest, that when the products of American ... labor are brought into the free and open market with the products of European and other foreign labor of the same kind, the labor itself is in the same market ; and that the tendency is to reduce the price of American labor to that of foreign labor. We say the tendency ... We have before indicated the reason why American labor, in such a case, will not come entirely down to the old level of European labor. The water of one cistern which is higher than that of another, will raise the other, by being let of into it, before both come to a common level. If the capacity of the two cisterns were equal, the common level would be found midway of the difference. But the American cistern is a very small one compared with all the rest of the world, and being let off, would fall immensely, while the other would scarcely seem to rise.[458]

This theory remained in the repertory of naive protectionist politicians for more than eighty years, and was still being voiced in the Republican National Platform as late as the 1932 elections. "The avowed object of protective tariffs," wrote Francis Amassa Walker in 1876, during the heyday of American protectionism, "has been to keep wages from sinking to the level of Europe and Asia. The allusions to 'pauper labor' which crowd the speeches of Clay, Stewart and Kelley have significance only as it is assumed that a day's labor in one place is the economical equivalent of a day's labor anywhere, and that one man's labor is effective in the same degree as that of any other man."[459]

After citing the example of an English wood-sawyer capable of performing as much work in a given period of time as thirty-two East Indians, Walker concluded: "In the contests of industry the civilized, organized, disciplined, and highly-equipped nations may safely entertain much the same contempt for barbarous antagonists as in the contests of war." The accumulation of human and material capital, not cheap labor, was responsible for the competitive cost-advantage enjoyed by sophisticated industrial powers.

We thus find, in the nineteenth century, American protectionists voicing the pauper-labor theory of wage equalization among nations in an attempt to scare U.S. workingmen into enacting protective tariffs. American free traders replied that the American workingman had nothing to fear from Iron-wage competition abroad, as pauper labor was ultimately more expensive on a unit-cost basis. Jacob Schoenhof, a free-trade Democrat, was employed by the State Department in Grover Cleveland's two Democratic administrations to travel around the world comparing wage rates and labor productivity, so as to confirm the thesis that variations in wage levels were more than offset by productivity differentials. His findings indicated that America's relatively highly-paid labor provided the nation with an international advantage in industrial production,

---

[458] Calvin Colton, *Public Economy for the United States* (New York: 1848), pp. 429f. See also pp. 65, 178–79. For a modern restatement of this theory, see Samuelson, *op. cit.*, p. 667 and Kindleberger, *op. cit.*, p. 33.

[459] Francis Amassa Walker, *The Wages Question* (New York: 1876), p. 41.

obviating the need for protective tariffs to support wage rates. "It is not by reducing wages that America is making her conquests," wrote Schoenhof, "but by her superior organization, greater efficiency of labor consequent upon the higher standard of living ruling in the country. High-priced labor means better food and better living, and these supply the American workman with the energy and nerve-power for which he is so justly celebrated. High-priced labor countries are everywhere beating 'pauper-labor' countries."[460] American industrial strategy should therefore make use of the country's high wage and productivity levels, and to foster, if possible, a kind of feedback mechanism of steadily increasing competitive advantage: the higher the wages for the U.S. laborer, the greater would be his productivity advantage over foreign workers, and the further U.S. unit production costs would decline relative to Europe's increasingly obsolete pauper labor. "The survival of the fittest," Schoenhof concluded, "is, therefore ... the result of a high wage rate; and a high standard of living in industrial countries, becomes a prerequisite to a low cost of production."[461]

The Energy Theory of Absolute Advantage among Nations

More sophisticated American protectionists had anticipated the high-wage argument for increasing productivity. In fact, it was E. Peshine Smith and Henry Carey that originally inspired the free-trade critics of the "pauper labor" argument for protective tariffs. Peshine Smith in particular had pressed this line of reasoning considerably further than was to be found in later literature, by emphasizing the role of superior educational attainments in securing inter- national cost advantage. Not only did highly paid labor outperform pauper labor in most physical tasks, he observed, but insofar as higher money wages enabled the American workingman to procure superior education for himself and his children, he accumulated the industrial skills needed to utilize energy- intensive machinery. And in the final analysis, cheap foreign labor was undersold more by highly productive American machinery than by highly productive American labor qua physical labor.

"The employment of machinery," wrote Alexander Hamilton already in 1790, "forms an item of great importance in the general mass of national in- dustry. It is an artificial force brought in aid of the natural force of man, and, to all the purposes of labor, is an increase of hands, an accession of strength,

---

[460] Jacob Schoenhof, *Wages and Trade in Manufacturing Industries in America and in Europe* (New York: 1884), p. 19. See also Schoenhof's definitive work on *The Economy of High Wages* (New York: 1892), p. 385.

[461] *The Economy of High Wages*, p. 39. The American protectionist E. Peshine Smith had already asserted, in his *Manual of Political Economy* (New York: 1853), p. 104, that "high proportional wages are the index of cheap production."

unencumbered, too, by the expense of maintaining the laborer."[462] The impact of this concept on U.S. national strategy and its economic doctrine cannot be overestimated, although it has been neglected by virtually all twentieth century historians of economic thought. "To illustrate this last idea," added Hamilton, "let it be supposed that the difference in price in two countries of a given quantity of manual labor requisite to the fabrication of a given article is as ten, and that some MECHANIC power is introduced into both countries which, performing half the necessary labor, leaves only half to be done by hand, it is evident that the difference in the cost of fabrication of the article in question in the two countries, as far as it is connected with the price of labor, will be reduced from ten to five in consequence of the introduction of that POWER."[463] The United States certainly could match Europe's natural advantages in water-powered machinery by virtue of "the uncommon variety and greater cheapness of situations adapted to mill-seats with which different parts of the United States abound." Thus, America's natural resources (its water power and abundant woods) competed to some extent with Europe's capital resources (its machinery).

Water-power considerations aside, England continued to widen her industrial advantage over the United States as a result of the superior productive power of her material capital, substituting steam-driven engines for manual labor. "Mr Clay had occasion to notice, as long ago as 1824," wrote Calvin Colton, "that some British authorities estimated the machine power of Great Britain as equal to two hundred millions of men. The number of operatives to apply this machinery has never amounted to one million. Here, then, is a nation, with a population of some twenty-five millions, with a producing power of two hundred millions. Its capabilities of producing wealth by artificial means, is so great, that its natural power is scarcely worthy of being brought into the account.... One man at home did the work of two hundred, less or more.... Science, which makes one man as powerful as two hundred, or a thousand, left to their natural powers, will and must prevail against numbers. That nation which cultivates the useful, mechanic, and manufacturing arts, all of which have their foundation in science, and which excels in them, other things being equal, will excel in strength, and maintain a superiority."[464] The

---

[462] Alexander Hamilton, *Report on the Subject of Manufactures* (1799), reprinted in Frank Taussig, ed., *State Papers and Speeches on the Tariff* (Cambridge: 1893), p. 17. Hamilton's document remained the germinal theoretical defense of protectionism for more than two generations.

[463] *Ibid.*, p. 35. For a more detailed analysis of the implications of this theory, see my dissertation on *E. Peshine Smith; A Study in Protectionist Growth Theory and American Sectionalism* (New York University: October, 1968).

[464] Calvin Colton, *Life and Times of Henry Clay* (New York: 1846), Vol. II, pp. 159f.

steam-engine could produce a manhour of work effort at a lower cost than could a man himself, as the cost of fueling and operating a machine was considerably less than feeding and sustaining the human body. This metaphor between man and machine permeated U.S. economic doctrine throughout the nineteenth century."[465]

Henry Mayhew computed that the total machine power of Britain had risen to the equivalent labor-power of 600 million human beings.[466] This was cheap power, and the key to England's world economic supremacy. America's industrialization program was therefore promoted by protectionists on the ground that industrial technology could undersell, by a widening margin, the increasingly obsolete employment of the human body as a supplier of work effort in production-not to mention the work effort supplied by horses, oxen and other beasts of burden. Nations that did not supplant their raw labor with machine power faced a widening cost-gap between themselves and the leading industrial and agricultural powers. No matter how lowly their labor might be paid, no matter to what squalor it might be reduced, the price of sustaining it still exceeded the machine costs of supplying a comparable man-hour or kilowatt-hour of work effort. Manual labor throughout the world inevitably lost out in competition with the power-driven forces of mass production. The result was increasing economic obsolescence and poverty in the countries slow to make the changeover to modern production techniques.

A modern conceptual approach to analyzing the cost technology of producing power by alternative methods may be found in a book by Zachariah Allen on the *Philosophy of the Mechanics of Nature, and the Sources and Modes of Action of Natural Motive Power*, published in 1852. In addition to computing the alternative operating costs of producing industrial energy by horsepower, manpower and steam power (both with coal and wood as fuels), Mr. Allen introduced the land-area constraints necessary to produce these various foods and fuels. The hay and corn needed to produce a day's horsepower of mechanical energy by means of horses cost 63 cents, and required 5 ¾ acres for their production. The wood fuel necessary to produce an equivalent of steam power was less expensive, but required 23 acres for its production. The needed coal to produce one horsepower of machine energy cost only 24 cents per pound,

---

[465] See for instance E. Peshine Smith's *Manual of Political Economy*, p. 53, Francis Amassa Walker, *The Wages Question*, pp. 58, 84, and Jacob Schoenhof, *The Industrial Situation* (New York: 18–), pp. 14f. The analogy seems to have come intermediately from Justus Liebig, *Complete Works on Chemistry*, trans. Lyon Playfair (Philadelphia, n.d.), pp. 76f, and originally from Belidor's *Architecture Hydraulique* (1739).

[466] E. Peshine Smith, *op. cit.*, p. 72. This calculation is attributed to Mayhew's *London Labour and the London Poor* (London: 1851), p. 439.

less than half the price of producing animal effort (no area constraint). The internal combustion engine was later to make even further cost savings. It was apparent that horses were doomed.

The ability of machines to supplant human labor as well as work animals in the drudgery of production, freeing it for higher tasks and in fact compelling it to be thus free under pain of economic obsolescence, was emphasized in almost every nineteenth-century treatise on steam engines. In this the mechanics and other writers of the period were in advance of most twentieth century economists, although Melman and Salter have analyzed in some detail the economies of substituting mechanical energy for labor power. Melman works out the economies of trading machine-hour cost for labor-cost, specifically in the area of materials handling,[467] and observes that "the fourfold increase in productivity of industrial workers in the United States over the last half century has been matched by a fourfold increase in the horsepower of the motor-driven machines which they use."[468] Salter analyzes the best-production technique, and specifies the point at which a changeover will occur from one mode of production to another.[469]

The Obsolescence Function in the International Economy: Industry

We have now seen how the factor-price equalization theorem was voiced and controverted over a century ago, and was then rediscovered and restated in what economists like to call "elegant" mathematical language and accepted on its own terms, as a geometric logical problem to be judged only on the basis of its own limiting assumptions. The thought of national trade policies being based on such an example of specious exercise is apalling. The theory's shortcoming may be indicated by posing the question of why the U.S. horse population has dwindled steadily following introduction of the internal combustion engine around the turn of the century. Economic theory seems able to explain this, but not the obsolescence of more human forms of labor services. The world horse population has died out because, as a producer of energy, particularly transport energy, it was higher-cost than alternative sources. Horses were no longer worth the cost of their food and shelter, and became a burdensome overhead rather than a net resource.

---

[467] Seymour Melman, *Dynamic Factors in. Industrial Productivity* (New York: 1956), pp. 40–44.
[468] *Ibid.*, p. 1.
[469] W. E. G. Salter, *Productivity and Technical Change* (Cambridge: 1960), pp. 23, 65–73.

Why, we may ask comparative advantage theorists, did horses not simply shift over to some other task ? Was there no alternative work for them to perform? The answer is clear: there were no alternative tasks for horses, and countries which had hitherto grown hay to feed their horse populations found it more efficient to export this hay or related grains and to import engines and motors. This explains why world horse-incomes have not equalized with those of manual laborers, as one might perhaps expect from the factor-price equalization theorem. Countries with comparatively large horse populations have not retained any comparative advantage in horse-intensive commodity lines, although the theory tells us that even if their cost structures are higher across the board, they must still be relatively low-cost producers of some class of commodities. It is up to today's "pure" trade theorists to tell us why this has not occurred.

In the race between machine and man as economic energy suppliers and servomechanisms, the machine will drive the raw laborer from the contest at that point where its costs of supplying industrial energy fall below the average wage which must be paid for unskilled labor to perform an equivalent amount of work effort. The minimum price of this unskilled labor is set by the price of human subsistence. At a lower factor return for work effort the manual laborer must be phased out of production, to remain unemployed until such time as he may acquire the working skills necessary to elevate himself to a tool user rather than a mere energy supplier. In fact, not only does the substitution of capital for manual labor as a source of energy free labor for higher, more skilled tasks, it positively drives him to elevate his status in production, by displacing him from the more menial tasks.

Figure 1 represents the Obsolescence Function as applied to manual labor.

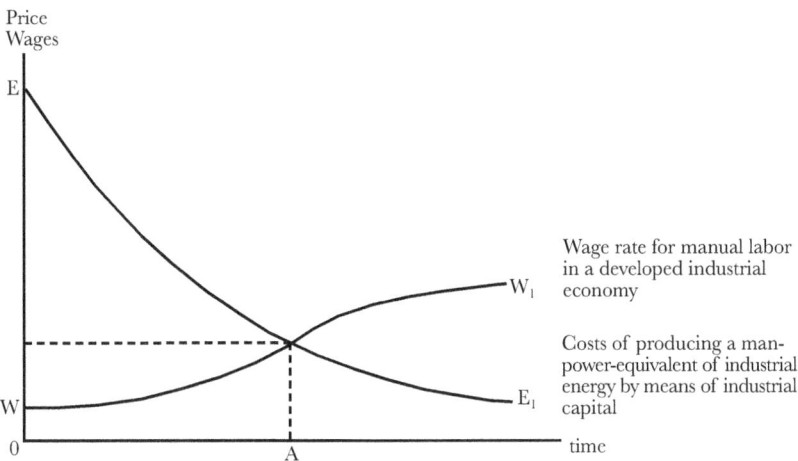

Fig. 1

Line WW_1 represents the wage rate for manual labor as it evolves in a developed industrial economy: it tends to rise because of the general scarcity of all labor during the early stages of industrialization, and then levels off as manual labor becomes increasingly obsolete. Line EE_1 represents the declining costs over time of producing a manpower-equivalent of industrial energy by means of capital equipment. In the last century the costs of producing a manpower-equivalent of energy by means of steam and electricity fell below the cost of using the human body as an energy-converter, that is, converting his 'fuel'—his food, clothing and related necessities—into a given flow of caloric work effort. Manual labor in the factories, and later on the farm, was supplanted by steam engines, electrical generators and their related servomechanisms, and the internal combustion engine.

The economic implications of the developments are far-reaching. In Ricardo's day, when England's industrial revolution was still gaining momentum, all that was demanded of the rural migrant newly arrived in the city was the ability to exert manual effort. Children worked as servomechanisms at their looms. Today, the willingness and ability to perform similar tasks no longer qualifies the rural migrant for employment. The exodus of farmboys, which contributed so strongly to Britain's industrial power two centuries ago, represents only a burden for the less developed countries of today. Eighteenth-century labor cannot find employment and happiness in this twentieth-century world.

The theory of obsolescence as it applies to the international economy is thus much more problematic than has been recognized by neo-classical economics. According to the assumptions of this latter theory, what little advantage as may be enjoyed by the backward countries derives from their low wage levels, and only on the naive (or, as economists like to say, "heroic") assumption that labor productivity is roughly similar among all nations. However, as we have now seen, low-paid laborers cannot afford to acquire the training or education necessary to raise their status in production at the rate required by twentieth-century technology. They therefore find themselves unemployed. Rather than being productive inputs they become welfare charges on their society, banding together with their unfortunate compatriots in the urban shantytowns now gobbling up Latin America.

The converse of the Obsolescence Function is what we may term the Complementarity Function between human and material capital. In order to be employable, the human laborer over time requires a rising complement of training and education. He finds his employability proportional to his ability to draw upon his training and acquired working skills to perform tasks which machinery could not perform at a lower cost. Already in 1853 Peshine Smith observed that, "as we rise to labour in connection with more complicated

346

machinery, the value of general intelligence becomes distinctly apparent."[470] In fact, as Schoenhof observed: "In almost every employment of an industrial nature a very great amount of training is requisite to make it effective or to make it serviceable at all. Only in times of a very great demand and scarcity of labor would any one employ crude labor in factories where skill is required."[471] This minimum necessary educational level was rising over time, as labor required an increasingly intensive training and education as a precondition for employment. Thus, accumulation of material capital in the United States has been conditional upon the concurrent accumulation of human capital. Failure to acquire this human capital results in human obsolescence. This helps explain why the average education of American labor has increased steadily over the decades. It has not been a luxurious consumption good, but a precondition for capitalizing the American economy.

The Obsolescence Function in the International Economy: Agriculture

Not only has manual labor in the backward countries been increasingly undersold by the powers of mechanized and computerized capital in the advanced nations, but the productive powers of their soil resources have also been increasingly undersold by the far less costly powers of U.S. farm capital, that is, by the fertilizers, agricultural machinery and related farm improvements which have characterized agriculture in the more developed nations. Today, "natural" or "virgin" soil fertility has become as obsolete an economic input as raw unskilled labor. What was competitive in past centuries is no longer competitive.

The treatment of soil as an economic input has always distressed economists. Particularly since Ricardo they have used arable land area as a proxy for soil, failing to recognize the extent to which soil is a bio-chemical entity whose fertility is a function of its mineral and related inputs. Land area, in the quantitative sense of acres subject to given climatic conditions, has been taken as representing the supply function of agricultural resources, particularly by proponents of the factor-proportions school. The effect of artificial fertility-inputs on the international agricultural supply function has been unduly neglected.

Ricardo was the major culprit in popularizing the erroneous concept that soil possessed "original and indestructible powers." Whatever fertility differentials existed in its virgin state, he believed, would remain fixed for all eternity. Any changes in yield-per-acre ratios following from capital improvements were presumed to take place proportionately on all soils within given nations—and by implication, among nations.

---

[470] Peshine Smith, *op. cit.*, p. 107. [471] *The Economy of High Wages*, p. 27.

At least he did not treat soil as a homogeneous and uniform entity among regions, as was the treatment accorded labor. Quite the opposite. In agriculture alone, and specifically with regard to soil inputs, was the role of differential productivity recognized by Ricardo and other classical British political economists. According to their theory of comparative advantage, each nation's agriculture was characterized by some yield-per-acre ratio, subject to deterioration in this ratio at the extensive margin. The more recently settled, sparsely populated nations were presumed to have the most fertile soils, as there was less pressure on their soil resources at the extensive margin. Thus, there appeared to be some natural equitability in international trade as between crop producers and industrial nations. The older and more densely populated nations would exchange their manufactures—the low cost of which presumably followed from their low wage levels—for the food and other primary products of the younger, less populated countries. Some countries were therefore "naturally" suited for industry, others for raw-materials production.

This concept of soil and natural resources was as unrealistic and static as was the classical concept of labor. By the 1840's, a more modern concept of soil as a chemical entity was being developed by Liebig, Thaer and Lawes. According to their theories, there was no such thing as original and permanent fertility. Soil could be depleted, as was clearly taking place in sparsely cultivated countries such as the United States, where the "farm and run" practice was the rule. Transcient families would "mine the soil" in one district and then move on to another.

Conversely, soil could be augmented by the application of nutrients. Whatever original fertility differentials as existed among nations could thus be overcome by sophisticated farm-management practices.[472]

This explained why soil productivity in Europe, as measured by output-per-acre, was superior to that in the United States, and why this condition persists today. In Europe, labor is substituted for land, so that Europe possesses an edge in per-acre productivity, the United States an edge in agricultural labor-productivity. This also explains why Europe and other industrial nations have not become the growing market for the products of the less developed, raw-materials exporters as was so widely anticipated in the last century. Today, each year's new basket of food contains fewer inputs of rural farm labor and simple "land area" and more of capital. Because this agricultural capital may be substituted for land and rural farm labor at ever-diminishing costs, as was

---

[472] For a controversion of the Ricardian concept of soil, see Liebig, *op. cit.*, Peshine Smith, *op. cit.*, and Daniel Lee's articles in the *Report of the U.S. Commissioner of Patents*, Vol. II: *Agriculture*, for the years 1849, 1851, and 1852.

revealed so sharply by the response of American farmers to the Soil Bank program, the unimproved land and untrained rural labor of the backward countries no longer constitute the resource that they seemed to represent in the nineteenth century. Instead, they are a form of obsolete social-economic overhead, to be supported by economic charity, not economic markets.

Figure 2 illustrates how the costs of artificial chemical sources of fertility have declined in comparison with the costs of cultivating virgin lands. Line CC_1 represents the cost of cultivating unimproved land, which is rising over time both because of land prices generally (in relation to other prices), and because of the gradual depletion of the soil resulting from land-extensive modes of cultivation. Line KK represents the unit cost of producing a similar market-basket of crops with modern, capital-intensive farm techniques. Capital supplants soil just as it has supplanted manual effort. The soil is transformed into a capital instrument, just as are its trained businessman-operatives.

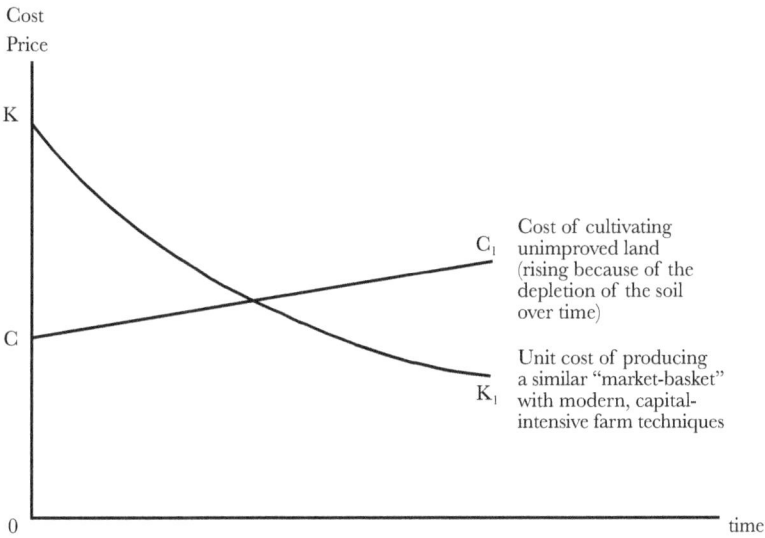

Fig. 2

This explains why it is precisely those countries which originally seemed to possess the greatest natural advantages that have today sunk into the most backward and obsolescent state. Originally fertile soils now become high-cost soils, and "naturally" rich mines tend to become high-cost mines. This is no anomaly but is the rule of economic evolution. The copper industry provides an illuminating example. As the quality of available copper ores has declined throughout the world, technological innovations have been developed to

349

substitute capital techniques for the original richness of ore-bodies. As events have worked out, the lower the copper content—generally, of the more recently opened mines—the lower are the unit costs of production. Thus, highly mechanized ore-bodies in the United States, whose copper content averages only 0.4 to 0.6 per cent, may be mined less expensively than the more labor-intensive copper operations of the Congo and Zambia, where 4 to 5 per cent copper is the rule. A similar development has occurred in the iron-ore industry, where pelletizing processes have been developed to exploit the lower-grade ore-bodies, with the result that the cost of iron has declined rather than risen.

These mineral examples thus parallel the evolution of food production costs over time. Contrary to the Ricardian theory of rent as applied to mining and agriculture, the lands and mines exploited in the earliest years do not find themselves recipients of any scarcity-rent, but instead suffer a negative quasi-rent (as Marshall termed it) of obsolescence. In this manner the nations least endowed with natural resources have conquered the most highly ("naturally") endowed nations.

We may now generalize our theory of limits as applied to the obsolescence function of labor and soil, as well as that of capital. Economic obsolescence in the less developed countries is a direct function of technological progress transpiring elsewhere. The more rapidly technological progress occurs in industry, agriculture and commerce, the faster will be the rate of obsolescence of all pre-existing capital, labor and soil. At some point the current operating costs of given "endowments" of manual labor, plots of soil, and obsolete capital exceed their contributions to marginal sales revenue. Their charges for maintenance, repair, and fuel in the case of obsolete capital, the minimum cost of subsistence in the case of manual labor, and the cost of maintenance and seed in the case of soil, can no longer be recaptured by the price of their products. Thus, by applying the theory of limits we may specify that point at which merely low-productivity capital, labor and soil become critically obsolete and unemployable altogether.

The Limited Concept of Technology Held by Most Economists

Technology for most economists represents simply the labor/capital and labor/output ratios used in producing given classes of commodities. I have selected the following statement only on the basis of its relatively recent publication as part of a National Bureau of Economic Research conference on *The Technology Factor in International Trade*. Output changes, remarks Ronald Jones, "could be represented by movements along a transformation curve.

Technological progress is seen to complicate matters further in two ways. First, the reduction in factor requirements is seen to act like an increase in the quantity of factors available ... Thus if factor prices were constant and only labor coefficients were reduced, the transformation schedule would be shifted outward and the output of the labor-intensive commodity would be increased while the output of the land-intensive commodity would be reduced."[473] But what is it that increases, to displace labor in the above example? If it is energy, what are the dynamics of its introduction? What happens to pre-existing plants using old techniques, which are too concrete to shift over to any alternative use? If the productivity increase derives from superior industrial organization, what are the relevant costs and benefits associated with this overhead expenditure?

Raymond Vernon, editor of the above volume, views technology simply as a thing-in-itself, something akin to phlogiston. In Jones's words, his concept of the "product cycle ... argues that advanced countries tend to have comparative advantage in producing those commodities that are newly being developed.... In simplified terms, this suggests a three factor model: capital, 'ordinary' labor, and a third factor that comprises a host of special skills on the part of labor or of capital equipment.... Advanced countries, such as the United States, have a relative abundance of this third factor and hence a comparative advantage in producing new commodities at early stages of production. Later stages are associated with a shift in factor intensities toward a relatively greater role played by capital and labor."[474] Again, this theory suffers from an inadequate definition of technology, and also of capital. Technology is conceived as novelty, not as the ability to substitute some new form of economic input for a pre-existing form, such as machine power for labor power and horse power, or artificial nitrates for virgin soil fertility. If labor, land or capital are displaced or economized in production, it must be obvious that this is costless at all, but reflects the substitution of some unspecified input, whose economies must be specified in order to understand the processes at work. Otherwise one cannot explain why countries have comparative advantages in research-intensive product lines, which may be subsidized by government military activities by private nonprofit foundations, or other factors which today's economic thought considers non-economic in nature.

---

[473] Ronald Jones, "The Role of Technology in the Theory of International Trade," in Raymond Vernon, ed., *The Technology Factor in International Trade* (New York: 1970. Universities-National Bureau Conference Series 22), p. 76.
[474] *Ibid.*, p. 84.

Application of the Obsolescence Function to Dual Economies: The Ghetto Function at Home and Abroad

Increasing capital productivity in the agricultural and industrial sectors of the developed nations, in the face of stagnant productivity in the less developed countries' domestic sectors, is the major explanation of increasing economic imbalance between rich and poor countries. Technological obsolescence of labor and land in the latter countries has been reinforced by the various forms of social and political obsolescence historically associated with backward economies. The effect of this widening imbalance is to transform the least developed countries into world mendicants. Similar forces are at work within the United States itself, as its sophisticated mainstream labor and capital compete with obsolete economic inputs.

Consider the slums that have mushroomed in the United States since the Korean War as backward rural and black labor have been displaced from its southern agricultural regions into northern and western large cities. The relative backwardness of minority-group labor in the United States reflects the economic elevation and technological progress that has characterized the non-black, mainstream labor force. Obsolete labor, finding itself culturally alien to the sophisticated urban economy into which it finds itself displaced, is not oriented toward acquiring the working skills and attitudes requisite for modern employment. Some portion of this minority labor force visibly falls too far behind its contemporaries to catch up under its own power, given existing social institutions. Its incomes are insufficient to enable it to finance the educational and related social expenditures needed to bring it up to a par with mainstream labor. Only an external transfusion of social resources can accomplish this end.

To be sure, there was prevalent misery and poverty in England's weaving towns during the first half-century of its industrial revolution. In fact, it was England's most highly skilled labor that was the first to be displaced by machines as power looms supplanted the male hand weavers, whose jobs could then be taken over by less highly skilled women. With the introduction of even simpler machinery, women were supplanted by children. Many observers believed that the quality of life and labor would become increasingly degraded rather than elevated by the spread of machine production.

Ultimately, however, England's industrial economy entered a more advanced phase of mechanization. Its capital became increasingly skill-intensive, and called once again for trained blue-collar operatives, as well as a new white-collar complement. Contrary to the forecasts of underconsumptionists, no vast displacement of labor ensued. Instead, there developed a normal state of chronic full employment for skilled labor (the Great Depression being essentially a monetary anomaly resulting from unique postwar conditions). The Luddites and their machine-wrecker contemporaries were therefore wrong concerning the domestic economy. Technological progress elevated the social and economic status of the working class as a whole, rather than condemning it to an existence of squalid unemployment.

But this has been the case only in the advanced nations, where techno-logical change has occurred slowly enough so that no great gap has developed between obsolescence and modernity. The ghetto function in the backward countries today, by way of contrast, is indeed a by-product of their overall obsolescence. The problem is that they are obsolescent on a nationwide scale. Their rural exodus, displaced from its traditional living areas to flood the old industrial and commercial capital cities, becomes a social overhead. This places an exponentially increasing per capita burden on the productive sectors of their societies. The burgeoning surplus of consumers who are not producers must somehow be supported out of domestic output—that is, they must receive some portion of society's income to finance their subsistence—or else subsist by foreign aid.

Private sector production costs in the backward countries are increased just as they are in New York City by the rising welfare-tax burden needed to support this obsolescent labor force. Increasing budgetary allotments are required in the form of transfer payments and welfare infrastructure expenditures. This increas-ing tax function further impairs the competitive position of such areas. A diminishing social surplus is available to devote to the educational and other infrastructure activities needed to modernize their backward labor and land resources so that they may find employment in the modern twentieth-century world.

Among the developed nations this emergence of a welfare class, accompa-nied by the transformation of major cities into welfare reservations, is unique to the United States. Its black and other minority-group labor was left on the land, in the slums and in the shoeshine stalls a century too long, and has been degraded too far to retain what cultural integrity it originally possessed, and which is a prerequisite for the development of modern work attitudes. America's urban ghettos are thus the result of its artificial division of labor into two broad groups, skilled whites and unskilled blacks. The latter are a racist incident to capitalism. The American economy could well have evolved with all its citizens, black and white alike, had it not chosen to suffer the expensive cultural luxury of being as sharply racist as it in fact was.

Some modest effort is now being made to modernize hitherto untapped minority group resources. In oligarchic backward countries, by way of contrast, a prolonged state of immiseration seems inevitable, so long as an open international economy is maintained which throws obsolescent labor and land into uneven combat with more modern producers in the advanced nations. To these more modern producers the international economy promises economies of scale in production and marketing, and therefore a regenerative feedback system of increasing sales and capital accumulation. To the backward countries it connotes a loss of markets, starting with their own home market. It means deprivation of economies of scale, and a virtual blocking off of balanced economic growth and self-sufficiency.

Some indication of the cruelty that this situation must inevitably breed was given a century ago in the debates over England's and Ireland's Poor Laws. James Phillips Kay, a physician who inspected the living habits of Manchester working-men, wrote that "the introduction of an uncivilized race does not tend even primarily to increase the power of producing wealth, in a ratio by any means commensurate with the cheapness of its labour, and may ultimately retard the increase of the fund for the maintenance of that labour. Such a race is useful only as a mass of animal organization, which consumes the smallest amount of wages. The low price of the labour of such people depends, however, on the paucity of their wants, and their savage habits. When they assist the production of wealth, therefore, their barbarous habits and consequent moral depression must form a part of the equation. They are only necessary to a state of commerce inconsistent with such a reward for labour, as is calculated to maintain the standard of civilization. A few years pass, and they become burdens to a community whose morals and physical power they have depressed; and dissipate wealth which they did not accumulate."[475] (The alternative, of course, is a transformation of their society which put them in this state.) Kay then quotes from Nassau Senior's *Letter to Lord Howick on a Legal Provision for the Irish Poor, &c., &c.*, which puts to shame the most reactionary attacks on the welfare and aid system being made today. The Poor Laws, Senior asserted, would "divide Ireland into as many distinct countries as there are parishes, each peopled by a population *ascripta glebae* multiplying without forethought; impelled to labour principally by the fear of punishment; drawing allowance for their children, and throwing their parents on the parish; considering wages not a matter of contract but of right; attributing every evil to the injustice of their superiors; and, when their own idleness or improvidence has occasioned a fall of wages, avenging it by firing the dwellings, maiming the cattle, or murdering the persons of the landlords and overseers; combining, in short, the insubordination of the freeman with the sloth and recklessness of the slave."[476]

---

[475] James Phillips Kay, *The Moral and Physical Condition of the Working Classes, Employed in the Cotton Manufacture in Manchester* (London: 1832), p. 52.
[476] Quoted *ibid.*, pp. 53f.

I cite these quotations not as antiquarian documents of the past, but as an indication of the political response to come if foreign aid and domestic welfare expenditures continue to take the form merely of income transfers rather than capital transfers to help elevate unskilled labor into human capital. It is to this problem that I address my concluding remarks.

Policy Conclusions

Three policies have been suggested for countries to increase their incomes. Most popular among academic economists and factor endowment theorists remains free trade. Poor countries are urged to modernize their economies only within the confines of laissez faire. They should open their markets so that they may reap the traditional gains from trade. These are the gains which Ricardo believed would benefit Portugal as it specialized in wine-making and left England to specialize in weaving and its associated industrial branches. Unfortunately for Portugal and other primary commodity exporters, the gains from this pattern of trade seem to have accrued almost exclusively to England and other developed nations. The external economies and diseconomies of such trade, which free traders have neglected from Ricardo's day down to the present, far outweigh the short-term economies of exchange.

The most immediate problem of taking the free trade option is that backward countries have little to trade except the products of their mines and their "cheap labor." The appearance of international trade masks what is basically a transfer function: They are lent foreign-aid funds to purchase goods in the aid-lending nations, while foreign affiliates of international firms produce their exports in isolated mineral and plantation enclaves. Thus, they pay for their imports not by exporting goods and services from their domestic economy, but with promissory notes and with exports produced by foreign-controlled firms, whose factor proportions reflect those of their parent country's economy rather than that of their host country. The poorer countries' ability to attract aid and capital inflows becomes increasingly political rather than economic in nature.

Modern capitalism began by opening up the world economy, fostering a commercial revolution whose effect was to monetize all areas of economic activity. Now that the catalyst of money and commerce has been implanted in all societies of the globe, its workings can be completed only by less developed countries closing themselves off into regional blocs. Suspension of free-market competition within some political context seems to be the only alternative to an aggravation of the Obsolescence and Ghetto Functions. Otherwise, the open international economy dictates that the backward countries must remain part of the "world village," gathered like serfs at the foot of the castle. They

are obliged to exchange their raw materials and to sell their domestic investment rights to foreigners, and to borrow increasing sums abroad to finance
their economic backwardness and its associated trade deficit. Their cost of
remaining members in good standing in the international economy ultimately
involves their total submission to this economy.

The result is that increasing portions of their economies become less and
less an integral part of this world economy. The bulk of their poor populations
is increasingly excluded from the world of technological advance. Thus, the
quality of human resources falls ever further below the rising minimum degree
necessary for employment in the world economy. The more the physical productiveness of agricultural and industrial capital in the developed nations
increases, the more the value of preexisting, increasingly obsolete agricultural
inputs abroad declines, and with it their factor incomes. At some point they are
rendered uncompetitive altogether. Under free trade, the world economy shrinks
more and more, until finally it is comprised exclusively of the developed nations
and their extractive export enclaves among the raw-materials exporters.

Some economists have advocated terms-of-trade insurance for the less
developed, primary-commodity exporters. In practice, this amounts to financing their general economic backwardness, not to modernizing their economies.
It enables them to go on servicing the raw-materials needs of the developed
nations, neglecting to modernize their agricultural and human resources. It is
just another form of income transfer, rather than the capital transfer called for.

The required capital transfer is not to be found in the poorer countries
redirecting their production towards manufacturing and other commodity lines
whose terms of trade appear to rise over time, a panacea endorsed by Commu-
nist planners as well as by the World Bank and other aid-lending cartels. For
by seeking to industrialize some part of their economies, the poor countries
may aggravate their internal obsolescence function, that is, their dual economies which mirror domestically the international dualism between rich and
poor countries. For them to proceed directly to the most modern agricultural
and industrial technology would be to expel their labor from the land and from
the workshops, leaving it nowhere to go to offer its obsolescent labor services,
except perhaps into the army. This would be the modern counterpart to England's Enclosure Movements of past centuries, only today the "hands" freed
will have nowhere to go. For hands are no longer needed for employment in
today's world, only brains.

The glib prescription to industrialize does not indicate what will happen to
that sector of the population which must necessarily lag behind. Nor does it
inquire as to which classes will reap the apparent benefits of industrialization,
or how these benefits will be shared within the country, or the extent to which

the new industrial islands will actually be composed in large part of foreign affiliates. The industrialization panacea has nonetheless gained some degree of popularity in the United States, as American firms have by now established affiliates in the less developed countries and find Prebisch's analysis a convenient argument for tariff barriers to guarantee profitable operations for these affiliates. Furthermore, industrialization tends to aggravate the rural exodus and the widening food deficits now plaguing the less developed countries. Partly for this reason it may well please the American farm lobby, as U.S. farm exports to these countries have mushroomed dramatically since World War II.

The thesis of this essay is that the key factor inputs in today's world are work effort and soil productiveness. The indicated policy conclusion of the foregoing analysis is protectionist. It emphasizes modernization of the backward countries' soil and human capital resources, with labor development being concentrated on the land instead of in the cities.

A century ago, many American workingmen voted for protective tariffs in order to prevent their per-diem wages from being equalized with those of lesser-paid foreign labor. As the above analysis has shown, they were somewhat confused as to just what was being equalized by the process of international trade. It was not compensation per diem, but compensation per unit of work-effort output, as well as compensation for the costs of acquiring the labor skills necessary to operate machines which took over an increasing share of labor's manual tasks. Today, the capital-poor countries find their self-interest to lie in interfering with the free flow of international trade precisely in order to suspend the "equilibrating" factor-price equalization process between work-effort supplied by capital and that supplied by untrained labor. For a transition period, they must also suspend the international competition between artificial sources of soil fertility in the developed nations and those of their own unimproved soils worked by outmoded agrarian methods. What is to be equalized in the realm of international trade is not per-diem wage rates, or per-acre land rents, but the price of the services of supplying work energy and simple servomechanism operations, as well as soil productiveness. These services can be supplied much less expensively by inputs of capital equipment than by raw labor, much less costly by artificial fertilizers than by unimproved soil. The result is that the annual returns to labor and land in the less developed countries are not improved, towards those levels which characterize laborers and farmers in the developed nations. We may call this the Factor-Price-Disparity Theorem.

Just as England's Enclosure Movements displaced people in favor of sheep, modern technology displaces people in the less developed countries from their traditional livelihoods. Technological efficiency takes precedence over humanity, and productivity becomes the new sacred cow to which backward societies are

357

sacrificed. The mechanism of this sacrifice is the international economy. Malnutrition spreads in Brazil and Colombia, in the face of rising coffee exports, all in the name of "gains from trade" and comparative advantage. The backward countries can only watch passively as the economic powers of alien and vastly more productive agricultural and industrial capital bring about mass unemployment on their land and in their cities. A similar process seems about to begin working within their domestic economy as well as within the international economy.

The competitive plight of backward countries today is thus much more serious than was that of the United States a century ago. Their quandary lies in the fact that modern industrial and agricultural technology requires the application of technical skills and work attitudes that can be built up only over a period of time. However, educational facilities currently available in the backward countries are far insufficient to educate their stream of new working-age population. Furthermore, in order to initiate a modern human capital-formation function new teachers must be withdrawn from the ranks of the potentially productive skilled labor force. In this lies the major source of pessimism as to economic prospects in the backward countries. The major limitation on their economic development does not lie in diminishing returns in agriculture, or in the dearth of natural resources — the bogies of old Malthusianism — but in the manpower constraints of their educational infrastructures.

Still, upgrading of their human capital resources and agricultural modernization are the two most essential paths of overcoming their international backwardness. Their indicated path today is similar to that followed by the United States following the Republican victory in the 1860 elections, when protectionists moved to supplement American labor with energy-intensive capital, so that the American workingman would be freed for higher, more sophisticated tasks. "The American System," wrote Peshine Smith, the economic spokesman for Secretary of State William Seward and later the third-ranking employee of the State Department, "rests upon the belief, that in order to make labor cheap, the laborer must be well fed, well clothed, well lodged, well instructed, not only in the details of his handicraft, but in all general knowledge that can in any way be made subsidiary to it. All these cost money to the employer and repay it with interest."[477] Agricultural extension services must be developed today as they were in the United States to modernize agriculture, something which is conditional upon a radical transformation of land tenure systems in the food-deficit countries.

---

[477] Peshine Smith, "The Law of Progress in the Relations of Capital and Labor," *Hunt's Merchants' Magazine*, Vol. XXVI (January 1852), p. 42.

These educational expenditures will obviously add further to the already strained budgets of the less developed countries. Unfortunately, the monetary impact of the resulting budget deficits will hardly aid them in fostering full employment. In fact, the very concept of full employment is sharply narrowed by the Obsolescence Function. The seemingly homogeneous group of laborers depicted in neo-classical economics is seen to be actually divided into two noncompeting groups. Skilled, increasingly capitalized and sophisticated labor competes against unskilled and increasingly obsolete manual labor. To acknowledge this duality is to foresake any simplistic theory of full employment. We find a tendency towards full employment of skilled labor, but declining employment opportunities for unskilled labor. Today, what Marx termed the army of the unemployed has turned out to be an army only of welfare recipients.

This means that there is no simple monetary or income-policy cure for the domestic ghetto or for urban ghettos in the backward countries. Labor retraining, including in many cases cultural retraining programs as well, is a precondition for the modernization of obsolescent labor which would otherwise remain a social overhead, unable by itself to inaugurate the rise in educational levels required by modern technology. Just as capitalists must either reinvest some portion of their income in cost-reducing technology or see their businesses go under, so too must labor. In the advanced nations, whose labor has succeeded in keeping pace with the march of technology, this labor has moved on to the more imaginative skills which are increasingly requisite for contemporary production. This elevation of labor in the advanced nations seems to have doomed to a status of unemployed obsolescence the uneducated classes in urban ghettos wherever they remain in the world economy.

INDEX

abolition, 12, 50, 98, 138, 147, 156

economists, academic, 188, 355

ad valorem duties, 39, 45, 46, 48, 73; see also tariffs

Adams, Brooks, 159

Adams, Henry C., 8, 156, 268

Adams, John Quincy, 19, 99

agricultural commodities, 202, 338

agricultural economy, 76

agricultural productivity, 6, 160, 302, 306, 323, 329

agronomy, 160, 192

Allen, Zachariah, 343

American Academy of Arts and Sciences, 215, 257

American Academy of Political and Social Science, 183

American Association for the Advancement of Science, 220

American Economic Association, 8, 25, 213, 259, 280, 296

American School, 1–5, 7f., 11, 15f., 18–21, 24, 26, 29, 35, 51, 91, 119, 155, 186, 291, 301, 302, 304f., 308

American Selling Price (system of import evaluation), 41

American Sociological Society, 213, 280

Andrews, Stephen Pearl, 149

Anglophobia, 138

Appleton, Nathan, 120, 157

art, role of, 278

Averroes (Ibn-Rushd), 252

backwoods theory, 32

Bacon, Francis, 85, 121

balance of payments, 190

Baldwin, James Mark, 272

bank see national bank

Bank of England, 218

Bank of the United States, 62

banking system, 37, 48, 141, 142, 301

Bastable, John, 268

Bastiat, Claude Frédéric, 2, 51, 196, 200, 234

Baxter, Robert Dudley, 220, 225

Bayard, Thomas Francis, 230

Beard, Charles, 310, 311

Bentham, Jeremy, 275, 290, 291

Benthamism, 280

Bigelow, Erastus Brigham, 3, 20, 22, 125–129

bilateral reciprocity, 191

Bodin, Jean, 250f., 254, 287

Böhm-Bawerk, Eugen, 165, 172

bond issues, 217

border states, 5, 43, 46, 307, 309

Boston memorial, 74f.

Boston protectionists, 6, 18f., 118

Bovay, Alvan E., 151

Bowen, Francis, 1, 3, 5f., 18, 24f., 85, 118–123, 137, 145, 157, 172, 177, 218

Bradsher, Earl L., 61

Brisbane, Albert, 148

British economic thought, 84f., 91, 121, 273, 296

Brown University, 13

Bryan, William Jennings, 310

Buchanan, James, 57f., 326

Buckle, Henry Thomas, 220, 250

Bunyan, John, 279

Burke, Edmund, 317

Butt, Isaac, 23

Cairnes, J. E., 194, 220, 225

Calhoun, John C., 40, 58

Cameron, Simon, 57, 58

capital

  capital efficiency, 231

  accumulation of capital, 30, 52, 53, 128

  dormant capital, 113, 114

  forms of capital, 91, 160, 161

  human capital, 347, 355, 357, 358

  latent capital, 89

  marginal efficiency of capital, 224

  productivity of capital, 164

  social capital, 114

capital-intensive production, 200

capitalism, 20, 53, 54, 281, 295, 353, 355

Carey, Henry Charles, 1, 3, 5, 7f., 19f., 22, 24, 34, 51f., 58, 60f., 75, 83, 92, 110, 117, 119, 153, 155f., 167, 170–180, 185, 202, 213, 218, 228, 230, 233, 246, 255, 257, 259, 263, 274, 291, 301, 305, 307f., 320, 327, 329, 341

361

www.ingramcontent.com/pod-product-compliance
Lightning Source LLC
Chambersburg PA
CBHW081801200326
41597CB00023B/4102